Lynn L. Wolff

W. G. Sebald's Hybrid Poetics

Interdisciplinary German Cultural Studies

Edited by
Scott Denham, Irene Kacandes and
Jonathan Petropoulos

Volume 14

Lynn L. Wolff

W. G. Sebald's Hybrid Poetics

Literature as Historiography

DE GRUYTER

ISBN 978-3-11-048599-8
e-ISBN 978-3-11-034055-6
ISSN 1861-8030

Library of Congress Cataloging-in-Publication Data
A CIP catalog record for this book has been applied for at the Library of Congress.

Bibliographic information published by the Deutsche Nationalbibliothek
The Deutsche Nationalbibliothek lists this publication in the Deutsche Nationalbibliografie;
detailed bibliographic data are available in the Internet at http://dnb.dnb.de.

© 2014 Walter de Gruyter GmbH, Berlin/Boston
Cover image: Lynn L. Wolff, Neues Museum Berlin
Typesetting: jürgen ullrich typosatz
Printing: Hubert & Co. GmbH & Co. KG, Göttingen
♾ Printed on acid-free paper
Printed in Germany

www.degruyter.com

For J.J.

Contents

Acknowledgments

A significant portion of this book was written in Berlin, a city that physically documents and testifies to Germany's turbulent history: from the iconic Kaiser Wilhelm Gedächtnis Kirche, left in ruins as a witness to the destruction wrought by World War II, to the recently constructed but still controversial Holocaust memorial, the "Denkmal für die ermordeten Juden Europas" located in the city center. David Chipperfield's design for the Neues Museum – at once a remnant and a monument – encapsulates a symbiosis of ruin and reconstruction that is an almost literal illustration of the presence of the past. A photograph from inside the museum thus serves as this book's cover image, echoing the salient feature of W. G. Sebald's works that this book explores: the simultaneous embodiment of history and critical questioning of historical representation.

This book began as a doctoral dissertation, which I completed at the University of Wisconsin, Madison in 2011. First and foremost, I would like to express my deepest gratitude to Hans Adler, who directed my dissertation and who has generously shared his knowledge, critical thought, integrity, and humor over many years. The members of my defense committee also deserve thanks for valuable suggestions for this publication: Michael Bernard-Donals, Sabine Gross, B. Venkat Mani, and Marc Silberman. My graduate studies were generously funded by various fellowships and assistantships, and I would like to extend my thanks to the University of Wisconsin's Department of German, Graduate School, Center for German and European Studies, and Institute for Research in the Humanities. I am particularly grateful to both the Fulbright Commission for granting me a research fellowship to spend a year in Berlin and the Alexander von Humboldt Foundation for funding my current position as a postdoctoral researcher at the Universität Stuttgart. For the honor of being included in the *Interdisciplinary German Cultural Studies* series and for their extremely valuable feedback, I thank Scott Denham, Irene Kacandes, and Jonathan Petropoulos as well as the anonymous readers of my manuscript. Manuela Gerlof and the helpful and meticulous staff at de Gruyter deserve my appreciation for bringing this book into its present form.

An early stage of this project's line of inquiry can be found in my article "Literary Historiography: W. G. Sebald's Fiction," published in *W. G. Sebald: Schreiben ex patria / Expatriate Writing,* ed. Gerhard Fischer, New York: Rodopi, 2009, 317–330. A very small section of the introduction appeared in "W. G. Sebald: A 'Grenzgänger' of the 20th/21st Century" in a special issue of *Eurostudia – Revue Transatlantique de Recherche sur l'Europe* 7.1–2 (2011) 191–198. A part of chapter six appeared as "The 'Solitary Mallard': On Sebald and Translation" in a special issue on W. G. Sebald edited by Richard Sheppard, *Journal of European Studies* 41:

3–4 (December 2011) 318–335; I am grateful to the *JES* for the permission to reprint it here.

Fellow Sebaldians Jo Catling, Helen Finch, Richard Hibbitt, Florian Höllerer, Dora Osborne, Richard Sheppard, Reinbert Tabbert, Ruth Vogel-Klein, and Markus Zisselsberger deserve my heartfelt thanks for their encouragement, feedback, and friendship. This study benefitted greatly from a month spent at the Deutsches Literaturarchiv in Marbach, working with Sebald's manuscripts, letters, and library. For their support and assistance I would like to thank the kind staff of both the library and archive and Marcel Lepper in particular for making this stay possible. A very short but fruitful stay in Cambridge allowed me to work with Michael Hulse's translations and his correspondence with Sebald held at Harvard University's Houghton Library. For their assistance with the Hulse papers and their enthusiasm for my project I thank Peter Accardo and Roger Stoddard, and for being such a gracious host, I thank Sophie Salvo. For the permission to cite from Sebald's estate, I would like to thank the DLA, Michael Hulse, and the Wylie Agency.

For advice and support at various stages of this project I thank colleagues and friends near and far: Brigitte Adler, Michael Bailey, Hartmut Böhme, John Dillion, Susan Stanford Friedman, Victoria Hill, Sarah Marcus, Angus Nicholls, Monika Peschken, Jonathan Pollack, and Sandra Richter. I would like to express my gratitude to "Aunt" Carolyn Berterello, Francine Conley, Angelika Czekay, Keith Hartmann, John Ricciardi, and Craig Streff for their positive encouragement many years ago. For their friendship and *savoir vivre*, my warmest thanks go to Marie Odile Beaubiat, Catherine and the late Joop van Couwelaar, Thyra E. Knapp, Joan Leffler, and Michel Martinez. Last, but certainly not least, I would like to thank my parents, Tom and Mary Wolff, for their love and support.

L.L.W, Stuttgart, July 2013

List of Abbreviations

Quotations from all of W. G. Sebald's primary works will be cited parenthetically in the body of the text, according to the following abbreviation system. English translations are provided in square brackets.

A   *Austerlitz* (Frankfurt am Main: Fischer Taschenbuch Verlag, 2003 [2001]).

AE   *Austerlitz*, trans. Anthea Bell (New York: Random House, 2001).

ALW   *Across the Land and the Water. Selected Poems, 1964–2001*, ed. Sven Meyer, trans. Iain Galbraith (London: Hamish Hamilton, 2011).

CS   *Campo Santo*, ed. Sven Meyer (Munich; Vienna: Hanser, 2003).

CSE   *Campo Santo*, ed. Sven Meyer, trans. Anthea Bell (New York: Random House, 2005).

DA   *Die Ausgewanderten. Vier lange Erzählungen* (Frankfurt am Main: Fischer, 2002 [1992]).

E   *The Emigrants*, trans. Michael Hulse (New York: New Directions, 1997 [1996]).

G   *"Auf ungeheuer dünnem Eis." Gespräche 1971 bis 2001*, ed. Torsten Hoffmann (Frankfurt am Main: Fischer, 2011).

Logis *Logis in einem Landhaus. Über Gottfried Keller, Johann Peter Hebel, Robert Walser und andere* (Frankfurt am Main: Fischer, 2003 [1998]).

LuL   *Luftkrieg und Literatur. Mit einem Essay zu Alfred Andersch* (Frankfurt am Main: Fischer, 2003 [1999]).

NH   *On the Natural History of Destruction*, trans. Anthea Bell (New York: Random House, 2003).

PC   *A Place in the Country. On Gottfried Keller, Johann Peter Hebel, Robert Walser and Others*, trans. Jo Catling (London: Hamish Hamilton, 2013).

RS   *Die Ringe des Saturn. Eine englische Wallfahrt* (Frankfurt am Main: Fischer, 2003 [1995]).

RoS   *Rings of Saturn*, trans. Michael Hulse (New York: New Directions, 1999 [1998]).

SG   *Schwindel.Gefühle* (Frankfurt am Main: Fischer, 2005 [1990]).

Ü   *Über das Land und das Wasser*, ed. Sven Meyer (Munich; Vienna: Hanser, 2008).

V   *Vertigo*, trans. Michael Hulse (New York: New Directions, 2000 [1999]).

Introduction
Why W. G. Sebald

The status of literature has long been a contentious one, ranging from deception and imitation at one extreme to cognition and invention at the other. Plato not only separated literature from philosophy but created a deep chasm between the two, and his assertion of literature's ontological and moral deficiencies established a long-standing suspicion of the discourse, traces of which are at times still perceptible today. Countering its inferiority and championing its philosophical value, Aristotle elevated the status of literature by highlighting its element of potentiality, and this distinction remains fundamental to our understanding of fictional literature and novels in particular.[1] Literature is now well known as a protean discourse, appearing in a seemingly inexhaustible variety of genres. Oftentimes, the variations of literary forms coincide with philosophy, theology, history, and other discourses. This variability of literature, then, demands that we inquire into the specificity of this discourse and attempt to delineate its center from its periphery. While such inquiries may lead us to question the concept of 'discourse' itself, we must not feel bound to clear and distinct definitions nor must we allege the 'purity' of the discourse, for both demands would require an unnecessary reduction if not inappropriate restriction of literature. A more productive avenue would be to explore the 'fuzziness', elusiveness, and near unlimited potential of literature, since these are qualities that have been essential in securing the survival of literature as one of the fundamental components of human culture, according to an understanding of human culture as an encompassing and indispensible tool for the survival of the human species. Through the physical, intellectual, and imaginative processes involved in reading, we experience the indisputable impact of literature: it affects us on sensate and emotional as well as cognitive and intellectual levels.[2] Literary discourse has the unique

---

1 Milan Kundera's exploration of the art of the novel, for example, clearly echoes Aristotle's distinction between literature and history made in chapter nine of his *Poetics*. Kundera writes, "Le roman n'examine pas la réalité mais l'existence. Et l'existence n'est pas ce qui s'est passé, l'existence est le champ de possibilités humaines, tout ce que l'homme peut devenir, tout ce dont il est capable." Milan Kundera, *L'art du roman* (Paris: Gallimard, 1986) 57. ["A novel examines not reality but existence. And existence is not what has occurred, existence is the realm of human possibilities, everything that man can become, everything he's capable of." Milan Kundera, *The Art of the Novel*, trans. Linda Asher (London; Boston: Faber and Faber, 1988) 42.]

2 It is not without reason that Charles Baudelaire deemed the human imagination the "Queen of the faculties" or that Immanuel Kant identified the imagination as essential to the process of human cognition insofar as it mediates between the senses and cognition. See Charles Baude-

potential to transfer experiences and ideas into linguistic representations, but it does not only document or demonstrate such a process of transfer, rather it can also reflect upon this process. By exploring the unique potential of literary discourse to produce, perform, and problematize this interdiscursive transfer from experience to representation, we can begin to approach the intangible and often elusive form of aesthetic knowledge or literary (re)cognition. In this way it will become clear how literature has the potential to both transmit and create knowledge in ways that other discourses cannot.

With regard to the transfer process from experience to representation, this book offers a new critical perspective on the perpetual problem of literature's relationship to reality and focuses in particular on the sustained tension between literature and historiography. The scholarly and literary works of W.G. Sebald (1944–2001) serve as striking examples for this discussion, for the way in which they challenge and ultimately eschew traditional forms of historiography and fiction. In the search for a truth that lies beyond 'facts,' Sebald confronts the border between history and literature and by extension between fact and fiction, bringing to the fore pressing ethical questions. In exploring the interplay of epistemology, aesthetics, and ethics in Sebald's works, this book reconsiders the fundamental concern since Kant, Nietzsche, Freud, and Wittgenstein of what we can *know* about the world we live in. Furthermore, the book shows how this concern gains greater urgency when brought together with the perennial mimesis/realism debate of how we can *represent* the world we live in. This book examines how Sebald explores and interrogates the past – predominantly the singular atrocity of the Holocaust but also other contentious moments in world history – while simultaneously engaging with the constitution of literary texts. What sets Sebald's works apart from other instances of post-World War II literature in German is their focus on the tension between the specific problem of coming to terms with Germany's Nazi past and the more universal concerns, common to literature and history alike, of attempting to understand the past and searching for ways to represent it.

The sustained tension between literature and historiography – from Aristotle's differentiation of two distinct discourses via the nineteenth-century historical novel to documentary fiction and "faction" of the twentieth and twenty-first centuries – is the problematic that frames this study of Sebald's œuvre. Marking

---

laire, "The Salon of 1859. Letters to the editor of the *Revue Française*," *Art in Paris 1845–1862. Salons and Other Exhibitions Reviewed by Charles Baudelaire*, trans. and ed. Jonathan Mayne (London: Phaidon Publishers [Greenwich, Conn.: New York Graphics Society Publishers], 1965) 144–216, here 155. See Immanuel Kant, *Critique of Pure Reason*, trans. and ed. Paul Guyer and Allen W. Wood (Cambridge: Cambridge University Press, 2000) 225 [A 95].

a shift away from literary representations of historical events and historiography that employs elements of the literary discourse, this book elucidates how Sebald's works demonstrate the emergence of a new hybrid form of literature *as* historiography, or what I term literary historiography. Sebald's hybrid form is not a mere fictionalization of history but rather a reconstruction of history that combines the reality of observation and the fictionality of representation. Put another way, Sebald fuses the work of both the historiographer and the poet from Aristotle's fundamental distinction made in chapter nine of his *Poetics*. Sebald's literary historiography illuminates the unique potential of literature to perform the interdiscursive transfer from experience to representation, that is, from event to narrative and from history to story. This study advances the notion of an anthropological necessity of literature and of fiction more broadly, and the in-depth examination of Sebald's works – embedded within larger historical contexts and theoretical considerations – reveals the singular truth value of literature.

The Borders of World Literature: Sebald the Author and the Phenomenon

Sebald's works have attracted remarkable academic and popular attention, and they have also prompted a variety of reactions ranging from skepticism and criticism to fascination and emulation. In short, Sebald can be seen as a "phenomenon" of contemporary literature written in German.[3] Contributing to Sebald's status as a "phenomenon" is, first, his subject position as a German who lived in England for the second half of his life and, second, the double role he occupied as both author and scholar. In an effort to get a grasp on this elusive and engaging author of the twentieth century, scholarship has fractured Sebald into the person, the author, the narrator,[4] an act which also risks turning the phenomenon of Sebald into a myth. The title of this introduction – "Why W. G. Sebald" – is written assertively *without* a question mark, for it is not my purpose to defend Sebald to those who question the persistent fascination with

---

3 With regard to the "industry" of secondary literature on Sebald, Martin Swales has asserted that "W.G. Sebald is in danger of becoming less a writer than a phenomenon." Martin Swales, Review of *W.G. Sebald. History – Memory – Trauma* (Berlin and New York: de Gruyter, 2006), *Arbitrium* 26.1 (2008) 128–130, here 128.
4 Jens Mühling, for example, distinguishes between person and author. Jens Mühling, "The Permanent Exile of W.G. Sebald," *Pretext* 7 (2003) 15–26.

this author.[5] Rather, I outline and assess what is "phenomenal"[6] about Sebald and his works, beginning with a brief overview of Sebald's life, since it is appropriate to first address the question "Who is Sebald?" before embarking upon the "why." This introduction also serves to locate Sebald vis-à-vis the borders of world literature by considering the implications of his national identity, the language of his literary production, and reception of his works. Theoretical considerations of world literature also enable me to reconsider the problematic notion of Sebald's "self-imposed exile," a description which has gained currency in research over the last ten years. After highlighting Sebald's border crossing – between discourses, genres, media, nations, and epochs – the rest of the book then excavates how this inscribes itself in a complex layering in his texts as a particular form of literary archaeology.

"World literature," as formulated by Franco Moretti, "is not an object, it's a *problem*, and a problem that asks for a new critical method."[7] In his essay on the philology of *Weltliteratur*, Erich Auerbach already pointed to world literature as a "problem," outlining an essential tension in the concept: once realized, it would at the same time be dissolved.[8] David Damrosch's solution to this "problem" suggests we understand world literature from the perspective of circulation and networks rather than focusing on individual literary works.[9] This move away from world literature as an object also involves a move away from nation as an organizing principle for the study of literature. Despite this shift, there remains a persistent need to identify an object or a nation, or to locate the world in the question of world literature.[10] With such attempts to broaden the discussion beyond the nation and beyond national literatures,

---

5 The fact that Sebald was a literary scholar has been a source of skepticism and reproach, especially in German academia. The oft-heard prejudice maintains that a literary scholar cannot also write good literature without falling back on a form of mannerism.

6 Scott Denham, "Foreword: The Sebald Phenomenon," *W. G. Sebald: History, Memory, Trauma*, eds. Scott Denham and Mark McCulloh (Berlin: de Gruyter, 2006) 1–6. Swales, Review of *W. G. Sebald. History – Memory – Trauma*, 128.

7 Franco Moretti, "Conjectures on World Literature," *New Left Review* 1 (2000) 54–68, here 55.

8 According to Auerbach, "'man will have to accustom himself to existence in a standardized world, to a single literary culture, only a few literary languages, and perhaps even a single literary language. And herewith the notion of *Weltliteratur* would be at once realized and destroyed.'" Auerbach cited in Peter Madsen, "World Literature and World Thoughts: Brandes/Auerbach," *Debating World Literature*, ed. Christopher Prendergast (London; NY: Verso, 2004) 54–75, here 55.

9 David Damrosch, "Introduction. Goethe Coins a Phrase," *What is World Literature?* (Princeton: Princeton University Press, 2003) 1.

10 "What is the 'world' in 'world literature'?" asks Carolyn Vellenga Berman in her considerations of this subject. Carolyn Vellenga Berman, "The Known World in World Literature: Bakhtin, Glissant, and Edward P. Jones," *Novel* 42.2 (2009) 231–238, here 231.

much in the spirit of Goethe's original idea of *Weltliteratur* (1827), one may risk reaching even beyond literature itself. For this reason, my analyses of Sebald's writings start at the level of the text and my consideration of Sebald as an author of world literature begin with his background and subject position as a writer. After all, even if world literature is not an object, we nevertheless need an object before working out a theory or a "new critical method" as Moretti states.

Sebald was an author deeply devoted to the ethical responsibilities and aesthetic possibilities of literary discourse. Born in Southern Germany at the end of World War II, Sebald spent the better part of his life grappling with Germany's recent past, and he did this "from abroad," living in England from 1966 until his death in December 2001. His texts, written in German, deal primarily with events of twentieth-century European history in general and the Holocaust in particular, with interwoven strands of eighteenth- and nineteenth-century history as well, such as the Napoleonic Wars, the silk trade, and colonialism. Encompassing world history, Sebald's texts present an example of world literature that problematizes but does not eclipse the nation. Sebald as an author represents a cosmopolitan consciousness that does not reject the specificity of the nation. The tension between the global and the local in Sebald's works, that is, between world history that transcends national concerns on the one hand and very specific moments in Germany history on the other, warrants their inclusion within the category of world literature. While Sebald's status as a "Holocaust author" has been fiercely debated, one cannot dispute the central position this atrocity holds in his works.[11] Sebald also goes beyond this particular twentieth-century European atrocity, in writing of the violence of the Belgian colonial oppression in the Congo, the capitalist exploitation of the Amazon forests, and the massacres caused by Napoleon's military campaigns. Furthermore, his texts explore how trauma is not limited to human experience; Sebald devotes much attention to conjecturing about the pain and suffering of animals and considering the destruction of nature as well. He does not privilege the human being above all other forms of life, rather his concern is for life in all forms: human, animal, and

---

[11] Although Sebald may not have liked being reduced to a "Holocaust" author, this is nevertheless a central theme in his works and a repeated topic of discussion in his interviews. He moreover chose to focus on this history, further pursuing the themes laid out in *Die Ausgewanderten* in his last work *Austerlitz*. He makes this explicit at the beginning and end of a two-page publicity flyer describing *Austerlitz*: "Along the lines first drawn in *The Emigrants*, this prose fiction work, which runs to some three hundred pages, recounts the story of Jacques Austerlitz [...]. Like the accounts in *The Emigrants*, *Austerlitz* is based on a real life story and includes photographic documentation." A: Sebald, DLA Marbach.

natural.[12] Thus, his concerns are as much ecological as they are global. By examining Sebald as an author of world literature – an author writing "literary works that circulate beyond their culture of origin"[13] – while also accounting for the specificity of his texts,[14] we can continue to work within the idea(l) of world literature, as Goethe envisaged, without dissolving it.

Sebald was born in 1944 as Winfried Georg, but as a university student he had a number of nicknames[15] and from his time in England on, he was known to his friends as "Max."[16] Although separated generationally from the tradition of post-

---

12 Hans-Walter Schmidt-Hannisa describes Sebald's "anti-specieist" approach to history, based on the way he represents the relationship between humans and animals in *Luftkrieg und Literatur* and *Die Ringe des Saturn*. By highlighting stories of animals as victims, Sebald counters "an anthropocentric perspective on history." Hans-Walter Schmidt-Hannisa, "Abberation of a Species: On the Relationship between Man and Beast in W. G. Sebald's Work," *W. G. Sebald and the Writing of History*, eds. Anne Fuchs and J. J. Long (Würzburg: Königshausen & Neumann, 2007) 31–44, here 32.

13 Damrosch, *What is World Literature?*, 4.

14 In his philology of *Weltliteratur*, Auerbach emphasizes the need to consider context, history, and culture in order to properly understand a body of literature. "[...] es sind die Bedingungen zu studieren, unter denen sie sich entwickelt hat; es sind die religiösen, philosophischen, politischen, ökonomischen Verhältnisse, die bildende Kunst und etwa auch die Musik in Betracht zu ziehen, und es sind auf all diesen Gebieten die Ergebnisse der ständig tätigen Einzelforschung zu verfolgen." Erich Auerbach, "Philologie der Weltliteratur," *Philologie der Weltliteratur. Sechs Versuche über Stil und Wirklichkeitswahrnehmung* (Frankfurt am Main: Fischer, 1992) 83–96, here 88. ["[...] one must study the conditions under which this literature developed; one must take into account religion, philosophy, politics, economics, fine arts and music; in every one of these disciplines there must be sustained, active and individual research." Erich Auerbach, trans. Maire and Edward Said, "Philology and *Weltliteratur*," *The Centennial Review* 13.1 (1969) 1–17, here 8.]

15 To his friend and roommate Albrecht Rasche, he was known as "Koki," for example. Interview with Albrecht Rasche, December 8, 2011, Freiburg im Breisgau.

16 Contrary to what several scholars and journalists have stated, "Maximilian" was not Sebald's third name. As Uwe Schütte rightly states, this inaccuracy is "eine vielfach nachgeplapperte Konjektur und ein Beispiel dafür, wie Sebald den sich bereits zu Lebzeiten um ihn bildenden 'Sebald-industrial complex' (Neil Pages) auch gerne mit schelmischer Freude in die Irre laufen ließ" [a conjecture that has repeatedly been parroted and an example for what can be called the 'Sebald-industrial complex' (Neil Pages) that built up around Sebald already during his lifetime and that he, with mischievous pleasure, let run wild]. See Uwe Schütte, *W. G. Sebald. Einführung in Leben und Werk* (Göttingen: Vandenhoeck & Ruprecht, 2011) 17. On Sebald's youth see Mark M. Anderson, "A Childhood in the Allgäu: Wertach, 1944–52," and on Sebald's university and early years in Manchester, see Richard Sheppard, "The Sternheim Years: W. G. Sebald's *Lehrjahre* and *Theatralische Sendung* 1963–75," both in *Saturn's Moons: A W. G. Sebald Handbook*, eds. Jo Catling and Richard Hibbitt (Oxford: Legenda, 2011) 16–41; 42–107. For additional detailed biographical accounts of Sebald's life, see Richard Sheppard, "Dexter – sinister: Some Observations on Decrypting the Mors Code in the Work of W. G. Sebald," *Journal of European Studies* 35.4

war German authors, his scholarly and literary texts offer a continuation of the question of *Vergangenheitsbewältigung* [coming to terms with the past, meaning Germany's Nazi past in particular] that was born out of this previous generation's literary productions. From an early age on, Sebald sensed a silence in postwar German society, a silence bound up in the repression of the Nazis' crimes and the complicity of ordinary people. He describes, "I think there was certainly what has often been described as a conspiracy of silence. [...] One had tacitly agreed to leave this behind and developed an attitude which was entirely forward-looking, which was bent on *not* remembering."[17] Sebald's engagement with questions of Germany's past first began in primary school after seeing footage of the liberation of the Bergen-Belsen concentration camp. In several interviews he recalls this formative moment, how the films were shown without explanation or discussion; the students were given no chance to ask questions (*G* 83; 226–227). As a student at the University of Freiburg, Sebald began to develop a critical perspective of the atrocities, and here his disillusionment crystallized in what he sensed as an "atmosphere of falseness"[18] in higher education, especially when the activities of professors during the Nazi era came to light. It was also during his time as a university student that the Auschwitz trials in Frankfurt widely publicized the crimes of the concentration camps. Sebald described the trials as "the first *public* acknowledgment that there was such a thing as an unresolved German past."[19] This delay in Sebald's exposure to the Holocaust can certainly be read as informing the slow excavation and revelation of the past in his literary works.[20]

Reproachful of Germany's "Gedächtnislosigkeit"[21] ["lack of memory"], Sebald took a teaching assistantship in England at the age of twenty-two, where he remained until a tragic automobile accident took his life in 2001. Sebald's position as "Lektor" at the University of Manchester was funded by the Deutscher Akademischer Austauschdienst for the year 1966–1967, which he then renewed for a second year after getting married in 1967. In the following year, 1968–1969 he

---

(2005) 419–463 and Sheppard's continuation piece "'Woods, trees, and the spaces in between:' A Report on Work Published on W.G. Sebald 2005–2008," *Journal of European Studies* 39.1 (2009) 79–128.

17 W.G. Sebald, "W.G. Sebald," Christopher Bigsby, *Writers in Conversation with Christopher Bigsby. Volume Two* (Norwich [U.K.]: Arthur Miller Centre for American Studies, 2001) 139–165, here 142–143.

18 Sebald in Bigsby, 147.

19 Ibid.

20 The reverse chronology in several of Sebald's works will be outlined in chapter four.

21 Sigrid Löffler, "Kopfreisen in die Ferne: ein Geheimtip; in Norwich, gar nicht hinter dem Mond, lebt und schreibt W.G. Max Sebald," *W.G. Sebald*, ed. Franz Loquai (Eggingen: Ed. Isele, 1997) 32–36, here 34.

returned to "the continent" and worked as a teacher at a private school in St. Gallen, Switzerland.[22] Feeling that his attempt as a teacher was a failure, he returned to Manchester where he pursued both his Master's and PhD in German literature[23] and was involved in directing the theater group of the university's German Department.[24] Some fifteen years later, Sebald was granted his Habilitation by the University of Hamburg, with a collection of essays that he then published as *Die Beschreibung des Unglücks* (1985). Sebald taught courses in nineteenth- and twentieth-century German prose fiction for close to thirty years in the school of English and American Studies at the University of East Anglia in Norwich, England. As part of his professional duties, he also founded and directed the British Centre for Literary Translation in 1989, housed at the UEA, Norwich. In his last years, profiting from his literary successes, Sebald was able to free himself from all teaching but occasionally offered courses in creative writing.

Sebald's first years in England had a deep impact on him; he became aware of a large number of exiles and entire Jewish communities who were forced to leave Germany during World War II. He recalls the gradual process of coming into contact with exiles and how his initial hesitations were rooted in the fear of saying the wrong things.[25] A parallel can be drawn here between Sebald's life and work: *Die Ausgewanderten* (1992) and *Austerlitz* (2001) – with their specific focus on the experience of exiles, mediated through German-born narrators – could be read as a literary reworking of Sebald's own past experiences, a literary reimagining of how he came into contact with exiles and how he came to learn about the German past through their life stories. Sebald's works are driven by a search for truth and a desire for authenticity, which he draws from his own experiences. He states,

---

22 See Reinbert Tabbert, "Max in Manchester. Außen- und Innenansicht eines jungen Autors," *Akzente* 50.1 (2003) 21–30, here 28, and Tabbert, "Tanti saluti cordiali. Max: W. G. Sebald … drei bislang unveröffentlichte Briefe an einen Studienfreund," *Literaturen* 5 (2004) 46–49, here 46. In his article for *Literaturen*, Tabbert cites a letter from October 2, 1968, in which Sebald paints a bleak picture of his teaching experience in St. Gallen. Convinced that his attempts to be a teacher were a failure, Sebald was nevertheless satisfied to have begun writing again ["'Ich habe wieder zu kritzeln begonnen'"].

23 He completed his Master's and PhD degrees at the University of Manchester under the supervision of Idris Parry, writing on Carl Sternheim and Alfred Döblin respectively. Idris Parry was born in Bangor, Wales, and taught at the University College of North Wales, Bangor, from 1947–1963. In his obituary of Idris Parry, Martin Durrell suggests that Sebald drew from his conversations with Parry for the descriptions of North Wales in *Austerlitz*, although Parry himself doubted this. See Martin Durrell, "Idris Parry: Scholar of German Literature," *The Independent (Obituaries)* Wednesday, March 26, 2008.

24 See Tabbert, "Tanti saluti cordiali," 47.

25 Carole Angier, "Wer ist W. G. Sebald? Ein Besuch beim Autor der *Ausgewanderten*," *W. G. Sebald*, ed. Franz Loquai (Eggingen: Ed. Isele, 1997) 43–50, here 45.

'I've grown up feeling that there's some sort of emptiness somewhere that needs to be filled by accounts, witnesses one can trust. I would never have encountered these witnesses if I had not left my native country at the age of twenty because the people who tell you the truth, or something at least approximating the truth did not live there any longer.'[26]

Besides voicing his criticism of postwar German society, Sebald emphasizes his central concern with authentic experience and authentic witnessing. His literary works moreover reveal just how difficult the endeavor of accessing this truth is.

In addition to the dominant theme of exile in his works, Sebald's decision to leave Germany in the 1960s and to eventually take up permanent residence in England has prompted scholars and critics to read his life in close connection to his subjects and to suggest his "self-imposed" or "voluntary" exile.[27] However, such designations are both problematic and, from Sebald's perspective, simply false. "Vom Exil kann man nicht reden" [One cannot talk of exile], Sebald stated succinctly in one interview (*G* 82), and in another interview he suggested an alternative way of describing his position in England, "Sagen wir es mal in Anführungszeichen – 'Auswanderung'" (*G* 131) [Let's put it this way in quotes: 'emigration']. While refusing this label himself, Sebald also expressed his awareness of the liminal status of his life and work in England. In the speech made on the occasion of his acceptance into the German Academy, he stated, "In England nur gastweise zuhause, schwanke ich auch hier zwischen Gefühlen der Vertrautheit und der Dislokation" (*CS* 250) ["Only a guest in England, I still hover between feelings of familiarity and dislocation there too" (*CSE* 208)]. In the same speech, Sebald also expressed a distance towards his homeland as well as his feelings of being "a traitor to [his] country and a fraud" (*CSE* 208). This liminal status must be emphasized, for it was only in the distance from Germany, while in England, that Sebald was able to form a critical perspective of his native country (see also *G* 66; 224).

In addition to Sebald's own resistance to the designation of "exile," this label is to be avoided, for it the way it collapses the historical perspective that his works

---

26 Quoted in Carol Bere, "The Book of Memory," *Literary Review* 46 (2002) 186.

27 James Atlas, "W.G. Sebald. A Profile," *The Paris Review* 41.151 (1999) 278–298, here 286; Arthur Williams, "W.G. Sebald: A Holistic Approach to Borders, Texts and Perspectives," *German-Language Literature Today: International and Popular?*, eds. Arthur Williams, Stuart Parkes, and Julian Preece (Oxford; New York: P. Lang, 2000) 99–118, here 103; Mark M. Anderson, "The Edge of Darkness: On W.G. Sebald," *October* 106 (2003) 102–121, here 103; John Zilcosky, "Sebald's Uncanny Travels. The Impossibility of Getting Lost," *W.G. Sebald: A Critical Companion*, eds. J.J. Long and Anne Whitehead (Seattle, WA: University of Washington Press, 2004) 102–120, here 116; Ronald H. McKinney, "W.G. Sebald and 'the Questionable Business' of Post-Holocaust Writing," *Philosophy Today* 49.2 (2005) 115–126, here 115.

precisely emphasize. Rather than identifying Sebald as an "exile," then, one alternative is to discuss his works in terms of *expatriate writing*. With an eye to the linguistic specificity of Sebald's success, Gerhard Fischer asserts,

> Sebald, after all, despite being an expatriate writer living in England for the better part of his life, wrote only in German [...]. His reputation rests primarily on his consummate mastery of the German language and the German literary tradition, which is quite unparalleled in contemporary writing.[28]

Fischer's conceptual program for thinking of Sebald as an expatriate writer is productive, insofar as he identifies in Sebald's works "a potentially emancipatory cultural memory that resists the push and pull of a single, hegemonic world culture."[29] The emphasis on an author's origins and his texts' linguistic material is therefore not to be seen as a reactionary emphasis on national identity but rather as an essential assertion of difference. Peter Madsen suggests a differentiated understanding of the relationship between language, nationality, and world literature that informs my understanding of Sebald as both a 'German' author and an author of world literature. Madsen writes,

> The construction of national identity, however, is in itself a mystifying (and potentially destructive) endeavour. The seemingly natural link between literature as a linguistic art form, national language and national identity is at odds with the fact that literature travels in translation and that all nations are heterogeneous culturally speaking. From the outset the idea of world literature goes against the grain of nationalism.[30]

The specificity of Sebald's works in German – in particular the intricate layering of visual and textual material and varying degrees of narrative mediation – will be explored throughout this book, and in the following I consider Sebald's relationship to language as a way to further situate his work within networks of world literature and world history.

On various occasions, Sebald expressed his complex relationship to language. Even after thirty years in England and being fluent in English, Sebald still considered English a foreign language. "I don't in the least feel at home in it. I use

---

28 Gerhard Fischer, "Editor's Note," *W.G. Sebald. Schreiben ex patria/Expatriate Writing*, ed. Gerhard Fischer [*Amsterdamer Beiträge zur neueren Germanistik* 72] (Amsterdam; New York: Rodopi, 2009) 12.

29 Gerhard Fischer, "Introduction: W.G. Sebald's Expatriate Experience and His Literary Beginnings," *W.G. Sebald. Schreiben ex patria/Expatriate Writing*, ed. Gerhard Fischer [*Amsterdamer Beiträge zur neueren Germanistik* 72] (Amsterdam; New York: Rodopi, 2009) 15–24, here 21.

30 Peter Madsen, "World Literature and World Thoughts: Brandes/Auerbach," *Debating World Literature*, ed. Christopher Prendergast (London; NY: Verso, 2004) 54–75, here 74.

it but it sounds quite alien to me," Sebald states in his interview with Christopher Bigsby.[31] Furthermore, Sebald refuses Bigsby's suggestion that he would "become a Joseph Conrad," feeling it was too late for him to change his "linguistic coat."[32] Sebald also describes the German language as "eine Art von Floß, auf dem ich sitze in diesem mir auch nicht vertraut gewordenen englischen Ausland" (*G* 253) [a sort of raft on which I sit in this English foreign country that is still not yet familiar to me]. Having grown up in Bavaria, Sebald considered the Southern German dialect his mother tongue, and he recounts having made his first efforts to learn, speak, and write standard "high" German when he entered the university in Freiburg in 1963 (*G* 254). Sebald wrote almost exclusively in German for his entire life, even while in England, however he did write a few poems in English for a collaborative project with Tess Jaray;[33] Sebald also translated poems by Michael Hulse, the English translator of his own prose works;[34] and he is listed as the translator of scholarly works by Richard Evans and Richard Sheppard.[35]

In a letter to Reinbert Tabbert, his friend and former roommate during his first year in Manchester, Sebald expressed his skepticism of teaching works in translation. Sebald also explained his reasons for turning down a job offer in the Department of Drama at the University of Bangor were based on the issue of teaching in translation. He wrote to Tabbert, perhaps ironically, in English, "'They wanted me to deal with nineteenth- and twentieth-century German and French drama via English translations exclusively. Besides providing a rather dubious basis for discussion this would have completely exiled me.'"[36] Despite both being native Germans, Sebald shifted between English and German in his letters to Tabbert and often inserted Latin and French phrases and sometimes even wrote in Alemannic. The inside jokes, cryptic allusions, and jabs at academia in these letters reveal the closeness of these two friends as well as Sebald's sense of humor. Sebald closed his letter of April 7, 1970,

---

31 Sebald cited in Bigsby, 148.
32 Ibid.
33 W.G. Sebald, illustrated by Tess Jaray, *For Years Now* (London: Short, 2001).
34 Michael Hulse, trans. W.G. Sebald, "An Botho Strauss in Berlin," "Raffles Hotel Singapur," *Sprache im technischen Zeitalter* 33 Nr. 134 (1995) 162–164.
35 Richard J. Evans; trans. W.G. Sebald, *Sozialdemokratie und Frauenemanzipation im deutschen Kaiserreich*, (Berlin: J.H.W. Dietz, 1979). Richard Sheppard, ed., *Die Schriften des Neuen Clubs 1908–1914* (Hildesheim: Gerstenberg, 1980 [Vol. 1], 1983 [Vol. 2]). In the foreword, Sheppard thanks Sebald for his help on polishing the German: "Aus diesem Grund sei hier den Personen und Institutionen gedankt [...] meinem Kollegen Dr. Max Sebald (Norwich/England), der das Nachwort durchgesehen und wesentlich ausgebessert hat [...]" (Vol. 2, p. 7).
36 Sebald cited in Tabbert, "Max in Manchester," 29. See also Tabbert, "Tanti saluti cordiali," 47.

> This summer I shall try to find the house of Consul Meyer in Bordeaux, where Hölderlin was Hofmeister for a couple of months. Probably will tell me more about him to look at the facade of this place, than to read the latest news from the intellectual stock-exchange. The Tui-business. Most of its agents can't think further than a London pigeon can fly. So they can't imagine Hölderlin, walking, in midwinter, from Frankfurt to Bordeaux.[37]

The biting sarcasm of this closing remark reveals both what Sebald values in literature and how he begins positioning himself as a young scholar vis-à-vis his discipline. Sebald fancied and fashioned himself as an academic outsider, writing and publishing a particular form of literary criticism that challenges or goes against the grain of traditional scholarship.[38] For example, he attracted some attention with the publication of his master's thesis on Carl Sternheim and the following polemical discussion that ensued in the newspaper *Die Zeit*.[39] Sebald's statement in his letter to Tabbert is more important for the way it concisely reveals Sebald's approach to literature and literary studies. Here we see how important it is for him that the reader has an imaginative, even empathetic, investment in his subject. The attempt to access the past through physical traces, such as architectural structures, is valued over intellectual, rational, and critical analysis. This is a position and a method that Sebald develops further in both his literary criticism and fiction.[40]

The understanding of world literature as literature that circulates beyond the borders of its production naturally raises the question of translation. "Everyone knows, of course," writes Hayden White,

> that there is no such thing as a perfect translation, but translatability has long been the mainstay of the humanistic philological approach to the comparative study of literature, the

---

37 Ibid.

38 Considering his vehemence against the "intellectual stock exchange," it is worth noting that Sebald pursued his Habilitation, which may indicate his desire to leave the British system to pursue a career in Germany. On Sebald's resistance to traditional literary criticism, see Uwe Schütte, "Against Germanistik: W. G. Sebald's Critical Essays," *Saturn's Moons: A W. G. Sebald Handbook*, eds. Jo Catling and Richard Hibbitt (Oxford: Legenda, 2011) 161–194.

39 See Valerij Poljudow, "Eins mit seinen Gegnern? Sebalds Sternheim-Polemik," *Die Zeit* Nr. 33 (August 14, 1970) 15. Sebald's response to Poljudow was published as well: W. G. Sebald, "Sternheims Narben," *Die Zeit* Nr. 35 (August 28, 1970) 46. Both of these articles are reprinted in Marcel Atze and Franz Loquai, eds. *Sebald. Lektüren* (Eggingen: Ed. Isele, 2005) 56–60.

40 Sebald's essay on Jean-Jacques Rousseau in *Logis in einem Landhaus*, which recounts his own travels to St. Peter's Island, Switzerland, reveals a similar method. See chapter two below. The idea of going to the house where Hölderlin was Hofmeister is also echoed in the scene where Austerlitz finds his childhood apartment in Prague, an act that (re)activates his long repressed memories. Austerlitz experiences deep sensate recognition while standing in the building, even before he knows that this is where he grew up.

principal device for representing the relation between one period and another in literary history, and the secret to that 'continuity in change' that is supposed to be the payoff of a specifically historical treatment of anything whatsoever.[41]

The question of translation is particularly pertinent to a discussion of Sebald's works, first for the thematic importance of transfer, translation, and transformation, second for the construction of the text both on linguistic and visual levels, and third with regard to the positive reception of Sebald in the Anglophone world. Therefore, a discussion of Sebald's works in translation ensures that the specificity of his poetics does not get occluded in political and cultural debates.[42] In other words, we do not want, as Damrosch warns, to "gain a work of world literature but lose the author's soul."[43] Considering translation is also essential for the fact that the German and English versions of Sebald's works differ in part so significantly that it has been suggested they be held apart as two distinct œuvres.[44] My analyses of Sebald's works throughout the book bear in mind the distinction between original and translation without making a 'fetish' of the original.

In the preface to their translation of Erich Auerbach's "Philology and *Weltliteratur*," Maire and Edward Said point precisely to one of the greatest challenges in translation – the historicity of terms that I invoked above with Hayden White – when they account for why they do not translate Goethe's concept of *Weltliteratur* as "world literature." The Saids state,

> An expedient such as 'world literature' betrays the rather unique traditions behind the German word. It is, of course, Goethe's own word which he used increasingly after 1827 for universal literature, or literature which expresses *Humanität*, humanity,[45] and this expression is literature's ultimate purpose. *Weltliteratur* is therefore a visionary concept, for it transcends national literatures without, at the same time, destroying their individualities.[46]

---

41 Hayden White, "Commentary: 'With no particular place to go:' Literary History in the Age of the Global Picture," *New Literary History* 39.3 (2008) 727–745, here 741.

42 I will return to the various levels of translation in Sebald's works in chapter six.

43 Damrosch, *What is World Literature?* 36.

44 McCulloh, "Introduction," 7.

45 "Humanity" would also fall under this category of "expedient." The English cognate betrays the complexity and multiple dimensions and specific cultural and historical context of the German word *Humanität* in the eighteenth and nineteenth centuries. See Hans Adler, "Herder's Concept of *Humanität*," *A Companion to the Works of Johann Gottfried Herder*, eds. Hans Adler and Wulf Koepke (Rochester, NY: Camden House, 2009) 93–116.

46 Auerbach, trans. Maire and Edward Said, "Philology and *Weltliteratur*," 1.

These thoughts on language and literature resonate with Auerbach's concluding remarks on philology and *Weltliteratur* that assert our philological home [*Heimat*] can no longer be the nation. The influence of his own exile becomes clear when he states,

> Gewiß ist noch immer das Kostbarste und Unentbehrlichste, was der Philologe ererbt, Sprache und Bildung seiner Nation; doch erst in der Trennung, in der Überwindung wird es wirksam. Wir müssen, unter veränderten Umständen, zurückkehren zu dem, was die vornationale mittelalterliche Bildung schon besaß: zu der Erkenntnis, daß der Geist nicht national ist.[47]
>
> [The most priceless and indispensible part of a philologist's heritage is still his own nation's culture and language. Only when he is first separated from this heritage, however, and then transcends it does it become truly effective. We must return, in admittedly altered circumstances, to the knowledge that prenational medieval culture already possessed: the knowledge that the spirit is not national.[48]]

While lifting the borders of national philology, or undoing the limit of nation on philological pursuits, Auerbach nevertheless reinforces the fundamental importance of language in these pursuits. Acknowledging the weight that comes with national and historical inheritance, Sebald insists on remaining aware of one's origin as it lends a degree of truth to one's writing.[49]

International and Transdisciplinary Reception

Sebald's works have been widely translated, and the Anglo-American reception of Sebald is in part responsible for his presence in the world literary market.[50] In

---

47 Auerbach, "Philologie der Weltliteratur," 96.

48 Auerbach, "Philology and *Weltliteratur*," 17.

49 In Rebecca Walkowitz's project of cosmopolitanism that purports to go beyond the nation, she asserts that to be cosmopolitan – this holds for both texts and for individuals – "means engaging in an intellectual program rather than inhabiting a cultural position." It is therefore perplexing that she speculates, and in part insists, on the "Britishness of Sebald's novels." Rebecca Walkowitz, "Introduction" and "Sebald's Vertigo," *Cosmopolitan Style. Modernism Beyond the Nation* (New York: Columbia University Press, 2006) 16 and 162, respectively.

50 Sebald's *Austerlitz*, for example, has been translated into over twenty languages. See also Juliane Römhild, "'Back in Sebaldland.' Zur Rezeption von W. G. Sebald in der britischen Tagespresse," *Zeitschrift für Germanistik* 15.2 (2005) 393–399. The reception of Sebald's works to a certain extent parallels Damrosch's account of the reception of Eckermann's *Gespräche mit Goethe*. Damrosch writes, "The book's rapid foreign success stands in sharp contrast to its early reception at home. [...] Eckermann's book thus provides an interesting example of a work that only achieves an effective presence in its country of origin after it has already entered world

recent years, the wide reception of Sebald's works has broadened out into a full-fledged multi-media resonance. Not only are there contemporary literary works that bear the influence of Sebald's style[51], but his works have also inspired photographic meditations[52], theater and radio productions[53], and both documentary and creative films.[54] An entire exhibition around Sebald and his works, displaying his handwritten manuscripts and image collections, was organized by the Literaturmuseum der Moderne, which is adjacent to the Deutsches Literaturarchiv [German Literature Archive] in Marbach, Germany, where his entire estate is held.[55] This exhibition drew significant crowds, and parts of it were also exhibited at the Centre Pompidou in Paris.

In addition to the wide international resonance of Sebald's works, one could also talk of a transdisciplinary reception that manifests itself in the various responses to his works in other forms, especially digital ones. This is evidenced in the various Sebald-related or Sebald-inspired blogs and websites, several of which track down the minutiae of Sebald's stories, in some cases even physically and photographically retracing the journeys described in the text. The title of one blog – "Stalking Sebald" – is probably the most revealing of this phenomenon.[56] This blogger visited and photographed several of the sites that are described in *Austerlitz*; the blog posts include these color photographs,

---

literature; in a movement that would hardly have surprised Goethe, the book's reception abroad set the stage for its subsequent revival at home." Damrosch, "Introduction," 32.

51 Most notable is Teju Cole's *Open City* (New York: Random House, 2011).

52 The contributions to *Searching for Sebald. Photography after W. G. Sebald*, ed. Lise Patt (Los Angeles: Institute for Cultural Inquiry and ICI Press, 2007) include scholarly articles and descriptions of artistic, in particular photographic projects inspired by Sebald's works.

53 A recent theater adaptation of *Die Ringe des Saturn* was directed by Katie Mitchell and performed at Halle Kalk, Schauspiel Köln, in Cologne, May 2012. Excerpts from Grant Gee's film (see below) were incorporated into this production. The radio program "Sebald's Apocalyptic Vision" recounted the conceptualization of and preparations for Mitchell's theater adaptation; this program aired on BBC Radio 3, June 8, 2013, 21:00–21:30.

54 Thomas Honickel's documentary film *W. G. Sebald. Der Ausgewanderte* (2007) traces Sebald's biography from his youth in the Allgäu to his life in Norwich, highlighting his life as an author and incorporating interviews with his former colleagues. Honickel's film *Sebald. Orte* (2007) is a more interpretative exploration of the places in Sebald's fictional works. *Patience – After Sebald* (2012), a film by Grant Gee, is a creative, collage-like filmic interpretation of Sebald's *Die Ringe des Saturn*.

55 The exhibition was on display from September 26, 2008 through February 1, 2009 and accompanied by the catalogue: *Wandernde Schatten. W. G. Sebalds Unterwelt*, eds. Ulrich von Bülow, Heike Gfrereis and Ellen Strittmatter (Marbach am Neckar: Deutsche Schillergesellschaft, 2008).

56 http://stalkingsebald.blogspot.com/ [accessed: June 22, 2013]

which are captioned by or embedded in the relevant passages – both in English and in German – from Sebald's text.[57] The design and content of this and other blogs is indicative of the way Sebald's texts fascinate many readers and inspire them to emulate his works. The visual reflection of Sebald's texts in the blogs is, however, not always matched by critical reflection. In fact, the 'imitation' of the text-image arrangements in Sebald's works and the long citations are left to speak for themselves without much, if any, additional commentary.[58] This current fascination with Sebald as manifested in digital forms can be connected to Sebald's own approach to literature, as voiced in his letter to Tabbert cited above. Sebald's own practice of seeking out physical traces is inscribed into his fictional texts insofar as his narrators and characters travel to particular geographical destinations in hopes of accessing knowledge or insight of the past, and their aimless wandering also often makes spontaneous discoveries and connections possible. It is perhaps no surprise then that Sebald's texts incite readers to carry out a similar practice.

What many of the authors of such blogs have in common is that they are self-proclaimed "amateurs"[59] who hold themselves at some distance from academic literary studies and practices. Christian Wirth, who set up the impressive website: www.wgsebald.de, introduced himself on the welcome page in an earlier version of the site as follows: "Der Betreiber dieser Seite ist Laie und Sebald-Leser"[60] [the operator of this site is a layman and Sebald reader], and currently on the site's "Impressum" [about section], Wirth describes the site as the "Produkt eines Amateurs, der viel Zeit und etwas Geld investiert" [product of an amateur, who invests a lot of time and a little bit of money into it].[61] As with all blogs, the posts are organized in reverse chronological order with the most recent items listed first, and they are characterized by an integration of visual and video material

---

57 No further posts have been added to this blog, as the author notes: "The blog had a natural end point once my perambulations round Europe had much or less covered all the spots described by Austerlitz and his author." A further blog called "Norwich," includes posts by a certain "Sébastien Chevalier," and is subtitled: "on the times and places in W. G. Sebald and others." http://norwitch.wordpress.com/ [accessed: June 22, 2013]

58 A more informative and reflective blog would be Terry Pitts' "Vertigo: Collecting and Reading W. G. Sebald," subtitled: "On literature and book collecting, with an emphasis on W. G. Sebald and novels with embedded photographs." http://sebald.wordpress.com/ [accessed: June 22, 2013]

59 For a discussion of Sebald and the question of "amateurs," see Ruth Franklin, "Sebald's Amateurs," *W. G. Sebald. History – Memory – Trauma*, eds. Scott Denham and Mark McCulloh (Berlin: de Gruyter, 2006) 127–138.

60 http://www.wgsebald.de/framestart.html [accessed: March 30, 2010]

61 http://www.wgsebald.de/impressum.html [accessed: June 22, 2013]

and the use of hypertext or tags. The blogging about Sebald's texts rewrites them in a hypertext format and rearranges the non-chronological progression, thus providing a way to keep track of and to visualize the repeated motifs, story lines, and formation of the text.[62] This particular response to Sebald's works – digital transcriptions, translations, and adaptations – is indeed ironic, since Sebald wrote everything by hand or with a mechanical typewriter and remained reluctant to even turn on a computer.

Beyond amateur blogging, Barbara Hui's LITMAP presents a more complex and technologically sophisticated effort to digitally "map" one of Sebald's texts.[63] With this project, Hui visualizes the literal border crossing in *Die Ringe des Saturn* to show the range of geographical and political space covered.[64] Interested in the "geospatial shape of the narrative," by which she means "the contours that emerge when the place names mentioned in the texts are plotted on [a] geospatial map image," Hui created the LITMAP in order for "humanities scholars to read literature spatially."[65] Her project conceives of geographical space in a positivist and empirical way, using "numerically precise data" to plot place names on the surface of the earth "with a certain degree of mathematical accuracy."[66] The LITMAP encompasses both the local and the global and enables a reader to oscillate between the two levels by zooming in and out, ultimately gaining insight into the particularities of places and the greater network in which these places are located.[67] Driven by a sense that notions of perception and comprehension are also in flux, Hui sees that "places denoted by markers on map images are not fixed, immobile, bounded entities with unified histories, but rather dynamic, socially defined 'moments.'"[68] As a result of the pervasiveness of such applica-

---

62 Before taking this idea too far, one could just view this hypertext approach as a modern form of the "Zettelkasten" [index card catalogue] in which one may still get lost but at least with fewer paper cuts.

63 http://barbarahui.net/litmap/ [accessed: June 22, 2013]; see also Barbara Hui, *Narrative Networks: Mapping Literature at the Turn of the 21ˢᵗ Century*, PhD dissertation, Comparative Literature, UCLA, 2010 and Barbara Hui, "Mapping Historical Networks in *Die Ringe des Saturn*," *The Undiscover'd Country. W. G. Sebald and the Poetics of Travel*, ed. Markus Zisselsberger (Rochester, NY: Camden House, 2010) 277–298.

64 For thematic border crossing, see Martin Klebes, "No Exile: Crossing the Border with Sebald and Améry," *W. G. Sebald: Schreiben ex patria/Expatriate Writing*, ed. Gerhard Fischer. (Amsterdam; New York, NY: Rodopi, 2009) 73–90.

65 http://barbarahui.net/the-litmap-project/ [accessed: June 22, 2013]

66 Ibid.

67 "Network" for Hui is concrete (physical), as well as abstract (colonial, imperial, migratory, and linguistic), and imaginary.

68 http://barbarahui.net/the-litmap-project/

tions like GoogleMaps and Google Earth, Hui argues, "geographical representations are becoming rapidly entrenched in our cultural consciousness" and that we "are growing accustomed to viewing and navigating our surroundings via the use of the geospatial applications."[69] Whether this is really how we navigate the space of a literary text remains to be seen, I would argue. What is certain, however, is that Sebald's texts do indeed lend themselves to such visualization and spatialization.

Hui's LITMAP creates and enables new readings of Sebald's *Die Ringe des Saturn* in particular and potentially all literature in general, by giving the reader an immediate geographical orientation to match the textual description. However, while employing cutting-edge technology, the project's innovation is limited. One may wonder how such a project differs from a world map marked up with push pins. Moreover, such spatial re-presentation runs the risk of de-contextualization and disorientation. Despite having the book's page numbers as reference points, it is likely that the reader will lose the actual context of the passage in the text's new spatial *re*-presentation. The result of such computerized (re)mapping or imaging as opposed to human visualization or imagining in the end levels the depth of the text's actual archaeological structure, compressing the layers onto one plane. Ironically, in spatializing *Die Ringe des Saturn* in a visual form, the LITMAP approach decontextualizes the narrative passages and erases the visual elements of the text. That is, the images integrated into the text, which are characteristic of Sebald's works and essential to his poetics, are neither reproduced nor referenced in this digital form.

Sebald's works combine text and image in such a way that heightens the emotional and intellectual engagement through the many questions they raise. Readers are prompted to ask: Is the text a novel, a travelogue, a biography, an autobiography? Why do these texts remind us of Kafka, Borges, Nabokov? What is the role of the images integrated into the text? What is fact and what is fiction? What is real and what is invented? The reader is engaged simultaneously on multiple levels, reflecting on the above questions while experiencing the text through the senses (visually and haptically) and actively imagining what is read. Moreover, the specific questions of genre, text/image, fact/fiction that are elicited by Sebald's works can in turn be connected to broader questions fundamental to the study of literature: What is genre and how do we define it? What is intertextuality? What is intermediality? What is literature's relationship to reality? How do we define 'truth' in literature? What are the aesthetic possibilities of literature and in particular at the end of the twentieth

---

69 Ibid.

century? It is a defining principle of Sebald's approach to literature to incorporate various fields while simultaneously questioning the interaction, overlap, and limits of these various ways of knowing.

Scope and Method

Within the framework of human culture as a constitutive tool necessary for human evolution and literature as a constitutive component of human culture, it is imperative that we keep an open perspective toward both the objects of our analyses (i.e., texts) and the way we approach them. This book operates within such an open theoretical framework to both re-examine the perennial question – what is literature good for? – and to illuminate Sebald's engagement with this question in his literary and critical works. The purpose of this book is thus two-fold: it excavates the nexus of epistemological, aesthetic, and ethical concerns that structure the foundation for Sebald's hybrid form of writing, and it positions his form of literary historiography with regard to the former question of literature's purpose and achievement. By way of this in-depth examination of Sebald's works, the book offers a broader consideration of the perpetual problem of literature's relationship to reality as it is exemplified in the particular tension between literature and historiography. The book also offers a new critical perspective on Sebald by elucidating his immanent poetics as they emerge across his œuvre and by situating them within the particular twentieth-century cultural context.

This book addresses Sebald's scholarly as well as fictional works to ultimately engage with fundamental concepts of literary discourse: mimesis, representation, narration, and translation. I approach and analyze Sebald's immanent poetics and his innovative form of literary historiography in his four main fictional prose works: *Schwindel.Gefühle, Die Ausgewanderten, Die Ringe des Saturn*, and *Austerlitz* and further contextualize this interdiscursivity with regard to his literary critical writing, primarily in *Logis in einem Landhaus* and *Luftkrieg und Literatur*. Considerations of Sebald's poetry in *Unerzählt* and *Über das Land und das Wasser* contribute to this book's comprehensive assessment of Sebald's poetics. Moving the perspective beyond Sebald's œuvre, this book both illuminates the potential of the literary discourse to perform the interdiscursive transfer from experience to representation and also makes the case that a historical perspective is necessary to humanity's understanding of itself.

Appropriate to the way in which Sebald's works challenge us to rethink the boundaries between genres, discourses, disciplines, and media, this book proceeds in a methodologically non-dogmatic way, which should not be confused with a "disobedient" approach.[70] The multiplicity of perspectives – historical, cultural, and narrative, among others – that Sebald employs on a thematic and more significantly on a discursive level, demands flexibility from both the reader and the scholar. This multiplicity forms an aesthetic principle of Sebald's prose and defies the reduction that one narrow theoretical framework imposes. My approach thus draws on hermeneutics, semiotics, narratology, and discourse theory, and thereby distinguishes itself from much existing scholarship that tends to level the complexity of Sebald's literary texts by narrowly viewing them through one theoretical or methodological lens. Devoting special attention to the intertextualities at stake in Sebald's works, this book sets itself apart from the comparative approaches and studies of influence that try to fit Sebald's works into a mold drawn from other authors, such as Barthes, Benjamin, and Adorno, to name but a few. In a similar vein, this work stands apart from the several Freudian-based analyses that reduce Sebald's fiction to aspects of trauma, mourning, and melancholia.[71]

Two complementary perspectives guide my definition and analysis of Sebald's literary historiography in his fictional prose works and posthumously-published poetry as well as in his essayistic and literary critical writing. *Textual hybridity* is the first perspective and encompasses both the various forms Sebald's texts adopt and the multiple levels of reference that one and the same text may embody. *Interdiscursivity* constitutes the second perspective, and with it I refer to the transfer and translation of knowledge among co-existing discourses. Furthermore, my approach has two interdependent dimensions: the in-depth *synchronic* analysis of Sebald's works opens up the possibility of examining broader *diachronic* developments in and beyond his works. This simultaneously synchronic and diachronic approach reveals on the one hand the intricacies of a single text – its construction, narrative techniques, and complex network of references – and on the other the structural commonalities and thematic threads that run across multiple texts. My approach to the problem of representing history within the

---

70 See Deane Blackler, *Reading W. G. Sebald: Adventure and Disobedience* (Rochester, NY: Camden House, 2007). Other scholars and artists have "performed" similarly "disobedient" readings. See for example, Natania Rosenfeld, "Enthrallments," *Hotel Amerika* 3.1 (2004) 19–23.

71 Quite common in current Sebald research is an emphasis placed on the connection between discussions of memory and mourning and, by extension, trauma theory. While often evocative, these at times far-reaching interpretations of Sebald's works tend to drift the furthest from the textual material. A refreshing counter example is Dora Osborne's recent "parallel examination" of Sebald and Christoph Ransmayr; based in close readings of select works by these two authors, Osborne shows both how Freud's case histories are intertextually 'present' in these works and how these authors adapt Freud's models in their literary works. See Dora Osborne, *Traces of Trauma in W. G. Sebald and Christoph Ransmayr* (Oxford: Legenda, 2013) 2.

literary discourse and to the question of the narrative formation of history is not strictly formal but rather requires the understanding of both author and context to fully develop the historical knowledge and perspective of the literary text. My approach to Sebald's works could further be described as an inductive approach that is supported with empirical investigation.

Over the last ten years, there has been an explosion of secondary literature on Sebald, and scholarship continues to appear at a rapid rate. The repetitive nature of commentary on Sebald's works is an inevitable result of so much being produced simultaneously.[72] Since the Sebald "boom" is a rather recent phenomenon, one can still, to a degree, maintain an overview of research literature. However, one may do well to heed Sebald's own caveat to resist "die Verschrecktheit der eigenen Meinung angesichts der Fülle von Sekundärliteratur," [the fear of one's own opinion in the face of abundant secondary literature,] which results in "eine letztlich auch inspirationslose Gründlichkeit beim Schreiben" [a thoroughness in writing that is ultimately uninspired].[73] Moreover, a significant amount of secondary literature devotes its attention to various themes and motifs in the works of Sebald, often resulting in an essayistic exposé that stops at a characterization of his works while raising related key questions. Interesting connections can indeed be found in such essays, but often a central thesis seems to be lacking.

The researcher interested in Sebald is confronted with not only secondary literature on Sebald but also a meta-level of Sebald criticism: review articles that comment critically on said secondary literature. A case-in-point is the fact that two major review articles appeared at approximately the same time: Richard Sheppard's article on eleven Sebald-related publications[74] and Markus Zisselsberger's review article of three major publications on Sebald.[75] It is almost unjust to

---

72 See Lynn Wolff, "'Das metaphysische Unterfutter der Realität:' Recent Publications and Trends in W.G. Sebald Research," *Monatshefte* 99:1 (2007) 78–101, here 78. See also Lynn Wolff, review of *W.G. Sebald: History, Memory, Trauma*, eds. Scott Denham and Mark McCulloh (Berlin: de Gruyter 2006) *Monatshefte* 100.2 (2008) 313–316.

73 Sebald cited in Florian Radvan, "W.G. Sebald – Schriftsteller und Scholar. Erinnerungen an einen Grenzgänger zwischen Literatur und Wissenschaft," *Kritische Ausgabe* Nr. 18 "Familie" (2010) 56–59, here 56.

74 Richard Sheppard, "'Woods, trees and the spaces in between:' A Report on Work Published on W.G. Sebald 2005–2008" *Journal of European Studies* 39.1 (2009) 79–128.

75 Markus Zisselsberger, "A Persistent Fascination: Recent Publications on the Work of W.G. Sebald," *Monatshefte* 101.1 (2009) 88–105. Zisselsberger's review article evaluates Claudia Öhlschläger, *Beschädigtes Leben. Erzählte Risse: W.G. Sebalds Poetische Ordnung des Unglücks* (Freiburg i. Br.; Berlin; Vienna: Rombach, 2006), J.J. Long, *W.G. Sebald: Image, Archive, Modernity* (Edinburgh: Edinburgh University Press, 2007), and Blackler (2007).

refer to the contributions by Sheppard as review articles, for they go far beyond an evaluation of recent scholarship. Sheppard weaves together meticulous readings of Sebald's literary and critical works with detailed biographical knowledge. Further broad meta-commentary on Sebald scholarship can be found in Jonathan Long's valuable bibliographical essay included in the volume *W.G. Sebald and the Writing of History*, which he co-edited with Anne Fuchs.[76] Long considers over one hundred individual works – both articles and books – by some eighty scholars written over the past fifteen years. While indicating the breadth of Sebald scholarship and providing an orientation among the main areas of research, Long focuses on research from 2000 to 2007 and refrains from explicitly evaluating each individual contribution. Providing a useful distinction for considering the proliferation of commentaries and in particular those that do not fall under the category of literary criticism, Zisselsberger differentiates between "a readerly fascination with Sebald and an intellectual interest in his work."[77] Although they must always be read with a critical distance, interviews also serve as a major source for both establishing Sebald's biography and characterizing his poetics.[78] The consideration of Sebald scholarship that follows is therefore limited to only

---

76 J.J. Long, "W.G. Sebald: A Bibliographical Essay on Current Research," *W.G. Sebald and the Writing of History*, eds. Anne Fuchs and J.J. Long (Würzburg: Königshausen & Neumann, 2007) 11–29.

77 Ibid., 89. The "readerly fascination" that Zisselsberger identifies is particularly applicable for the blogs and digital visualizations and transcriptions of Sebald's works I discussed above. Silke Horstkotte also suggests differentiating between Sebald's professional readers and "Sebald-Neulinge" [Sebald novices] whom she qualifies as those, "die sich offenbar (noch) nicht in die Sebald-Forschung eingelesen haben" [who apparently are not (yet) familiar with Sebald scholarship]. Silke Horstkotte, Review of *Verschiebebahnhöfe der Erinnerung. Zum Werk W.G. Sebalds*, eds. Ingo Wintermeyer and Sigurd Martin (Würzburg: Königshausen & Neumann, 2007) *Monatshefte* 100.3 (2008) 451–455, here 454.

78 A recent edition of interviews, many of which were previously unpublished, promises to serve as an important reference work for future Sebald scholarship. See *"Auf ungeheuer dünnem Eis". Gespräche 1971 bis 2001*, ed. Torsten Hoffmann (Frankfurt am Main: Fischer, 2011). In addition to Bigsby cited above, see *The Emergence of Memory: Conversations with W.G. Sebald*, ed. Lynne Sharon Schwartz (New York; London; Melbourne; Toronto: Seven Stories Press, 2007). Schwartz's collection has also appeared in French translation as *L'Archéologue de la mémoire: Conversations avec W.G. Sebald*, ed. Lynne Sharon Schwartz, trans. Patrick Charbonneau and Delphine Chartier (Arles: Actes Sud, 2009). See also, Torsten Hoffmann, "Das Interview als Kunstwerk. Plädoyer für die Analyse von Schriftstellerinterviews am Beispiel W.G. Sebald," *Weimarer Beiträge* 55.2 (2009) 276–292. Sheppard has voiced a caveat on reading Sebald's interviews as a source of "evidence" when interpreting his texts. Sheppard warns the reader, "never believe Sebald the interviewee when he is solemnly stating facts rather than expressing opinions, and even then be sceptical." See Sheppard, "'Woods, trees and the spaces in between,'" 97.

the most relevant publications as they relate to the central problem of literature's relationship to history and historiography in Sebald's works.[79]

"We need to see Sebald not only as a chronicler of post-Holocaust trauma but as a historian of the longue durée of modernity if we are fully to understand why his work matters," writes Jonathan Long in the last sentence of his study *W. G. Sebald: Image, Archive, Modernity*, a significant contribution to the field of Sebald research.[80] The strength of this work lies in Long's emphasis on the historical dimension of Sebald's works, which moves research beyond trauma studies.[81] Numerous publications over the past few years engage with "History" and the "historical" in Sebald's works, be it by investigating the historical events he thematizes, by scrutinizing his sources, or by analyzing his presentation of such material that problematizes the entire historiographical endeavor. Anne Fuchs' trailblazing study on the poetics of memory in Sebald's prose works suggests ways of defining Sebald's concept of history; in particular, she highlights how history, for Sebald, can no longer be told as a process of causal developments but rather must be seen as a network of disasters.[82] She also suggests that Sebald reverses historical perspective: "Nicht mehr die Gegenwart ist Richtschnur der Vergangenheit, sondern die obsoleten Überreste der Vergangenheit werden zum Maßstab der Gegenwart" [The present is no longer the guideline of the past, rather the obsolete remains of the past become the standard of the present.][83] Several of these investigations, however, like much of the literature on Sebald, have remained thematic rather than discursive in nature. Antje Tennstedt's comparative intertextual analysis of Claude Simon and Sebald underscores the tension between individual memory and official historiography, but she keeps the question of historiography as the thematic back-

---

79 Recent relevant publications that due to time constraints could not be considered in their entirety include: Christina Hünsche, *Textereignisse und Schlachtenbilder. Eine sebaldsche Poetik des Ereignisses* (Bielefeld: Aisthesis Verlag, 2012); Fridolin Schley, *Kataloge der Wahrheit. Zur Inszenierung von Autorschaft bei W. G. Sebald* (Göttingen: Wallstein, 2012); Peter Schmucker, *Grenzübertretungen: Intertextualität im Werk von W. G. Sebald* (Berlin [u.a.]: de Gruyter, 2012). (Spectrum Literaturwissenschaft, 28); Ben Zimmermann, *Narrative Rhythmen der Erzählstimme. Poetologische Modulierungen bei W. G. Sebald* (Würzburg: Königshausen & Neumann, 2012).
80 Long, *W. G. Sebald*, 174 (first italics mine).
81 In addition to the historical, Long makes a point of emphasizing both metaphysical and geophysical dimensions in Sebald's works. Ibid., 21.
82 Anne Fuchs, *"Die Schmerzensspuren der Geschichte." Zur Poetik der Erinnerung in W. G. Sebald's Prosa* (Cologne: Böhlau, 2004) 53.
83 Ibid., 54.

ground to her investigation.[84] I see my intervention in Sebald studies as developing such a historical view and also taking up Long's specific call to consider Sebald not only as a chronicler but as a historian.[85] I do not stop there, however, and would agree with Ben Hutchinson who insists on Sebald's status as an artist rather than a "verkappter Historiker"[86] [historian in disguise]. By emphasizing the difference between the artist and the historian, Christopher Bigsby also justifies the enterprise of interviewing authors about their work: "Creative writers are not historians but there is a history contained in their work and, of course, in their lives. The story of story making is also a story worth reading."[87]

The problem of representation, historical representation in particular, is a central focus of Sebald's works and hence secondary literature. Many articles discuss Sebald's project in terms of a metaphysics of history, however this is often not defined and can lead to near-endless permutations when trying to characterize this so-called metaphysics.[88] Several scholars have focused on Sebald's understanding of history as informed by Walter Benjamin[89] as well as by Horkhei-

---

84 Antje Tennstedt, *Annäherungen an die Vergangenheit bei Claude Simon und W.G. Sebald* (Am Beispiel von *Le Jardin des Plantes, Die Ausgewanderten* und *Austerlitz*) (Freiburg im Breisgau: Rombach, 2007).

85 Michael Braun refers to Sebald as "der melancholische Chronist" [the melancholy chronicler]. Michael Braun, "Im Schatten des Saturn. Die melancholische Geschichtsschreibung des W.G. Sebald," *Der zertrümmerte Orpheus. Über Dichtung* (Heidelberg: Das Verlag Wunderhorn, 2002) 51. Uwe Schütte also sees Sebald as a chronicler, specifically of the history of catastrophe and of German-Jewish lives. Cf. Uwe Schütte, *Sebald. Einführung*, 13 and 30.

86 Ben Hutchinson, *W. G. Sebald – Die dialektische Imagination* (Berlin: de Gruyter, 2009) 19.

87 Christopher Bigsby, *Writers in Conversation with Christopher Bigsby. Volume Two* (Norwich [U.K.]: Arthur Miller Centre for American Studies, 2001) viii.

88 In an attempt to specify what is meant by "metaphysics of history," a phrase used by several of the authors in Fuchs and Long's volume, Helen Finch writes, "This 'metaphysics' both restores repressed memory and points towards an esoteric level in his account of historical events. In Sebald's view, conventional narratives of history serve only to conceal further this 'truer' metaphysical level." The outlines of this definition, however, become blurred by the further qualifications of Sebald's "metaphysical poetics," "secular metaphysics," and the "neo-Romantic aspect of Sebald's metaphysics." See Helen Finch, "'Die irdische Erfüllung': Peter Handke's Poetic Landscapes and W.G. Sebald's Metaphysics of History," *W.G. Sebald and the Writing of History*, eds. Anne Fuchs and J.J. Long (Würzburg: Königshausen & Neumann, 2007) 179–197, here respectively 180, 181, 182, 181.

89 See for example Irving Wohlfarth, "Anachronie. Interferenzen zwischen Walter Benjamin und W.G. Sebald," *IASL. Internationales Archiv für Sozialgeschichte der Deutschen Literatur* 33.2 (2008) 184–242. The volume *W.G. Sebald and the Writing of History*, eds. Anne Fuchs and J.J. Long (Würzburg: Königshausen & Neumann, 2007) further establishes Sebald as an intellectual heir to Walter Benjamin, particularly with regard to Benjamin's concept of history as developed in his *Über den Begriff der Geschichte*. See Lynn Wolff, review of *W.G. Sebald and the*

mer and Adorno's *Dialektik der Aufklärung*.[90] Graham Jackman characterizes Sebald's "cautious, 'archaeological' method" that "exemplifies a mode of memorialising the victims which constitutes an alternative to the necessarily evaluative techniques of discursive historiography."[91] Similarly, in an essay on the representation of the "Kindertransport" in literary texts, Mona Körte describes Sebald's prose as "an alternative to the dwindling number of survival autobiographies, on the one hand, and official history on the other," and his method as one that destabilizes traditional historiography.[92] Together with these concluding thoughts, Körte also asserts that "Sebald is one of many authors whose prose has been elevated by literary critics to a position of 'poetic historiography.'"[93] Körte, however, does not name any of these "many authors" nor does she provide any references to said literary critics. In his article on Sebald's "miniature histories," Long reminds us of the "mediated nature of so-called personal memory," and points to the fact that Sebald's texts themselves constantly allude to this dimension of the individual or subjective experience of history: "the workings of memory are inseparable from external prosthetic mnemotechnical aids and the metaphors that derive from them: photographs, cinema, paintings, archival documents, and so on."[94] Through comparisons to Maurice Blanchot, Georges Perec, and Paul Celan, Jan Ceuppens highlights how Sebald privileges the "petite histoire" over representative historical narratives.[95] Mary Cosgrove identifies the problem in *Austerlitz* with master narratives as rooted in "their neglect of the subjective experience of history,"[96] an assessment that equally applies to Sebald's entire œuvre. According to Russell J. A. Kilbourn, shifting the focus to the

---

Writing of History, eds. Anne Fuchs and J. J. Long, (Würzburg: Königshausen & Neumann, 2007). *Monatshefte* 100.3 (2008) 455–457.

90 See for example Graham Jackman, "'Gebranntes Kind?' W. G. Sebald's 'Metaphysik der Geschichte,'" *German Life and Letters* 57.4 (2004) 456–471. Stephan Seitz frames his investigation of Sebald's method of bricolage with the philosophy of history developed by Benjamin and Adorno. Stephan Seitz, *Geschichte als bricolage – W. G. Sebald und die Poetik des Bastelns* (Göttingen: V & R Unipress, 2011).

91 Graham Jackman, "Introduction," *German Life and Letters* 57.4 (2004) 343–353, here 351–352.

92 Mona Körte; trans. Toby Axelrod, "Bracelet, Hand Towel, Pocket Watch: Objects of the Last Moment in Memory and Narration," *Shofar* 23.1 (2004) 109–120, here 119.

93 Ibid.

94 J. J. Long, "W. G. Sebald's Miniature Histories," *W. G. Sebald and the Writing of History*, eds. Anne Fuchs and J. J. Long (Würzburg: Königshausen & Neumann, 2007) 111–120, here 113.

95 Jan Ceuppens, "Tracing the Witness in W. G. Sebald," *W. G. Sebald and the Writing of History*, eds. Anne Fuchs and J. J. Long (Würzburg: Königshausen & Neumann, 2007) 59–72.

96 Mary Cosgrove, "Sebald for our Time: The Politics of Melancholy and the Critique of Capitalism in his Work," *W. G. Sebald and the Writing of History*, eds. Anne Fuchs and J. J. Long (Würzburg: Königshausen & Neumann, 2007) 91–110, here 107.

representations of history "foregrounds the artificiality, the constructedness, of history," and that for Sebald, "the reading or interpretation of such representations *as* representations (such texts as texts, in context, *intertextually*) is of fundamental importance, since the 'thing itself,' an objective account of the *past* – or, for that matter, of *identity* – always escapes capture in the present."[97] In what follows, I will further elucidate how Sebald challenges such objective accounts of the past and how he inscribes the process of historical reconstruction through a literary mode within his fictional prose works.

Beyond the relationship of history and literature, several research areas and approaches can be identified within the scholarship on Sebald, and these stem from the central themes in his works. Questions have been posed regarding Sebald's "Jewishness"[98]; his personal status as an "exile," and specifically in relation to his literary exile figures;[99] how his works can be read as an illustration of Marianne Hirsch's concept of "postmemory;"[100] how he attempts to represent the Holocaust;[101] and what function the visual material integrated

---

97 Russell J.A. Kilbourn, "'Catastrophe with Spectator:' Subjectivity, Intertextuality and the Representation of History in *Die Ringe des Saturn*," *W.G. Sebald and the Writing of History*, eds. Anne Fuchs and J.J. Long (Würzburg: Königshausen & Neumann, 2007) 139–162, here 160.

98 Leslie Morris, "How Jewish is it? W.G. Sebald and the Question of 'Jewish' Writing in Germany Today," *The New German Jewry and the European Context: The Return of the European Jewish Diaspora*, ed. Y. Michal Bodemann (Houndmills, U.K.; New York: Palgrave Macmillan, 2008) 111–128; Stuart Taberner, "German Nostalgia? Remembering German-Jewish Life in W.G. Sebald's *Die Ausgewanderten* and *Austerlitz*," *Germanic Review* 79.3 (2004) 181–202; Ralf Jeutter, "'Am Rand Der Finsternis:' The Jewish Experience in the Context of W.G. Sebald's Poetics," *Jews in German Literature since 1945: German-Jewish Literature?*, ed. Pól O'Dochartaigh (Amsterdam, Netherlands: Rodopi, 2000) 165–179.

99 Susanne Finke, "W.G. Sebald, der fünfte Ausgewanderte," *W.G. Sebald*, ed. Franz Loquai (Eggingen: Ed. Isele, 1997) 214–227 and Sigrid Löffler, "W.G. Sebald, der Ausgewanderte," *Kritiken, Portraits, Glossen* (Vienna, u.a.: Deuticke, 1995) 72–78.

100 See chapter five for list of articles and a further discussion of this concept.

101 Noam M. Elcott, "Tattered Snapshots and Castaway Tongues: An Essay at Layout and Translation with W.G. Sebald," *Germanic Review* 79.3 (2004) 203–23; J.J. Long, "History, Narrative, and Photography in W.G. Sebald's *Die Ausgewanderten*," *Modern Language Review* 98.1 (2003) 117–137; Carol Bere, "The Book of Memory: W.G. Sebald's *The Emigrants* and *Austerlitz*," *Literary Review: An International Journal of Contemporary Writing* 46.1 (2002) 184–92; Jan Ceuppens, "Im zerschundenen Papier herumgeisternde Gesichter. Fragen der Repräsentation bei W.G. Sebalds *Die Ausgewanderten*," *Germanistische Mitteilungen* 55 (2002) 79–98; Silke Horstkotte, "Pictorial and Verbal Discourse in W.G. Sebald's *The Emigrants*," *Iowa Journal of Cultural Studies* 2 (2002) 33–50; Stefanie Harris, "The Return of the Dead: Memory and Photography in W.G. Sebald's *Die Ausgewanderten*," *German Quarterly* 74.4 (2001) 379–91; Katharina Hall, "Jewish Memory in Exile: The Relation of W.G. Sebalds *Die Ausgewanderten* to the Tradition of the Yizkor Books," *Jews in German Literature since 1945: German-Jewish Literature?*, ed. Pól O'Dochar-

into his verbal texts has.[102] Two major book publications have analyzed the intertextuality of Sebald's works, both with an emphasis on narratology.[103] Additionally, numerous articles have appeared on intertextuality, some of which couple intertextuality with intermediality.[104] The various comparative

---

taigh (Amsterdam, Netherlands: Rodopi, 2000) 153–164; Ann Parry, "Idioms for the Unrepresentable: Postwar Fiction and the Shoah,"*The Holocaust and the Text. Speaking the Unspeakable*, eds. Andrew Leak and George Paizis (Basingstoke, England; New York, NY: Macmillan; St. Martin's, with Institute for Romance Studies and Institute for English Studies, School of Advanced Study, University of London, and Wiener Library, 2000) 109–124, et al.

102 See chapter three for a discussion of Sebald's use of images and chapter six for a discussion of intermedial translation.

103 See Susanne Schedel, *'Wer weiss, wie es vor Zeiten wirklich gewesen ist?' Textbeziehungen als Mittel der Geschichtsdarstellung bei W.G. Sebald* (Würzburg: Königshausen & Neumann, 2004) and Tennstedt, *Annäherungen an die Vergangenheit*. Narratology is one of four aspects that make up Tennstedt's approach to Simon and Sebald, and she outlines two sides of intertextuality: on the one hand, as a politically subversive potential and on the other, as a hermeneutic technique.

104 See two articles by Marcel Atze, "Casanova vor der Schwarzen Wand. Ein Beispiel intertextueller Repräsentanz des Holocaust in W.G. Sebalds *Austerlitz*," *Sebald. Lektüren*, eds. Marcel Atze and Franz Loquai (Eggingen: Ed. Isele, 2005) 228–243 and "Koinzidenz und Intertextualität. Der Einsatz von Prätexten in W.G. Sebalds Erzählung 'All'estero,'" *W.G. Sebald*, ed. Franz Loquai (Eggingen: Ed. Isele, 1997) 151–175. The proceedings of a 2007 conference on Sebald organized by Irene Heidelberger-Leonard were published as Irene Heidelberger-Leonard and Mireille Tabah, eds., *W.G. Sebald. Intertextualität und Topographie* (Berlin: LIT Verlag, 2008). See in particular Jo Catling, "W.G. Sebald: ein 'England-Deutscher'? Identität – Topographie – Intertextualität," 25–53 and Ruth Vogel-Klein, "Französische Intertexte in W.G. Sebalds *Austerlitz*," 73–92. Further articles include Michaela Holdenried, "Zeugen – Spuren – Erinnerung. Zum intertextuellen Resonanzraum von Grenzerfahrungen in der Literatur jüdischer Überlebender. Jean Améry und W.G. Sebald," *Autobiographisches Schreiben in der deutschsprachigen Gegenwartsliteratur 2. Grenzen der Fiktionalität und der Erinnerung*, eds. Christoph Parry and Edgar Platen (Munich: iudicium, 2007) 74–85; Silke Horstkotte, "Prozessionen und Trauerzüge. Intertextualität und Intermedialität in W.G. Sebalds *Die Ringe des Saturn*," *Nachbilder. Fotografie und Gedächtnis in der deutschen Gegenwartsliteratur* (Cologne; Weimar; Vienna: Böhlau, 2009) 43–75; Judith Kasper, "Intertextualitäten als Gedächtniskonstellationen im Zeichen der Vernichtung: Überlegungen zu W.G. Sebalds *Die Ausgewanderten*," *Wende des Erinnerns? Geschichtskonstruktionen in der deutschen Literatur nach 1989*, eds. Barbara Beßlich, Katharina Grätz, Olaf Hildebrand [*Philologische Studien und Quellen* 198] (Berlin: Schmidt, 2006) 87–98; Russell J.A. Kilbourn, "Kafka, Nabokov...Sebald: Intertextuality and Narratives of Redemption in *Vertigo* and *The Emigrants*," *W.G. Sebald. History – Memory – Trauma*, eds. Scott Denham and Mark McCulloh (Berlin: de Gruyter, 2006) 33–63; Patrick Lennon, "In the Weavers' Web: An Intertextual Approach to W.G. Sebald and Laurence Sterne," *W.G. Sebald. History – Memory – Trauma*, eds. Scott Denham and Mark McCulloh (Berlin: de Gruyter, 2006) 91–104; Claudia Öhlschläger, "Unschärfe. Schwindel. Gefühle. W.G. Sebalds intermediale und intertextuelle Gedächtniskunst," *Mémoire. Transferts. Images./Erinnerung. Übertragungen. Bilder*, ed. Ruth Vogel-Klein, *Recherches germaniques* Hors Série 2 (2005) 11–23; Ann Pearson, "'Remembrance ... Is Nothing Other Than a Quotation:'

approaches to Sebald's works are not surprising when one considers this underlying intertextuality of his œuvre.[105]

Despite the abundant secondary literature on Sebald, there are significant gaps with regard to the specificity of his poetics. Zisselsberger identifies an irony in Long's Foucault-focused study "not only because its academic rhetoric and theoretical approach 'discipline' Sebald's work – through its subordination to theory – but also because it replicates the kind of 'scholarly' engagement with texts in which 'literature' gets increasingly lost and from which Sebald therefore tried to distance himself."[106] Martin Swales has also lamented the lack of specifying the *literary* achievement of Sebald's works in current research. That is, the question "How, specifically, does he write?" has not been answered sufficiently.[107] Hutchinson's book on Sebald and the "dialectical imagination" attempts to answer this question by focusing on Sebald's style in particular. My book also strives to fill this significant lacuna, approaching Sebald's literary achievements by elucidating the discursive fusion found across his works. By starting from the construction of the texts, I am able to outline underlying structures or highlight their absence, rather than imposing a pre-existing structure onto the individual texts. Sebald's emphasis on elements and aspects rather than concepts or theories influences the way I reference theory in my approach to his works. That is, I refer to theoretical considerations in order to open up aspects of Sebald's œuvre rather than reading his works through one particular 'lens.'

The Intertextual Fictions of W. G. Sebald," *Comparative Literature* 60.3 (2008) 261–278; Oliver Sill, "'Aus dem Jäger ist ein Schmetterling geworden.' Textbeziehungen zwischen Werken von W. G. Sebald und Vladimir Nabokov," *Poetica* (1997) 596–623; Martin Swales, "Intertextuality, Authenticity, Metonymy? On Reading W. G. Sebald," *The Anatomist of Melancholy. Essays in Memory of W. G. Sebald*, ed. Rüdiger Görner (Munich: iudicium, 2003) 81–87.

105 A selection of comparative approaches includes Dora Osborne, *Traces of Trauma in W. G. Sebald and Christoph Ransmayr* (Oxford: Legenda, 2013); Daniel L. Medin, *Three Sons: Franz Kafka and the Fiction of J. M. Coetzee, Philip Roth and W. G. Sebald* (Evanston, IL: Northwestern University Press, 2010); Anneleen Masschelein, "Hand in Glove: Negative Indexicality in André Breton's *Nadja* and W. G. Sebald's *Austerlitz*," *Searching for Sebald. Photography after W. G. Sebald*, ed. Lise Patt (Los Angeles: Institute for Cultural Inquiry and ICI Press, 2007) 360–387; J. J. Long, "Disziplin und Geständnis. Ansätze zu einer Foucaultschen Sebald-Lektüre," *W. G. Sebald. Politische Archäologie und melancholische Bastelei* (Philologische Studien und Quellen. H. 196), eds. Michael Niehaus and Claudia Öhlschläger (Berlin: Schmidt, 2006) 219–239; Marcel Atze, "Die Gesetze von der Wiederkunft der Vergangenheit. W. G. Sebalds Lektüre des Gedächtnistheoretikers Maurice Halbwachs," *Sebald. Lektüren*, eds. Marcel Atze and Franz Loquai (Eggingen: Ed. Isele, 2005) 195–211; Eluned Summers-Bremner, "Reading, Walking, Mourning: W. G. Sebald's Peripatetic Fictions," *JNT: Journal of Narrative Theory* 34.3 (2004) 304–334 (on Sebald and Lacan).

106 Zisselsberger, "A Persistent Fascination," 103.

107 Swales, review of *W. G. Sebald. History – Memory – Trauma*, 129.

Focusing on the individual or the individualization of history rather than a collective or totalizing concept – making history accessible to others as literature, but not merely through a functionalization of literature – is essential to understanding Sebald's concept of literature. Central questions of my investigation are: What is particular about Sebald's writing? How is he 'translating' history into literature? How and where does he emphasize this process? Where are his sources apparent? Where does he cover them up? The reader of Sebald's texts is often left wondering what is fact and what is fiction, which photographs can be considered *objets trouvés* and which may contain Sebald's own reflection, which newspaper articles and journal entries are real and which are 'forged.'[108] These questions prove productive in initiating the reader's engagement with not only the text but also broader questions of memory, history, and authenticity.

Chapter one lays the foundation for the book's thesis: Sebald's œuvre embodies a new type of historiography that comes into being only in the literary mode. In a first step, I sketch in broad strokes the diachronic development of literature's relationship to historiography from antiquity to the present, highlighting moments of discursive differentiation and destabilization as well as disciplinary developments. In a second step, I situate Sebald within a genealogy of authors and historians concerned not only with Germany's recent past but also with the form in which this past can most appropriately be recounted. Reading Sebald with and against authors of post-World War II literature, this chapter establishes the innovativeness of Sebald's fiction by showing how it diverges from documentary fiction on the one hand and the historical novel on the other.

Moving from the external to the internal contextualization of Sebald's œuvre, chapter two continues to elucidate the broader frame of the book by mapping the development of Sebald's literary historiography with regard to his literary scholarship and in particular his essayistic criticism that borders on autobiography in *Logis in einem Landhaus* and *Luftkrieg und Literatur*. Of particular significance in this respect is the manuscript of the original lectures on poetics given in Zurich in 1997 out of which the publication *Luftkrieg und Literatur* emerged. My analysis of the manuscript, which is part of Sebald's estate now held at the Deutsches Literaturarchiv in Marbach, Germany (DLA), contributes to a re-contextualization and re-evaluation of the political polemic that his lectures ignited with the contentious thesis that no (sufficient) literary representations were written about the Allied air raids on German cities at the end of World War II. The far-reaching

---

108 See Adrian Daub, "'Donner à Voir:' The Logics of the Caption in W.G. Sebald's *Rings of Saturn* and Alexander Kluge's *Devil's Blind Spot*," *Searching for Sebald. Photography After W.G. Sebald*, ed. Lise Patt (Los Angeles: Institute for Cultural Inquiry and ICI Press, 2007) 306–329.

concerns discussed in this chapter and at the heart of Sebald's form of literary historiography are the ethical imperative of literature and the challenge of writing history as a transfer from experience into language.

Expanding the discussion of the narrative formation of history to include the role of images and the imagination, chapter three offers new ways to consider the text-image relationship that makes Sebald's works immediately recognizable. Sebald's text-image constellations are central to creating his distinctive tone and to presenting his particular worldview. Giving rise to questions of genre, influence, and reference, the tension between text and image proves productive in further initiating the reader's engagement with the overarching questions of memory, history, and authenticity. To draw out the implications of these questions and the effect of the dynamic text-image relationship, I differentiate among multiple levels of reality in Sebald's works. I frame my analyses within three broader historical and theoretical discussions: the concept of mimesis, the development of photography, and the representability of the Holocaust. In these considerations, I engage with the writings of Charles Baudelaire, Siegfried Kracauer, Walter Benjamin, Bertolt Brecht, Roland Barthes, Susan Sontag, Theodor W. Adorno, Saul Friedländer, and Georges Didi-Huberman. This chapter further illuminates the ethical imperative of literature by connecting the fundamental problem of art's relationship to reality to the specific problem of the Holocaust's representability, which is arguably Sebald's foremost concern. Ultimately, the investigation of the visual materials and their relationship to the text connects the two main concerns of the book. That is, the question of representation occupies a pivotal position in the book, as it forms the discursive space shared by both literature and historiography.

In chapter four I first shed light on Sebald's unique theory of time that allows for the simultaneity of past, present, and future. I then draw out the implications that such a theory has for the chronology of narrative texts in particular and on our understanding of the past in general. I show how the co-presence of various points of time within one physical space – be it geographic, architectural, or narrative – rather than a chronological ordering creates the effect of a tableau rather than flow in Sebald's literary works. To do this, I focus particular attention on *Austerlitz*, the last fictional prose work to be published during Sebald's lifetime and certainly his most complex with regard to narrative structure. This work presents explicit discussions of time, while placing both thematic and discursive emphasis on history and historiography. Based in large part on archival material in Sebald's estate (DLA), I elucidate the tension between the necessity of a specific chronology to make the narrative possible and Sebald's way of erasing the traces of this chronology to intentionally create a non-linear narrative progression. This narratological analysis thus reveals not only how Sebald works against chronology and 'order' but also how his narrative techniques align with his concept of providing an unofficial and alternative form of historiography within fictional literature.

Chapter five further develops the considerations of the individual's relationship to 'reality' by examining the representation of memory as a dynamic process and the conceptualization of memory as largely dependent on imagination. To substantiate a main strand of my argument that Sebald's concept of history is not to be reduced to an overriding metaphysics, I highlight his focus on the individual or the individualization of history as opposed to a collective or totalizing concept. Moreover, by framing this discussion with a critical reconsideration of theories of memory and structures of testimony, this chapter reveals the potential of literary discourse to respond to the complex and often contentious epistemological, aesthetic, and ethical dimensions involved in representing the past.

Using theories of translation (Willis Barnstone, George Steiner, Edith Grossman, et al.), chapter six defines and distinguishes among the multiple levels of translation in Sebald's four major fictional prose works and in *Über das Land und das Wasser*, a collection of poetry edited and published posthumously. This differentiated exploration of translation further illuminates the specificity of Sebald's poetics and what can appropriately be characterized as his conservative innovation. I first discuss issues of textual translation such as Sebald's syntax, style, tone, and deployment of specialized terminology. I then elucidate questions of intra- and intertextual translation, and the complicating factor of Sebald's use of intermediality. Third, I present metaphorical translation, conceptualized as the root of representation, as the overarching concern that drives Sebald's writing, and I relate this back to the problem of historical representation with which my book begins. In addition to textual analysis, I incorporate into this discussion the comments made by several of Sebald's translators (Anthea Bell and Michael Hulse on their English translations and Patrick Charbonneau on his French translations) as well as Sebald's own changes and 'corrections' to their translations. The considerations in this chapter are based in large part on my analysis of the manuscripts and correspondence between Hulse and Sebald housed at Harvard University's Houghton Library. The chapter ultimately reveals translation as a key concept for defining the particularity of the literary discourse to enact, thematize, and reflect upon the process of capturing experience in writing.

The conclusion briefly revisits the text-image relationship for the way it echoes the broader concerns of the book: the interaction yet irreducibility of distinct discourses and the resulting tension between construction and reconstruction, creation and recreation, imagination and memory. By exploring the particular tension between literature and historiography, as both illustrated and problematized across Sebald's œuvre, this book takes the reader on a journey that reveals the potential of the literary discourse to process, produce, and perform the interdiscursive transfer from experience to representation. The conclusion brings this journey to a close at a panoramic look-out point that reconsiders how Sebald's œuvre illustrates interdiscursivity while creating a transdiscursive form. That is, I make clear how Sebald's literary historiography not only brings two discourses into contact but more significantly retains the dialectic potential of the relationship between literature and historiography. The new literary form that emerges out of this dialectic tension across Sebald's works reveals an interdiscursive vision of literature and a transdiscursive ideal of "literary knowledge." This is the vanishing point, where a type of aesthetic knowledge or a unique form of literary (re)cognition emerges, making it possible to re-evaluate and redefine how we understand both the past and our place in the present.

Chapter 1
Literature as Historiography in Context

The first part of this chapter traces the sustained contact between historiography and literature from Aristotle's differentiation of two distinct discourses to the discursive fusion in twentieth- and twenty-first-century fictional forms. Since this is both a long and well-documented relationship, I aim to highlight select moments in order to focus on a new literary form that emerges from the close connection between history and literature. I explore the tension inherent in the simultaneous in- and co-dependence of these two discourses, arguing that their sustained contact is rooted in the fact that neither history nor fiction is a stable concept. Furthermore, the discursive difference – whether reinforced in narrative historiography of the eighteenth and nineteenth centuries or destabilized by the "linguistic turn" of structuralism and postmodernism – remains an organizing principle for both literature and historiography across the ages. Despite and precisely because of the instability of both history and fiction, made most acute in theories of postmodernism, truth and authenticity persist as core values to both.[1] The parallels between and overlapping of literature and history will be discussed here, that is, the literary dimension of historiography and the historicity of literature.[2]

The second part of this chapter takes a closer look at the way in which Sebald's literary texts bring history and literature into dialogue with one another and the ethical dimensions of such a practice. The authenticity or feeling of authenticity in Sebald's texts, that is, an authenticity based on emotional connec-

---

1 One of Frank Ankersmit's many contributions to the discussion of the relationship between history and literature points to the truth value of both and raises the question of "whether historical writing can contribute to a better understanding of the novel." See Frank Ankersmit, "Truth in History and Literature," *Narrative* 18.1 (2010) 29–50, here 29. This refreshing starting point moves in a direction similar to the considerations outlined below. I diverge from Ankersmit insofar as my investigation is not limited to the historical novel. Furthermore, I maintain that literature dealing with historical concerns should not be viewed as an instrumentalization of the historical discipline but rather considered for how it can transmit and more significantly create knowledge of the past.

2 Ansgar Nünning has written about this extensively. See for example, Ansgar Nünning, *Von historischer Fiktion zu historiographischer Metafiktion. Band I Theorie, Typologie und Poetik des historischen Romans* (Trier: Wissenschaftlicher Verlag Trier, 1995) and Ansgar Nünning, "'Verbal Fictions?' Kritische Überlegungen und narratologische Alternativen zu Hayden Whites Einebnung des Gegensatzes zwischen Historiographie und Literatur," *Literaturwissenschaftliches Jahrbuch* 40 (1999) 351–380.

tion rather than rational reflection or factual reference,[3] suggests that literature not only possesses a truth value in itself but can also be a means of accessing and transmitting historical truth. In considering the relationship between historiography and literary discourse from a diachronic perspective, this chapter responds to the question of the sustainability of traditional concepts and the emergence of new ones. Furthermore, I articulate this book's central claim that Sebald's œuvre forges a new discourse of literary historiography, a new type of historiography that comes into being only in the literary mode and that reveals literature's privileged position for exploring, preserving, and understanding the past.[4] Through this analysis of Sebald's fiction I show how literature aims at and claims a certain kind of truth, as history does, and that this is a further reason this relationship can be seen as one of co-dependence, which has persisted over time, albeit in differing forms.

Literature versus Historiography across the Ages

Today it may seem like common theoretical knowledge that history, like literature, is a discourse that does not exist a priori. History, as opposed to literature, presents a particular challenge insofar as it can be understood to mean multiple things. In defining the concept, Reinhart Koselleck points to history as both an event and the recounting of this event, as well as the collection of examples, from which one can learn in order to live a just and wise life.[5] Echoing Koselleck, Hayden White writes of "the diversity of meanings that the term *history* covers in current usage." That is,

> [history] applies to past events, to the record of those events, to the chain of events that make up a temporal process comprising the events of the past and present as well as those of the future, to systematically ordered accounts of the events attested by the record, to explanations of such systematically ordered accounts, and so forth.[6]

---

3 This is evoked in particular through Sebald's use of photography and will be elucidated in chapter three.
4 For an earlier exploration of these ideas, see Lynn Wolff, "Literary Historiography: W.G. Sebald's Fiction," *W.G. Sebald: Schreiben ex patria/Expatriate Writing*, ed. Gerhard Fischer (Amsterdam; New York: Rodopi, 2009) 317–332.
5 Reinhart Koselleck, "Einleitung" in "Geschichte, Historie," *Geschichtliche Grundbegriffe. Historisches Lexikon zur politisch-sozialen Sprache in Deutschland*, vol. 2, eds. Otto Brunner, Werner Conze, and Reinhart Koselleck (Stuttgart: Klett, 1975) 593–595, here 594.
6 Hayden White, *The Content of the Form. Narrative Discourse and Historical Representation* (Baltimore; London: Johns Hopkins University Press, 1987) 147.

This diversity of meanings makes it all the more difficult to formulate a consistent definition of the discourse of history, but this is not only a consideration of our current understanding of history or just a result of the "linguistic turn." Rather, this challenge can be traced back to the beginnings of history. When Herodotus, the "father of history," wrote of *historia* (ἱστορία), he used the word to signify knowledge in general as well as investigation and the result of research, i.e., the recording and reporting of knowledge.[7] Thus we see how history, from its inception, has been defined both by the material sources (artifacts and documents) and by the documenter and documentation process (historian and historiography). Written history, based on material sources, in turn becomes a document or a form of documentation that serves as the basis for later histories.

Despite the multiplicity of referents bound to this one signifier, a "thread of distinction" between literature and history as formulated by Aristotle in his *Poetics*, still influences our current understanding of history.[8] In chapter nine of his *Poetics*, Aristotle states,

> The poet and the historian differ not by writing in verse or in prose. [...] The true difference is that one relates what has happened, the other what may happen. Poetry, therefore, is a more philosophical and a higher thing than history: for poetry tends to express the universal, history the particular.[9]

This fundamental distinction has indeed carried through from Herodotus to modern historiography. The idea of history that dominated from Herodotus' time through the nineteenth century is that the "history" already exists, i.e., is inherent in the past events and experiences, and it is the task of the historian to tell this history. Here, the task of the historian can be seen as one of documentation, or even transcription and transmission from an occurrence to the account of this occurrence, that is, from "event" (*Geschehen*) to "history" (*Geschichte*), to use Karlheinz Stierle's distinction.[10] The innovation of Stierle's model is the introduction of a third stage in this progression of writing history, namely the "text of history" (*Text der Geschichte*). Elizabeth Deeds Ermarth problematizes the way that both history and historical thinking, while an essential anthropolo-

---

7 Koselleck, "Einleitung," 595.

8 Cf. White, *The Content of the Form*, 147.

9 See Aristotle, Chapter Nine, *Poetics*, *Aristotle's Theory of Poetry and Fine Art*, ed. S.H. Butcher (New York: Dover Publications, 1951) 35.

10 Karlheinz Stierle, "Geschehen, Geschichte, Text der Geschichte," *Geschichte: Ereignis und Erzählung*, eds. Reinhart Koselleck and Wolf-Dieter Stempel, (*Poetik und Hermeneutik* 5) (Munich: Fink, 1973) 530–534.

gical constant, have become naturalized. She describes how "[...] thinking historically is like breathing. It is automatic. It is 'natural.' We talk about 'history' as if it were something objective – Out There, like rocks and stones and trees: a natural medium *in* which all things exist, causalities unfold, and time is productive."[11] Ermarth formulates an urgent call to "develop alternative ways of using the past, and alternative explanations of how time passes and what it produces" and reiterates the importance of "preserv[ing] our relation to the past."[12] In the considerations that follow, I will develop just how literature presents a privileged mode of critically approaching and engaging with the past in order to preserve our relation to it.[13] Several elements are at stake in the distinction between literature and history and will be discussed throughout this book, namely questions of reality, possibility, truth, experience, knowledge, representation, and imagination. Through my analyses of Sebald's works, I illuminate the particular way in which literary discourse responds to and engages with these questions.

The development of a modern, totalizing concept of history can be located in the eighteenth century, and towards the end of this century, history achieves the status of a leading political and social concept.[14] Fundamental to this modern concept of history is its status as a "Kollektivsingular" [collective singular], that is, the accumulation of individual histories.[15] Reinhart Koselleck has traced the development of this modern concept of history – how *Geschichte*, in the sense of an event or sequence of events, gradually took precedence over *Historie*, in the sense of the report of what has occurred – and the convergence

---

11 Elizabeth Deeds Ermarth, "The Trouble with History," *Historisierte Subjekte – Subjektivierte Historie. Zur Verfügbarkeit und Unverfügbarkeit von Geschichte*, eds. Stefan Deines, Stephan Jaeger, Ansgar Nünning (Berlin; New York: de Gruyter, 2003) 105–120, here 105.

12 Ibid., 105 and 120.

13 It is significant that Ermarth points to the way in which history should aspire to literature, yet she holds the discourses distinct: "We need a history that can do what literature can do, once it is freed from historical imperatives: recognize and give priority to the multiplicity of systems and to the volatility of meaning. We need a history that recognizes the power of associative relationships and that does not dismiss such relationships as 'irrational.' We need a history that recognizes there is more to reason that rationality, and that psychic and emotional reason operate differently from the rational, linear and productive mechanisms of history" (ibid., 115).

14 See Daniel Fulda and Silvia Serena Tschopp, "Einleitung. Literatur und Geschichte: Zur Konzeption des Kompendiums," *Literatur und Geschichte. Ein Kompendium zu ihrem Verhältnis von der Aufklärung bis zur Gegenwart*, eds. Daniel Fulda and Silvia Serena Tschopp (Berlin; New York: de Gruyter, 2002) 1–10. See also Koselleck, "Einleitung," 593.

15 Reinhart Koselleck, "Historia Magistra Vitae. Über die Auflösung des Topos im Horizont neuzeitlich bewegter Geschichte," *Natur und Geschichte. Karl Löwith zum 70. Geburtstag*, eds. Hermann Braun and Manfred Riedel (Stuttgart: Kohlhammer, 1967) 196–219, here 203.

within the concept of history of these two dimensions.[16] History then becomes "the great obsession of the nineteenth century,"[17] to speak with Foucault, while also coming into its own as a distinct discipline. The discipline of history is then elevated to attain the status of a science. Moreover, history becomes more broadly conceptualized in the nineteenth century to be seen as "the result of all-encompassing historical and social forces, rather than of the actions of individual kings or statesmen."[18] What marks historiography of the nineteenth century is the certainty that "unambiguous answers could be provided,"[19] and that the past could be presented "as it really was" – "wie es eigentlich gewesen" – as famously formulated by Leopold van Ranke. Modern historiography includes three main types of historical representation: the annals (a list of events), the chronicle (a chronological account up until the chronicler's present), and "the history proper" (an account that conveys not only chronology but also a structure and meaning).[20] The difference between the annals and the chronicle reveals a development in both form and content, from a list to a more comprehensive and narratively-coherent text.[21] This difference in form, or level of narrativity, is connected to the status of both what historians claim and how they claim it.[22] Historians of the nineteenth century certainly recognized the possibility for differing points of view, but in general, a common conviction persisted. As Hayden White states,

> The idea was to 'tell the story' about 'what had happened' without significant conceptual residue or ideological preformation of the materials. If the story were rightly told, the explanation of what had happened would figure itself forth from the narrative, in the same way that the structure of a landscape would be figured by a properly drawn map.[23]

---

16 Cf. ibid., 201–202.

17 Michel Foucault, "Of Other Spaces," trans. Jay Miskowiec, *Diacritics* 16.1 (1986) 22–27, here 22.

18 Frank R. Ankersmit, *Historical Representation* (Stanford: Stanford University Press, 2001) 149.

19 Hayden White, *Metahistory. The Historical Imagination in Nineteenth Century Europe* (Baltimore: Johns Hopkins University Press, 1973) 1.

20 White, *The Content of the Form*, 4–5.

21 Cf. White, *The Content of the Form*, 16.

22 Ibid., 19. White writes, "For the annalist there is no need to claim the authority to narrate events, since there is nothing problematical about their status as manifestations of a reality that is being contested. Since there is no 'content,' there is nothing to narrativize, no need for them to 'speak themselves' or be represented as if they could 'tell their own story.'"

23 White, *Metahistory*, 142.

While this position made it possible for the discipline of history to be elevated to that of a science, it is precisely these claims that are challenged in the twentieth century.[24]

The principle of nineteenth-century historiography to present the past "as it was," has come to be seen as a narrative itself, an ironic development from historiography as science to the extreme view of history as fiction. According to White, this emphasis on narrative has been established by historians and was even argued as the mark of the discipline's objectivity,

> It is historians themselves who have transformed narrativity from a manner of speaking into a paradigm of the form that reality itself displays to a 'realistic' consciousness. It is they who have made narrativity into a value, the presence of which in a discourse having to do with 'real' events signals at once its objectivity, its seriousness, and its realism.[25]

The "linguistic turn," as it applies to the historical discourse, challenges the empirical basis for historical knowledge insofar as language is seen to constitute reality. Presence and first-hand experience are no longer considered guarantors of truth, objectivity, or direct representation, since the translation from experience into language is contestable. Influenced by White, scholars have emphasized the rhetorical performance and analyzed the poetic aspects of historical representation. However, the value of a narrative historiography has long been recognized. It is not only accuracy or veracity that is valued in historians' writings, but it is their ability to tell a vivid story, to make the reader a "spectator" of sorts, a spectator who also experiences an emotional reaction to the subject. Koselleck asserts the anthropological foundation of telling (hi)stories ("Geschichten-Erzählen") and the necessity of such (hi)stories for memory on individual and collective, personal and political levels.[26] In addition to being an anthropological constant, White also sees narrative as a formal constant, suggesting it be seen as a solution to "the problem of how to translate knowing into telling."[27] Like

---

24 White refers to several authors and texts that challenge these claims, including Claude Lévi-Strauss' *The Savage Mind* [*La pensée sauvage*, 1962]. Sebald draws on the key notion of "bricolage" to describe his own method of researching and writing. One could therefore conjecture that Sebald's skepticism towards the authoritative gesture of historical accounts is in part influenced by Lévi-Strauss.

25 White, *The Content of the Form*, 24.

26 Koselleck, "Einleitung," 594.

27 White, *The Content of the Form*, 1. White also establishes the etymological connection between narration and knowing, referring to the Latin *gnārus* ('knowing,' 'acquainted with,' 'expert') and *narrō* ('relate,' 'tell') from the Sanskrit root *gnâ* ('know'). For the anthropological and formal basis of narrative, i.e., that it is "a human universal," White relies on Roland Barthes' assertion that narrative "is simply there like life itself [...] international, transhistorical, transcul-

Aristotle, Joseph Addison distinguishes between the work of the poet and that of the historian. The writer of poetry, according to Addison, is freer to use his imagination, whereas the historian – as well as "natural philosophers, travelers, geographers, and in a word, all who describe visible objects of a real existence" – is "obliged to follow nature more closely."[28] Addison's plea for narrative historiography as opposed to a chronology that lists or recounts facts makes clear that the role of the historian was to tell both an accurate history and an engaging story. He writes,

> It is the most agreeable talent of an historian to be able to draw up his armies and fight his battle in proper expressions, to set before our eyes the divisions, cabals and jealousies of great men, and to lead us step by step into the several actions and events of his history. We love to see the subject unfolding itself by just degrees, and breaking upon us insensibly, that so we may be kept in a pleasing suspense, and have time given us to raise our expectations, and to side with one of the parties concerned in the relation. I confess this shews more the art than the veracity of the historian [...].[29]

While White does not deny reality, historical or otherwise, his definition of the real is problematic insofar as it is dependent on a form of representation: "These events are real not because they occurred but because, first, they were remembered and second, they are capable of finding a place in a chronologically ordered sequence."[30] This relates to what White terms a "prefigurative act" in his *Metahistory*, an act that is "*poetic* inasmuch as it is precognitive and precritical in the economy of the historian's own consciousness."[31] White draws out the implication of this notion of the historian's prefigurative act, "In the poetic act which precedes the formal analysis of the field, the historian both creates his object of analysis and predetermines the modality of the conceptual strategies he will use

---

tural." White quotes from Barthes, "Introduction to the Structural Analysis of Narratives," *Image, Music, Text*, trans. Stephen Heath (New York: Hill & Wang, 1977) 79. This problem, both epistemological and aesthetic, is exactly what preoccupies and drives Sebald to write fictional literature.

28 Joseph Addison, *Spectator* No. 420 (Wednesday, July 2, 1712), *The Papers of Joseph Addison, Esq. in the Tatler, Spectator, Guardian, and Freeholder*. Together with his *Treatise on the Christian Religion*. To which are prefixed *Tickell's Life of the Author*, and extracts from *Dr. Johnson's Remarks on his Prose Writings*. With original notes never before published. Vol. III of IV (Edinburgh: William Creech, 1790) 282.

29 Ibid., 282–283. Addison's account previews the way that Austerlitz's history teacher André Hilary presents their history lessons such that the students become spectators to the theater of war. See discussion below.

30 White, *The Content of the Form*, 20.

31 White, *Metahistory*, 31.

to explain it."[32] Such claims stretch the possibilities of the historical discourse and the power of history and ultimately risk denying any sort of historical reality that exists outside of language. I see this as the danger in the above definition of the real formulated in *The Content of the Form*, i.e., that an event only becomes "real" when it has been recorded. By this logic, would natural disasters that predated human script or human existence be any less real? Does an earthquake only become real when scientists have recorded and measured it? I would have to disagree on the simple basis that ignorance, in short, does not change reality.

Ankersmit makes an important distinction between the significance of the "linguistic turn" for historiography and the use of literary theory as a tool for understanding historiography. Recapitulating White's central thesis that our understanding of the past is determined by the historian's presentation of the past, more precisely in the language he uses, Ankersmit writes, "historical knowledge is as much 'made' (by the historian's language) as it is 'found' (in the archives)."[33] White's axiom – "thought remains the captive of the linguistic mode in which it seeks to grasp the outline of objects inhabiting its field of perception"[34] – is certainly rooted in the philosophy of language; however, Ankersmit makes clear that literary theory as opposed to philosophy of language is the main source of inspiration for White.[35] What is more, Ankersmit contests the usefulness of literary theory in dealing with the central problem of historical theory – "the problem of how the historian accounts for or represents past reality" – for it does not deal with the question of "how a text may represent a reality other than itself and about the relationship between the text and reality."[36] In his double role as scholar and author, Sebald wrote fictional prose works that achieve just what Ankersmit thinks literary theory falls short of doing. In a literary form, Sebald poses questions about the representation of reality and the relationship between the text and reality.

Developments in the twentieth century, in particular theoretical reflections rooted in what has become known as the "linguistic turn," destabilize the discursive distinction between history and literature that was solidified during the nineteenth century. Theories of postmodernism emphasize the similarities between literature and history rather than insisting on their fundamental differ-

---

32 Ibid.
33 Ibid., 30.
34 White, *Metahistory*, xi.
35 Ankersmit, *Historical Representation*, 63–64. Ankersmit clarifies this difference: "The literary theorist 'naturalizes' language, whereas the philosopher of language will always 'semanticize' language and its relationship to the world" (65).
36 Ibid., 68.

ences. Building on the work of Hayden White, Linda Hutcheon asserts that "the realist novel and Rankean historicism share many similar beliefs about the possibility of writing factually about observable reality."[37] Hutcheon further outlines the convergence of the two disciplines:

> They have both been seen to derive their force more from verisimilitude than from objective truth; they are both identified as linguistic constructs, highly conventionalized in their narrative forms, and not at all transparent, either in terms of language or structure; and they appear to be equally intertextual, deploying the texts of the past within their own complex textuality.[38]

It is curious that Hutcheon does not problematize the novelistic genre in her discussion and definition of postmodern historiographic metafiction. However, this may very well be an illustration of what she later asserts of postmodernism: "It uses and abuses the very beliefs it takes to task; it installs and only then subverts the conventions of genre."[39] In a later work, Hutcheon points to the "provocative blurring of boundaries and crossing of borders" as defining aspects of postmodernism or as "givens for postmodern art forms."[40] "Postmodern historiographic metafiction" is thus the category Hutcheon carves out for "novels that are intensely self-reflexive but that also both re-introduce historical context into metafiction and problematize the entire question of historical knowledge," with which Hutcheon indicates an ontological problem.[41] Significantly, Hutcheon revises this assertion, broadening the category in later discussions within the context of representing the Holocaust. In her analysis of Art Spiegelman's *Maus*, she reestablishes a connection between truth and postmodernism when she asserts,

> The ontological and the epistemological are therefore of equal concern: the past did exist, the Holocaust did happen, but *Maus* explores *how* we know that, as well as *what* we can know about it from one man's testimony and one man's very real suffering. There are no universal claims to truth here, but this does not mean that no truth exists.[42]

---

37 Linda Hutcheon, "The Pastime of Past Time: Fiction, History, Historiographic Metafiction," *Genre*, Special Topics 12: *Postmodern Genres*, ed. Marjorie Perloff, XX.3–4 (1987) 285–305.
38 Ibid., 285.
39 Hutcheon, "Pastime of Past Time," 286.
40 Linda Hutcheon, "Literature Meets History: Counter-Discursive 'Comix,'" *Literatur und Geschichte in der Postmoderne*. Eds. Stephan Kohl, Karl Reichl, Hans Sauer, Hans Ulrich Seeber and Hubert Zapf. Special Issue of *Anglia. Zeitschrift für Englische Philologie* 117.1 (1999) 4–14, here 4.
41 Hutcheon, "The Pastime of Past Time," 285–286.
42 Hutcheon, "Literature Meets History," 12.

Since one of the key aims of this book is to elucidate how Sebald's œuvre presents a new narrative form that emerges out of the tension between the two existing discourses of literature and history, it is necessary to differentiate his works in relation to competing categories and literary genres. Engaging with the question of "postmodern or not?" that some scholars have posed with regard to Sebald's works does not afford us much insight into the specificities of Sebald's fictional prose, especially since the concept of postmodernism is itself rather elusive.[43] It is, however, productive to consider the category sketched out by Hutcheon, while at the same time heeding Ansgar Nünning's reminder that Hutcheon's "story," i.e., account of historiographic metafiction, is itself just one of many competing "'narratives of postmodernism.'"[44] A reason to refer back to Hutcheon's category is the way her considerations play out in practice. Much of what she argues with respect to Spiegelman's *Maus* would hold true for Sebald's works, especially the technique of distancing and the achievement of a certain degree of realism in the narrative. For instance, she writes of *Maus,*

> Yet, however documentary or realist its mode, it always reminds us of the *lack* of transparency of both its verbal and visual media. Its consistent reflexivity, pointing to the utter non-objectivity of the historian or biographer, here raises precisely the issues that have obsessed theorists of historiography for several decades now [...]. Far from being ahistorical because of challenges to some of the assumptions grounding traditional historiography, self-conscious narratives like *Maus* enact critical commentaries on the very 'making' of history, from what Hayden White calls its 'narrativizing' to the nature of its documentary archive. Problematizing notions of teleology as well as objectivity, of causality as well as totality, *Maus's* double narrative line *simultaneously* asserts the validity of the testimonial and questions the reliability of modes of representation; it accepts both the truth and the vagaries of memory.[45]

---

43 Nünning emphasizes the plurality of postmodernism but offers Hans Bertens' succinct characterization of what can be understood under the concept: "'a deeply felt loss of faith in our ability to represent the real.'" Nünning, "Crossing Borders and Blurring Genres," 219. See Hans Bertens, *The Idea of the Postmodern. A History* (London & New York: Routledge, 1995) 11.

44 Nünning, "Crossing Borders," 219. Here Nünning is referring to John Mepham, "Narratives of Postmodernism," *Postmodernism and Contemporary Fiction*, ed. E. J. Smyth (London: Batsford, 1991) 138–155. In a later article, Nünning broadens and differentiates the scope of the postmodern historical novel beyond the category of "historiographic metafiction" put forward by Hutcheon. See Ansgar Nünning, "'Beyond the Great Story:' Der postmoderne historische Roman als Medium revisionistischer Geschichtsdarstellung, kultureller Erinnerung und metahistoriographischer Reflexion." *Literatur und Geschichte in der Postmoderne*. Eds. Stephan Kohl, Karl Reichl, Hans Sauer, Hans Ulrich Seeber and Hubert Zapf. *Anglia. Zeitschrift für Englische Philologie* 117.1 (Special Issue) (1999) 15–48.

45 Hutcheon, "Literature Meets History," 11.

There are self-reflexive moments in Sebald's works, primarily in his use of images, and historical context is indeed indispensible. Rather than problematizing "the entire question of historical knowledge," Sebald's works are problematizing historical representation from an epistemological and aesthetic point of view. He is concerned with our access to the past rather than with the question of its existence, and while interrogating different forms of historical representation, his works at the same time present new ways of representing the past.[46]

Further formal categories to consider include historiographic metafiction and metahistorical novels, a distinction Ansgar Nünning makes as follows,

> In contrast to historiographic metafiction which addresses problems related to the writing of history explicitly in metafictional comments, metahistorical novels focus on the continuity of the past in the present, on the interplay between different time levels, on forms of historical consciousness, and on the recuperation of history.[47]

While comprehensible, this differentiation seems artificial when one tries to fit a complex literary text into one or the other category. Furthermore, the distinction itself becomes blurred when Nünning on the one hand emphasizes how metahistorical novels treat history as a literary theme and on the other states, "Instead of portraying a historical world on the diegetic level of the characters, metahistorical novels are generally set in the present but concerned with the appropriation, revision and transmission of history."[48] This concern with the transmission of history brings us close to the defining aspect of historiographic metafiction that "addresses problems related to the writing of history," cited above. That is, metahistorical novels "highlight the process of historical reconstruction and the protagonists' consciousness of the past rather than a represented historical world as such,"[49] whereas the "hallmark of explicit historiographic metafiction is that historiographical issues are directly thematized by narrators or characters."[50] I began this book by asserting my non-dogmatic approach to Sebald's works, and here it becomes clear that there are limitations to such theoretical constructs. Before getting lost in the various permutations of the concept of "metahistory," I would like to invoke Mieke Bal's broader understanding of the term "metahistorical" as "a critical examination of what historicity means – and can mean" and

---

46 As will be discussed below, I defend Sebald's assertion that he is not writing novels, and in this aspect, his works also resist Hutcheon's mold.
47 Nünning, "Crossing Borders," 224.
48 Ibid.
49 Ibid.
50 Ibid., 228.

how this concept functions in both reappraising the past and maintaining a critical view of how we construct this past.[51]

Whether we talk of historiographic metafiction or metahistorical novels, these forms are not the only ones that have a privileged access to the (re)construction of the past in the twentieth century. Ankersmit describes a "personalization or privatization of our relationship to the past," which is manifested in the "sudden predominance of the notion of memory" in twentieth-century historical representation.[52] Aleida Assmann points to the separation of history from memory that occurred alongside the professionalization of the discipline of history in the nineteenth century as well as the way the two have begun to converge again since the 1980s.[53] Oral history has played a significant role in this development and is relevant to the discussion at hand, for it is a form of historical investigation that reveals both a desire for more immediate access to the past and an awareness of the role human influence plays in the construction of the past.[54] Assmann points to the connection between oral history and Holocaust research in particular, namely the revaluation of survivor testimonies, highlighting how such forms of witnessing both document the past from an intimately personal perspective and serve a memorial function.[55] In a similar vein to oral history, "Alltagsgeschichte," or history of the everyday, has been an important development in reconsidering the role of personal memory in official forms of historiography. Andrea Albrecht highlights how historians of the everyday undertake microhistorical investigation of letters, memories, and interviews of contemporary witnesses, referring to Christopher Browning's *Ordinary Men* as a significant contribution to the development of this methodology.[56] The following section further develops the way

---

51 Mieke Bal, *Quoting Caravaggio. Contemporary Art, Preposterous History* (Chicago; London: University of Chicago Press, 1999) 19.

52 Ankersmit, *Historical Representation*, 154.

53 Aleida Assmann, *Der lange Schatten der Vergangenheit. Erinnerungskultur und Geschichtspolitik* (Munich: C.H. Beck, 2006) 44, 47.

54 On the relationship between oral history and literature in *Austerlitz*, see Bettina Mosbach and Nicolas Pethes, "Zugzwänge des Erzählens: Zur Relation von Oral History und Literatur am Beispiel W.G. Sebalds Roman *Austerlitz*," *Bios: Zeitschrift für Biographieforschung und Oral History* 21.1 (2008) 49–69.

55 Ibid., 49.

56 Christopher R. Browning, *Ordinary Men. Reserve Police Battalion 101 and the Final Solution in Poland* (New York: Harper Collins, 1992). In her article on Uwe Timm's *Am Beispiel meines Bruders*, Albrecht provides an overview of the development of oral history and "Alltagsgeschichte" in the 1970s to frame her analysis of Timm's text, an autobiographical novel which combines the literary pursuit of representing individual emotions and experiences with an interest in the history of the everyday. Albrecht furthermore points to a connection between Timm and Walter Benjamin in the way non-chronological representation reflects the fragmentary and

authors of postwar literature in German have continued to reflect upon and shape historical thinking within their works.

Toward a Genealogy of a Present Past

Postwar literature in German is marked by a tension between two central concerns, namely *Vergangenheitsbewältigung* – the so-called "coming to terms with the past," meaning Germany's Nazi past in particular – and the aesthetic and ethical (im)possibility of representing the Holocaust. The turn of the millennium has seen both a renewed interest in postwar literature and a surge in the production of literary texts that continue to deal with aspects and effects of the Second World War, often from a specifically generational perspective.[57] Decisive for this renewed interest in postwar literature were Sebald's lectures on poetics and their published form as *Luftkrieg und Literatur* (1999). The controversial thesis put forward by Sebald in these lectures brought widespread attention to him, as he was seen as initiating a public debate around war atrocities experienced by Germans during the Allied air raids at the end of World War II. Or, as it has been more polemically phrased: Sebald is seen as having initiated the debate on "German victimhood."[58] Both postwar and contemporary authors dealing with the Second World War and the Holocaust often test the limits of literature in order to approach the past, demonstrating the different ways that literature tells not only a story but also history. One could imagine the constellation of these authors as plotted along a continuum, the poles of which being, roughly, fact and fantasy or documentation and imagination. The ethical dimension of such literary engagements with World War II can be seen as a constant along this continuum, that is, the question of how to appropriately represent this moment in history as well as the past more generally is repeatedly posed both implicitly and explicitly in these texts. These authors, who demonstrate the different ways that literature tells (hi)-

---

episodic nature of memory. However, Timm's literary project remains distinct from Benjamin's insofar as he is not writing against the work of historians as Benjamin did. Cf. Andrea Albrecht, "Thick descriptions. Zur literarischen Reflexion historiographischen Erinnerns 'am Beispiel Uwe Timms,'" *Erinnern, Vergessen, Erzählen. Beiträge zum Werk Uwe Timms*, ed. Friedhelm Marx unter Mitarbeit von Stephanie Catani and Julia Schöll (Göttingen: Wallstein Verlag, 2007) 69–89, here 73, 86–87.

57 See for example Friederike Eigler, *Gedächtnis und Geschichte in Generationenromanen seit der Wende* (Berlin: Schmidt, 2005); Erin McGlothlin, *Second-Generation Holocaust Literature: Legacies of Survival and Perpetration* (Rochester, NY: Camden House, 2006).

58 Chapter two develops an alternative reading of these lectures by situating them within the broader context of Sebald's poetics.

stories – the double meaning implicit in the German word *Geschichte* – include first and foremost the pioneers of documentary literature and proponents of a history from below. These include the narrating documentarian Alexander Kluge and the collecting chronicler Walter Kempowski. Both Kluge and Kempowski are known for their relentless productivity and multi-volume works. Kempowski's *Chronik des deutschen Bürgertums*, comprising nine individual novels; his four-volume "Kollektives Tagebuch" [Collective Diary] for the years 1941–1945 referred to as the *Echolot*-project; and his so-called "Befragungsbücher" [Survey Books] – *Haben Sie Hitler gesehen?* and *Haben Sie davon gewusst?* – which collect the answers from hundreds of citizens; all contribute to his chronicle and archive of the German people. Located at the other end of the spectrum from documentary literature would be the inventive ventriloquist Marcel Beyer (*Flughunde; Spione*) and the fantastic satirist Edgar Hilsenrath (*Der Nazi und der Friseur; Jossel Wassermanns Heimkehr*). Both of these authors start from a historical basis to re-imagine alternative historical possibilities. Somewhere in the middle of this continuum would be the genre of historical novels, novels that recount historical events from the perspective of minor figures; and as representatives one could name both Günter Grass (*Die Blechtrommel*) and Bernhard Schlink (*Der Vorleser*). Perhaps most closely comparable to Sebald's works are those of Uwe Timm that link (auto)biography and history with reflections on the writing process (*Am Beispiel meines Bruders; Der Freund und der Fremde*; and *Halbschatten*).

In the attempts to approach and engage with history to ultimately understand past events and experiences, it becomes difficult to preserve the distinctions among the processes of seeing, remembering, and imagining. It is perhaps for these reasons that certain postwar authors have shifted their focus away from the visual toward the aural, focusing not on the sense of sight but on both sound and its opposite: silence. Two examples include Beyer's *Flughunde* and Timm's *Halbschatten*.[59] "Der Graue" [The gray one] in Timm's novel guides the narrator through the Berlin Invaliden Cemetery, directing his – and by extension our – attention to the voices that can be heard but that have grown progressively quieter over time: "Viele kann man kaum noch verstehen, und die meisten sind längst verstummt"[60] [Many can hardly be understood, and most have long since gone silent]. One could think of these voices in the cemetery as "Quasselstimmen" [gabbing voices], like those described in the prologue to Hilsenrath's *Jossel Wassermanns Heimkehr*.[61] While thousands of photographs were collected for

---

59 Marcel Beyer, *Flughunde* (Frankfurt am Main: Suhrkamp, 1995); Uwe Timm, *Halbschatten* (Cologne: Kiepenheuer & Witsch, 2008).
60 Timm, *Halbschatten*, 28.
61 Edgar Hilsenrath, *Jossel Wassermanns Heimkehr* (Munich: Piper, 1993) 21–32.

Kempowski's *Echolot* project, it was the voices – "ein eigenartiges Summen" [a curious humming] that he recalled hearing in the Bautzen prison yard – that inspired him to make an archive of unpublished biographies.[62] Kempowski himself situates his archive project on the border between history and literature,[63] and he admits his own difficulty with photographs as documents, expressing how photographs disturb "das innere Bild"[64] [the inner image].

By considering Sebald in relation to these authors and their literary projects, one can begin to develop a genealogy of authors concerned not only with Germany's recent past but also with the form in which this past can most appropriately be recounted. The different degrees of discursive hybridity of these works, or the range they present from documentary literature to fictional and fantastical reworkings of the past help determine the specificity of Sebald's literary form that uses documents but eschews the category of documentary literature, a form that is steeped in historical concerns but that cannot be contained within the category of the traditional historical novel.

Literary Historiography: A Method of Interdiscursive Writing

History and literature form a nexus in Sebald's works, and his discursive hybridity needs both. Distinct from narrative historiography and historical fiction, Sebald's texts trouble the fundamental distinction between the historian or historiographer and the poet as famously described by Aristotle in chapter nine of his *Poetics*. The poet, according to Aristotle, differs from the historian who chronicles events as they happened, by writing not only of how things *were* but of how things *could be*. The poet has both the room to be inventive and the freedom to tell stories that do not stem from past occurrences or that are based on what already exists in the world. This element of potentiality is the essential difference for Aristotle and the reason why he extols poetry as more philosophical than history.[65] Since the possible is the source of reality, according to Aristotle,[66] reality can then be seen

---

62 For his own reflections on the *Echolot* project, see Walter Kempowski, *Culpa. Notizen zum Echolot. Mit Seitenhieben von Simone Neteler und einem Nachwort von Karl Heinz Bittel* (Munich: btb, 2007 [2005]).

63 Cf. ibid., 181.

64 Ibid., 281.

65 Karlheinz Stierle identifies the allegorical basis for this potential of fictional texts to illustrate the general in the particular. Stierle, "Geschehen, Geschichte, Text der Geschichte," 533.

66 The possible is also "one of the provinces of truth," according to Baudelaire. Charles Baudelaire, "The Salon of 1859. Letters to the editor of the Revue Française," *Art in Paris 1845–1862. Salons*

as part of or encompassed by the possible. In this sense, presenting the possible remains a more comprehensive act than representing reality.

By troubling the boundaries between the two separate and at times disparate discourses of literature and history, Sebald's prose works combine the possibility and potentiality of fiction with direct references to an extra-textual reality, as lived by individuals, recounted in historical texts, or evidenced in artifacts. Sebald's integration of certain kinds of images, photographs in particular, demonstrates this potentiality valued so highly by Aristotle. Ontologically tied to an extra-textual reality, photographs testify to a past existence, yet Sebald's narratives show that it is only through literature that the documentary nature of photography can be unfolded. At the same time, the narratives Sebald spins around a photo-graph are not always tied to an extra-textual reality nor do they necessarily have anything to do with the original physical reality of the photograph.[67]

"Historiographie und Literatur gehen ihre eigenen Wege, manchmal parallel zueinander, manchmal so weit voneinander entfernt, daß sie einander kaum noch rufen hören" [Historiography and literature go their own ways, sometimes parallel to one another, sometimes so far apart from one another that they can hardly hear the other calling], writes Ruth Klüger in an essay that explores the interface ["Schnittstelle"], between literature and history. She describes how the relation-ship can be seen from two perspectives: literature using history as material ["Stoff"] for its own purpose and literature written in the service of history.[68] Klüger focuses her discussion on Holocaust literature and ultimately sides with literature that deals with history as "eine Form der Wirklichkeitsbewältigung" [a way to overcome reality], asserting that if literature or film functions only as a servant to history, then it inevitably turns into kitsch.[69] While interested in the sustained contact between

---

and Other Exhibitions Reviewed by Charles Baudelaire, trans. and ed. Jonathan Mayne (London: Phaidon Publishers [Greenwich, Conn.: New York Graphics Society Publishers], 1965) 144–216, here 156.

67 This is in the sense of Roland Barthes' *"that-has-been,"* or "ça-a-été" in the original French formulation. The notion that the photograph captures the "that-has-been" is particular to this medium and, as Barthes sees it, "the very essence, the *noeme* of Photography." Explaining the specificity of the photographic referent, Barthes writes: "I call 'photographic referent' not the *optionally* real thing to which an image or sign refers but the *necessarily* real thing which has been placed before the lens, without which there would be no photograph." Roland Barthes, *Camera lucida. Reflections on Photography* (New York: Hill and Wang, 1981 [French original 1980]) 76. See chapter three for a continued discussion of this point.

68 Ruth Klüger, *Dichter und Historiker. Fakten und Fiktionen*, Mit einem Vorwort von Hubert Christian Ehalt [Lecture given on March 24, 1999 as part of the "Wiener Vorlesungen im Rathaus."] (Vienna: Picus Verlag, 2000) 17.

69 Ibid., 50–51.

the two discourses, Klüger's argument ultimately reifies the separate spheres of literature and history. The complexity of Sebald's works arises from the way he blurs this clear separation. Although a sense of the historical pervades his prose, he insists on the legitimacy and independent status of the literary discourse, never relegating it to the status of a mere servant of history. If literature were a servant to historiography, it would ultimately be subsumed by this discipline. Moreover, it would be limited to reflecting historical reality and recounting past events as accurately as possible. Sebald's works exemplify how literature remains an independent discourse with inexhaustible potential. The complex structure of his works makes multiple readings and interpretations both possible and necessary.

While defending literature's "autonomy," Sebald goes beyond the fundamental distinction between literature and historiography as it was established by Aristotle in antiquity and reinforced by the disciplinary divide of the nineteenth century which elevated the status of historiography to that of a science. In the following I examine what constitutes both history and literature for Sebald in order to establish how this discursive tension forms the fundament of his fiction; I consider which events, individuals, and historians he thematizes as well as the implicit and explicit critiques of history that he develops. Considering in particular how Sebald "reconstructs" history and what implications this has for the literary discourse in relation to historiography, I show how Sebald ultimately fuses the two qualitatively different discourses of literature and history to reveal an interdiscursive form of literature. Such a vision of literature can also be seen as Sebald's method, which translates into a new form of "literary historiography:"[70] a rewriting of history that incorporates certain heretofore unconsidered or underestimated sources, that offers new perspectives on history and storytelling (or story-making), and that privileges the literary discourse as a means of approaching, translating, and ultimately representing experiences, emotions, and events. His search for meaning and for a truth that lies beyond facts drives Sebald to confront and ultimately break down this borderline, to create a new polydiscursive form of writing. As Sebald describes it:

---

70 The term "literary historiography" has been used by James E. Young to express the interrelated concerns of both literary and historical interpretation. That the study of the Holocaust is by nature an interdisciplinary endeavor is a starting point for Young and the basis for his assertion that the two separate disciplines (literary and historical) conjoin to form one field of study: *literary historiography*. Young's book is rooted in narratological and socio-historical approaches to literary texts, films, and monuments. Sebald's project in contrast is a distinctly literary one. See James E. Young, *Writing and Rewriting the Holocaust. Narrative and the Consequences of Interpretation* (Bloomington and Indianapolis: Indiana University Press, 1988).

That temptation to work with very fragmentary pieces of evidence, to fill in the gaps and blank spaces and create out of this a meaning which is greater than that which you can prove, led me to work in a way which wasn't determined by any discipline. It wasn't history, it wasn't literary criticism, it wasn't sociology, but it was all of these things together.[71]

The hybridity of Sebald's fiction is not marked by the ultimate dissolving of generic boundaries or a leveling out of the difference between fiction and reality or historiography and literature, but rather by the fact that these borders often become more apparent.[72] The blurring of boundaries has practical implications for publishing, and viewing fact and fiction as hybrids rather than alternatives has moral implications as well. Sebald makes the ethical dimension of the porous boundaries between fact and fiction explicitly and implicitly clear in all of his writing.[73]

Sebald's literary historiography is not a mere fictionalization of history but rather a reconstruction of history that attempts to represent the past while simultaneously channeling the potentiality of literature in the Aristotelian sense. A field of tension is created by the barriers that exist to reproducing the past on the one hand and the persistent drive to represent past history on the other. Sebald's emphasis on the individuality and idiosyncrasy of living beings only adds to this tension. Reconstruction for Sebald, moreover, is not limited to the human realm of individuals who perished or were killed but also encompasses entire cultures or species, natural landscapes, and even architectural structures that were destroyed. Heinz Ludwig Arnold highlights the different facets of Sebald's prose that contribute to this tension between literature and historiography in his works: "der fließende Übergang von der Realität des Geschauten in die Fiktionalität seiner Darstellung; und die Verbindung von Eklektizismus und Intuition: die Auswahl der vermittelten Gegenstände, Inhalte, Themen – und das reflexive Hineinversenken in ihre mögliche, denkbare Geschichte" ["the fluid transition from the reality of what is seen to the fictionality of its representation; and the connection between eclecticism and intuition: the array of mediated objects, contents, themes – and the reflexive immersion in the possible, imaginable (hi)story"].[74] These aspects, the reality of observation and the fictionality of representation, or, to use Aristotle's fundamental differentiation between history

---

71 Christopher Bigsby, "W. G. Sebald," *Writers in Conversation with Christopher Bigsby. Volume Two* (Norwich [U.K.]: Arther Miller Centre for American Studies, 2001) 139–165, here 153.
72 See Nünning's reflections on postmodern literature in "'Verbal Fictions?'" in particular 379–380.
73 The ethical imperative and the role of the author in engaging his readers are the two main aspects I focus on in chapter two in order to characterize Sebald's concept of literature.
74 Heinz Ludwig Arnold, ed., "W. G. Sebald," *Text + Kritik* 158 (2003) 3–4.

and literature: writing about what *has* happened and writing or imagining what *could* happen, are essential to Sebald's work. However, he does not present such a clear-cut delineation between these modes of representation. Sebald's hybrid discourse emerges in part from our difficulty in clearly differentiating between these modes of representation.

The particular challenge in defining Sebald's prose as a form of literary historiography, moreover, lies in the fact that both history and literature are in and of themselves "contested concepts."[75] Joseph W. Turner has argued against comparison as an approach to defining historical fiction, since "neither history nor fiction is itself a stable, universally agreed upon, concept."[76] With this in mind, then, my approach to what constitutes both history and literature and historical and literary representation in Sebald's œuvre focuses on the works themselves and gathers additional support from assertions Sebald made in interviews.[77] Taking my cue from Sebald's works, I make connections to what is broadly understood as *official* history in full awareness of the myriad forms this history can take and the various forms the (re)presentations of history have taken over time.

There is a historical basis in Sebald's prose, with extratextual references to historical events and individuals; and "reconstructing history" can even be argued as the impetus or "the raison d'être of Sebald's fiction."[78] The fact that a more broadly conceptualized idea of "the past" dominates Sebald's works is rooted in his fundamental skepticism towards traditional modes of historiography. At the same time, it is this obsession with the past that drives Sebald to engage with the established forms in which it has been presented. Sebald explicitly thematizes the problem of representing history in a pictorial mode, such as in the form of a diorama or panorama, both of which are characterized by the presentation from an impossible perspective. The emphasis throughout Sebald's œuvre is clearly on storytelling as opposed to the events as they are first experienced and on the story itself rather than who is telling it or whether it is 'real.' The self-referentiality of his works, that is, the thematization of representa-

---

75 Joseph W. Turner, "The Kinds of Historical Fiction: An Essay in Definition and Methodology," *Genre* 12 (1979) 333–355, here 335.
76 Ibid., 333.
77 Sebald's assertions will not be taken for granted as authorial "truth," since elements of his own self-stylization must also be taken into consideration. See Torsten Hoffmann, "Das Interview as Kunstwerk. Plädoyer für die Analyse von Schriftstellerinterviews am Beispiel W.G. Sebald," *Weimarer Beiträge* 55.2 (2009) 276–292.
78 Mark R. McCulloh, *Understanding W.G. Sebald* (Columbia, SC: University of South Carolina Press, 2003) 109.

tion within a representational text, is one of the defining aspects of his literary historiography.

Despite history's inherent conceptual and discursive complexity, it is possible to establish what constitutes history for Sebald by considering the following questions that emerge from his works: Which events are recorded? Whose lives are recounted? How are these events and people represented? Who are the historians that record and recount? Implicit in these questions are their reformulation in the negative: Which events are *not* recorded? Whose lives are *not* recounted? If not by historians, then from whom or from which sources do we learn about the past? Is there another perspective from which history could or should be told? This second set of questions further reinforces the position of fundamental skepticism towards official forms of history that underlies Sebald's works. Sebald is concerned with the historian's background and agenda or investment in his material much in the same way that he is concerned with an author's motivation, as can be seen in his literary critical work and essays.[79]

Sebald's fictional works emphasize the individual experience of the past, recounted through oral testimony or written in journals; as compared with and often preferred over official representations of historic events, in the form of monuments or accepted national narratives. Across his œuvre, Sebald approaches history, or a more broadly conceptualized idea of the past, through idiosyncratic, coincidental, and personal experiences.[80] Sebald's texts offer an approach to history via idiosyncratically imaginative connections and open up the possibility of retrieving personal memory, individual identity even, via investigations of architectural, institutional, and historical structures. In this way, Sebald's works develop a discourse of "deep associations" that connect individuals to their surroundings and to a greater history. In an interview with Volker

---

[79] This can lead Sebald into moralizing and pathologizing judgments of an author's work. See his essay on Alfred Andersch in *Luftkrieg und Literatur* as well as his volume of essays on nineteenth- and twentieth-century German-language authors, *Die Beschreibung des Unglücks. Zur österreichischen Literatur von Stifter bis Handke* (Salzburg; Vienna: Residenz-Verlag, 1985). Martin Klebes offers insights into Sebald's literary criticism from the 1970s and 1980s by questioning the unconventional way in which Sebald tries to "recover the connections between an author's life, his *biography*, and his textual production" (68). Klebes not only considers Sebald's analyses of such authors as Carl Sternheim, Alfred Döblin, and Ernst Herbeck, among others – in particular Sebald's interest in the textual manifestation of these authors' mental conditions – but he also turns Sebald around on himself to reveal the limitations of such an approach. See Martin Klebes, "Sebald's Pathographies," *W.G. Sebald: History – Memory – Trauma*, eds. Scott Denham and Mark McCulloh (Berlin: de Gruyter, 2006) 65–75.

[80] See discussion of Ermarth above and her call for alternative forms of history that approximate literature.

Hage in 2000, Sebald describes his view of history that stands in contrast to the nineteenth-century ideal outlined above. He states,

> Wir wissen ja inzwischen, dass Geschichte nicht so abläuft, wie die Historiker des 19. Jahrhunderts uns das erzählt haben, also nach irgendeiner von großen Personen diktierten Logik, nach irgendeiner Logik überhaupt. Es handelt sich um ganz andere Phänomene, um so etwas wie ein Driften, um Verwehungen, um naturhistorische Muster, um chaotische Dinge, die irgendwann koinzidieren und wieder auseinanderlaufen. Und ich glaube, dass es für die Literatur und auch für die Geschichtsschreibung wichtig wäre, diese komplizierteren chaotischen Muster herauszuarbeiten. Das ist nicht auf systematische Weise möglich (G 187).
>
> [We now know that history does not function as the historians of the nineteenth century told us, that is, not according to a logic dictated by great individuals, not according to any kind of logic at all. History has more to do with completely different phenomena, with something like drifting, with natural historical patterns, with chaotic things that for a certain time coincide and then later go their separate ways. And I believe that it would be important for literature as well as for historiography, to work out these complicated chaotic patterns. This is not possible in systematic ways.]

The histories Sebald concerns himself with are not limited to those of particular nations or national groups but rather include predominantly personal histories, that is, biographies. Most of the individual stories he recounts are of invented, fictionalized, or composite figures, inspired by several people who existed in an extra-literary sense.[81] In several cases, Sebald also includes the stories of authors of varying ethnicities and nationalities: Franz Kafka, Joseph Conrad, Stendhal (Henri Beyle), Michael Hamburger, Jean Améry, among others. In this way Sebald is not only writing "literary historiography" but also rewriting literary history by emphasizing different aspects of these well-known authors and recontextualizing them and their works in a new way.

In this chapter, *Austerlitz*, Sebald's last fictional prose work to be published during his lifetime, will serve as the exemplary case of his discursive synthesis of literature and historiography. *Austerlitz* tells the story of the eponymous character's search for his past and eventual reconstruction of his own identity. This reconstruction of Austerlitz's individual history is at the same time an indirect approach to representing the Holocaust. The complex constellation of historical event, individual experience, and the literary presentation of such events and experiences imbricates questions of perception, memory, representation, and translation as well, all of which form the nexus of concerns present across Sebald's works that will be developed throughout this book.

---

81 Cases of composite figures will be discussed further in chapter three in relation to the levels of reality in Sebald's fiction.

As will be seen below and developed in further detail in chapter four, the question of perspective – in both a literal and figurative sense – is essential to the problem of writing history. The way in which Sebald's texts criticize the impossible vantage point from which history is represented, reveals how they clearly privilege a "history from below." Bertolt Brecht's poem, "Fragen eines lesenden Arbeiters," captures the problem of history written from the vantage point of the victors. The questions asked by poem's narrative voice – a worker who reads – problematize the position that only "great men make history." In this political poem, Brecht distinguishes those who do the planning from those who do the actual building, and he thereby criticizes the type of historiography that ignores and even erases socio-economic reality. While Brecht's poem presents a class-centered view of history, Sebald's concern is for those individuals whom history has forgotten or deemed unimportant. Whereas Brecht may have wanted to underline the socio-economic reality as determining both the individual and history, Sebald's focus is on the individual, idiosyncratic experience of the past and how such experiences are worthy of recuperation in a historical form. A connection can nevertheless be drawn here between Brecht and Sebald: as if in direct response to the critique Brecht voices in his poem – that history remembers only the names of great men – Sebald's texts often do not explicitly name the "great" figures of history but rather allude to them only indirectly.[82] The following examples from *Austerlitz* underline the intentional omission of the names of historical heavyweights.[83] Adolf Hitler is referred to as "der Reichskanzler" and twice as the "Führer" (*A* 245, 246–247) [*AE* 167, 168–169], while the name "Hitler" is only mentioned in the alliterated list: "Hitler und Heß und Himmler" (*A* 247) [*AE* 169]. Austerlitz refers to Napoleon without naming him as follows, "am Tag der Verbannung des Kaisers auf die Insel St. Helena" (*A* 378) ["on the day when the Emperor was exiled to the island of St. Helena" (*AE* 266)].[84] Austerlitz refers to the new Bibliothèque nationale de France as "die den Namen des französischen Präsidenten tragende neue Nationalbibliothek" (*A* 391) ["the new Bibliothèque

---

82 Brecht, too, does not "name names" but refers generally to kings and generals.

83 A similar practice can be found in Sebald's interviews, for example he does not name Hitler but rather refers to him as "der größte Feldherr aller Zeiten, der Führer des dritten deutschen Reiches" (*G* 261) [the greatest general of all times, the leader of the third German Reich].

84 Sebald also refers to Napoleon without naming him in *Logis in einem Landhaus* as "der Kaiser, der überall in Europa das Unterste zuoberst gekehrt hatte" (*Logis* 77) ["the Emperor who had turned the world upside down all over Europe" (*PC* 69)]. Napoleon is identified by name, when Austerlitz describes his history teacher André Hilary's "Napoleonbegeisterung" (*A* 105) ["enthusiasm for Napoleon" (*AE* 69)]. Hilary, however, refers to him differently, as Austerlitz tells the narrator "der von ihm so genannte korsische Komet" (*A* 105) ["the Corsican comet, as he put it" (*AE* 69)].

Nationale bearing the name of the French President" (*AE* 275)]. Compared with the many other details listed in his description of the library, the omission of François Mitterrand's name is indeed conspicuous, and it is clear that the president shall remain nameless.[85] This practice of withholding names also extends to not explicitly naming causes of destruction, as can be seen in Michael Hamburger's memories of Berlin in ruins, recounted in *Die Ringe des Saturn*. Simon Ward points to Sebald's use of the passive as "a technique that Sebald often employs in the context of the ruin, and that implies the absence of, or at least *a refusal to name*, an active agent in the process of ruination."[86]

The problem of representation, in particular historical representation, is fundamental to Sebald's œuvre as a whole, and treated both explicitly and implicitly in his literary and critical works. That history can be told objectively or "realistically" is never taken for granted, but rather doubt and suspicion are continually cast upon purported verisimilitude in the representation of history. The problem of representation, in particular historical representation, is explicitly formulated in *Die Ringe des Saturn*, Sebald's third major fictional prose work. The narrator calls the purported truth of historiography into question when he asserts, "schon zeigen sich in der Historiographie die unbestreitbaren Vorteile einer fiktiven Vergangenheit" (*RS* 91) ["in historiography, the indisputable advantages of a fictitious past have become apparent" (*RoS* 71)].[87] This counterfactual formulation shows that to preserve the truth of historiography, extralinguistic reality must necessarily be fictitious. The narrator turns this assumption around when he describes pictorial representations of great battles in history, asserting them to be "pure Fiktionen" (*RS* 95) ["without exception figments of the imagination" (*RoS* 76)]. The narrator names examples of paintings that "trotz einer durchaus erkennbaren realistischen Absicht, keinen wahren Eindruck davon zu vermitteln [vermögen]" (*RS* 95) ["fail to convey any true impression of how it must have been" (*RoS* 77)]. The clause, "trotz einer durchaus erkennbaren realistischen Absicht" ["despite a thoroughly recognizable realistic intention"] is unfortunately missing from

---

85 There are two additional instances where the president is mentioned without naming Mitterrand explicitly (see *A* 392 [*AE* 276] and *A* 409 [*AE* 289]). Andrew Shields also points out that the "spektakuläre[] Reichsparteitagsfilm" (*A* 247) ["spectacular film of the Party rally" (*AE* 169)] is mentioned without naming Leni Riefenstahl as the filmmaker, explaining that this is because the film rather than the director is the main concern. See Andrew Shields, "Neun Sätze aus *Austerlitz*," *Akzente* 50.1 (2003) 63–72, here 67.

86 Simon Ward. "Responsible Ruins? W. G. Sebald and the Responsibility of the German Writer," *Forum for Modern Language Studies* 42.2 (2006): 183–199, here 189, my emphasis.

87 This comment by the narrator is inserted at the end of a long passage in which he seamlessly quotes from Jorge Luis Borges' *Tlön, Uqbar, Orbis Tertius*.

the English translation; this brief side comment is significant insofar as it points to an essential difference between what is realistic (*realistisch*) and what is real (*wahr*).[88] Directly below this sentence is a black and white reproduction of one such pictorial representation, as if to reinforce the preceding statement. Moreover, the narrator asserts the impossibility of imagining the pain and suffering endured and the shortcomings of our imagination in comprehending the preparations for the battle.

> Die erlittene Pein, das gesamte Werk der Zerstörung übersteigt um ein Vielfaches unser Vorstellungsvermögen, ebenso wie es nicht auszudenken ist, was für ein enormer Aufwand an Arbeit – vom Schlagen und Zurichten der Bäume, von der Gewinnung und der Verhüttung des Erzes und dem Schmieden des Eisens bis zum Weben und Vernähen der Segel – vonnöten gewesen sein muß, um die ja von vornherein größtenteils zur Vernichtung bestimmten Fahrzeuge zu bauen und auszurüsten (*RS* 96).
>
> [The agony that was endured and the enormity of the havoc wrought defeat our powers of comprehension, just as we cannot conceive the vastness of the effort that must have been required – from felling and preparing the timber, mining and smelting the ore, and forging the iron, to weaving and sewing the sailcloth – to build and equip vessels that were almost all predestined for destruction (*RoS* 78).]

In short, historical representation is characterized as necessarily fictional and insufficient. Similarly, statistical or factual information alone, although highly regarded in official forms of historiography, cannot reveal a greater meaning of the events, precisely because they reveal nothing of the emotional experience.

The problem of accessing the past is rooted in the broader problem of subjectivity and even more precisely the problem of accessing another person's emotions, thoughts, and experiences. The narrator in *Die Ringe des Saturn* uses the example of a herring to show how despite the quantifications of a natural scientist, the truth remains: "Doch in Wahrheit wissen wir nichts von den *Gefühlen* des Herings" (*RS* 75, my emphasis) ["that we don't know what the herring *feels*" (*RoS* 57, my emphasis)]. The detailed account of the herring, based on historical and scientific research, revealed nothing of the herring's sensate experience. Sebald returns to this problem in *Austerlitz*, revealing it to be one of his overarching concerns. Austerlitz echoes the sentiments of the narrator in *Die Ringe des Saturn* when describing the moths that fly up to the walls of his house and remain there until they die, as if paralyzed by having lost their way. Austerlitz states, "Manchmal beim Anblick einer solchen in meiner Wohnung zugrunde gegangenen Motte frage ich mich, was für eine Art Angst und Schmerz sie in der Zeit ihrer Verirrung wohl *verspüren*" (*A* 141, my emphasis). ["Sometimes, seeing

---

88 This distinction will be discussed with regard to the concept of *mimesis* in chapter three.

one of these moths that have met their end in my house, I wonder what kind of fear and pain they *feel* while they are lost" (*AE* 94, my emphasis).] Across Sebald's œuvre, we find narrators and characters focusing on the minutiae of experience, the details of what might have been *seen*, but being careful not to carry this over into the emotional realm of identification that allows one to assume what might have been *felt*. In this way, Sebald points to the epistemological and aesthetic questions involved in writing history and in particular the history of the Holocaust. The awareness and inscription of these dual concerns in his works reveal the underlying ethical dimension of Sebald's form of literary historiography. These problems of historical representation implied in *Die Ringe des Saturn* are presented explicitly in Sebald's lectures on poetics, given in Zurich in 1997.[89] Aside from the fact that these lectures sparked debates over the controversial status of Germans as victims in the Allied air raids at the end of World War II, these passages in *Luftkrieg und Literatur* and *Die Ringe des Saturn* reiterate Sebald's skepticism of official forms of historical knowledge and the nexus of epistemological, aesthetic, and ethical concerns behind this skepticism.

Sebald further illustrates the problem of representation through his particular emphasis on the concept of perspective. His narrator points to the dominance of a "Vogelperspektive" ["bird's-eye view"] in historical paintings, giving the specific example of Jacob van Ruisdael's *View of Haarlem with Bleaching Fields*, which Ruisdael painted "auf einem künstlichen, ein Stück über der Welt imaginierten Punkt" (*RS* 103) ["his vantage point was an imaginary position some distance above the earth" (*RoS* 83)]. The narrator then indicates one of the implications of viewing events from this imaginary perspective: people are remarkably absent from our view and understanding of the world (*RS* 113–114, *RoS* 91–92). In visiting the historical memorial site of the Battle of Waterloo, and in particular after viewing a large panorama, the narrator has the following reaction: "Das also, denkt man, indem man langsam im Kreis geht, ist die Kunst der Repräsentation der Geschichte. Sie beruht auf einer Fälschung der Perspektive. Wir, die Überlebenden, sehen alles von oben herunter, sehen alles zugleich und wissen dennoch nicht, wie es war" (*RS* 151–152). ["This then, I thought, as I looked round about me, is the representation of history. It requires a falsification of perspective. We, the survivors, see everything from above, see everything at once, and still we do not know how it was" (*RoS* 125).] This falsified perspective is not criticized from a moral point of view; "falsified" here is not meant in the sense of moral deception. Rather, the perspective is problematized for the way it obscures our access to the

---

89 The structurally and rhetorically similar passages in *Luftkrieg und Literatur* and *Die Ringe des Saturn* will be discussed further in chapter two.

past and for the way it deceives us into thinking that we can *see* and, by extension, *know* everything. This falsified perspective, then, which is also an impossible perspective, is ultimately an illusion that prevents us from knowing the past; and without knowledge there is no possibility of understanding the past.

Different from the explicit critique of historical representation in *Die Ringe des Saturn, Austerlitz* offers a more complex presentation of historiography. The "falsified" perspective of history and its vivid presentation are essential to the lectures given by Austerlitz's high school history teacher and later mentor André Hilary. Austerlitz recalls Hilary's lessons on Napoleon, which were dramatic representations that intentionally created an overview perspective: "aus der Höhe überblickend, mit dem Auge des Adlers, wie er einmal nicht ohne Stolz angemerkt hat" (*A* 106) ["surveying the entire landscape of those years from above with an eagle eye, as he once and not without pride remarked" (*AE* 70)]. Austerlitz describes Hilary's vivid presentation as if he were painting a picture ("Hilary malte uns ein Bild," *A* 108) that enabled the classmates to *hear, see,* and even *feel* in their own bodies the events unfold as he narrated them ("hörten," "sahen," "vernahmen wahrhaftig, wie wir glaubten," "spürten...im eigenen Leib," *A* 108). Although history is an attempt to represent reality – "Wir versuchen, die Wirklichkeit wiederzugeben..." (*A* 109) – Hilary acknowledges the limits of the historian's ability to report accurately ("wirklich") and the difference between representing and re-enacting the past.[90] Moreover, Hilary emphasizes how we rely on clichés and set images in our attempts to imagine the past:

> Unsere Beschäftigung mit der Geschichte, so habe Hilarys These gelautet, sei eine Beschäftigung mit immer schon vorgefertigten, in das Innere unserer Köpfe gravierten Bildern, auf die wir andauernd starrten, während die Wahrheit irgendwoanders, in einem von keinem Menschen noch entdeckten Abseits liegt (*A* 109).
>
> [Our concern with history, so Hilary's thesis ran, is a concern with preformed images already imprinted on our brains, images at which we keep staring while the truth lies elsewhere, away from it all, somewhere as yet undiscovered (*AE* 72).]

One question that remains unanswered in this passage is where these images originate, suggesting the possibility that one is even born with them. Austerlitz recognizes this same phenomenon in himself: he has read many descriptions of

---

90 As in other instances in the text, the pronoun "wir" could apply to Austerlitz, the narrator, or the reader. "Wir versuchen, die Wirklichkeit wiederzugeben, aber je angestrengter wir es versuchen, desto mehr drängt sich uns das auf, was auf dem historischen Theater von jeher zu sehen war [...]" (*A* 109) ["We try to reproduce the reality, but the harder we try, the more we find the pictures that make up the stock-in-trade of the spectacle of history forcing themselves upon us [...]" (*AE* 71)].

the "Dreikaiserschlacht" (*A* 109) ["battle of the Three Emperors" (*AE* 72)], but the only thing that has remained in his memory is "*das Bild* vom Untergang der Alliierten" (*A* 109, my emphasis) ["the picture of the final defeat of the Allies" (*AE* 72)]. All of his attempts to comprehend (*begreifen*) the events of this battle crystallize in the one scene that he already described. Austerlitz describes being able to *see* various aspects of the scene, even repeating the verb "sehen" four times, and he recognizes that the perspective from which he sees the action is not his own but based on that of the Marshall Davout.[91] Austerlitz remembers Hilary often repeating how, "... sollte man wirklich [...] in irgendeiner gar nicht denkbaren systematischen Form, berichten, was an so einem Tag geschehen war, [...] so brauchte es dazu eine endlose Zeit" (*A* 108) ["[...] it would take an endless length of time to describe the events of such a day properly, in some inconceivably complex form [...]" (*AE* 71)]. Hilary, therefore, is not only presenting the past to his students, but he is also reflecting upon the act of representation. This narration and meta-narrative reflection within the fictional form parallels Sebald's own literary strategy.

The barrier between the past and the present is further asserted in one of the key passages, when Austerlitz visits the Ghetto Museum in Terezín (Theresienstadt). Here, Austerlitz is physically, mentally, and emotionally overwhelmed by the photographs and descriptions found there. Proceeding in an ekphrastic way and recounting that which Austerlitz has told him, the narrator details the photographs and documents presented in the Ghetto Museum. However, none of these visuals are reproduced in the text, thus denying the reader a double role as a 'viewer'. Austerlitz recalls to the narrator how he

> [...] habe nicht meinen Augen getraut und habe verschiedentlich mich abwenden und durch eines der Fenster in den rückwärtigen Garten hinabsehen müssen, zum erstenmal mit einer Vorstellung von der Geschichte der Verfolgung, die mein Vermeidungssystem so lange abgehalten hatte von mir und die mich nun, in diesem Haus, auf allen Seiten umgab (*A* 286).
>
> [[...] could not believe my eyes, and several times had to turn away and look out of a window into the garden behind the building, having for the first time acquired some idea of the history of the persecution which my avoidance system had kept from me for so long, and which now, in this place, surrounded me on all sides (*AE* 198).]

After the experience of being "wie geblendet von den Dokumenten" (*A* 286) ["blinded by the documentation" (*AE* 198)] at the Ghetto Museum and not having found any 'real' trace of his mother there, Austerlitz nevertheless obtains his first idea of the history of the persecution endured during the Holocaust, a

---

91 Austerlitz describes how the myopic Davout relied on glasses that were fashioned around his head in a peculiar way with two ribbons (*A* 110) [(*AE* 72)].

history to which he is also personally connected. To develop his first vague notions of this history into deeper knowledge and understanding, Austerlitz delves into H.G. Adler's historical and sociological account of Theresienstadt.[92] It is the experience of reading rather than his physical presence in Terezín that helps Austerlitz find an access to his own identity which is inextricably linked to this past history.[93] In a parallel situation, at the end of *Austerlitz*, the narrator, as if still searching for ways to approach Austerlitz's past, revisits the fortress of Breendonk; but rather than observing his surroundings, he spends the entire afternoon until dusk, reading Dan Jacobson's memoir/biography *Heshel's Kingdom*, a book which Austerlitz had given him during their last meeting. In this way of reading about the past, rather than trying to experience the past "on location," *Austerlitz* reaffirms to a certain extent the importance of historiographical enterprises.[94]

The Building Blocks of a Hybrid Form: Genre, Narration, Structure

The complex constellation of historical event, individual experience, and the poietic presentation of both events and experiences is at the heart of Sebald's work and reveals why his texts elude established genre traditions. His prose has been described as "a mosaic of several forms,"[95] and identified as possessing a "generic hybridity."[96] Furthermore, Sebald's texts demonstrate a generic multiplicity in the way that they draw on elements of biography, autobiography,

---

92 H.G. Adler, *Theresienstadt 1941–1945. Das Antlitz einer Zwangsgemeinschaft. Geschichte, Soziologie, Psychologie* (Tübingen: Mohr, 1955).

93 On the intertextual references to Adler's text in *Austerlitz*, see Marcel Atze, "W.G. Sebald und H.G. Adler. Eine Begegnung in Texten," *W.G. Sebald. Mémoire. Transferts. Images./Erinnerung. Übertragungen. Bilder*, ed. Ruth Vogel-Klein, *Recherches germaniques* Hors série N. 2 (2005) 87–97, especially 90.

94 The fact that Adler also wrote fiction may contribute to the fact that his *Theresienstadt* is appreciated differently than other historiographical accounts. See H.G. Adler, *Eine Reise* (Vienna: Zsolnay, 1999).

95 Carol Bere, "The Book of Memory: W.G. Sebald's *The Emigrants* and *Austerlitz*," *Literary Review* 46 (2002) 184–192.

96 J.J. Long, "History, Narrative, and Photography in W.G. Sebald's *Die Ausgewanderten*," *The Modern Language Review* 98 (2003) 117. J.J. Long elucidates the hybridity he sees in Sebald's writing by linking the question of genre to Marianne Hirsch's definition of "postmemory." In his analysis of *Die Ausgewanderten*, he states, "The hybridity of the text, then, also manifests itself in the relationship between the narrating subject and the past he represents. The narratives are reducible neither to memory nor to history; they partake of both while being neither" (122).

memoir, travelogue, and even mystery novel[97]; thus, his fictional prose cannot be simply considered historical novels in a traditional sense[98] but rather need to be seen as their own genre, perhaps most appropriately termed "faction," as Peter Craven has argued.[99] By incorporating images, photographs in particular, in a complex manner and simultaneously reflecting on this within the literary form of his texts, Sebald thematizes the acts of seeing, remembering, and knowing, while also raising fundamental questions of literature's relationship to 'truth' and 'reality.' The theoretical and aesthetic questions pertinent to photography in general and relevant to Sebald's unique text–image constellation in particular are those of realism, authenticity, and the documentation and writing of history. These questions will be explored in depth in chapter three, but the problems emerging from the specific difference between the verbal and pictorial discourses are mentioned here for the way they underline the necessarily interdiscursive dimension of Sebald's works. At the basis of this discussion is the problem of signification, that is, the difficulties inherent in a semiotic presentation of human experiences. The discussion of representation is further complicated by Sebald's particular blending of fact and fiction, through which he not only implicitly problematizes the fact-fiction binary but also reveals it to be a false dichotomy in itself. The indeterminate status of Sebald's prose, according to traditional genre distinctions, will foreground my discussion of the aesthetic nature of his texts, as it is inextricably linked with the problem of representation.

To begin with the most basic indicator of genre, one need not look any further than the cover or title page of Sebald's books. While none of his works were published with a standard genre distinction, some include a descriptive subtitle. His first major literary work to be published, *Nach der Natur*, is subtitled "Ein Elementargedicht" as if to qualify the work; however, this subtitle in fact neither reflects the epic nature nor the triptych structure of the poem. Sebald's invented word (and subsequent genre), *Elementargedicht*, is moreover difficult to translate

---

97 McCulloh likens the structure of Sebald's narratives to mystery novels. McCulloh, *Understanding W.G. Sebald*, 115. See also Elinor Shaffer who uses the term "detective narrative" in describing Sebald's prose. Elinor Shaffer, "W.G. Sebald's Photographic Narrative," *The Anatomist of Melancholy. Essays in Memory of W.G. Sebald*, ed. Rüdiger Görner (Munich: iudicium, 2003) 51–62, here 57.

98 Todd Samuel Presner characterizes Sebald's fiction as a new form of "modernist realism," pointing in particular to the "techniques of literary modernism" that differentiate his texts from "the conventional narrative strategies of the historical novel." Todd Samuel Presner, "'What a Synoptic and Artificial View Reveals:' Extreme History and the Modernism of W.G. Sebald's Realism," *Criticism* 46.3 (2004) 341–360, here 345.

99 Peter Craven, "W.G. Sebald: Anatomy of Faction," *Heat. Literary International* 13 (1999) 212–224, here 220.

into English and consequently has been left out of Michael Hamburger's English translation. The subtitle of the German edition of *Die Ausgewanderten* (*The Emigrants*)[100] reads "Vier lange Erzählungen" ("four long stories"), and the German edition of *Die Ringe des Saturn* (*The Rings of Saturn*)[101] is subtitled "Eine englische Wallfahrt" ("an English pilgrimage"). In both cases the subtitle is left out of the English translations by Michael Hulse. Both *Schwindel.Gefühle* (*Vertigo*) and *Austerlitz*[102] were published without a genre designation and without a descriptive subtitle like the works mentioned above. Thus, readers who pick up Sebald's works are not given an easy orientation. These non-standard subtitles or absent genre distinctions engage the reader from the outset, and the question of categorization or characterization of his works must moreover be constantly reconsidered throughout one's reading.

The double role taken on by Sebald's narrators – "nicht nur der gewissenhafte Archivar der Geschichte, sondern auch der phantastische Imaginator von Geschichten"[103] [not only the diligent archivist of history, but also the imaginative inventor of (hi)stories] – enacts the fusion of writing literature and writing history by blurring the boundary between documenting history and making stories. Although Sebald's prose combines paraphrases and citations from other works[104] in a way that reveals the influence of documentary fiction, his emphasis lies on the imaginative potential of literature.[105] The unmarked integration of quotes into the narrative, much in the same way that images are integrated without comment

---

100 The four autonomous yet interrelated stories of *Die Ausgewanderten* read like biographies, although the individuals never existed in 'real life.' The stories are interrelated insofar as the first person narrator in each section grapples above all with questions of memory and history.

101 Both German original and English translation of *Die Ringe des Saturn* begins with a sort of table of contents dividing the text into ten parts. However, the body of the work is not divided into sections, and the page numbers indicated in the contents only reflect the page on which each section approximately begins.

102 In a rather glaring oversight, the Fischer Taschenbuch Verlag first published the paperback edition with *Roman* (novel) on the front cover. This error has been corrected in later printings.

103 Franz Loquai, "Erinnerungskünstler im Beinhaus der Geschichte. Gedankenbrosamen zur Poetik W. G. Sebalds," *W. G. Sebald*, ed. Franz Loquai (Eggingen: Ed. Isele, 1997) 259. I assume both meanings – history and stories – are implicit in Loquai's quote, due to the nature of Sebald's work.

104 Atze characterizes Sebald's works as a "Mischform aus Paraphrase und Zitat," "W.G. Sebald und H.G. Adler," 92.

105 Arthur Williams states, "[Sebald] is concerned with the retrieval of the past from the spaces uncharted by traditional historiography, which can be successfully attempted only if technology and scholarship combine with humanity's most powerful tool, the imagination."Arthur Williams, "'Das Korsakowsche Syndrom:' Remembrance and Responsibility in W.G. Sebald," *German Culture and the Uncomfortable Past. Representations of National Socialism in Contemporary*

or caption, also reveals this fusion of historiography and literature that is unique to Sebald's prose. Intertextuality in addition to intermediality indeed lends Sebald's works a documentary quality, yet his project must be held distinct from documentary fiction. That is, it is not his main purpose to create a fiction that is historically substantiated through documentation, but rather a new form of historiography that is consciously literary and that problematizes both the writing process and the standards by which we judge authenticity, documentary status, historical truth, and even truth in general.

Narration for Sebald involves not only story-telling but also encompasses story-making, which will ultimately be linked to the problem of representing history and memory in general and the Holocaust in particular. Each of Sebald's four fictional prose works is narrated by a first-person narrator. While it is difficult to determine whether the identity of the narrator is identical in the case of the four separate stories of *Die Ausgewanderten*, such a distinction may not even be necessary. More significant is the fact that the narrators are the same *type* across this text and, one can even argue, across his entire œuvre.[106] Searching for the past and attempting to remember are themes that structure both *Die Ausgewanderten* and *Austerlitz*. This searching, however, often renders the narrator practically invisible, in part because of the way the telling (representation) is emphasized. Sebald therefore inserts "reminders" of the various narrative voices.[107] This act at one and the same time thematizes the actual mediation of the telling and reinforces the distance among the author, narrator, and narrated subjects who narrate themselves.

There is a structural similarity among all of Sebald's narratives in that they are anything but linear. The non-linear, "circuitous"[108] narrative progression of *Austerlitz* is made clear from the very beginning of the narrative. The narrator quotes Austerlitz as he begins his story, as if to provide the reader with a disclaimer against expecting a linear narrative: "Es ist nicht einfach gewesen, aus der Befangenheit mir selbst gegenüber herauszufinden, noch wird es einfach

---

Germanic Literature. Warwick Studies in the Humanities, ed. Helmut Schmitz (Aldershot, UK: Ashgate, 2001) 65–86, here 68.

106 The role of Sebald's narrators and the frequent equation of Sebald with his narrators in secondary literature point to the intertwining of different layers of reality in Sebald's texts and the larger problem of the literary text's relationship to reality and will therefore be discussed in further detail in chapter three.

107 Examples of the sort, "so sagte Věra, sagte Austerlitz," (*A* 244) ["Vera told me, said Austerlitz" (*AE* 180)] abound across Sebald's works. See the further discussion of this aspect of Sebald's prose in chapter four.

108 Bere, "The Book of Memory," 190.

sein, die Dinge jetzt in eine halbwegs ordentliche Reihenfolge zu bringen" (*A* 69). ["It hasn't been easy to make my way out of my own inhibitions, and it will not be easy now to put the story into anything like proper order" (*AE* 44).] This way in which Austerlitz begins his story, acknowledging his difficulty in reconstructing the past, also relates to how Sebald conceptualizes time in such a way that dissolves linear progression and allows for the simultaneity of past, present, and future.[109] Moreover, Austerlitz's personal story with its multiple starting points begins almost seventy pages into the book, working against a clearly demarcated narrative frame. The narrative progression is further prolonged as details are introduced and then "forgotten" or brushed aside only to be pursued, unfolded, and revealed in their full complexity and interconnectedness at later points in the text.

Sebald further challenges his readers with complex hypotaxis in long sentences and lengthy paragraphs that run over pages.[110] His hypotactic structure, comprised of relative and subordinate clauses and participial constructions, brings about a hastened reading to arrive at the subject or object of the sentence, and with this comes the necessity to return and reread passages. The longest sentence in *Austerlitz* runs over ten pages (*A* 339–349) [(*AE* 236–244)], and there are more or less no paragraphs in the over four hundred pages that make up the German edition. Additional paragraph or section breaks have been inserted into the English edition of *Austerlitz*, but even here there is a paragraph that runs over sixty-five pages (*AE* 162–227). The geographical space covered in these pages corresponds to the locations where the discussions between Austerlitz and the narrator take place as well as to where Austerlitz travels. The geographical range includes Prague, Marienbad, Terezín, various cities in Germany, as well as Antwerp, Terneuzen, London, and Paris. The only "breaks" afforded to the reader come in the form of images inserted into the text, and even here, the reader must be attentive to the possible relationships between the visual and the textual and the multiple meanings that can be drawn from these different text-image constellations. Further "pauses" come in the narration in the form of inserted commentary made by the narrator, marking either that Austerlitz has become apparently overwhelmed in his recollections or that both Austerlitz and the narrator have become caught up in the narration and lost contact with the present world around them.[111]

---

109 See chapter four for a discussion of Sebald's theory of time.

110 Sebald's style and the particular challenge these hypotactic constructions pose not only to his readers but also to his translators will be discussed in chapter six.

111 For example, the narrator states: "Im Gegensatz zu dem Onkel Evelyn, so nahm Austerlitz seine ihn offenbar sehr bewegenden Erinnerungen an Andromeda Lodge nach einer Weile wieder auf..." (*A* 132) ["Unlike Uncle Evelyn, said Austerlitz after a while..." (*AE* 88)], or "So sehr hatte

A gradual and often indirect excavation of the past is characteristic of Sebald's prose in general, and "apparently random details,"[112] mentioned as if in passing, often resurface as connections are made between individual characters and the greater events of history. When it comes to researching and reconstruct ing the stories of emigrants and exiles, this is coupled with hesitation and uncertainty in the ability to tell another's story. The narrative voice(s) across *Die Ausgewanderten* share and voice similar concerns. For example, in the fourth part of *Die Ausgewanderten*, the narrator describes his approach to recounting Max Aurach's story as follows

> Es war ein äußerst mühevolles, oft stunden- und tagelang nicht vom Fleck kommendes und nicht selten sogar rückläufiges Unternehmen, bei dem ich fortwährend geplagt wurde von einem immer nachhaltiger sich bemerkbar machenden und mehr und mehr mich lähmenden Skrupulantismus. Dieser Skrupulantismus bezog sich sowohl auf den Gegenstand meiner Erzählung, dem ich, wie ich es auch anstellte, nicht gerecht zu werden glaubte, als auch auf die Fragwürdigkeit der Schriftstellerei überhaupt. Hunderte von Seiten hatte ich bedeckt mit meinem Bleistift- und Kugelschreibergekritzel. Weitaus das meiste davon war durchgestrichen, verworfen oder bis zur Unleserlichkeit mit Zusätzen überschmiert. Selbst das, was ich schließlich für die ‚endgültige' Fassung retten konnte, erschien mir als ein mißratenes Stückwerk (*DA* 344–345).
>
> [Often I could not get on for hours or days at a time, and not infrequently I unravelled what I had done, continuously tormented by scruples that were taking tighter hold and steadily paralysing me. These scruples concerned not only the subject of my narrative, which I felt I could not do justice to, no matter what approach I tried, but also the entire questionable business of writing. I had covered hundreds of pages with my scribble, in pencil and ballpoint. By far the greater part had been crossed out, discarded, or obliterated by additions. Even when I ultimately salvaged as a 'final' version seemed to me a thing of shreds and patches, utterly botched (*E* 230–231).]

This statement is made only a few pages before the end of this collection of four long stories, signaling to the reader to be skeptical of what is written, i.e., to critically reconsider everything he has just read. This skepticism is not aimed at discounting the text, but rather it is meant to bring forth the epistemological, ethical, and aesthetic questions central to Sebald's works: in how far can we know the past and in which ways can we ethically approach and aesthetically represent

---

sich Austerlitz in seiner walisischen Geschichte und ich mich im Zuhören verloren, daß wir nicht merkten, wie spät es geworden war" (*A* 145). ["Austerlitz had been so deeply immersed in his Welsh tale, and I in listening to him, that we did not notice how late it had grown" (*AE* 96).] In omitting the narrator's comment that Austerlitz was obviously moved by his own memories of Andromeda Lodge, the English translation curiously reduces the degree of Austerlitz's emotional investment, to which the narrator is highly sensitive.

112 Craven, "Anatomy of Faction," 215.

this past? These questions gain further weight when we consider them within the context of the paradigmatic atrocity of the Holocaust, the implicit concern at the center of these stories.

Overcoming the Obstacles in Representing the Past

The problem of historical representation is rooted in questions of transfer from the objective, i.e., non-semiotic real into the arbitrary signs of language. In other words, the process of writing history can be subsumed under a broader process of semioticization, understood as the attempt to overcome the chasm between lived experiences and the representation of these experiences in language. Considering historical semioticization, in particular, is to be aware of "the difference and distance between historical documents and the truth of past lived experience."[113] The process of translation that is at work in historiography becomes evident when we consider the different interpretations that can be made from the same sources and documents. History itself becomes an interpretation (and an argument) insofar as the writing of history informs our ideas and concepts of the past and insofar as the process of narrativization transforms the actions and events of the past into a story that follows a logic of its own.

Here we can revisit Hayden White's definition of the historical work as "a verbal structure in the form of a narrative prose discourse that purports to be a model, or icon, of past structures and processes in the interest of *explaining what they were by representing them*."[114] I would like to draw attention to White's footnote to this assertion, as it provides a link to the broader considerations of this book. White connects the claim of the historical work to be an explanation through representation to "the most vexed problem in modern (Western) literary criticism, the problem of 'realistic' literary representation."[115] The problem of modern historiography is, according to White, "the nature of 'realistic' representation," and his central question deals with the "'artistic' elements of 'realistic' historiography."[116] Sebald is writing very much in this vein of problematizing 'realistic' representation, but the significant difference is that Sebald explores these questions of historical representation *within* literary discourse. More pre-

---

113 Helmut Schmitz, "'... only signs everywhere of the annihilation.' W.G. Sebald's *Austerlitz*." *On Their Own Terms. The Legacy of National Socialism in Post-1990 German Fiction* (Birmingham: University of Birmingham, University Press, 2004) 291–321, here 304.
114 White, *Metahistory*, 2 emphasis HW.
115 Ibid., footnote 4 on page 2.
116 Ibid., 3.

cisely, he develops a hybrid form within which to explore these questions, a hybrid discourse that combines fact, fiction, and theory and that moves between description and reflection. Furthermore, Sebald's works demonstrate a fundamental skepticism toward totality, upon which the explanatory function of traditional historiography is based. His works also challenge the hierarchy of significance asserted in historical texts. As will be seen in later chapters, Sebald also inscribes himself into his fictional texts, as if to underline the connections he creates between the individual and a larger, more all-encompassing history. Sebald's literary historiography, in particular this self-inscription in the fictional text and historical context, could be seen as a response to Ankersmit's claim that historical reality "is only encountered in our attempts to define our relationship to our past, in our attempt to 'write ourselves' by writing history."[117] Such connections across time and space and between 'reality' and 'fiction' that are an achievement of the literary discourse also reveal the limits of the historical discourse.

There is a materiality of history embodied in artifacts and documents, and there is also a texture of history created by layers of interpretation. When we move from event to history to story – as outlined by Stierle in his model of the historical writing process from "Geschehen" to "Geschichte" to "Text der Geschichte" – we might also see this as a translation from the discourse of history into the discourse of literature. In this process, a further layer must be considered, one that does not cover up but rather surrounds: aura. The integration of images in literary texts contributes to this aura, especially when the images do not depict something per se but rather convey what one could call an "atmosphere."[118] Sebald uses extra-literary source material and events and makes intertextual references as well. In this way, he combines all three stages of Stierle's model to create his own (hi)-stories. This book is thus concerned with the narrative formation of history in Sebald's works as it depends on both images and the imagination. The photographs in *Austerlitz*, for example, possess an inherent power to provoke memory and activate the process of remembering, but most importantly the text demonstrates the necessity of a human voice to interpret these images. The efforts to interpret photographs can complicate and at times paralyze the endeavor of writing: revealing that this process of representation – the translation of a past reality or personal experience into arbitrary signs – is by no means a process that one can take for granted as natural or fluid. Not only photographs, but images in general, possess an element of potential that only language can develop; only in

---

117 Ankersmit, *Historical Representation*, 261.
118 The complex interplay between text and image in Sebald's works is discussed in detail in chapter three.

language can the documentary nature be brought to life and made accessible to the viewer and reader.

In this way, Sebald's literary historiography is more than a product or a new discourse, it can also be seen as a mode of reading and research. The two-fold time of research – the author's and the reader's – adds a further layer to be considered. The author pieces together his story from multiple sources, including articles, events, images, and verbal stories, and the reader then reconstructs not only the story but the construction of the story. The work of the reader follows the work of the author and thus mirrors his approach. In working through the intra-, inter-, and extratextual layers of the text we engage with history, its sources, and its transformation into a new hybrid discourse. A new form of transdiscursive knowledge, a specifically *aesthetic* knowledge, emerges from this way of working through both material and text.

Chapter 2
Conscious Historiography and the Writer's Conscience

Writing on the Border between Literary Studies and Literature

While Sebald's public literary career did not begin until the late 1980s, he was already writing poetry as a high school student and working on a novel as a university student. An exhibit at the Literaturhaus in Stuttgart, dedicated to Sebald's speech that marked the opening of this venue on November 17, 2001, displayed Sebald's earliest creative collaborations with schoolmate and longtime friend, the visual artist Jan Peter Tripp, including an issue of *Der Wecker*, a student magazine of the Oberstdorfer Oberschule, from 1962.[1] Thus, his literary and scholarly interests and endeavors should be seen as running parallel, rather than as in a sequence. Sebald can perhaps be best characterized as a "Grenzgänger" [border crosser] as Florian Radvan, one of his former PhD students at the University of East Anglia, has described him; for Sebald not only crossed but also blurred and dissolved the borders between literary criticism and literature, English and German, words and images, fiction and reality, biography and autobiography.[2] This moving between academic and literary writing can also be gleaned from a brief glance at his publication history. Sebald's first literary work to be published was a three-part poem, *Nach der Natur. Ein Elementargedicht* (1988), translated by Michael Hamburger as *After Nature* (2002). The four major fictional prose works with which Sebald earned his literary renown are *Schwindel.Gefühle* (1990), translated by Michael Hulse as *Vertigo* (2000); *Die Ausgewanderten. Vier lange Erzählungen* (1992), translated, also by Hulse, as *The Emigrants* (1996); *Die Ringe des Saturn. Eine englische Wallfahrt* (1995), the last work translated by Hulse as *The Rings of Saturn* (1998); and *Austerlitz* (2001), translated by Anthea Bell with the same title and published in the same year. *Unerzählt*, a collaboratively-planned project with Jan

---

1 See the publication that accompanied the exhibit: Florian Höllerer, ed., *W.G. Sebald. Zerstreute Reminiszenzen. Gedanken zur Eröffnung eines Stuttgarter Hauses.* Warmbronn: Verlag Ulrich Keicher, 2008.

2 Florian Radvan, "W.G. Sebald – Schriftsteller und Scholar. Erinnerungen an einen Grenzgänger zwischen Literatur und Wissenschaft," *Kritische Ausgabe* 13. Jahrgang Nr. 18 (2010) 56–59, here 58. Sven Meyer also notes Sebald's own preference for literary "Grenzgänger," such as Bruce Chatwin. Sven Meyer, "Im Medium der Prosa. Essay und Erzählung bei W.G. Sebald," *Mémoire. Transferts. Images./Erinnerung. Übertragungen. Bilder*, ed. Ruth Vogel-Klein, *Recherches germaniques* Hors Série 2 (2005) 173–185, here 180.

Peter Tripp, was published posthumously in 2003 and translated by Michael Hamburger as *Unrecounted* (2004). This book combines short poems by Sebald, ranging anywhere from four to ten lines, and etchings of pairs of eyes by Tripp. Sebald completed a collaborative project with British artist Tess Jaray that was similar to the one he undertook with Tripp, and in some respects the poems in *For Years Now*[3] read as English versions of the poems that later appear in *Unrecounted*. *For Years Now* juxtaposes bright screen prints by Jaray, which she explains were "conceived in relation to selected extracts from [Sebald's] *The Rings of Saturn* and *Vertigo*,"[4] with short poems by Sebald. These are the only poems that Sebald wrote in English.

In addition to both poetry and fictional prose, Sebald wrote many scholarly studies related to literature written in German, primarily on nineteenth- and twentieth-century Austrian, Swiss, and German writers. Both *Die Beschreibung des Unglücks* (1985) and *Unheimliche Heimat* (1991) bring together Sebald's essays on Austrian writers, including Adalbert Stifter, Thomas Bernhard, Peter Handke, Gerhard Roth, and Hermann Broch, among others.[5] Sebald was also interested in writers such as Jean Améry, Elias Canetti, Franz Kafka, Vladimir Nabokov, and Bruce Chatwin, and wrote essays on their works and lives. *Campo Santo* (2003), also translated by Bell as *Campo Santo* (2005), is a posthumously published collection of Sebald's unfinished and abandoned project to write about the island of Corsica. The volume also includes several previously published essays and speeches. *Logis in einem Landhaus* (1998), a collection of essays on Swiss authors, translated by Jo Catling as *A Place in the Country* (2013), and *Luftkrieg und Literatur* (1999), translated by Bell as *On the Natural History of Destruction* (2003), a revised version of a series of lectures on poetics given by Sebald in Zurich in 1997, will be discussed in further detail below.

In an interview with Christopher Bigsby, Sebald described how he was drawn away from academic writing to writing in a "more tentative sort of way,"

> I moved from the straight monograph to essayistic exploration, dealing with my subjects in an elliptical sort of way. But even so I constantly came up against a *borderline* where I felt, well, if

---

3 W.G. Sebald; illustrated by Tess Jaray, *For Years Now* (London: Short, 2001).

4 Tess Jaray, "A Mystery and a Confession. What did Sebald find in Marienbad?" *Irish Pages* 1.2. "The Justice Issue" (2002/2003) 137–139, here 137.

5 W.G. Sebald, *Die Beschreibung des Unglücks. Zur österreichischen Literatur von Stifter bis Handke* (Salzburg; Vienna: Residenz-Verlag 1985). W.G. Sebald, *Unheimliche Heimat. Essays zur österreichischen Literatur* (Salzburg; Vienna: Residenz-Verlag, 1991).

I could go a little bit further it might get very interesting, that is, if I were allowed to make things up.[6]

Richard Weihe notes that the tension between being a scholar of literary studies and a writer of fiction was probably the most productive source for Sebald's work as an author and how, as a writer of fiction, Sebald was free and able, "Metaphern zu verwenden, Leben und Werk im Sinne des sonst verpönten Biografismus als Einheit zu verstehen, und vor allem die Subjektivität des Schreibenden zu betonen, indem er laut und deutlich 'ich' sagt"[7] [to use metaphors, to understand life and work as a unity, as opposed to the usually frowned upon biographism, and above all to emphasize the subjectivity of the writer by pronouncing 'I' loudly and clearly]. This move from literary criticism to literature is not without risks however. Academics who make a "career change" to writing fiction are, to put it mildly, often viewed with suspicion. Radvan notes that, "Als Hochschullehrer, der auch literarisch schrieb, wäre [Sebald] in der deutschen Akademie wohl misstrauisch beäugt, wenn nicht belächelt und wären seine Texte als 'Professorenprosa' abgetan worden"[8] [Sebald, as a university professor who also writes literature, would be viewed suspiciously if not with a smirk within German academia, and his texts would be dismissed as 'professor prose']. This clichéd image of an academic turned author has been attached to Sebald, although he was working simultaneously on scholarly and literary projects for the greater part of his life. This skeptical and even dismissive attitude towards "professors-turned-authors" has certainly contributed to the slower reception of his works in Germany, as opposed to the very positive reception outside of Germany, especially in England and the United States but also in France.

Letters both to and from Sebald are revealing of his two sides: the literary scholar and the author. His correspondence with various publishers and journals during the 1970s and 1980s is particularly illuminating of the way in which Sebald walked on a tightrope between the two sides of scholarly and literary writing.[9] In particular, one can see how he bristled against the constraints of form and methodology in place at that time. What comes through in these letters are the broader political, critical, and methodological standards that dominated "Germa-

---

6 Christopher Bigsby, "W. G. Sebald," *Writers in Conversation with Christopher Bigsby. Volume Two* (Norwich [U.K.]: Arther Miller Centre for American Studies, 2001) 139–165, here 152, my emphasis.
7 Richard Weihe, "Wittgensteins Augen. W. G. Sebalds Film-Szenario *Leben Ws*," *fair. Zeitung für Kunst und Ästhetik* Nr 7.4 (2009) 11–12, here 12. This "I" of the text – the "intradiegetic narrator" (Gérard Genette) – must of course not be confused with the "I" of the extra-textual author.
8 Radvan, "W. G. Sebald – Schriftsteller und Scholar," 58.
9 A: Sebald, DLA Marbach.

nislik" at that time and the power such institutions possessed in determining what was considered both important and 'true.' In several letters, Sebald argues that his essayistic approach enables different connections and insights. His various unsuccessful attempts to publish his work reveal his interest in new forms of literary scholarship and his refusal to work within or adapt his work to established formal and methodological standards. Ultimately, it is Sebald's blending of genres in a literary form that proves to be the key to his success. Sebald's attention to history – in particular how historical events are recorded and recounted – and to literature – in particular the constitution of literary texts and how this bears on truth and reality – are consistent across his works, informing both his judgments of other literary works and the creation of his particular form of literary historiography. In order to elucidate this point, I examine Sebald's *Logis in einem Landhaus* and *Luftkrieg und Literatur* in further detail.

Literary Portraits as Self-Portrait: *Logis in einem Landhaus*

Logis in einem Landhaus brings together essays by Sebald on the Swiss authors Johann Peter Hebel, Eduard Mörike, Gottfried Keller, and Robert Walser, the French philosopher Jean-Jacques Rousseau, and the visual artist Jan Peter Tripp. In this collection of "biographical meditations,"[10] we get a glimpse not only into the lives and works of these individuals but also into what Sebald values in life and literature and art more broadly. As stated in his foreword, Sebald regards this volume as his "Tribut an die vorangegangenen Kollegen in Form einiger ausgedehnter und sonst keinen besonderen Anspruch erhebenden Marginalien" (*Logis* 7) ["a tribute to these colleagues who have gone before me, in the form of these extended marginal notes and glosses, which do not otherwise have any particular claim to make" (*PC* 3)]. In an earlier interview with Ralph Schock in 1993, Sebald explained his literary strategy of paraphrasing other works or integrating quotations but leaving them unmarked, likening this method to the way that painters commonly refer to or take up motifs from each others' works, "sozusagen als Geste der Ehrerbietung. Und das ist etwas, was ich also auch sehr gerne mache als Schreibender" (*G* 98) [so to say as a gesture of reverence. And that is something that I also like to do as a writer]. Moreover, in these essays we find an illustration of Sebald's desire to make a personal connection to other authors, be it through their texts or through physical traces. By way of the connections that Sebald both

---

10 Jo Catling, "Silent Catastrophe. In Memoriam W.G. (Max) Sebald 1944–2001," http://www.new-books-in-german.com/featur27.htm [accessed: June 22, 2013]

makes and uncovers in writing these portraits, he is also writing his own autobiography to a degree. Uwe Schütte's designation of Sebald's method across these essays as one of "Auto(r)biografie" [aut(h)o(r)biography] is indeed quite apt.[11] Sebald contrasts the stasis of a geographical and physical location with the flux of personalities, 'real' individuals who occupy a particular time and place. Forever emphasizing the distance between the present and the past, that is, our access to past events and experiences, what emerges from such investigations as these portraits is that deep connections do exist across space and time.

Sebald's piece on Rousseau contains, quite appropriately, the most autobiographical elements of all the essays in *Logis in einem Landhaus*, considering Rousseau is the founder of modern autobiography.[12] Sebald describes the "Rousseaubegeisterung" (*Logis* 49) ["Rousseau mania" (*PC* 43)] that brings people to St. Peter's Island, "um den Ort in Augenschein zu nehmen" (*Logis* 48) ["to see for themselves" (*PC* 41)]. He recounts how many of the visitors to the island felt compelled to leave their own trace. He then imagines how this interest shifts away from the philosopher toward in general interest in the previous visitors and into a desire to gain insight into the experiences of these unknown individuals. Sebald writes,

> Manche dieser Besucher haben mit dem Federmesser ihre Namen oder Initialen und das Datum ihres Besuchs in die Türpfosten und in die Sitzbank in der Fensternische des Rousseauzimmers geschnitten, und *gerne möchte man, wenn man mit dem Finger die Kerben im Holz nachfährt, wissen, wer sie gewesen und wohin sie gegangen sind* (*Logis* 49, my emphasis).
>
> [A number of these visitors, too, carved their initials or the date of their visits with a penknife on to the door-jambs and window-seat of the Rousseau room, and as one runs a finger along these grooves in the wood, one wishes one could know who they were and what has become of them (*PC* 43).]

In contrast to the Rousseau enthusiasts, Sebald also spots other visitors to the island who have no apparent interest in the philosopher; he contrasts his own

---

11 Uwe Schütte, *W.G. Sebald. Einführung in Leben und Werk* (Göttingen: Vandenhoeck & Ruprecht, 2011) 239. Claudia Albes offers a detailed consideration of the genre of these essays that reveal "Sebald's personal relationship to the writers he reveres." See Claudia Albes, "Between 'Surface Illusionism' and 'Awful Depth': Reflections on the Poetological and Generic Ambivalence of W.G. Sebald's *Logis in einem Landhaus*," *Journal of European Studies*, Special Issue: W.G. Sebald, ed. Richard Sheppard 41.3–4 (2011) 449–465, here 450.

12 Ulrich von Bülow describes how Sebald used the material from his "Korsika-Projekt" [Corsica Project] as a "Steinbruch" [quarry], from which he drew on for parts of *Austerlitz* and individual essays; this piece on Rousseau is one such example. Ulrich von Bülow, "Sebalds Korsika-Projekt," *Wandernde Schatten. W.G. Sebalds Unterwelt*, eds. Ulrich von Bülow, Heike Gfrereis, and Ellen Strittmatter (Marbach am Neckar: Deutsche Schillergesellschaft, 2008) 211–224, here 220.

acute perception to their lack of interest, but he must also admit that the connection he feels – "als sei ich zurückversetzt in die vergangene Zeit" (*Logis* 50) ["as if I had been transported back to an earlier age" (*PC* 43)] – is indeed only an illusion.

Sebald's essay on Johann Peter Hebel also demonstrates a careful approach to the past, one which acknowledges the distance in time and space separating us from past events and experiences. In this portrait, Sebald does not simply provide the historical context for an analysis of the author's works, but rather reveals the complexity of historical context in itself. Referring to the "Weltbegebenheiten" [world events] that Hebel lists in a text included in his *Rheinischer Hausfreund* from 1814, Sebald writes, "Wir heutigen können *etwas ahnen* von dem Entsetzen, das den Kalendermacher überfiel, als er in diesen schon offenen Schlund der Geschichte hinabschaute [...]" (*Logis* 33, my emphasis) ["In our own times we can *get a sense* of something of the horror which befell the Almanac author as he gazed down into the already gaping maw of history" (*PC* 27, my emphasis)]. It is our power of imagination and our ability to conjecture that enable us to *sense* the past and even gain an experience of it. In tracing Hebel's enthusiastic support of Napoleon which eventually wanes as the Napoleonic Wars continue, Sebald encourages the reader to reconsider present assessments of the past.

> Eine Weile zumindest waren also auch Hebels politische Hoffnungen auf den Franzosenkaiser gerichtet. Damit war er unter den fortschrittsgesinnten Konservativen seiner Zeit nicht allein. Die von Napoleon geschlagenen Schlachten erschienen zunächst, auch in Deutschland, in einem anderen Licht als das grauenvolle Blutbad der Revolution. Sie waren nicht behaftet mit dem Stigma des Bürgerkriegs und der irrationalen Gewalt, sondern quasi überstrahlt von einer höheren Vernunft und dienten, so wollte man meinen, der Ausbreitung des Gleichheitsgedankens und der Toleranz (*Logis* 31).
>
> [For a while at least, then, Hebel's political hopes too were pinned on the French Emperor. Among the progressively minded conservatives of his day, this view was by no means unusual. The battles fought by Napoleon appeared initially, even in Germany, in a different light from the horrifying bloodbath of the Revolution. They were not tainted by the stigma of civil war and irrational violence, but appeared almost as if suffused in the light of a higher reason, and served, so it was believed, to promote the dissemination of the ideas of equality and tolerance (*PC* 25–26).]

Several scholars have pointed to Napoleon as a key figure in Sebald's works, seeing in him the starting point of a downward trajectory of violence and destruction that finds its nadir in the twentieth-century atrocity of the Holocaust.[13]

---

13 See for example Claudia Öhlschläger, "'Die Bahn des korsischen Kometen.' Zur Dimension 'Napoleon' in W. G. Sebalds literarischen Netzwerk," *Topographien der Literatur. Deutsche Literatur im transnationalen Kontext*. DFG-Symposium 2004, eds. Hartmut Böhme, Inka Mülder-Bach, Bernhard Siegert, and Horst Wenzel (Stuttgart: Metzler, 2005) 536–558.

Sebald's essay on Hebel, however, complicates this potentially reductive assessment (see *Logis* 35/*PC* 29).[14]

One can draw a web of thematic connections across the first five essays of *Logis in einem Landhaus* that culminates in Sebald's tribute to Robert Walser.[15] On the one hand, this essay reads like an explicit poetics with forthright assertions of what Sebald values in writing. On the other hand, it reads like an autobiography with declarations of his worldview. Sebald traces several aspects of Walser's biography and writing, but this author remains elusive, according to Sebald, "eine singuläre, unerklärte Gestalt" (*Logis* 131) ["a singular, enigmatic figure" (PC 120)], of whom one cannot write a proper (hi)story or biography, but rather only a legend. Because Walser eludes systematic treatment, Sebald sees most criticism becoming "ein persönlicher Tribut" (*Logis* 133) ["an act of *hommage*" (*PC* 123, italics Catling)] and acknowledges that his comments will be no exception.

> Wie soll man auch einen Autor verstehen, der Humoresken verfaßte aus reiner Verzweiflung, der fast immer dasselbe schrieb und sich doch nie wiederholte, dem die eigenen, an Winzigkeiten geschärften Gedanken unfaßbar wurden, der ganz auf dem Erdboden war und rückhaltlos in der Atmosphäre sich verlor, dessen Prosa die Eigenheit hat, sich aufzulösen beim Lesen, so daß man sich bereits ein paar Stunden nach der Lektüre kaum mehr erinnern kann an die ephemeren Figuren, Vorkommnisse und Dinge, von denen da die Rede gewesen ist (*Logis* 132–133).
>
> [How is one to understand an author who was so beset by shadows and who, none the less, illumined every page with the most genial light, an author who created humorous sketches from pure despair, who almost always wrote the same thing and yet never repeated himself, to whom his own thoughts, honed on the tiniest details, became incomprehensible, who had his feet firmly on the ground yet was always getting lost in the clouds, whose prose had the tendency to dissolve upon reading, so that only a few hours later one can barely remember the ephemeral figures, events and things of which it spoke (*PC* 122).]

Since he finds it difficult to get closer to Walser, to establish "[w]er und was Robert Walser *in Wahrheit* gewesen ist" (*Logis* 139, my emphasis) ["[w]ho and what Robert Walser really was" (*PC* 128)], Sebald turns to photographs. However,

---

14 Going beyond a thematic analysis, Mark M. Anderson outlines how Napoleon structures Sebald's concept of realism. See Mark M. Anderson, "Napoleon and the Ethics of Realism: Hebel, Hölderlin, Büchner, Celan," *Journal of European Studies*, Special Issue: W.G. Sebald, ed. Richard Sheppard 41.3–4 (2011): 395–412.

15 Jo Catling's translation of Sebald's essay on Walser is also included as an introduction to the English translation of Walser's novel *Geschwister Tanner*. See W.G. Sebald, "Le Promeneur Solitaire. A Remembrance of Robert Walser," trans. Jo Catling, *The Tanners*, Robert Walser, trans. Susan Bernofsky (New York: New Directions, 2009) 1–36.

rather than presenting us with an indisputable, unequivocal truth, the photographs Sebald chooses from various stages in Walser's life and Sebald's way of reading Walser's physiognomy in connection to his psychological state only increases the enigmatic aura around this author. Sebald mentions the last photograph taken of Walser when he was found dead in the snow but clearly out of respect and discretion chooses not to include this image in his text.[16]

In considering the unique aspects of Walser's language, Sebald's readers will recognize several similarities to Sebald's own style, aspects which Sebald's translators have also highlighted as posing a particular challenge. I quote the following passage at length to demonstrate both Sebald's style and Jo Catling's masterful translation. Sebald writes,

> Das spielerische, bisweilen auch verbohrte Auspinseln absonderlicher Details gehört zu den auffälligsten Eigenheiten der Walserschen Sprache. Die durch überspannte Partizipialkonstruktion oder durch Verbalkumulationen wie 'haben helfen dürfen zu verhindern' mitten im Satz entstehenden Wortstrudel und Turbulenzen; Neologismen wie zum Beispiel 'das Manschettelige' oder 'das Angstmeierliche', die gleich Tausendfüßlern unter unserem Blick davonwuseln; 'das Nachtvogelhaftscheue, in der Finsternis die Meere Überfliegende, in sich Hinabwimmernde,' von dem der Erzähler des Räuberromans in gewagter Metaphorisierung behauptet, daß es über einer Frauenfigur Dürers schwebe; Bizarrerien wie das unter der entzückenden Last einer verführerischen Dame gyxelnde Sofa; die an längst außer Gebrauch gekommene Dinge erinnernden Regionalismen; die fast manische Geschwätzigkeit – all das sind Elemente der Elaboration, deren Walser sich befleißigt, weil er befürchtet, zu geschwind fertig zu werden, wenn er, seiner Neigung gemäß, nichts als eine schön geschwungene Linie ohne Seitenzweige und Blüten aufs Blatt brächte. Tatsächlich ist der Umschweif für Walser eine Überlebensfrage (*Logis* 142–143).

> [The playful – and sometimes obsessive – working in with a fine brush of the most abstruse details is one of the most striking characteristics of Walser's idiom. The word-eddies and turbulence created in the middle of a sentence by exaggerated participial constructions, or conglomerations of verbs such as 'haben helfen dürfen zu verhindern' ('have been able to help to prevent'); neologisms, such as for example 'das Manschettelige' ('cuffishness') or 'das Angstmeierliche' ('chickenheartedness'), which scuttle away under our gaze like millipedes; the 'night-bird shyness, a flying-over-the-seas-in-the-dark, a soft inner whimpering' which, in a bold flight of metaphor, the narrator of *The Robber* claims hovers above one of Dürer's female figures; deliberate curiosities such as the sofa 'squeach-

---

16 Whereas Sebald exercises discretion with regard to this photograph, Jürg Amann reproduces two photographs from different angles of the dead Walser in his literary biography of the author. See Jürg Amann, *Robert Walser. Eine literarische Biographie in Texten und Bildern* (Zurich; Hamburg: Arche, 1995) 166 and 173. This photograph seems to have a legendary status of its own. Benjamin Kunkel writes, "Someone had the sang-froid to snap a photograph: footprints in the snow lead to a tall man lying with one arm thrown behind his head, for all the world as if his last gesture had been to toss off the hat that lies a few feet away." Benjamin Kunkel, "Still Small Voice. The Fiction of Robert Walser," *The New Yorker* (August 6, 2007) 68–71, here 71.

ing' ('gyxelnd') under the charming weight of a seductive lady; the regionalisms, redolent of things long fallen into disuse; the almost manic loquaciousness – these are all elements in the painstaking process of elaboration Walser indulges in, out of a fear of reaching the end too quickly if – as is his inclination – he were to set down nothing but a beautifully curved line with no distracting branches or blossoms. Indeed, the detour is, for Walser, a matter of survival (*PC* 131).]

Further aspects of Walser's writing that Sebald considers are tempo, irony, and his characters. He discusses specific works, in particular *Der Räuber* and *Kleist in Thun*, but he also mentions *Die Geschwister Tanner* and Walser's "Mikrogramme."[17] Sebald also finds affinities between Walser and Nikolai Gogol, and this connection is made via Vladimir Nabokov's observations on Gogol's characters. Sebald writes,

> Beide, Walser und Gogol, verloren nach und nach die Fähigkeit, ihr Augenmerk auf das Zentrum des Romangeschehens zu richten und verschauten sich statt dessen auf eine fast zwanghafte Weise in die an der Peripherie ihres Gesichtsfeldes in Erscheinung tretenden seltsam irrealen Kreaturen, über deren vorheriges und weiteres Leben wir nie auch nur das geringste erfahren (*Logis* 146).
>
> [Both of them gradually lost the ability to keep their eye on the centre of the plot, losing themselves instead in the almost compulsive contemplation of strangely unreal creations appearing on the periphery of their vision, and about whose previous and future fate we never learn even the slightest thing (*PC* 134).]

J. M. Coetzee aptly identifies that "Walser's texts are driven neither by logic nor by narrative but by moods, fancies, and associations: in temperament he is less a thinker or storyteller than an essayist."[18] It is perhaps no coincidence that Susan Sontag was drawn to Sebald's works and praised him so highly when one reconsiders the admiration she expressed for Robert Walser in her foreword to a collection of his stories in English translation. Sontag begins by lauding Walser as "one of the important German-language writers of this century."[19] One may

---

17 A selection of microscripts from Walser's *Aus dem Bleistiftgebiet. Mikrogramme 1924–1933* (1985–2000) have recently been published in English translation. Robert Walser, *Microscripts*, trans. and with an introduction by Susan Bernofsky, afterword by Walter Benjamin (New York: New Directions/Christine Burgin, 2010).
18 J. M. Coetzee, "The Genius of Robert Walser," *The New York Review of Books* 47.1 (November 2, 2000). This article reviews two translations of Walser's texts: *Jakob von Gunten*, trans. Christopher Middleton (New York: New York Review Books, 1999); *The Robber*, trans. Susan Bernofsky (Lincoln: University of Nebraska Press, 2000). Walser's essay *Kleist in Thun* demonstrates this particulary well.
19 Robert Walser, *Selected Stories*, with a Foreword by Susan Sontag, trans. Christopher Middleton and others (New York: Farrar, Straus, Giroux, 1982) vii–ix, here vii.

even wonder if Sebald himself learned from or emulated Sontag's form of essayistic writing. Just as Sontag sees Walser as "the missing link between Kleist and Kafka,"[20] we might see Sontag as the missing link between Walser and Sebald.

Reflecting on the connections he sees between Walser and his own grandfather prompts Sebald to ask "Was bedeuten solche Ähnlichkeiten, Überschneidungen und Korrespondenzen?" (*Logis* 137–138) ["What is the significance of these similarities, overlaps and coincidences?" (*PC* 127)]. He wonders,

> Handelt es sich nur um Vexierbilder der Erinnerung, um Selbst- oder Sinnestäuschungen oder um die in das Chaos der menschlichen Beziehungen einprogrammierten, über Lebendige und Tote gleichermaßen sich erstreckenden Schemata einer uns unbegreiflichen Ordnung? (*Logis* 138).
>
> [Are they rebuses of memory, delusions of the self and of the senses, or rather the schemes and symptoms of an order underlying the chaos of human relationships, and applying equally to the living and the dead, which lies beyond our comprehension? (*PC* 127)]

One may also consider that these connections attest to our desire for such order, a desire so strong that it necessitates the creation of order via our own invented connections. Sebald identifies the affinities between Walser and his grandfather, yet several affinities between Walser and Sebald become apparent along the way, leading the reader to transfer Sebald's comments on Walser back to Sebald himself. Sebald also acknowledges his relationship to other authors and his way of incorporating their words into his own works,

> Ich habe immer versucht, in meiner eigenen Arbeit denjenigen meine Achtung zu erweisen, von denen ich mich angezogen fühlte, gewissermaßen den Hut zu lüften vor ihnen, indem ich ein schönes Bild oder ein paar besondere Worte von ihnen *entlehnte*, doch ist es eine Sache, wenn man einem dahingegangenen Kollegen zum Andenken ein Zeichen setzt, und eine andere, wenn man das Gefühl nicht loswird, daß einem zugewinkt wird von der anderen Seite (*Logis* 139, my emphasis).
>
> [I have always tried, in my own works, to mark my respect for those writers with whom I felt an affinity, to raise my hat to them, so to speak, by borrowing an attractive image or a few expressions, but it is one thing to set a marker in memory of a departed colleague, and quite another when one has the persistent feeling of being beckoned to from the other side (*PC* 128)].

One particular affinity between Walser and Sebald, in addition to their use of language mentioned above, is their interest in other authors and their attempts to rework these lives into a literary form. Walser wrote not only his essay on

---

20 Ibid.

Kleist but short pieces on Georg Büchner and Jakob Michael Reinhold Lenz as well.[21]

In the last few pages of this essay on Walser, Sebald mentions, as if in passing, the first work he read by Robert Walser. In his characteristic way, Sebald does not give the title of this story but simply states "das über Kleist in Thun" (*Logis* 162) ["his piece on Kleist in Thun" (*PC* 148)]. Significantly, Sebald takes the title for his volume from the first sentence of Walser's story, which begins, "Kleist hat Kost und Logis in einem Landhaus auf einer Aareinsel in der Umgebung von Thun gefunden"[22] [Kleist found board and lodging in a country house on the Aare Island in the vicinity of Thun]. Sebald presents this story in more general terms: "in dem die Rede ist von den Qualen eines an sich und seinem Handwerk verzweifelnden Menschen und von der rauschhaft schönen Landschaft ringsum" (*Logis* 162) ["where he talks of the torment of one despairing of himself and his

---

21 In a collection of essays by Walser, we find a portrait of Georg Büchner entitled "Büchners Flucht" [Büchner's Flight] and a short play entitled "Lenz," which presents among other scenes, Lenz visiting Goethe in Straßburg and Weimar. See *Aufsätze von Robert Walser* (Leipzig: Kurt Wolff Verlag, 1913) 171–172; 176–183. Walser's play juxtaposes Lenz and Goethe as opposing representatives of Sturm und Drang [Storm and Stress] and Classicism, as can be seen in how Walser ventriloquizes the two here:

> Goethe: Unser Auge ist eine seltsame Maschine. Es greift und läßt alles wieder fahren. [...] Ist nicht Ordnung immer wieder das Schöne? (178) [The human eye is a curious machine. [...] Is order not always equivalent to the beautiful?]

> Lenz: In unsere deutsche Literatur muß der Sturm fahren, daß das alte, morsche Haus in seinen Gebälken, Wänden und Gliedern zittert. Wenn die Kerls doch einmal natürlich von der Leber weg reden wollten. Mein 'Hofmeister' soll sie in eine gelinde Angst jagen. Jagen, stürmen. Man muß klettern. Man muß wagen. In der Natur ist es wie ein Rauschen und Flüstern von Blut. Blut muß sie in ihre aschgrauen, blassen, alten Backen bekommen, die schöne Literatur. Was: schön. Schön ist nur das Wogende, das Frische. Ah, ich wollte Hämmer nehmen und drauflos hämmern. Der Funke, Goethe, der Funke. Die 'Soldaten,' bilde ich mir ein, müssen so etwas wie ein Blitz werden, daß es zündet (178–179). [The storm must rage in our German literature, so that the old, rotten house shakes in its beams, walls, and elements. If only the fellows wanted to speak freely and naturally from the gut. My 'Tutor' should chase a mild fear in them. To chase, to storm. One must climb. One must dare. In nature it is like a rushing and whispering of blood. Blood must flow in the ashen, pale, old cheeks of beautiful literature. What: beautiful. Only what is churning and fresh is beautiful. Ah, I wish I could take a hammer and hammer straight on. The spark, Goethe, the spark. The 'Soldiers,' I imagine, must become something like a flash of lightening that can start a fire.]

22 Robert Walser, "Kleist in Thun," *Geschichten von Robert Walser. Mit Zeichnungen von Karl Walser* (Leipzig: Kurt Wolff Verlag, 1914) 135.

craft, and of the intoxicating beauty of the surrounding landscape" (*PC* 148)]. In a way that is characteristic of his indirectness, Sebald does not state explicitly that the "Handwerk" ["craft"] refers to writing or the profession of this "Menschen" ["someone"] as that of an author.

Sebald recounts how he began reading Walser in the second half of the 1960s (*Logis* 162/*PC* 149), an act which is connected to the fact that he found a sepia photograph, picturing the house on the Aare Island in which Kleist lived in spring 1802. He found this photograph, coincidentally, in one of the three volumes of Keller's biography written by a certain "Bächtold."[23] According to Sebald's story, he purchased this biography at an antiquarian shop and surmises that it belonged to the estate of an exiled Jew – "die mit einiger Gewißheit aus dem Nachlaß eines aus Deutschland vertriebenen Juden stammte" *Logis* 162) ["which had almost certainly belonged to a German-Jewish refugee" (*PC* 149). This web of connections leads Sebald to the following conclusion,

> Langsam habe ich seither begreifen gelernt, wie über den Raum und die Zeiten hinweg alles miteinander verbunden ist, das Leben des preußischen Schriftstellers Kleist mit dem eines Schweizer Prosadichters, der behauptet, Aktienbrauereiangestellter gewesen zu sein in Thun, das Echo eines Pistolenschusses über dem Wannsee mit dem Blick aus einem Fenster der Heilanstalt Herisau, die Spaziergänge Walsers mit meinen eigenen Ausflügen, die Geburtsdaten mit denen des Todes, das Glück mit dem Unglück, die Geschichte der Natur mit der unserer Industrie, die der Heimat mit der des Exils (*Logis* 163).
>
> [Since then I have slowly learned to grasp how everything is connected across space and time, the life of the Prussian writer Kleist with that of a Swiss author who claims to have worked as a clerk in a brewery in Thun, the echo of a pistol shot across the Wannsee with the view from a window of the Herisau asylum, Walser's long walks with my own travels, dates of birth with dates of death, happiness with misfortune, natural history and the history of our industries, that of *Heimat* with that of exile (*PC* 148, italics Catling).]

Sebald has made similar comments in interviews. In particular in his interview with Christopher Bigsby, he recounts,

> While I was sitting in my pushchair and being wheeled through the flowering meadows by my mother, the Jews of Corfu were being deported on a four-week trek to Poland. It is the simultaneity of a blissful childhood and those horrific events that now strikes me as incomprehensible. I know now that these things cast a very long shadow over my life.[24]

---

23 Sebald is most likely referring to Jakob Baechtold, *Gottfried Kellers Leben. Seine Briefe und Tagebücher* (Berlin: W. Hertz, 1894–1897).
24 Sebald in Bigsby, 144.

One could see this as the underlying force of Sebald's fictional and in part scholarly writing: to illustrate, reenact, elucidate, and even create such connections.

Logis in einem Landhaus closes with an essay on questions of realism, focusing on the works of Jan Peter Tripp, Sebald's longtime friend and artistic collaborator who also shared his appreciation for Gottfried Keller and Robert Walser. In comparison to the rest of the essays in the volume, which seem woven together through their thematic connections, the essay on Tripp reads almost like an afterword. This final essay also stands apart from the others, for Tripp is a visual artist rather than a writer, although he is an artist with a pronounced literary sensibility. Authors of world literature form the subject of several of his works, including a recent cycle entitled "The Unknown" of twenty-five small-format paintings, depicting famous authors as well as politicians and performers at stages in their lives prior to their fame.[25] In addition to his collaboration with Sebald on *Unerzählt*, Tripp has recently produced a volume of his own visual works and poems by Hans Magnus Enzensberger; Justine Landat designed the volume, bringing together the images and texts, which were created independently.[26] Sebald provides his own explanation for why he ends with this essay on Tripp, "weil ich an seinen Bildern gelernt habe, daß man weit in die Tiefe hineinschauen muß, daß die Kunst ohne das Handwerk nicht auskommt und daß man mit vielen Schwierigkeiten zu rechnen hat beim Aufzählen der Dinge" (*Logis* 7) ["because from his pictures I have learned how it is essential to gaze far beneath the surface, that art is nothing without patient handiwork, and that there are many difficulties to be reckoned with in the recollection of things" (*PC* 3)]. In this collection of essays, Sebald formulates a concept of literature that is also evident in his own literary works, one that Schütte appositely describes as follows, "Das feine, ephemere Gewebe der Literatur verstand Sebald als einen ganz zentralen Bestandteil jener allumfassenden Ordnung, weshalb auch ihr genaues Studium uns dabei hilft, das Unbegreifbare – vielleicht – zu begreifen"[27] [Sebald understood the fine, ephemeral web of literature as a very central component of an all encompassing order, and the exacting study of literature helps us to – perhaps – comprehend the incomprehensible].

---

25 These twenty-five paintings were on display at the Literaturhaus in Stuttgart from May 22, 2013 through June 25, 2013. http://www.literaturhaus-stuttgart.de/event/2627-2-the-unknown/ [accessed June 22, 2013].

26 Hans Magnus Enzensberger, Jan Peter Tripp, Justine Landat, *Blauwärts. Ein Ausflug zu dritt* (Frankfurt am Main: Suhrkamp, 2013).

27 Schütte, *Sebald. Einführung*, 242.

From Polemic to Poetics: *Luftkrieg und Literatur*

I now turn my attention to Sebald's very controversial *Luftkrieg und Literatur*, not to engage with the morally-charged discussions of "German victimhood"[28] or with the debates around the taboo status of representing the Allied air raids in postwar German literature, but rather to consider this volume as it was originally conceived: a published version of Sebald's lectures on poetics given in Zurich in 1997. In this way, I argue that these lectures present a willful (mis)reading of the past in an attempt to get at a larger issue: Sebald's selective presentation of postwar literature and intentionally-skewed perspective ultimately emphasize the broader concern of transferring traumatic events and experiences into a linguistic form. This concern is not a problem of literary versus historical representation but demands that we consider the step before: the translation process from experience into language. I focus here on the apparent paradox between Sebald's poetics and his practiced aesthetics. That is, what Sebald argues for in his lectures – a synoptic and artificial view of history – is exactly what is criticized in his fictional prose works. And what Sebald problematizes in *Luftkrieg und Literatur* – the eyewitness account – is what seems to be privileged in the form of individual memory and experience that dominates his fictional texts. I would like to suggest that this potential aporia – between what Sebald advocates meta-discursively and what he accomplishes intra-discursively – functions in the same vein as certain narrative strategies employed in his literary texts. Ultimately this aporia points to the fundamental discursive tension in his work between history and literature. Instead of criticizing an allegedly contradictory constitution of the text, I suggest considering this hybridity of history and literature as essential to his approach to the past and constitutive for his entire body of work. The textual realization of this hybridity consists in what I outlined above: literary historiography, which is not history as illustrated within literature or a historiography supported by elements of the literary discourse, but rather a new type of historiography that comes into being *only* in the literary mode.

I choose not to focus my attention on Sebald's actual thesis, which has been duly noted and passionately disputed by literary scholars and journalists.[29] One

---

28 For an insightful discussion of this term, see Annette Seidel-Arpaci, "Lost in Translations? The Discourse of 'German Suffering' and W. G. Sebald's *Luftkrieg und Literatur*," *A Nation of Victims? Representations of German Wartime Suffering from 1945 to the Present*, ed. Helmut Schmitz (Amsterdam: Rodopi, 2007) 161–179.

29 Susanne Vees-Gulani's *Trauma and Guilt: Literature of Wartime Bombing in Germany* (Berlin and New York: de Gruyter, 2003) unequivocally refutes Sebald's claim that the Allied air raids had been taboo in German literature. See also Timm Menke, "W. G. Sebalds *Luftkrieg und Literatur*

only has to think of Volker Hage's *Zeugen der Zerstörung. Die Literaten und der Luftkrieg*, an over-300-page collection of essays and interviews on this subject.[30] Nevertheless, it might be helpful to briefly recall the central aspects of the thesis: Sebald asserts a lack of literary representations of the Allied air raids on Germany at the end of World War II, suggesting that this lack is indicative of a psychological state of repression – in the terms of Alexander and Margarethe Mitscherlich's groundbreaking work *Die Unfähigkeit zu trauern. Grundlagen kollektiven Verhaltens* (1977) – and that this lack ultimately points to an unspoken taboo.[31] Let me highlight just one article that disputes the assertion that there was no open discussion of the air raids due to repression or branding the event a taboo subject. Marcel Atze critically examines newspaper coverage of the Frankfurt Auschwitz trials from 1963–1965, showing that the trial documentation focused not only on the crimes committed at Auschwitz but also discussed the attacks on Hamburg and Dresden by British and American forces.[32] The "Überlagerung der Diskurse Holocaust und Luftkrieg" [overlap of the discourses Holocaust and air raids], which Atze argues is already apparent in public news media of the 1960s, demands a more differentiated discussion, rather than sweeping assertions of a conspiracy of silence, such as those voiced by Sebald on several occasions.[33]

---

und die Folgen: Eine kritische Bestandsaufnahme," *Bombs Away! Representing the Air War over Europe and Japan*, eds. Wilfried Wilms and William Rasch [*Amsterdamer Beiträge zur Neueren Germanistik* 60] (Amsterdam: Rodopi, 2006) 149–163; Gregor Streim, "Der Bombenkrieg als Sensation und als Dokumentation. Gert Ledigs Roman *Vergeltung* und die Debatte um W.G. Sebalds *Luftkrieg und Literatur*," *Amsterdamer Beiträge zur neueren Germanistik* 57.1 (2005) 293–312; Graham Jackman, "Introduction," and "'Gebranntes Kind?' W.G. Sebald's 'Metaphysik der Geschichte,'" *German Life and Letters* 57.4 (2004) 343–353; 456–471.

30 Volker Hage, *Zeugen der Zerstörung. Die Literaten und der Luftkrieg. Essays und Gespräche* (Frankfurt am Main: S. Fischer, 2003).

31 See Wilfried Wilms, "Speak no Evil, Write no Evil: In Search of a Usable Language of Destruction," *W.G. Sebald. History – Memory – Trauma*, eds. Scott Denham and Mark McCulloh (Berlin: de Gruyter, 2006) 183–204 and "Taboo and Repression in W.G. Sebald's On the Natural History of Destruction," *W.G. Sebald: A Critical Companion*, eds. J.J. Long and Anne Whitehead (Seattle, WA: University of Washington Press, 2004) 175–189.

32 See Marcel Atze, "'...und wer spricht über Dresden?' Der Luftkrieg als öffentliches und literarisches Thema in der Zeit des ersten Frankfurter Auschwitz-Prozesses 1963–1965," *Sebald. Lektüren*, eds. Marcel Atze and Franz Loquai (Eggingen: Ed. Isele, 2005) 105–115, also published in *W.G. Sebald. Politische Archäologie und melancholische Bastelei*, eds. Michael Niehaus and Claudia Öhlschläger [*Philologische Studien und Quellen* 196] (Berlin: Schmidt, 2006) 205–217.

33 See for example his interview with Michael Silverblatt, "A Poem of an Invisible Subject," *The Emergence of Memory: Conversations with W.G. Sebald*, ed. Lynne Sharon Schwartz (New York, London, Melbourne, Toronto: Seven Stories Press, 2007) 77–86, here 84. See also Charles Simic, "Conspiracy of Silence," *New York Review of Books* 50.3 [February 27] (2003) 86–96.

There is perhaps an important distinction to be made between "public" and "private" discussions of Holocaust atrocities and the Allied air raids. Sebald makes clear that the conspiracy of silence he is claiming is within a private sphere: "I grew up in postwar Germany where there was — I say this quite often — something like a conspiracy of silence, i.e., *your parents never told you anything about their experiences because there was at the very least a great deal of shame attached to these experiences.*"[34]

The lacuna in German literature that Sebald diagnoses is more complex than a mere moral reproach, as *Luftkrieg und Literatur* has often been (mis) understood, and points to the aesthetic deficiencies of the literary representations that do exist. Beyond an aesthetic dimension, Sebald's concern is one of the epistemological dimension of history, or the problem of how we can access or gain knowledge of the past beyond the documents and accounts that serve as a basis for such historical knowledge. In addition to this epistemological barrier there are linguistic limits as well, that is, the question of transfer from an extra-linguistic 'real' into the arbitrary signs of language, or what I described in chapter one as a process of semioticization. Also pointing to a problem of narrativization, Aleida Assmann asserts that the experience of the bombings was not distilled into a common, national narrative.[35] That this process of narrativization did not occur in the immediate postwar period is not surprising to Assmann, rather she finds surprising that Sebald in a sense expected there to be a national narrative in addition to literary representations of the air raids.

From the outset it must be stated that it is somewhat problematic to refer to Sebald's *Luftkrieg und Literatur* as a published form of his Zurich lectures on poetics or even as a revised version.[36] First of all, a shift in rhetoric almost always

---

34 Sebald in Silverblatt, "A Poem of an Invisible Subject," 84–85, my emphasis.

35 Cf. Aleida Assmann, *Der lange Schatten der Vergangenheit. Erinnerungskultur und Geschichtspolitik* (Munich: C. H. Beck, 2006) 184–185.

36 Significantly, the English edition of *Luftkrieg und Literatur* includes two additional essays by Sebald on Peter Weiss and Jean Améry, both of which touch on the problem of representation and the process of translating experiences into language and literature that is at the heart of these lectures on poetics. See W. G. Sebald, "The Remorse of the Heart. On Memory and Cruelty in the Works of Peter Weiss," (*NH* 169–191). This essay was first published as "Die Zerknirschung des Herzens. Über Erinnerung und Grausamkeit im Werk von Peter Weiss," *Orbis litterarum* 41.3 (1986) 265–278, and included in *Campo Santo* (*CS* 128–148). See also W. G. Sebald, "Against the Irreversible. On Jean Améry," (*NH* 143–167). This essay was first published as "Mit den Augen des Nachtvogels. Über Jean Améry," *Études Germaniques* 43.3 (1988) 313–327, and also included in *Campo Santo* (*CS* 149–170).

occurs from the oral lectures to their printed form.[37] In the case of Sebald's lectures, the revisions appear to be significant and substantial. He omits the first lecture altogether, drastically summarizing it and integrating it into the third section of the published volume, what he calls the "Nachschrift" (*LuL* 6) ["postscript" (*NHD* viii)].[38] The manuscript for this first lecture reveals Sebald's sensitivity to the challenge an author faces when giving such lectures about their writing. The first line of this manuscript, which could also be read as a title, reads: "Warum ich keine Poetikvorlesung im eigentlichen Sinn halten kann" [Why I cannot give a lecture on poetics in the usual sense] – Sebald proceeds, "weil ich fürchte, mich in meinem eigenen Haus zu verlaufen, oder aus dem Tritt zu kommen wie jener sprichwörtliche Tausendfüßler bei der Betrachtung über seine Art, sich fortzubewegen"[39] [since I fear that I will get lost in my own house, or that I will fall out of step, like the proverbial millipede who becomes frozen mid-step at the moment he starts to think about how it is he moves forward]. This first lecture furthermore contains a heavy reliance on and quotation from his own works and reveals a strong focus on his own biography, supporting a common phenomenon of such lectures on poetics. Sebald describes not only *how* he writes, but also emphasizes *why* he writes as well as the conditions of his writing. One must also keep in mind that Sebald already alluded to the problems outlined in *Luftkrieg und Literatur* in an essay called "Zwischen Geschichte und Naturgeschichte. Über die literarische Beschreibung totaler Zerstörung," published in the journal *Orbis litterarum* in 1982.[40] Furthermore, Sebald approaches the issue in his literary

---

37 In his book on the *Poetikvorlesung* [lectures on poetics] as a literary genre, Paul Michael Lützeler identifies this genre as a particular development within postwar German culture that can also be connected to the long tradition of authors writing about their works. Paul Michael Lützeler, "Einleitung. Poetikvorlesungen und Postmoderne," *Poetik der Autoren. Beiträge zur deutschsprachigen Gegenwartsliteratur* (Frankfurt am Main: Fischer Taschenbuch Verlag, 1994) 8.
38 For a detailed comparison between the lecture manuscript and the published version of *Luftkrieg und Literatur*, see Mario Gotterbarm, "Ich und der Luftkrieg. Sebalds erste Zürcher Vorlesung als Autofiktion," *Jahrbuch der deutschen Schillergesellschaft* 55 (2011) 324–345, especially 337. Reading the first Zurich lecture as exemplary of the phenomenon of "autofiction," Gotterbarm elucidates how Sebald develops a way to legitimate his engagement with the topic of the air raids, especially as someone who was born after the events and who necessarily can have no real memories of them but whose consternation is nonetheless genuine (cf. Gotterbarm, 325).
39 A: Sebald, DLA Marbach.
40 W.G. Sebald, "Zwischen Geschichte und Naturgeschichte. Über die literarische Beschreibung totaler Zerstörung," *Orbis litterarum* 37 (1982) 345–366. Republished in *Campo Santo* (69–100). Both Andreas Huyssen and Simon Ward have noted this basis for *Luftkrieg und Literatur*. Andreas Huyssen, "Rewritings and New Beginnings: W.G. Sebald and the Literature on the Air War," *Present Pasts: Urban Palimpsests and the Politics of Memory* (Stanford, CA: Stanford University Press, 2003) 138–157. Simon Ward, "Responsible Ruins? W.G. Sebald and the Responsibility of

works as well: in *Die Ringe des Saturn* the gardener of Somerleyton Hall discusses the Allied air raids with the narrator, and in Sebald's three-part *Nach der Natur*, the voice of the poem connects his own conception with that of the bombings.[41]

In the third part of *Luftkrieg und Literatur*, Sebald also provides a postscript to the Zurich lectures. Here he acknowledges the fragmentary nature of the lectures and the need to complete and correct his observations. In this sort of rebuttal, while acknowledging the many responses he received and highlighting some texts and authors he did not know and which have perhaps been unjustly forgotten, such as *Die Stalinorgel* and *Die Vergeltung*, both by Gert Ledig, Sebald ultimately reiterates his assertion of a lack in German literature, judging existing representations of the air raids as both quantitatively and qualitatively insufficient in the sense that these texts are incomparable to the actual collective experiences of the time. "Gewiß gibt es den einen oder anderen einschlägigen Text, doch steht das wenige uns in der Literatur Überlieferte sowohl in quantitativer als auch in qualitativer Hinsicht in keinem Verhältnis zu den extremen kollektiven Erfahrungen jener Zeit (*LuL* 75–76)." ["Yes, there are a few relevant texts, but what little has been recorded in literature, in terms of both quantity and quality, stands in no relation to the extreme collective experiences of the time" (*NHD* 70).] One must ask if Sebald sees something unique to the experience of the air raids or if what he describes here is a fact of every situation "reflected" in textual form, literary or otherwise. Will literature, according to such an assessment, always come up short, or is this a way of preserving its particularity as a discourse by marking and thereby maintaining the problem of representation, i.e., the irreconcilable difference between the 'real' and a text?

To assert such a literary insufficiency or inadequacy requires that Sebald formulate what an appropriate form of representation would look like, and this is where the issue becomes problematic. If one considers what Sebald suggests in

---

the German Writer," *Forum for Modern Language Studies* 42.2 (2006) 183–199. Ward, for example, marks a development in Sebald's "literary method" and his view of the writer's responsibility from the 1982 essay to the 1997 lectures: "Sebald implies that literature has a responsibility towards the victims of the kind of traumatic experience that should not be subordinated to an overriding metaphysics." See Ward, "Responsible Ruins?," 186. Several aspects of Sebald's fictional prose point to the fact that he does not subordinate "historical experience to an overriding metaphysics" (Ward, 191), although there are scholars that argue the contrary. See essays in *W. G. Sebald and the Writing of History*, eds. Anne Fuchs and J.J. Long, (Würzburg: Königshausen & Neumann, 2007).

41 On the presence of the air raids in Sebald's literary works, see Susanne Vees-Gulani, "The Experience of Destruction: W.G. Sebald, the Airwar, and Literature," *W.G. Sebald. History – Memory – Trauma*, eds. Scott Denham and Mark McCulloh (Berlin: de Gruyter, 2006) 335–349, especially 347.

Luftkrieg und Literatur in comparison with his own literary works, several contradictions become apparent, especially with regard to perspective, immediacy, and explicitness.[42] The synoptic and by necessity artificial view – "since no eyewitness could have had a synthetic view of the destruction"[43] – that Sebald sanctions in *Luftkrieg und Literatur* is exactly what is criticized in his fictional prose works.[44] To approach a definition of what Sebald means by "synoptic and artificial," one must look more closely at the text within the text: Sebald's (literary) description of "Operation Gomorrah," the air raid on Hamburg on July 28, 1943. It should be noted that this passage also presents a shift in discourse within *Luftkrieg und Literatur* from essay to fictional prose and back to essay. Sebald's "synoptic" view is made up of a combination of perspectives. His description is explicit in detail, even bordering on the grotesque, and shifts from aerial to ground view and oscillates from far to near. Such a direct representation is what Sebald works against in both *Die Ausgewanderten* and *Austerlitz*. Although immediate and explicit, the view Sebald suggests in *Luftkrieg und Literatur* is also an impersonal one, which further contrasts with the emphasis on telling an individual (hi)story that one finds in his stories of emigrants and exiles as a way of approaching a larger history. One way to reconcile *Luftkrieg und Literatur* with Sebald's fiction would be to see the impersonal – even anti-empathetic – viewpoint and the shifting perspective as impediments to inappropriate identification insofar as

---

42 These aspects have been touched upon by Todd Samuel Presner and Anne Fuchs, for example. See Todd Samuel Presner, "'What a Synoptic and Artificial View Reveals:' Extreme History and the Modernism of W.G. Sebald's Realism," *Criticism* 46.3 (2004) 341–360; Anne Fuchs, "A *Heimat* in Ruins and the Ruins as *Heimat*: W.G. Sebald's *Luftkrieg und Literatur*," *German Memory Contests. The Quest for Identity in Literature, Film, and Discourse since 1990*, eds. Anne Fuchs, Mary Cosgrove, and Georg Grote (New York: Camden House, 2006) 287–302.

43 Presner, "'What a Synoptic and Artificial View Reveals,'" 351. Carolin Duttlinger reads this combination of perspectives thus: "the imaginary eye of the writer is supposed to transcend the limitations of individual sources in order to reconstruct the past with greater accuracy and immediacy." Carolin Duttlinger, "A Lineage of Destruction? Rethinking Photography in *Luftkrieg und Literatur*," *W.G. Sebald and the Writing of History*, eds. Anne Fuchs and J.J. Long (Würzburg: Königshausen & Neumann, 2007) 163–177, here 167. Duttlinger's assertions are based on the assumption that the 'facts' are there, i.e., they exist extratextually, and one only has to get "close enough" to them in order to write an 'accurate' or 'true' history.

44 To recall the key example in *Die Ringe des Saturn*: the narrator expresses skepticism toward historical representation, "die Kunst der Repräsentation der Geschichte" (*RS* 152) ["the representation of history" (*RoS* 125)], for it depends upon a "Fälschung der Perspektive" (*RS* 152) ["falsification of perspective" (*RoS* 125)]. See discussion in chapter one.

both strategies create a distance from the subject.[45] In an interview with Volker Hage from 2000, Sebald again takes up the fundamental problem of writing and emphasizes the necessity of a distanced approach:

> Die Reproduktion des Grauens oder besser: die Rekreation des Grauens, ob mit Bildern oder mit Buchstaben, ist etwas, das im Prinzip problematisch ist. Ein Massengrab läßt sich nicht beschreiben. Das heißt, man muß andere Wege finden, die tangentieller sind, die den Weg über die Erinnerung gehen, über das Archäologisieren, über das Archivieren, über das Befragen von Personen – ein weiteres Indiz dafür, daß die Literatur zu diesem Thema nicht unbedingt aus der unmittelbaren Nachkriegszeit hätte kommen müssen (*G* 180).
>
> [The reproduction of horror, or better: the recreation of horror, whether with images or with letters, is something that is in principle problematic. A mass grave cannot be described. That is, one must find other ways that are more tangential, ways that proceed via memories, via archaeologizing, via archiving, via interviewing people – a further indication of why it was not necessarily possible for literature on this topic to be written in the immediate postwar period.]

In *Luftkrieg und Literatur*, Sebald asserts the limitations of individual sources. He does not write off eyewitness reports of the firebombing, but he does point to the limits of such reports, since they so often use "stereotype Wendungen" (*LuL* 32) ["clichés" (*NHD* 24)]. The stereotypes or clichéd phrases used by witnesses can only ever pale in comparison to the actual catastrophe and often only serve to cover up and to "neutralize" the experiences, which exceed all powers of comprehension, as Sebald describes, "die über das Fassungsvermögen gehenden Erlebnisse" (*LuL* 32) ["experiences beyond our ability to comprehend" (*NHD* 25)]. Sebald is not criticizing the individual sources but their de-individualization through clichés. The incomprehensibility of the reality experienced is made understandable, and assimilated into one's memory, when it is transformed into a previously given narrative form or in the form of a cliché. Authenticity, according to Sebald's argument, cannot be achieved in "Normalsprache" (*LuL* 32) ["everyday language" (*NHD* 25)]. Anyone who was able to survive the bombings only managed to do so with psychological and emotional damage: the experience of the air raids led "zwangsläufig zu einer Überladung und Lähmung der Denk- und Gefühlskapazität" (*LuL* 33) ["must inevitably have led to overload, to paraly-

---

45 Further differences between this passage in *Luftkrieg und Literatur* and Sebald's fictional prose works include the following aspects: In his fictions, Sebald creates distance on the discursive level rather than on the level of the story. Whereas time is marked specifically in this passage in *Luftkrieg und Literatur*, it is indicated more vaguely in *Austerlitz*, for example. While the style and syntax of the description of the bombing of Hamburg differs from Sebald's own literary descriptions – the description in *Luftkrieg und Literatur* is characterized by shorter sentences – it is couched in Sebald's more characteristic complex, hypotactic sentence structure.

sis of the capacity to think and feel in those who succeeded in escaping" (*NHD* 25)]. It is ironic here that this attempt to describe the experience of psychological and emotional damage is in itself a somewhat clichéd description of sensory overload or of a paralyzing of the senses and cognition.[46] Quoting from an earlier essay by Sebald on Jean Améry and Primo Levi,[47] Mark M. Anderson highlights the epistemological problem with which Sebald begins *Luftkrieg und Literatur* and to which he returns when discussing the difficulty in expressing the experience of the firebombing in "Normalsprache":

> [...] even direct witnesses of Nazi crimes, that is, 'the people who knew what went on' in the death camps, cannot give us a 'true understanding' ('keinen wahren Begriff') of their experience, since the original memory trace is too disturbed. Writing 'translates' this chaotic, pre-linguistic trace within the mind's recording faculty ('Gedächtnis') into an ordered, discursive 'recollection' ('Erinnerung') that distorts and betrays its truth content in the very act of mediation.[48]

Sebald does not reproach or discount eyewitness reports as such, but describes a double-bind in which the survivors of the air raids are caught. The experience escapes comprehension and any attempts to describe the event fall back on clichéd formulations and thus cannot be compared to the actual event. Moreover, Sebald sees a form of repression in eyewitness accounts, assessing such formulaic reports to be "eine Geste zur Abwehr der Erinnerung" (*LuL* 32) ["a gesture sketched to banish memory" (*NHD* 25)]. Rather than reading this turning away from memory as a moral reproach, Sebald is again emphasizing that such accounts, clichéd as they may be, are a manifestation of the limits of comprehension and the challenges to assimilate such an event as the air raids into one's experiences. The chasm that gapes between experience and representation is barely bridged by the process of semioticization, in itself a problematic if not

---

46 Sebald refers to Alexander Kluge's "Der Luftangriff auf Halberstadt am 8. April 1945," which includes an American military psychologist's assessment that "'die Bevölkerung [hätte], bei offensichtlich eingeborener Erzähllust, die psychische Kraft, sich zu erinnern, genau in den Umrissen der zerstörten Flächen der Stadt verloren.'" (*LuL* 31; Kluge 106) ["'the population, although obviously showing an innate wish to tell its own story, [had] lost the psychic power or accurate memory, particularly within the confines of the ruined city.'" (*NHD* 24)]. See Alexander Kluge, "Der Luftangriff auf Halberstadt am 8. April 1945," *Neue Geschichten. Hefte 1–18 'Unheimlichkeit der Zeit'* (Frankfurt am Main: Suhrkamp, 1977) 33–107.

47 W. G. Sebald, "Überlebende als schreibende Subjekte. Jean Améry und Primo Levi, ein Gedenken," *Zeit und Bild: Frankfurter Rundschau am Wochenende* (January 28, 1989) ZB3.

48 Mark M. Anderson, "Documents, Photography, Postmemory: Alexander Kluge, W. G. Sebald, and the German Family," *Photography in Fiction*, eds. Silke Horstkotte and Nancy Pedri, special issue of *Poetics Today* 29.1 (2008) 129–151, here 147–148.

practically impossible endeavor. Further emphasizing this core problem of literature, we find similar formulations by Heinrich Böll, whose text *Der Engel schwieg* is one of few that Sebald praises in *Luftkrieg und Literatur*. Böll touches upon this problem of translation from experience to language in his own lectures on poetics, which he held in Frankfurt in 1966. Böll succinctly states: "Das Wahrnehmbare, täglich Erlebte, ist offenbar nicht so leicht in Sprache zu fassen"[49] [That which we perceive, that which is experienced daily, is apparently not that easy to capture in language].

While the graphic and even grotesque description of corpses lying in pools of their own fat may seem incongruous to Sebald's characteristically indirect approach to depictions of atrocity – he never actually describes the horrors of World War II in his fictional prose – this type of description actually supports his general argument regarding the problem of representation. On the one hand, certain eyewitness accounts seem "clichéd," because the experiences have been assimilated into pre-established narrative forms. On the other hand, if words are found to describe events that defy comprehension, like the account of a woman carrying the burned corpse of a child in a suitcase, this attempt at representation unavoidably seems grotesque or lacking in authenticity. Sebald responds to this scene recounted by Friedrich Reck, stating, "weiß man sie doch in kein Wirklichkeitsraster einzuordnen und zweifelt irgendwie an ihrer Authentizität" (*LuL* 94) ["it is also hard to fit it into any framework of reality, so that one feels some doubt of its authenticity" (*NHD* 88)].

Despite the apparent paradox between Sebald's prescribed "synoptic and artificial view" and the criticism of such representations within his fictional prose, there are elements of his analytic and aesthetic process in *Luftkrieg und Literatur* that remain consistent with his literary works, like his citation practice. Although Sebald gives some bibliographic information in endnotes throughout *Luftkrieg und Literatur*, his citation practice remains one of integration rather than indication. This also provides a point of consistency between the Hamburg passage – which can itself be seen as a literary text within the larger essay form of *Luftkrieg und Literatur* – and his fictional prose texts. One can assume that the details given – weight and number of bombs, time of attack, speed of the fire storm, space and height that it covered – must come from military records, although no records are cited. Only towards the end of the description does Sebald allude to a source, namely reports by bomber pilots, but even here, there are no direct citations. He writes, "Eine wabernde Hitze, von der die Bomberpiloten berichteten, daß sie sie gespürt hätten durch die Wandungen ihrer Maschinen, ging lange noch von den

---

49 Heinrich Böll, *Frankfurter Vorlesungen* (Cologne: Kiepenheuer & Witsch, 1966) 48.

qualmenden, glosenden Steinbergen aus" (*LuL* 35). ["A wavering heat, which the bomber pilots said they had felt through the sides of their planes, continued to rise from the smoking, glowing mounds of stone" (*NHD* 27).] A further connection can be made between Sebald's lectures on poetics and the analytic and aesthetic strategies he uses in his literary works by examining the opening passage of *Luftkrieg und Literatur*. Here, we find an expression of the epistemological barrier to historical understanding, which is also a central concern of his literary texts. He writes,

> Es ist schwer, sich heute eine auch nur halbwegs zureichende Vorstellung zu machen von dem Ausmaß der während der letzten Jahre des zweiten Weltkriegs erfolgten Verheerung der deutschen Städte, und schwerer noch, nachzudenken über das mit dieser Verheerung verbundene Grauen. Zwar geht aus den *Strategic Bombing Surveys* der Alliierten, aus den Erhebungen des Bundesamts für Statistik und anderen offiziellen Quellen hervor, daß allein die Royal Air Force in 400 000 Flügen[50] eine Million Tonnen Bomben über dem gegner- ischen Gebiet abgeworfen hat, daß von den 131 teils nur einmal, teils wiederholt angegriffe- nen Städten manche nahezu gänzlich niedergelegt wurden, daß an die 600 000 Zivilperso- nen in Deutschland dem Luftkrieg zum Opfer fielen, daß dreieinhalb Millionen Wohnungen zerstört wurden, daß bei Kriegsende siebeneinhalb Millionen obdachlos waren, daß auf jeden Einwohner Kölns 31,4, auf jeden Dresdens 42,8 Kubikmeter Bauschutt kamen, doch was all das in Wahrheit bedeutete, das wissen wir nicht (*LuL* 11).
>
> [Today it is hard to form an even partly adequate idea of the extent of the devastation suffered by the cities of Germany in the last years of the Second World War, still harder to think about the horrors involved in that devastation. It is true that the strategic bombing surveys published by the Allies, together with the records of the Federal German Statistics Office and other official sources, show that the Royal Air Force alone dropped a million tons of bombs on enemy territory; it is true that the 131 towns and cities attacked, some only once and some repeatedly, many were almost entirely flattened, that about 600,000 German civilians fell victim to the air raids, and that three and a half million homes were destroyed, while at the end of the war seven and a half million people were left homeless, and there were 31.1 [sic][51] cubic meters of rubble for every person in Cologne and 42.8 cubic meters for every inhabitant of Dresden – but we do not grasp what it all actually meant (*NHD* 3–4).]

After listing various statistics that may quantify the damage and destruction caused by the air raids, Sebald asserts that we are unable to grasp what this actually means. The rhetorical construction of this passage, which highlights the barrier between empirical "facts" and (emotional) knowledge, is reminiscent of

---

50 It is unclear why this statistic is left out of the English translation.
51 Sebald takes this statistic from Hermann Glaser, *1945. Ein Lesebuch* (Frankfurt am Main: Fischer, 1995) (*LuL* 149) [(*NHD* 193)]. Glaser writes, "Laut Statistik kamen in Dresden 42,8 Kubikmeter Trümmer auf jeden Einwohner (inklusive der Toten), in München 6,5 cbm, in Stuttgart 8,5 cbm, in Berlin 12,6 cbm, in Köln 31,4 cbm." *Ein Lesebuch*, 22.

the oft-cited "herring passage" in *Die Ringe des Saturn* (*RS* 75).[52] This acknowledgment of knowing facts yet not claiming to possess understanding or access to the past or to another being's experience provides a generative force for Sebald's literary historiography: this fusion of the historian's knowledge of what happened and the writer's imagination of what could have been or what could be. The thesis that literary representations of the air raids are lacking and those that exist are aesthetically insufficient, then, can be read on the one hand as a necessary impossibility and on the other as a disappointment that no attempts or experiments were made to break out of the limits of existing linguistic and narrative structures. The necessary combination of perspectives to represent the past, which Sebald suggests in his "synoptic view," hinges directly on the need for a new discourse, to which Sebald's literary works can be seen as a response: taken together they reveal his attempts to create a new hybrid form of literary historiography.

Sebald challenges his readers in multiple ways. There is the dissonance between text and image, there is the porous boundary between authenticity and artificiality or between fact and fiction, and there is the closeness of Sebald the author to his nameless first-person narrators. The fact that Sebald's prose form defies traditional genre classification and can be characterized as a "hybrid poetics" reflects his understanding of the literary discourse and his attempt to create a new form that not only is interdiscursive but also embodies a fusion of both literature and history. While Sebald's literary *style* of writing may be "unashamedly traditional,"[53] conventional, or reminiscent of nineteenth-century writers,[54] as many scholars claim, there is innovation on both the *formal* level and the *discursive* level. The specifics of Sebald's hybrid form of writing, what I term his literary historiography, emerge out of the tensions created between *Luftkrieg und Literatur* and his fictional prose texts.[55] Todd Samuel Presner's illuminating reading of Sebald's "synoptic view" of history situates the techniques used by Sebald to represent extreme historical events as those of literary modernism and characterizes Sebald's suggested form of literature as a "new modernist realism."[56]

---

52 See discussion in chapter one.
53 Ward, "Responsible Ruins?," 192.
54 Among many others, Sebald's English translator, Anthea Bell, has made this remark.
55 Simon Ward mentions Sebald's development of his own literary discourse and his own mode of writing, which productively incorporates "the 'semantic potential' of fragments of the past (such as photographs, testimony)," not in an attempt to "write a critical history," but rather to write literature that "is disrupted through the interplay of fictional invention and historical detail, intertextuality and quotation." Ward, "Responsible Ruins?," 192.
56 Presner, "'What a Synoptic and Artificial View Reveals,'" 345.

However, we fall short if we only read this text as an explicit poetics. Reading *Luftkrieg und Literatur* as an implicit poetics, or as part of an immanent poetics that develops across Sebald's œuvre, helps develop a clearer picture of Sebald's understanding of the literary discourse, in particular as it relates to other discourses, such as historiography. Furthermore, reading *Luftkrieg und Literatur* as an implicit poetics and working through the tensions created between this text and his fictional prose, the reader becomes engaged on several levels. The critical engagement of the reader, not only with the literary text itself, but also with the contentious past at the center of these texts reveals the ethical dimension and imperative of Sebald's works.

Rather than seeing Sebald's suggestions for an "appropriate" literary representation of the Allied air raids as contradicted in his literary texts, one could acknowledge the close proximity of literature and historiography through this contradiction. Ultimately, any and all attempts to reconstruct the past or a reality of the past are per se artificial. In this sense, the representation of history, although the subject of critique in Sebald's literary texts, depends indeed on a falsification of perspective, just as the synoptic view suggested in *Luftkrieg und Literatur* must be artificial ["künstlich"]. Moreover, if one does not take the "synoptic view" literally, assuming, for example, that the multiplicity of perspectives are exclusively visual, one can see such an approach at work in Sebald's literary texts: he brings together information from multiple and varied sources, and such intertextuality and intermediality become characteristic for his fictional prose.

Luftkrieg und Literatur most explicitly diagnoses the problem of representation – both literary and historical[57] – as opposed to questions of description or invention, to which all of Sebald's fictional narrators are highly sensitive. The problem of a semiotically-mediated representation is at the fundament of Sebald's thesis in *Luftkrieg und Literatur*. This must not be understood as a prohibition in the sense that certain scholars have argued with regard to the Holocaust's "unrepresentability."[58] Rather, Sebald is marking the chasm between sensate experience and the linguistic formulation of such experiences, and he gives several examples of those who have failed in their attempts. He quotes Lord Solly

---

57 The short-comings Sebald asserts are not only on the side of literature: "es [ist] uns bisher nicht gelungen, die Schrecken des Luftkriegs durch historische oder literarische Darstellungen ins öffentliche Bewußtsein zu heben" (*LuL* 100) ["we have not yet succeeded in bringing the horrors of the air war to public attention through historical or literary accounts" (*NHD* 93)].

58 Elie Wiesel holds the representation of the Holocaust as a privilege of the survivors. Ruth Franklin cites Wiesel, "'Only those who lived it in their flesh and in their minds can possibly transform their experiences into knowledge.'" See Ruth Franklin, *A Thousand Darknesses. Lies and Truth in Holocaust Fiction* (Oxford: Oxford University Press, 2010) 86.

Zuckerman who was unable to carry out his plans to write a natural history of destruction, from which the title for the English translation of *Luftkrieg und Literatur* was taken: "My first view of Cologne cried out for a more eloquent piece than I could ever have written," writes Zuckerman in his autobiography *From Apes to Warlords*.[59] What is actually at stake here is not only the problem of historical or literary representation, i.e., a genre-specific problem, but rather the step before, the question of transfer from the objective, i.e., non-semiotic real into the arbitrary signs of language. Not only this process of semioticization, but the fact that Sebald is reflecting upon this problem within his literary texts, can be seen as his attempt to make visible and thereby overcome the irreconcilable chasm between experience and text.

The discursive tension between history and literature in Sebald's works parallels another tension: the experience of reading Sebald's works. Despite the many strategies Sebald employs to create distance or space for reflection – between the narrators and the subjects of the narrative or between the readers and the texts – the reader nevertheless responds emotionally to the stories he reads. This emotional reaction should not be equated with an easy identification with the subjects, however. The haunting, often suffocating atmosphere Sebald creates and the isolation and helplessness the figures feel when trying to remember or to write their experiences, transfers from the pages of the text to the reader. In an engaged reading of Sebald's works, it is difficult to remain indifferent, and despite the distance created by Sebald between his narrators and subjects, an intense form of witnessing takes place, a witnessing of Germany's past and a witnessing on behalf of the victims of this past.[60] Sebald's particular blend of representation and reflection upon this representation, that is, always with a critical regard towards this drive to representation, characterizes his literary historiographical project. While thematizing the problems of representation, both literary and historical, Sebald ultimately demonstrates the power of the literary discourse to form human experiences, emotions, and events into a story or "history." Sebald's texts offer us an interdiscursive view of art, substantially altered from Theodor W. Adorno's claim,

---

59 Lord Solly Zuckerman, *From Apes to Warlords* (London: [Hamish Hamilton], 1978) 322. Another example provided by Sebald is that of Hans-Dieter Schäfer, a Germanist in Regensburg who had a plan to write a Berlin novel: "Doch nie, sagt Schäfer, gelang es mir beim Schreiben, 'die furchtbaren Ereignisse in all ihrer Gewalt zurückzurufen'" (*LuL* 97). ["Yet he says that as he wrote he never succeeded 'in recalling the full force of those dreadful events'" (*NHD* 91).] In a footnote, Sebald refers to the source of this statement: Hans-Dieter Schäfer, *Mein Roman über Berlin* (Passau: refugium, 1990) 29.

60 See chapter five for a further discussion of witnessing and testimony.

Der Begriff einer nach Auschwitz auferstandenen Kultur ist scheinhaft und widersinnig, und dafür hat jedes Gebilde, das überhaupt noch entsteht, den bitteren Preis zu bezahlen. Weil jedoch die Welt den eigenen Untergang überlebt hat, bedarf sie gleichwohl der Kunst als ihrer *bewußtlosen Geschichtsschreibung.*[61]

[The concept of a culture that has arisen after Auschwitz is both illusionary and absurd, and for this reason, every creation that emerges has a bitter price to pay. Since the world has survived its own downfall, it needs art as its form of unconscious historiography.]

Sebald's fiction is an art that is *consciously* writing and rewriting history, thus a *conscious* historiography, but not only that, it is a historiography that is *consciously and purposefully* literary.

The Author's Role and the Reader's Engagement

"*A quoi bon la littérature?*" (*CS* 247) ["What is literature good for?"]. Sebald posed this question in his speech at the opening of the Stuttgarter Literaturhaus,[62] but it is a question implicit across his entire œuvre and representative of his deep devotion to the ethical responsibilities and aesthetic possibilities of the literary discourse. In response to this question, Sebald offers the following answer, "Einzig vielleicht dazu, daß wir uns erinnern und daß wir begreifen lernen, daß es sonderbare, von keiner Kausallogik zu ergründende Zusammenhänge gibt [...]" (*CS* 247). ["Perhaps only to help us to remember, and teach us to understand that some strange connections cannot be explained by causal logic [...]" (*CSE* 204).] Sebald's narratives reconceptualize boundaries of time, space, and memory though not necessarily according to a rationally explicable system. His narratives are ones of conjecture; attempts at explanation are prefaced with a provisional "perhaps," a tentative "it seems to me," or a suggestive "it might be." Through what appear to be coincidences, the individual finds insights into his

---

61 Theodor W. Adorno, "Jene zwanziger Jahre" *Kulturkritik und Gesellschaft II. Gesammelte Schriften*, vol. 10.2, ed. Rolf Tiedemann (Frankfurt am Main: Suhrkamp, 1977) 506, my emphasis.

62 W.G. Sebald gave this speech on November 17, 2001, and it has since been published and reprinted in various places. This speech was published first in the *Stuttgarter Zeitung*. It was also previously published under the same title in: *Betrifft: Chotjewitz, Dorst, Hermann, Hoppe, Kehlmann, Klein, Kling, Kronauer, Mora, Ortheil, Oswald, Rakusa, Sebald, Walser, Zeh*, eds. Florian Höllerer and Tim Schleider (Frankfurt am Main: Suhrkamp, 2004) 11–16. The speech was reprinted in *Campo Santo* under the title "Ein Versuch der Restitution," and the English translation was published not only in the English translation of *Campo Santo* but also as "An Attempt at Restitution. A Memory of a German City," trans. Anthea Bell, *The New Yorker* (December 20 & 27, 2004) 110–114.

identity and connections to a greater historical framework. Moreover it is through literature, in particular in the form of nonlinear narratives, that such non-rational insights or even epiphanies can be made. Sebald reveals such connections by way of his narrators who traverse varied landscapes across countless countries, speak multiple languages, and often merge with their subjects. They explore and observe artifacts that range from massive architectural structures such as war fortresses to delicate, forgotten photographs, found by chance between the pages of a well-worn book. Be they official representations of history presented in museum dioramas, classical paintings of famous battles, or personal accounts of the past, like a journal or a childhood photograph, all of these traces are considered and contemplated by Sebald's narrators and characters. But it is often the most incidental detail that captures one's attention, while the historical artifacts, traditionally accepted as "authentic," are skeptically questioned.

Sebald justifies further his choice to write literature with this succinct answer, "Es gibt viele Formen des Schreibens; einzig aber in der literarischen geht es, über die Registrierung der Tatsachen und über die Wissenschaft hinaus, um einen Versuch der Restitution" (CS 248). ["There are many forms of writing; only in literature, however, can there be an attempt at restitution over and above the mere recital of facts, and over and above scholarship" (*CS* 205).] This assertion alludes to the essential tension in Sebald's writing: the relationship between history and literature, documentation and imagination, rational explanations and defiantly non-rational insights. What Aristotle understands by "the universal," also entails his concept of realism; he stipulates that what may happen must occur "according to the law of probability or necessity."[63] One could cite the role of coincidence in Sebald's texts as proof of his divergence from Aristotelian realism insofar as encounters and connections do not depend upon a "law of probability or necessity." Yet these coincidences in his works, *Austerlitz* in particular, seem to affirm Aristotle's assertion that "coincidences are most striking when they have an air of design."[64] Though not immediately

---

63 Aristotle, Chapter Nine, *Poetics, Aristotle's Theory of Poetry and Fine Art,* ed. S.H. Butcher (New York: Dover Publications, 1951) 35.

64 Ibid., 39. This seems to be the reason why Arbogast Schmitt in his recent translation of the *Poetics* translates that the poet writes "was geschehen *müsste*" [what must have happened], whereas Fuhrmann and Gigon – the former standard translations of the *Poetics* in German – preferred "könnte" [could]. See Aristoteles, *Poetik,* Übersetzt und erläutert von Arbogast Schmitt (Aristoteles, *Werke,* in deutscher Übersetzung. Band 5) (Berlin: Akademie Verlag, 2008) 14, my emphasis. Aristoteles, *Poetik,* Griechisch/Deutsch, Übersetzt und herausgegeben von Manfred Fuhrmann (Stuttgart: Reclam, 1994) 29. Aristoteles, *Poetik,* Übersetzung, Einleitung und Anmerkungen von Olof Gigon (Stuttgart: Reclam, 1967) 36.

apparent or rationally explicable, the chance meetings between Austerlitz and the narrator among other coincidences nevertheless possess what could be called an extra-rational logic,[65] or a "hidden order of things."[66]

The potentiality of literature is what makes it a more universal discourse than history, according to Aristotle. This potentiality must not be misunderstood as an extreme position of denying the possibility of objective facts or equating history with fiction.[67] The horrors of World War II and the Holocaust for example, though not directly experienced by Sebald, are a very real part of history; and, one could even argue, central to understanding his entire œuvre.[68] In one interview, Sebald spoke of the millions of victims sent to the gas chambers, who must not be remembered as an anonymous mass but as individuals. "'Es ging immer um die Millionen, die da durch die Gaskammern geschleust wurden. Das waren aber nicht anonyme Massen, sondern immer einzelne Menschen, die tatsächlich auf der anderen Seite des Flurgangs gelebt haben.'"[69] [It has always been about the millions who were sent to the gas chambers. They were not anonymous masses, but rather individuals who had actually lived across the hallway.] There are common threads between this statement made in 1993 – before the publication of *Austerlitz* and before his comments made at the opening of the Literature House in Stuttgart – and Sebald's literary historiographical project. First, Sebald is working toward the rehabilitation of an individual's story and the emotional and mental experience of rediscovering one's own past, which is simultaneously connected to a greater "history." The ethical imperative of literature thus demands the responsibility of the author towards his subjects as well as the engagement of its readers.[70]

---

65 Christopher Bigsby has also suggested "a kind of associational logic" in Sebald's prose, meaning a logic like that of dreams. Bigsby, "W. G. Sebald," 148–149.

66 Mark McCulloch, *Understanding W. G. Sebald* (Columbia, S. C.: University of South Carolina Press, 2003) 122.

67 Ernst Breisach cites the work of Hayden White and Dominick LaCapra, among others, as tending to see history as merging into fiction. See Ernst Breisach, *Historiography. Ancient, Medieval, & Modern* (Chicago and London: The University of Chicago Press, Second Edition, 1994) 335.

68 This assertion holds true without pigeonholing Sebald as a "Holocaust author." See also Jackman, "'Gebranntes Kind?'" 466.

69 Cf. Atze, "W. G. Sebald und H. G. Adler," 93.

70 The way Sebald engages his readers is a further point of connection to Bertolt Brecht, in particular his project of Epic Theater that strove to activate the audience members and engage them in critical thought about the actions and interactions on stage.

Literature as a kind of historiographical enterprise and the documentary character of his texts provokes the question of why Sebald chose not to write historical monographs or reports. Sebald himself offers this answer:

'Was die historische Monographie nicht leisten kann, ist, eine Metapher oder Allegorie eines kollektiven Geschichtsverlaufes zu produzieren. Aber erst in der Metaphorisierung wird uns Geschichte empathetisch zugänglich. [...] Das soll aber nicht heißen, daß ich dem Romanhaften das Wort rede. Ich habe einen Horror vor allen billigen Formen der Fiktionalisierung. Mein Medium ist die Prosa, nicht der Roman.'[71]

['Historical monographs cannot produce a metaphor or allegory for the collective course of history. It is only in this process of metaphorization that history becomes empathetically accessible. [...] This of course does not mean that I am making a case for the novel. I find all cheap forms of fictionalization horrific. My medium is prose, not the novel.']

That Sebald refers to himself as a writer of prose rather than a novelist, has certainly to do with what Stanley Corngold has described as a "reflex of his shame at what he sees as the trawling for aesthetic effects in other people's suffering."[72] This is also a desire to avoid any presumptuous sentimentalization of history in general and of the Holocaust in particular. Furthermore, the designation of "prose writer" is also a better match with his particular "hybrid" prose style since it incorporates multiple genres, rather than being limited to the form of the novel.[73] In a *Spiegel* interview of 2001, Sebald states, "Ich glaube, dass gerade an der Nahtstelle zwischen Dokument und Fiktion literarisch die interessantesten Dinge entstehen"[74] [I believe that this interface of the documentary and the fictional is exactly where the most interesting things emerge].[75] This interface (*Nahtstelle*) can be seen as the site of both chronologi-

---

71 Cf. Sigrid Löffler, "'Wildes Denken.' Gespräch mit W. G. Sebald," *W. G. Sebald*, ed. Franz Loquai (Eggingen: Ed. Isele, 1997) 135–137, here 137.

72 Stanley Corngold, "Sebald's Tragedy," *Rethinking Tragedy*, ed. Rita Felski (Baltimore: The Johns Hopkins University Press, 2008) 218–240, here 219.

73 Sebald's practice of referring to himself as a writer of prose rather than novelist is also reminiscent of Brecht's use of "Stückeschreiber" (a mistranslation of the English term "playwright") rather than "Dramatiker," when referring to himself.

74 Martin Doerry and Volker Hage, "'Ich fürchte das Melodramatische,'" Interview in *Der Spiegel* 11 (March 12, 2001) 230.

75 Similarly, in an interview with Volker Hage from 2000, Sebald notes how the question of fact versus fiction (and specifically the question of what is fiction, what is citation, and what is invented citation in the works of Alexander Kluge) is a very productive one. In response to the common question of the degree of authenticity in the lives he describes in his works, Sebald remarks, "Das ist ja gerade das Geheimnis der Fiktion, daß man nie genau weiß, wo die Trennungslinie verläuft" (*G* 180) [That is precisely the secret of fiction, that one does not exactly know where the line of distinction runs].

cal documentation and creative potentiality, an interface that brings together the two separate endeavors of history and literature as described in Aristotle's *Poetics*.

Sebald activates his readers through the tension between text and image, his prose form that defies easy genre classification, and his autobiographically-inflected albeit nameless first-person narrators, just to name a few aspects. This critical engagement of the reader, not only with the literary text itself, but also with the contentious past at the center of these texts, namely the Holocaust, reveals a further ethical dimension and imperative of Sebald's œuvre. While the indirect presence of the Holocaust in Sebald's works does assume from readers a knowledge of this historical atrocity, Sebald's prose does not "exile" the Holocaust itself by using words like "Auschwitz" in a metonymic way to encompass the entire horror of the "Final Solution," devised by the Nazis to exterminate the Jews. By avoiding such a mode of representation, Sebald works against leveling the complexity of the Holocaust in both historical and literary terms. He challenges a superficial understanding of the Holocaust and standardized reactions, by focusing on the individual experience and problematizing our access, understanding, and representation of this paradigmatic atrocity of the twentieth century.

Chapter 3
What is (in) an Image? Mimesis, Representability, and Visual History

Art and Reality

As touched upon in the previous chapters, the photograph is tied to an extratextual reality insofar as this reality is inscribed into the image through the physical and chemical process of its creation. This technical documentation of an external reality does not however guarantee a statement of truth about what is pictured.[1] That is, while every photograph may document, not every photograph has a documentary status. Just as photographs possess the potential for documentation, they also have the potential for falsification; and Sebald's texts demonstrate how literature can explore and develop this double potential of photographs to both document and falsify reality. Just as Sebald places historical figures alongside fictional characters to explore the ontological status of the 'real,' his use of photographs illustrates the multiple relationships among intra-, inter-, and extratextual realities at play in fictional representations. In short, photography and photographs in his works provide a site for theoretical musings on the larger problems of history and memory. By connecting the fundamental problem of art's relationship to reality to the specific question of the Holocaust's representability – one of Sebald's core concerns – this chapter also explores the ethical dimension of literature. But before exploring the complex and dynamic relationship between verbal and pictorial discourses in Sebald's works, let us first develop the fundament for these further considerations.

Reality is not a given fact but a problem. This can be seen in the way that what has been considered reality has changed drastically over time from antiquity to modernity. The Platonic model of reality encompassed exclusively the world of ideas, to which man had no direct access, for ideas existed independently of perception. Since nothing could be added to the world of ideas, this model moreover only allowed for reproductions. The separation of the world of appearances

---

1 One must think of Bertolt Brecht's description of a photograph of a Krupp's factory and his assertion that the photograph cannot reveal what the factory truly is, i.e., its historical, social, and economic context. See discussion below. Bertolt Brecht, "Der Dreigroschenprozeß. Ein soziologisches Experiment," Vol. 21, *Schriften* 1, *Werke*, Große kommentierte Berliner und Frankfurter Ausgabe, eds. Werner Hecht, Jan Knopf, Werner Mittenzwei, and Klaus-Detlef Müller (Berlin; Weimar; Frankfurt am Main: Suhrkamp, 1992) 448–514.

from the world of ideas was also linked to the separation of the body from the soul and implied a clear hierarchy as well. The status of firstness was reserved for ideas, and ideas were the exclusive creation of the phyturge: the creator, 'poet,' on the ontological level.[2] Objects were located one step lower in this hierarchy, since they were seen as imitations of ideas, brought forth by the demiurge, a craftsman valued only insofar as he is useful. Artworks, i.e., objects derived from objects, were the result of mimesis and neither real nor useful and moreover disdained insofar as they could deceive.[3] While clearly asserting the deficits and dangers of art, Plato did not formulate a ban on all imitation. He, like Aristotle after him and all the way to Benjamin in the twentieth century, recognized the anthropological drive to imitate.[4] This ontological deficit of art that Plato describes in *The Republic* is based on the fact that art deals only with secondary appearances (*Schein*) and can therefore have no being (*Sein*) of its own. Twice-removed from reality, art cannot possess truth; hence it is also marked by an epistemological flaw. This stigma of 'thirdness' is an aspect of both imitation and imagination, since both are only able to bring forth copies. Their products are thus always valued less than original ideas and viewed as being remote from truth. In their potential to deceive, they are moreover marked by a moral deficit. Since truth, goodness, and beauty are linked for Plato, ethics and aesthetics are connected as well. Millennia away from Plato's concept of reality, we nevertheless still engage in discussions that range from the moral to the ontological when considering the relationships between art and life, fiction and authenticity.

Eighteenth-century aesthetics and nineteenth-century romanticism have shifted our view of reality away from the Platonic model, and creative endeavors have since been valued as contributing to the world of ideas. Reason has further been subordinated to imagination, which can be seen in claims for art that moves against and beyond imitation. Harry Mulisch, for example, makes a playful plea for the artistic ideal of mimesis that encompasses more than mere imitation: "the

---

2 See Hans Blumenberg, "'Nachahmung der Natur.' Zur Vorgeschichte der Idee des schöpferischen Menschen," *Wirklichkeiten in denen wir leben. Aufsätze und eine Rede* (Stuttgart: Reclam, 1993) 68ff.

3 The concept of mimesis has been reconsidered in recent years by Classical philologists, such as Stephen Halliwell, in order to reveal its multiple dimensions and break down the reductionist equation: mimesis = imitation. Stephen Halliwell, *The Aesthetics of Mimesis. Ancient Texts and Modern Problems* (Princeton, N.J.: Princeton University Press, 2002).

4 For Aristotle, man is not only capable of imitation but he can also draw pleasure from it. Further illuminating the anthropological basis for imitation is Walter Benjamin's "Lehre vom Ähnlichen" and "Über das mimetische Vermögen," *Walter Benjamin. Gesammelte Schriften* 2.1, eds. Rolf Tiedemann and Hermann Schweppenhäuser (Frankfurt: Suhrkamp, 1977 [both texts from 1933]) 204–210 and 210–213.

stupid duplication of reality – that is: the proof of [the artist's] complete super-fluousness."[5] The understanding of imagination shifted from a reproductive to a productive faculty and has come to be seen as the dominant faculty – the "queen" of the faculties, according to Charles Baudelaire – in human practices of art. A good painter, for Baudelaire, masters technique but also has an unlimited imagination and must strive to paint not what he sees but what he feels and dreams.[6] Baudelaire distinguishes between two camps of artistic expression, the "realists" who copy nature, not wanting to interfere with or alter the nature they paint, and the "imaginative," who paint with their soul, wanting to "illuminate things with [their] mind."[7] In outlining different types of painting – religious, historical, fantasy, portrait, and landscape – Baudelaire asserts the important role of the viewer, again emphasizing the significance of the imagination. He writes, "If an assemblage of trees, mountains, water and houses, such as we call a landscape, is beautiful, it is not so of itself, but through me, through my own grace and favour, through the idea or the feeling which I attach to it."[8] The diorama is somewhat different than the painting; it is not what the viewer brings to the object, but rather the construction itself appears to be stronger than the viewer. He states that the diorama's "brutal and enormous magic has the power to impose a genuine illusion upon me!"[9] Baudelaire identifies a certain degree of truthfulness in both the diorama and the theater, precisely in the directness of their illusion. He states, "These things, because they are false, are infinitely closer to the truth; whereas the majority of our landscape-painters are liars, precisely because they have neglected to lie."[10]

---

5 Harry Mulisch, trans. Paul Vincent, *The Discovery of Heaven* (New York: Penguin, 1997 [1992]) 386.

6 See Charles Baudelaire, "The Salon of 1859. Letters to the editor of the *Revue Française*," *Art in Paris 1845–1862. Salons and Other Exhibitions Reviewed by Charles Baudelaire*, trans. and ed. Jonathan Mayne (London: Phaidon [Greenwich, Conn.: New York Graphics Society Publishers], 1965) 144–216, here 155 and 162.

7 Ibid., 162.

8 Ibid., 194.

9 Ibid., 202. One could relate this to the description of the Waterloo diorama in Sebald's *Die Ringe des Saturn*. See discussion in chapter one.

10 Ibid., 203. Baudelaire's argument certainly applies to realist literature and aspects of this will be taken up in chapter four in relation to the impossibility of the narration in Sebald's works. That is, the tension between the gesture of direct, reported speech on the one hand and the countless details that would defy anyone's memory on the other point to the constructedness of the narration. It is this tension between realism and illusion, I would argue, that ultimately evokes a form of authenticity.

Vast changes have occurred in our understanding of reality since Plato, but the desire to represent reality, in particular to capture what one sees in an 'accurate' or exact form, has remained constant since antiquity. 'Photographic' representations in the broadest sense of the term, using light to draw an image, [Greek: *photos* = light + *graphein* = to draw] can be traced back to antiquity. Pliny tells the fable of a Corinthian girl who captured her parting lover in the form of a silhouette ["Schattenriß"]. The invention of the camera obscura dates back to the Renaissance and provided a way to temporarily transpose a replication of reality. In the late eighteenth century one can read a literary prophecy of photographic representation in Charles François Tiphaigne de la Roche's novel *Giphantie* from 1760, which recounts the "fixing of transient images" of nature by the action of light.[11] Nature, in this novel, is described anthropomorphically, following an age-old topos, as a painter "with a sure and nevererring hand."[12] These images then are said to be exact copies, equivalent to the original object in nature, thus surpassing any representations of the same nature by painters, as far as accuracy is concerned. Interestingly, such exact representations have a purported allegorical purpose: one image of a storm, for example, is said "to represent allegorically the troublesome state of this world, and mankind's stormy passage through the same."[13] Despite the change in artistic medium – from painting to a type of light drawing – the function thus remains the same, namely to rise above the 'real' in order to make a more general statement about man and the world.

The advent of photography's invention in 1839, with Louis Jacques Mandé Daguerre's eponymous "Daguerreotypes," brought about a renewed relevance to discussions of the relationship between reality and representation. The risk that painting would become obsolete is sensed, since, if painting reproduces nature and photography does this better, faster, and more accurately, then why not abolish painting? Baudelaire's scathing critique of the development of photography – voiced in his letters to Jean Morrel, the editor of the *Revue Française*, regarding the Salon of 1859 – scorned this new medium as "the refuge for every would-be painter, every painter too ill-endowed or too lazy to complete his studies [...]."[14] Baudelaire's critique turns the tables on the relationship between the light images "painted" by nature and man's imitations of nature by painting, as described by Tiphaigne de la Roche in his 1760 novel. According to Baudelaire,

---

11 "Photography Predicted. Tiphaigne de la Roche. 1760," *Photography. Essays & Images. Illustrated Readings in the History of Photography*, ed. Beaumont Newhall (New York: The Museum of Modern Art, 1980) 13–14, here 13.
12 Ibid., 14.
13 Ibid.
14 Baudelaire, "The Salon of 1859," 153.

A revengeful God has given ear to the prayers of this multitude. Daguerre was his Messiah. And now the faithful says to himself: 'Since photography gives us every guarantee of exactitude that we could desire (they really believe that, the mad fools!), then photography and art are the same thing.' From that moment our squalid society rushed, Narcissus to a man, to gaze at its trivial image on a scrap of metal. A madness, and extraordinary fanaticism took possession of all these new sun-worshippers. Strange abominations took form.[15]

The theoretical problem at the core of Baudelaire's idea of modern art and poetry is not only the competition between art and technology but an anxiety over its negative influence on the imagination. At its invention, photography appears to fulfill all of the qualities of mimesis, understood as an imitation or exact reproduction of nature, which, according to Baudelaire, is valuable for those with a weak memory or for those pursuing certain scientific studies. His tirade continues,

Let [photography] hasten to enrich the tourist's album and restore to his eye the precision which his memory may lack; let it adorn the naturalist's library, and enlarge microscopic animals; let it even provide information to corroborate the astronomer's hypotheses; in short, let it be the secretary and clerk of whoever needs an absolute factual exactitude in his profession – up to that point nothing could be better. Let it rescue from oblivion those tumbling ruins, those books, prints and manuscripts which time is devouring, precious things whose form is dissolving and which demand a place in the archives of our memory – it will be thanked and applauded. But if it be allowed to encroach upon the domain of the impalpable and the imaginary, upon anything whose value depends solely upon the addition of something of a man's soul, then it will be so much the worse for us![16]

It is not that Baudelaire sees no merit in photography, but he insists on its separation from the arts. Unsurprisingly, he is not willing to theorize photography as an art form on par with painting. Moreover, he accuses photography as the culprit for the degeneration or "impoverishment of the French artistic genius"[17] and alludes to the ultimate detrimental effect this technical progress will have on imagination.

The discussions around the development of photography in the nineteenth century initiated further questions around modes of authentic reproduction and

---

15 Ibid., 152–153.
16 Ibid., 154. There is a certain overlap between the legitimate uses of photography named by Baudelaire and the types of photographs and images used by Sebald. Sebald goes beyond Baudelaire, however, in showing just how problematic a discourse photography is – photographs do not simply reflect reality, they cannot make incontestable statements of truth, and they do not provide unambiguous proof of memory.
17 Ibid., 153.

more broadly the questions I have been invoking here: what is reality? What is realism?[18] What is art?[19] In Baudelaire's reflections on art, he clearly separates aesthetics and truth, asserting that beauty can exist without being true, "The exclusive taste for the True (so noble a thing when it is limited to its proper applications) oppresses and stifles the taste of the Beautiful."[20] This separation marks a development away from eighteenth-century aesthetics, yet the way in which Baudelaire defines the sense of sight is indebted to the advancements made by Kant: it is the individual who shapes what he sees within the process of perception. Kant's revolutionary *Critique of Pure Reason* makes clear that there are no 'given' objects, but rather that objects are constituted within the subject's perception. On the one hand, seeing is a mechanical process distinguished from dreams and on the other it encompasses both imagination and modification, elements on which the artist must rely.[21] Baudelaire's attack on photography aside, what is implied in his remarks is the changing view of art in relation to reality. Plato's hierarchy has been reversed in this modern idea of art as a creative cultural practice that is mediated through the artistic subject and that embodies the infinite and the possible. Poets and painters are now the only ones whose works have the potential to create new ideas and change society.

Since its invention and especially in response to the harsh critiques such as those voiced by Baudelaire, photography has had to legitimate its own existence in comparison to other discourses and art forms. Photography first becomes an object of theoretical discussions in the 1930s.[22] Siegfried Kracauer's essay "Die Photographie" (1927), Walter Benjamin's "Kleine Geschichte der Photographie" (1931) and "Das Kunstwerk im Zeitalter seiner technischen Reproduzierbarkeit" (1936), and Bertolt Brecht's "Dreigroschenprozeß" (1931), consider the particularities of this medium with regard to popular media, politics, and art. Moreover they consider the effect that new technological media have on how we perceive art. Susan Sontag's *On Photography* and Roland Barthes' *Camera Lucida*, provide later twentieth-century examples of treatises on photography as an art.[23] John Berger's reflections

---

18 While definitions of reality are historically contingent, *Realism* is limited to the epoch of the nineteenth century, and 'realism' encompasses a perennial problem of the arts.

19 Realist art relies on the pretension that there is an objective reality outside of itself.

20 Baudelaire, "The Salon of 1859," 151.

21 See ibid., 154–155.

22 Dominique Baqué, *La photographie plasticienne. Un art paradoxal* (Paris: Editions du Regard, 1998) 91.

23 Susan Sontag, *On Photography* (New York: Farrar, Straus and Giroux, 1973) and Roland Barthes, trans. Richard Howard, *Camera lucida. Reflections on Photography* (New York: Hill and Wang, 1981).

on photography also integrate those who distinguish it from other art forms; he cites Man Ray in this regard: "'I photograph what I do not wish to paint, and I paint what I cannot photograph.'" Berger also differentiates between two uses of photography, "[a]n ideological use, which treats the positivist evidence of a photograph as if it represented the ultimate and only truth. And in contrast, a popular but private use which cherishes a photograph to substantiate a subjective feeling."[24]

Asserting his historical position one hundred years after the invention of photography, Benjamin sets out to cut through the fog ("Nebel") that has surrounded the beginnings of photography.[25] The time has now come, asserts Benjamin, to begin answering certain historical and philosophical questions, questions which still preoccupy us today. This delay, according to Benjamin, is in part rooted in a philistine concept of art that has suppressed photography, restricting it to an inferior status within the hierarchy of the arts. In what is clearly a response to Baudelaire, Benjamin writes of the fetishistic and anti-technical concept of art that has determined the arguments of theoreticians of photography for nearly one hundred years.[26] Benjamin points to the tension that exists between the controlled technical mastery involved in taking a photograph and the magical value viewers find in looking at the photograph.

> Aller Kunstfertigkeit des Photographen und aller Planmäßigkeit in der Haltung seines Modells zum Trotz fühlt der Beschauer unwiderstehlich den Zwang, in solchem Bild das winzige Fünkchen Zufall, Hier und Jetzt, zu suchen, mit dem die Wirklichkeit den Bildcharakter gleichsam durchgesengt hat, die unscheinbare Stelle zu finden, in welcher, im Sosein jener längstvergangenen Minute das Künftige noch heut und so beredt nistet, daß wir, rückblickend, es entdecken können.[27]
>
> [No matter how artful the photographer, no matter how carefully posed his subject, the beholder feels an irresistible urge to search such a picture for the tiny spark of contingency, of the Here and Now, with which reality has so to speak seared the subject, to find the inconspicuous spot where in the immediacy of that long-forgotten moment the future subsists so eloquently that we, looking back, may rediscover it.[28]]

---

24 John Berger, *Another Way of Telling* (New York: Vintage, 1995) 111.

25 Walter Benjamin, "Kleine Geschichte der Photographie [1931]," *Walter Benjamin. Gesammelte Schriften* 2.1, eds. Rolf Tiedemann and Hermann Schweppenhäuser (Frankfurt: Suhrkamp, 1977) 368–385, here 368. Despite the title of his essay, Benjamin does not provide "a precise chronological or technological history, but a reflection on the impact of the cultural innovation of photography," as Dant and Gilloch observe. See Tim Dant and Graeme Gilloch, "Pictures of the Past. Benjamin and Barthes on Photography and History," *European Journal of Cultural Studies* 5.1 (2002) 5–23, here 10.

26 Cf. Benjamin, "Kleine Geschichte der Photographie [1931]," 369.

27 Ibid., 371.

28 Walter Benjamin, "A Short History of Photography," trans. Phil Patton, *Artforum* 15.6 (1977) 46–61.

This tension connects to Benjamin's concept of "Aura," which he defines in this essay as, "Ein sonderbares Gespinst von Raum und Zeit: einmalige Erscheinung einer Ferne, so nah sie sein mag"[29] ["A strange weave of space and time: the unique appearance or semblance of distance, no matter how close the object may be"]. The technology of the photograph, specifically "das Verhältnis des Photographen zu seiner Technik"[30] ["the photographer's attitude to his techniques"], is still the decisive factor in photography, but Benjamin also sees its creative potential as opposed to only a reproductive ability.[31] Benjamin writes, "Hat die Photographie sich aus Zusammenhängen herausbegeben, wie sie ein Sander, eine Germaine Krull, ein Bloßfeldt geben, vom physiognomischen, politischen, wissenschaftlichen Interesse sich emanzipiert, so wird sie 'schöpferisch'" ["Where photography has moved away from contexts imposed upon it by practitioners such as Sander, Germaine Krull, or Blossfeldt, where it has emancipated itself from physiognomical, political, or scientific concerns, it becomes 'creative'"]. Bestowing praise on Eugène Atget for both his precision and his efforts to unmask reality, Benjamin writes, "Atget war ein Schauspieler, der, angewidert vom Betrieb, die Maske abwischte und dann daran ging, auch die Wirklichkeit abzuschminken"[32] ["Atget was an actor who, disgusted with the profession, wiped off the mask and then set about removing the make-up from reality too"]. This is not to say that Benjamin naïvely thinks Atget presents a naked truth in his photographs, rather he sees Atget as a forerunner of surrealist photography, by initiating a new way of looking as well as "eine heilsame Entfremdung zwischen Umwelt und Mensch"[33] ["a salutary estrangement between man and his surroundings"].

Alongside such serious theoretical considerations, photography begins to gain value as an independent art form, and this is marked by its relationship to literature. In modernist and postmodernist literary texts we find characters who are photographers, and photographs themselves provide the starting point for fictional texts.[34] The narration of photographs within literary discourse offers a

---

29 Ibid., 378.
30 Ibid., 377.
31 Ibid., 383.
32 Ibid., 377.
33 Ibid., 379.
34 Heinz Lehmbäcker tells of his "fotographische und freundschaftliche Beziehungen zu Uwe Johnson" [photographic and friendly relationships to Uwe Johnson] and how one snapshot served "als Anregung fürs Bücherschreiben" [as a stimulus for writing books]. In his *Jahrestage*, Johnson describes the scene captured in this image and then explicitly states that the photograph also exists. Heinz Lehmbäcker and Uwe Johnson, *Mecklenburg. Zwei Ansichten*. Mit Fotografien von Heinz Lehmbäcker und Texten von Uwe Johnson (Frankfurt am Main and Leipzig: Insel Verlag, 2004) 175; 176; 178–179. J.J. Long cites Günter Grass' *Die Blechtrommel*, Christa Wolf's *Kind-*

modern form of ekphrasis, and authors, like Sebald, go a step further by incorporating actual reproductions of photographs in their texts.[35] Sebald's œuvre illustrates this new "photo-textual aesthetic,"[36] to borrow Paul Hansom's term. The particular questions pertinent to photography and especially relevant to Sebald – for he is explicitly raising such questions by way of both his narrative style and also his innovative integration of images – are those of realism, authenticity, the documentation of history, and subsequently the writing of this history, i.e., historiography. This discussion of literature's relationship to reality is further complicated due to the prominent though often implicit role the Holocaust plays in Sebald's texts, as will be shown below.

The individual's relationship to the past and one's attempt to gain access through physical presence and geographic proximity point to the problem of realism and are at the center of Sebald's personal and idiosyncratic approach to both the reading and writing of literature and history. Playfully raising the questions of how and to what degree we have access to reality, Sebald's works further interrogate our relationship to reality and require a discussion of what is meant by the 'real.'[37] Since several of the details that Sebald uses to lend an air of authenticity to his narratives are taken from other texts, we might have to specify the 'real' in his works as an intertextual one. These details drawn from other sources, literary and fictional sources in particular, are moreover in themselves mediated, i.e., not directly related to or reflecting reality. The construction of Sebald's texts thus points to the extreme position of Arno Schmidt, as formulated in his *Die Schule der Atheisten*: "Die 'wirkliche Welt'?: ist, in Wahrheit, nur die Karikatur unsrer Großn

---

heitsmuster, Thomas Bernhard's *Auslöschung*, and Peter Schneider's *Vati* as further examples of how the description of a photograph serves as a starting point for literary works. J. J. Long, "History, Narrative, and Photography in W. G. Sebald's *Die Ausgewanderten*," *Modern Language Review* 98.1 (2003) 117.

35 The instances of this seem to be increasing. Two further examples include Stephan Wackwitz, *Ein unsichtbares Land* (Frankfurt am Main: Fischer, 2003) and Maria Cecilia Barbetta, *Änderungsschneiderei Los Milagros* (Frankfurt am Main: Fischer, 2008). Indicating that this phenomenon is also an international one, Terry Pitts' blog, referenced in the introduction, takes as its focus not only Sebald's works but also "novels with embedded photographs," as the blog's subtitle reads. http://sebald.wordpress.com [accessed: June 22, 2013]

36 Paul Hansom, "Introduction," *Literary Modernism and Photography*, ed. Paul Hansom (Westport, CT; London: Praeger, 2002) xvii.

37 Lilian R. Furst identifies the blurred boundary between fact and fiction as an "integral strand of realism" in Sebald's writings but that his use of photographs actually subverts this tradition. Lilian R. Furst, "Realism, Photography, and Degrees of Uncertainty," *W. G. Sebald. History – Memory – Trauma*, eds. Scott Denham and Mark McCulloh (Berlin: de Gruyter, 2006) 219–229, here 221–222.

Romane!"[38] [The 'real world'?: is, in truth, only a caricature of our great novels!]. According to this position that holds reality as a reflection of fiction, art would have ontological precedence over the real, extratextual world.[39] For Schmidt, the writer is a "Wortweltenbauer"[40] [one who builds worlds out of words], whose creations are not bound by the limits of fiction, that is, an intratextual reality. Fictional writing creates reality, an extratextual reality that Schmidt values more highly: "Wir finden allmählich in Büchern mehr, als in der Natur oder in Menschen. Und zumal das an=studieren von umfangreichen Wortwelten kann die gleiche Bereicherung hinsichtlich Scharfsinnsübung, Einsichten & Erregungen, kurz echte innere Erfahrungen ergeben"[41] [We gradually find more in books than in nature or in humans. And above all, the studying of comprehensive word-worlds can result in an enrichment of our ingenuity, insights & inspirations, in short real inner experiences]. Literature is thus the ultimate reality, or, to quote Schmidt's character Leonard Jhering in *Julia, oder die Gemälde*: "[I]ch habe im Zimmer weit größere Freiheit, als draußen, und die Welt der Kunst & Fantasie ist die Wahre, der rest is a nightmare!"[42] [I have much greater freedom in my room than outside, and the world of art & imagination is the true one, the rest is a nightmare!]. Here we have an expression of the absolute reversal of Plato's world of ideas: only the artist creates the real, and only his works have an ontological primacy. In this respect, literature that references literature, in an intertextual way for example, would not be a fiction but rather *reality*. A further dimension of this perspective is the tension between influence and originality, or as Jonathan Lethem has it in his essay "The Ecstasy of Influence. A Plagiarism": "Literature has always been a crucible in which familiar themes are continually recast."[43] As indicated in the subtitle, this text is indeed a

---

38 Bernd Rauschenbach, "Was 'Worte' sind, wißt Ihr –?" "*Arno Schmidt? – Allerdings!*" *Eine Ausstellung der Arno Schmidt Stiftung Bargfeld. Im Schiller-Nationalmuseum, Marbach am Neckar. 30. März–27. August 2006*, ed. Deutsches Literaturarchiv Marbach, (Deutsche Schillergesellschaft, 2006) 33–50, here 33. Rauschenbach quotes Schmidt from his *Die Schule der Atheisten*, *Bargfelder Ausgabe* IV, 2 (Zurich: Haffmans, 1994) 181, henceforth quoted as BA.

39 Cf. Lenz Prütting, "Arno Schmidt," *Kritisches Lexikon der Gegenwartsliteratur* 35. Nlg. (Stand 1.4.1990) 1–22, here 19.

40 Rauschenbach quotes Schmidt (BA II, 2, 104), "Was 'Worte' sind," 33.

41 Ibid., Rauschenbach quotes Schmidt's *Sitara* [1962] (BA III, 2, 267).

42 Arno Schmidt, *Julia, oder die Gemälde. Scenen aus dem Novecento*, BA IV, 4 (Zurich: Haffmans, 1992) 14. Christoph Jürgensen sees Schmidt's characters as deciding against the validity of the outside world and for an apotheosis of imagination ["gegen die Gültigkeit der Außenwelt und für eine Apotheose der Phantasie"]. Chistoph Jürgensen, "*Der Rahmen arbeitet.*" *Paratextuelle Strategien der Lektürelenkung im Werk Arno Schmidts* (Göttingen: Vandenhoeck & Ruprecht, 2007) 250.

43 Jonathan Lethem, "The Ecstasy of Influence. A Plagiarism," *Harper's Magazine* (2007) 59–71, here 59.

plagiarism, that is, a text about influence stitched together from other texts on the subject. Lethem provides a key to the essay, naming the sources from which he draws and which he adapted for his text.[44] While provocative and playful, the use of the term "plagiarism" to describe both conscious and unconscious influence and intertextuality ultimately falls short as a way of getting at the complex operation of writing and the complex result of the literary text. David Shields' recent manifesto *Reality Hunger* presents and demonstrates an argument similar to Lethem's, although Shields is more reticent/consequent, depending upon one's perspective, in revealing his sources.[45]

Sebald integrates historical facts and aspects of literary history in his stories, and these stories take place in 'real' geographic settings.[46] Yet, his texts are founded on the awareness of a separation or border between the 'realism' of the text and the reality that exists outside of the text. Due to Sebald's references and descriptions of factual, historical events, like the Napoleonic Wars, the silk trade, and the Holocaust, in combination with fictional descriptions of 'invented' characters, the term "faction" seems an appropriate characterization of his works.[47] Susan Sontag wrote of Sebald's texts, in her now-famous review that is attributed with putting Sebald on the literary map in the Anglophone world:

> Fiction they are, not least because there is good reason to believe that much is invented or altered, just as, surely, some of what he relates really did happen – names, places, dates and all. Fiction and factuality are, of course, not opposed. One of the founding claims for the novel in English is that it is a true history. What makes a work of fiction is not that the story is untrue – it may well be true, in part or in whole – but its use, or extension, of a variety of devices (including false or forged documents) which produce what literary theorists call 'the effect of the real.' Sebald's fictions – and their accompanying visual illustration – carry the effect of the real to a plangent extreme.[48]

---

44 The statement I quoted above, for instance, is taken from Michael Maar's *The Two Lolitas*.

45 David Shields, *Reality Hunger* (New York: Knopf, 2010). Shields writes in the appendix to his manifesto, "A major focus of *Reality Hunger* is appropriation and plagiarism and what these terms mean. I can hardly treat the topic deeply without engaging in it. [...] However, Random House lawyers determined that it was necessary for me to provide a complete list of citations; the list follows (except, of course, for any sources I couldn't find or forgot along the way)" (209).

46 With aspects of literary history, I am referring to how he writes about other authors, such as Stendhal (Henri Beyle), Franz Kafka, Joseph Conrad, and Vladimir Nabokov, among others. These authors are explicitly described and named as well as alluded to indirectly.

47 Peter Craven, "W. G. Sebald: Anatomy of Faction," *HEAT* 13 (1999) 212–224, here 220.

48 Susan Sontag, "A Mind in Mourning," *Times Literary Supplement* (February 25, 2000) 3–4, here 3.

Sontag's mention of the "effect of the real" of course refers back to Roland Barthes' concept of "l'effet de réel," which he develops in a concise yet greatly influential essay on Gustave Flaubert's short story "Un cœur simple."[49] The question of what is fact and what is fiction in Sebald's texts inevitably arises for readers, and this productive tension will be demonstrated below. However, one must be careful not to become obsessed by this question. In response to degree of fictionality in *Die Ausgewanderten*, Sebald states,

> Alles Wichtige entspricht der Wahrheit. Die großen Ereignisse – etwa der Lehrer, der seinen Kopf auf die Eisenbahnschienen legt – die könnte man für arrangiert halten, aus Gründen des dramatischen Effekts. Tatsächlich aber sind sie alle wahr. Die Erfindung kommt meist auf der Ebene kleiner Details ins Spiel, um *l'effet du réel* zu erzielen.[50]
>
> [Everything important corresponds to the truth. The main events – the teacher, who lays his head down on the train tracks – one could take this as contrived for dramatic effect. But actually they are all true. Invention comes mostly on the level of small details, to create an effect of the real.]

Yet a detail that is not so small, the journal of Ambros Adelwarth – which serves as the central documentary source for the story of this third emigrant – is mostly written, that is, made up by Sebald himself.[51] The "Ereignis" [event] to which Sebald refers, the teacher's suicide, is not the only 'true' aspect; the teacher himself is also rooted in an extratextual individual,[52] like the emigrant Max Aurach, which will be elucidated below.

The photographs and documents inserted in the narrative are an essential part of Sebald's fiction and raise further questions about authenticity and the degree of factuality in Sebald's texts. These insertions not only point to the extratextual reality but also the process behind the genesis of the text. As J.J. Long states, "The drawings and notebooks reproduced thematize the problems of writing and representation, and our inability to fix a multifaceted reality on paper."[53] When we read Sebald's texts we must be aware of "the ontological hide-and-seek that Sebald plays with his readers, which both invites and thwarts

---

49 Roland Barthes, "L'effet de réel," *Communications* 11 (1968) 84–89.

50 Carole Angier, "Wer ist W.G. Sebald? Ein Besuch beim Autor der *Ausgewanderten*," *W.G. Sebald*, ed. Franz Loquai (Eggingen: Ed. Isele, 1997) 48. Whether Sebald's change from "de" to "du" is intentional or not, it is nevertheless worth noting. The "de" implies that reality itself is the effect, whereas "du" would imply that reality causes the effect.

51 Cf. ibid., 49.

52 The second "emigrant" Paul Bereyter, the narrator's beloved school teacher, is loosely based on Sebald's teacher Armin Mueller. Cf. *Saturn's Moons: W.G. Sebald – A Handbook* (Oxford: Legenda, 2011) 38.

53 Long, "History, Narrative, and Photography," 134.

attempts to separate fact from fiction."[54] Sebald achieves this by ascribing new realities to the photographs and documents he uses. As will be explored in more detail below, context determines to a great degree how we read a photograph. What we know outside of a photograph – both dependent on and independent of the photograph itself – causes us to make claims; yet in the particular case of the photographs inserted into these fictional texts we must remind ourselves to separate the photograph from the reality it depicts. The faces in the photographs beckon us to connect them to the names and identities described in the text, but we must also question whether such direct correspondences exist. If there is a direct link between the individuals in the images and those whom Sebald's narrators describe, then these "stories" become biographies. If there is no correspondence between text and image in an extratextual sense, then what is the status of the text? To say the figures are "made up" would seem to trivialize Sebald's prose to the level of "mere" fiction, and the themes, particularly the memory of the Holocaust would keep us from describing his works as anything but trivial.

Representing the Holocaust and Photographs of Auschwitz

We recognize how fraught our understanding of reality is when considering the problem of the Holocaust's representability. The reality of the Holocaust is incontestable; but the related epistemological, ethical, and aesthetic questions demand that we consider how an access to this reality can be achieved. Ulrich E. Simon, for example, questions the reality of the Holocaust insofar as the evil of the atrocity defies rational understanding and insofar as the survivors themselves resist pursuing or providing rational explanations. He writes, "What is evil? Is it a real thing? To what extent is Auschwitz real? Is it not its unreality which is its evil? It is not for nothing that so many prisoners despaired of understanding it and admonished themselves not even to seek a rational explanation."[55] If the Holocaust defies representation, as some have argued, then how can it be proven philosophically? Jean-François Lyotard's *Le différend* investigates and interrogates this question and the philosophical means that we have to prove the existence of the Holocaust.[56] Furthermore, the problem of the Holocaust's representability raises a broad range of ethical and aesthetic questions, such as the legitimacy and appro-

---

54 Ibid., 117–118.
55 Ulrich E. Simon, *A Theology of Auschwitz* (London: Victor Gollancz, 1967) 19.
56 Jean-Fraçois Lyotard, *Le différend* (Paris: Minuit, 1983).

priateness of certain forms of representation and the identity and intention of the creator of such representations. The comparison of the memorial sites at Auschwitz and Majdanek, in particular the displays of shoes, can help illustrate this point. At Auschwitz, hundreds of thousands of shoes are carefully arranged in mounds behind a wall of glass and illuminated by electric light so as to emphasize the mass, all of which contributes to the museum-like quality of this display. At the Majdanek memorial site, masses of shoes are also displayed, but, rather than being encased behind protective glass, they are spread out in low-standing, rusted metal cages, only discernible as shoes from the thin rays of natural sunlight that shine through the cracks in the barrack walls and the open door. As artifacts, these shoes serve the same evidentiary function, pointing to the victims who were murdered in the camps. As aestheticized objects, the shoes are invested with varying degrees of pathos. By contrasting these two different presentations, we gain a critical distance to the past and perhaps also an understanding of the challenges to representing the murder of millions in the Holocaust.

Transforming the experience of the camps into knowledge of the Holocaust has been seen as both a privilege and a responsibility of the survivors, as expressed by Elie Wiesel in particular.[57] Certainly, an understanding – in the affective or physical sense – of the starvation, exhaustion, extreme temperatures, sickness, disease, and violence experienced daily by the prisoners within the concentration and extermination camps is impossible for anyone without first-hand experience. Nevertheless, we can all engage with the question of how this historical human atrocity is to be communicated in a way that provides some sort of insight. Furthermore, critically examining existing representations, be they memoirs or testimonies, novels, short stories, or films, ensures that the memory of the Holocaust will not be forgotten. In a recent study of "lies and truth in Holocaust fiction," Ruth Franklin presents a case for a continued, ethical engagement with the past and the Holocaust in particular.[58] She divides her book into two parts, the first on "witnesses" – with chapters on Tadeusz Borowski, Primo Levi, Elie Wiesel, Piotr Rawicz, Jerzy Kosinski, and Imre Kertész – and the second on "those who came after" – with chapters on Thomas Keneally/Steven Spielberg, Wolfgang Koeppen, W.G. Sebald, Bernhard Schlink, and the so-called "Second Generation." This division makes clear the precedence of presence, that, indepen-

---

57 Cf. Jakob Lothe, Susan Rubin Suleiman, and James Phelan, "Introduction: 'After' Testimony: Holocaust Representation and Narrative Theory," *After Testimony. The Ethics and Aesthetics of Holocaust Narrative for the Future*, eds. Jakob Lothe, Susan Rubin Suleiman, and James Phelan (Columbus: The Ohio State University Press, 2012) 1–19, here 4, 16–17.
58 Ruth Franklin, *A Thousand Darknesses. Lies and Truth in Holocaust Fiction* (Oxford: Oxford University Press, 2011).

dent of form or genre – testimony versus novel, for example – the works written by the "witnesses" possess an ontological primacy. In considering the texts of the second group, identity also plays a role, but the question of the author's intention gains greater weight and ethical significance, that is, it often becomes the determining factor in the evaluation of the works' ethical achievements or trespasses. This study reveals a key component in the analysis of Holocaust literature: how an author's identity and intention becomes inextricable from their subject. Overall, Franklin's analyses of these works makes clear that the precedence of presence does not necessarily guarantee literary quality and aesthetic value (or even of truthfulness, showing for example how the survivor and witness Jerzy Kosinski has in a sense created a falsified memoir with his work *The Painted Bird*). While not discounting the truth-value of survivor testimony, Franklin does acknowledge the volatility of memory, making clear that memoirs and testimony are not exempt from criticism and interpretation. Despite my reservations at how Franklin assesses the "second" and "third" generations,[59] I highlight Franklin's book, because its broader claim about the power of literary discourse corresponds to how I understand Sebald's works and their ethical engagement with the past. Franklin states, "We need literature about the Holocaust not only because testimony is inevitably incomplete, but because of what literature uniquely offers: an imaginative access to past events, together with new and different ways of understanding them that are unavailable to strictly factual forms of writing."[60] Moreover, Franklin makes clear that the dilemmas inherent in Holocaust writing, in particular finding an adequate and appropriate way to transform experience into language (and then literature), is a "question to which everyone who writes – or reads – about the Holocaust must find his or her own answer."[61]

In the case of memorial sites – either former camps or new museums and monuments – one could discuss a reciprocal relationship between the site and the viewer that is similar to the relationship between author/reader and text described above. A memorial or museum may have a particular mission, vision,

---

59 Irene Kacandes rightly objects to Franklin's problematic accusation of "identity theft" by members of the "second" generation in her essay "Identity Theft: True Memory, False Memory, and the Holocaust," *The New Republic* (May 31, 2004) 31–37. Cf. Irene Kacandes, "'When facts are scarce': Authenticating Strategies in Writing by Children of Survivors," *After Testimony. The Ethics and Aesthetics of Holocaust Narrative for the Future*, eds. Jakob Lothe, Susan Rubin Suleiman, and James Phelan (Columbus: The Ohio State University Press, 2012) 179–197, here 180. Franklin's essay appears in a revised form as "Identity Theft: The Second Generation" in her book *A Thousand Darknesses*, 215–234.
60 Ibid., 13.
61 Ibid., 47.

agenda, or narrative,[62] yet there is still room for the visitor to develop an individual interpretation and critical response based on his or her own reaction. The actual possibility for an 'original' or 'sincere' emotional response is contestable, however, and one could even argue that the word "Holocaust" has transcended the meaning of the actual atrocity and only evokes certain standardized reactions.[63] Independent of how much one may actually know of the Holocaust, a common response is often evoked by words and phrases, like "Auschwitz," "Kristallnacht," or "Arbeit macht frei,"[64] for example. "Auschwitz" often serves as a metonymy for the genocide of the Jews, such as in Adorno's infamous dictum that to write poetry after Auschwitz would be barbaric. Frank R. Ankersmit suggests an almost blinding force of this metonymy: "What can even remotely resemble the horrors we associate with those terrible names: Sobibor, Treblinka, Majdanek, Chelmno, Stutthof, and, above all, Auschwitz-Birkenau? These are names having such a deep and profound resonance in our minds that we even have difficulty in believing that places actually existing on our globe correspond to them [...]."[65] It is precisely at this moment that literature can intervene, serving as sites of remembrance, resistance, and reinvention. Sebald's works do just this: the narrative structure, challenging syntax, self-reflexivity, and meta-narrative comments on representation resist easy consumption and demand more from the reader than traditional historical novels, for example. His works can also function as a site where postmemory works itself out or even is created, if we follow Marianne Hirsch's definition of postmemory as the instance or space in which one experiences a strong emotional connection to a past from which one may be distanced generationally.[66]

The representation of the Holocaust not only poses aesthetic and ethical challenges as touched on above, but it is also a semiotic problem: the unique-

---

62 The United States Holocaust Memorial Museum, for example, encourages identification between the museum visitor and the victims of the Holocaust. See Edward Linenthal, *Preserving memory. The Struggle to Create America's Holocaust Museum* (New York: Penguin Books, 1997).

63 A. O. Scott identifies a new genre of "Holocaust" films with standardized plots and messages. See A. O. Scott, "Never Forget. You're Reminded" *The New York Times* (November 23, 2008) AR1.

64 The iconic value of "Arbeit macht frei" was reiterated and reinforced when the steel words were stolen from the main entrance gate to Auschwitz on December 19, 2009.

65 Frank R. Ankersmit, *Historical Representation* (Stanford: Stanford University Press, 2001) 184. Without naming, i.e., needing to name Auschwitz or any other specific camps and internment sites, Dan Jacobson asserts that some of these names are "infamous; they have become metonyms for an entire epoch." Dan Jacobson, *Heshel's Kingdom* (London, New York: Penguin, 1999) 158.

66 Marianne Hirsch, *Family Frames. Photography, Narrative, and Postmemory* (Cambridge, MA. and London, England: Harvard University Press, 1997). See chapter five for an extension of these ideas.

ness and dimensions of the atrocity challenge what can be represented in linguistic signs. Paul Celan's "Todesfuge" (1945) still provides one of the best examples of this, pointing to the linguistic challenge of representing the Holocaust by way of fractured syntax, the adaptation of linguistic signs to a musical form, and the contradiction of everyday language. In her consideration of "Todesfuge" among other examples of Holocaust poetry, Susan Gubar highlights the constructedness of these poems, stating "these are fabricated words, not factual testimonies or even mimetic representations of testimonies."[67] The poems point to their own constructedness "by drawing our attention to the disparity between testimonial utterance and poetic forms that are always mediated, always consciously constructed."[68] Testimonials must also be viewed as constructions to a degree rather than direct transcriptions of the past, which will be developed in chapter five.[69]

Discussions of representing and in particular imagining the Holocaust have been reconsidered in recent years after an exhibition in France and a subsequent publication by the art historian Georges Didi-Huberman. Didi-Huberman's *Images in Spite of All. Four Photographs from Auschwitz*[70] retraces the steps of how four photographs were taken clandestinely from inside the gas chamber at crematorium V in Auschwitz in August 1944: how the prisoners of the Sonderkommando obtained the camera, the conditions under which the photographs were taken, and how the camera made it back to the Polish Resistance by September 1944. Didi-Huberman's book is not only a history of these four images but it is also one of the most striking interventions to "address the unimaginable and refute it,"[71] which is precisely what he sees these photographs as doing. He writes, "A single look at this *remnant of images*, or erratic corpus of *images in spite of all*, is enough to sense that Auschwitz can no longer be spoken of in those absolute terms – generally well intentioned, apparently

---

67 Susan Gubar, "The Long and Short of Holocaust Verse," *New Literary History* 35.3 (2004) 443–468, here 449.

68 Ibid. This also leads Gubar to assert "verse as the most unrealistic of languages" (450).

69 Eva Hoffman illustrates and also traces this process of "translation" from event to the story of the event. See Eva Hoffman, *After Such Knowledge. Memory, History, and the Legacy of the Holocaust* (New York: Public Affairs, 2004). It is precisely the process of translation that occurs in such formulations of past experiences and memories that Sebald thematizes in his hybrid form of literary historiography.

70 Georges Didi-Huberman, *Images in Spite of All. Four Photographs from Auschwitz* (Chicago & London: University of Chicago Press, 2008). [*Images malgré tout* (Paris: Les Éditions de Minuit, 2003).]

71 Ibid., 19.

philosophical, but actually lazy – 'unsayable' and 'unimaginable.'"[72] These photographs were not only an act of resistance, taken in the attempt to reveal the truth of the camps to the outside world, but also an act of resistance against the Nazi's attempt to obliterate human life and memory.[73] Didi-Huberman makes the following assertions,

> If the horror of the camps defies imagination, then *each image* snatched from such an experience becomes all the more necessary. If the terror of the camps functions as an enterprise of generalized obliteration, then *each apparition* – however fragmentary, however difficult to look at and to interpret – in which a single cog of this enterprise is visually suggested to us becomes all the more necessary.[74]

Ultimately Didi-Huberman reverses the problem of Auschwitz as unimaginable by asserting the *necessity* of our imagining it, despite our restriction to the image and the limitations of this medium. While this point is well taken and proves very productive, it is perhaps overstated, for one cannot properly read these four photographs without the contextual knowledge, as I will outline below.

Two of the photographs show members of the Sonderkommando loading bodies into an open-air incineration pit, the third photograph shows a group of women being chased in the direction of the gas chamber, and the fourth shows what appears to be the tops of trees and sky. All four photographs are reproduced in Didi-Huberman's text. But before Didi-Huberman focuses on reconstructing the history of these photographs and before he provides a meticulous reading of the photographs, he also recounts the "hell" that was the work of the Sonderkommando, basing these accounts on testimonies and memories, in particular those collected in Filip Müller's *Eyewitness Auschwitz*.[75] Although not explicitly stated by Didi-Huberman, this knowledge of the Sonderkommando provided by written and oral testimony is absolutely essential to one's reading of the photographs and one's attempts at understanding both the images and their context. Even with knowledge of the atrocities and horrors of the Holocaust, Müller's account is still shocking. It is against this backdrop that Didi-Huberman establishes the gravity of these images: the dimension of what they depict, the risk that was involved in capturing them, and the necessity in the first place of giving form "to this

---

72 Ibid., 25. He adopts "lazy" from Annette Wieviorka, *Déportation et genocide. Entre la mémoire et l'oubli* (Paris: Plon, 1995 [1992]) 165.
73 This attempt even entailed the "obliteration of the tools of the obliteration," thus, the SS destroyed crematorium V in January 1945. Didi-Huberman, *Images in Spite of All*, 21.
74 Ibid., 26, emphasis Didi-Huberman.
75 Filip Müller, trans. Susanne Flatauer, *Eyewitness Auschwitz. Three Years in the Gas Chambers* (New York: Stein and Day, 1979).

unimaginable reality."[76] This cooperation between written and visual testimony is related to the "paradoxical condition" of the photographs,[77] that is, the co-presence or co-existence of truth and obscurity. The truth lies in the direct documentation taken from close range, the obscurity in the blurred image and the fact that we cannot actually see the incineration pit. Hence, without the knowledge gained from the written account, we would be incapable of reading the images in the detailed way that Didi-Huberman masterfully demonstrates.

The problematic nature of photographs lies in our relationship to them: "we often ask too much or too little of the image," according to Didi-Huberman.[78] We demand 'the whole truth' from photographs, and with such an expectation the image will always be 'inadequate' or 'inexact.' We also demand too little from photographs when we do not reflect upon them critically but rather consider them a 'simulacrum' or 'document,' and thereby ignore their specificity and substance.[79] Didi-Huberman highlights both the specificity and the substance of the four photographs, in particular the details that were cropped away in efforts to make the images "presentable" and to emphasize "'what there is to see,'" efforts that ultimately "make them *icons* of horror."[80] Thus, Didi-Huberman's approach to reading the images works against such erasure of the photographs' context and complexity. Challenging standard ways of reading photographs, Didi-Huberman states, "The *mass of black* that surrounds the sight of the cadavers and the pits, this mass where *nothing is visible* gives in reality a *visual mark* that is just as valuable as all the rest of the exposed surface."[81] That is, the black mark is actually the space of the gas chamber, the place from where the photograph was clandestinely taken, "the space of possibility, the condition of existence of the photographs themselves."[82] By erasing this physical frame, the context of the danger and the risk in taking the photograph is also erased. This artificial focus on the 'object,' or the content (*histoire*) of the photograph – the Sonderkommando and the corpses – erases the

---

76 Didi-Huberman, *Images in Spite of All*, 9.

77 Ibid., 32. Didi-Huberman subsumes this "paradoxical condition" under the "*dual mode* of all images that so often troubles historians and turns them away from such 'material.'"

78 Ibid., 32–33.

79 Cf. ibid., 33. Here, Didi-Huberman seems to understand a document not as piece of evidence but rather as something already invested with meaning.

80 Ibid., 34, emphasis D-H.

81 Ibid., 35, emphasis D-H. Robert Harvey describes the "axiom driving Didi-Huberman's reading of the four photographs" as follows: "even in the worst of circumstances for making an image and the promise of future perception – extreme dimness, ageusia, blindness, dumbfoundedness, and so on – there is *always* something to be seen." See Robert Harvey, *Witnessness: Beckett, Dante, Levi and the Foundations of Responsibility* (London; New York: Continuum, 2010) 103, emphasis RH.

82 Ibid., 36.

form (*discours*) of the photograph – the context, that is, the conditions under which it was taken. For this reason, Didi-Huberman insists on the value of the last photograph that 'only' depicts the trees above, as it reveals further information about the photographer and the situation, "the impossibility of aiming the camera, the risk undergone, the urgency, the fact that he may have been running, the awkwardness, the sun in his eyes, and perhaps breathlessness too."[83] Reference to Jean-Paul Sartre's notion of the image being "an act and not a thing" reinforces the fact that a photograph is not "a mere container of information."[84] This brings us then to both Sebald's use of images in his texts and his narrative principle of emphasizing both the *histoire* and *discours* while also pointing to the complex relationship of one to the other. This will also reveal the ethical dimension behind Sebald's insistence of writing prose rather than novels.

Direct representations of the Holocaust, that is to say, describing life in the concentration camps, the details of a prisoner's physical pain and hunger, or a victim's emotional experiences of humiliation and fear, for example, are nowhere to be found in Sebald's writings. There is a simple answer to this, namely that the subjects in his texts escaped such experiences in the camps; many were able to survive the Nazi era by having gone into exile. In developing characters who are exiles, Sebald does not evade this intensely debated question of the Holocaust's representability, but rather points precisely to this problem. As Stephan Seitz aptly remarks, Henry Selwyn and Max Aurach, two of Sebald's "emigrants," may not be eyewitnesses to a particular event, but their life (hi)stories nevertheless testify to disaster; and through this form of indirect testimony, the past is revealed to be a history of catastrophe.[85] In the conclusion to his study, Seitz points to the imbrications of ethical and aesthetic concerns in the representation of such a history of catastrophe and how "literarische Geschichtsschreibung zum Schauplatz des Eingedenkens wird" [literary historiography becomes the stage for remembrance].[86] Sebald is fully aware of, if not obsessed with, this question of representability, the Holocaust's in particular, history in general, and an even more broadly conceptualized idea of the past.[87] His literary form reflects this: it is

83 Ibid., 37.

84 Ibid., 113. Didi-Huberman cites Jean-Paul Sartre, *L'imagination* (Paris: PUF, 1981 [1936]) 152.

85 Cf. Stephan Seitz, *Geschichte als bricolage. W. G. Sebald und die Poetik des Bastelns* (Göttingen: V & R Unipress, 2011) 177.

86 Ibid., 170.

87 For related discussions, especially regarding the moral dimension of the fact versus fiction debate, see Berel Lang, "The Post-Holocaust vs. the Postmodern. Evil Inside and Outside History," *Holocaust Representation. Art within the Limits of History and Ethics* (Baltimore: Johns Hopkins University Press, 2000) 140–157.

simultaneously representational and reflexive, thematizing its act of representation. Sebald writes adamantly against any sort of sentimentalization of the Holocaust, which he sees as presumptuous; and such an exploitation of the atrocity is especially prevalent in novels, according to Sebald. Particular to his works, and what will form a bridge between this chapter and the following ones, is how Sebald couples this question of representability with memory's suspect and unreliable nature. Furthermore, Sebald's unique use of photographs and photographic reproductions of other documents, such as pages from a dairy or a passport, raise questions of authenticity in his narrative form and in literary representations altogether. Sebald translates his critique of official forms of historiography into practice in the way in which he endows 'factional' stories with the weight usually attributed to historical accounts.[88] His works exemplify this process, by blending 'facts' and 'fiction' while trying to cope with the problematic source of memory, be it individual or collective, and the repression, recollection, and representation of this memory.

Untangling Fact from Fiction: Sebald's Extratextual Materials

Due to the present enthusiasm for the "pictorial" or "iconic" turn not only in German studies but in cultural studies in general, a fair share of scholars have reveled in Sebald's works for their illustration of the complex and complementary cooperation of images and texts.[89] Although not always in the same form

---

[88] In the previous chapters, I traced the development of Sebald's engagement with the question of representability: how he raises such questions in *Die Ausgewanderten*, later formulates these questions in *Die Ringe des Saturn*, and illustrates possible answers in *Austerlitz*. While *Die Ringe des Saturn* does not deal with the Holocaust per se, it is very much concerned with history and the representation of history.

[89] Various articles have treated Sebald's use of photography in particular, and almost every analysis of his works mentions this particular blend of verbal and pictorial discourses as the defining characteristic of his prose. See for example, Heiner Boehncke, "Clair obscur. W.G. Sebalds Bilder," *W.G. Sebald. Text + Kritik* (2003) 43–62; Richard Crownshaw, "Reconsidering Postmemory: Photography, the Archive, and Post-Holocaust Memory in W.G. Sebald's *Austerlitz*," *Mosaic* 37.4 (2004) 215–236; Carolin Duttlinger, "Traumatic Photographs: Remembrance and the Technical Media in W.G. Sebald's *Austerlitz*," *W.G. Sebald. A Critical Companion*, eds. J.J. Long and Anne Whitehead (Seattle, WA: University of Washington Press, 2004) 155–171; Noam M. Elcott, "Tattered Snapshots and Castaway Tongues: An Essay at Layout and Translation in W.G. Sebald," *Germanic Review* 79.3 (2004) 203–223; Andrea Gnam, "Fotografie und Film in W.G. Sebalds Erzählung *Ambros Adelwarth* und seinem Roman *Austerlitz*," *Verschiebebahnhöfe der Erinnerung: Zum Werk W.G. Sebalds*, eds. Sigurd Martin and Ingo Wintermeyer (Würzburg: Königshausen & Neumann, 2007) 27–47; Stefanie Harris, "The Return of the Dead: Memory and Photography in W.G. Sebald's

or format, the combination of word and image is present throughout Sebald's œuvre: from his first published poem *Nach der Natur. Ein Elementargedicht*; through all four major fictional prose works *Schwindel.Gefühle, Die Ringe des Saturn, Die Ausgewanderten*, and *Austerlitz*; as well as in his collections of essays *Logis in einem Landhaus* and *Luftkrieg und Literatur*. Sebald is of course not the first German-language author to use photographs in his literary texts; one must think of Rolf Dieter Brinkmann, Alexander Kluge,[90] Monika Maron,[91] Wolfgang Hildesheimer, and Bertolt Brecht[92], among others. Yet, these authors use images in ways that differ from Sebald. Moreover the ends to which these authors use images and the specific questions they raise via the effect of the text-image relationship differ from Sebald's approach.

One can draw various points of connection among Sebald, Barthes, and Kluge with regard to their ideas on the relationship between photography and history. Tim Dant and Graeme Gilloch refer to Barthes' history of *Michelet* (1954) which attempts to "evoke[] the emotional tone of Michelet and his reactions to the world."[93] Barthes accomplishes this by bringing together various elements, "images, bibliographic details, the historical facts, the testimonies and the quota-

---

Die Ausgewanderten," German Quarterly 74.4 (2001) 379–91; Silke Horstkotte, "Fantastic Gaps: Photography Inserted into Narrative in W. G. Sebald's *Austerlitz," Science, Technology and the German Cultural Imagination*, eds. Christian Emden and David Midgley (Berlin: Peter Lang, 2005) 269–286; Silke Horstkotte, "Pictorial and Verbal Discourse in W. G. Sebald's *The Emigrants," Iowa Journal of Cultural Studies* 2 (2002) 33–50; Samuel Pane, "Trauma Obscura: Photographic Media in W. G. Sebald's *Austerlitz," Mosaic* 38.1 (2005) 37–54; Alexandra Tischel, "Aus der Dunkelkammer der Geschichte. Zum Zusammenhang von Photographie und Erinnerung in W. G. Sebalds *Auster-litz," W. G. Sebald. Politische Archäologie und melancholische Bastelei*, eds. Michael Niehaus and Claudia Öhlschläger [*Philologische Studien und Quellen* 196] (Berlin: Schmidt, 2006) 31–45; Markus Weber, "Die fantastische befragt die pedantische Genauigkeit. Zu den Abbildungen in W. G. Se-balds Werken," *W. G. Sebald. Text + Kritik* (2003) 63–74; et al.

90 See for example Thomas von Steinaecker, *Literarische Foto-Texte. Zur Funktion der Fotografien in den Texten Rolf Dieter Brinkmanns, Alexander Kluges und W. G. Sebalds* (Bielefeld: transcript Verlag, 2007). Steinaecker makes a significant contribution to the contextualization of Sebald's works in relation to other twentieth-century authors experimenting with the integration of other media within the literary form.

91 See Silke Horstkotte's two similar articles, "Fotografie, Gedächtnis, Postmemory. Bildzitate in der deutschen Erinnerungsliteratur," *Lesen ist wie Sehen. Intermediale Zitate in Bild und Text*, eds. Silke Horstkotte and Karin Leonhard. (Cologne; Weimar; Vienna: Böhlau, 2006) 177–195, and "Photo-Text Topographies: Photography and the Representation of Space in W. G. Sebald and Monika Maron," *Poetics Today* 29.1 (2008) 49–78.

92 A differentiated discussion of Sebald's specific integration of images in comparison to other authors, such as Wolfgang Hildesheimer or Bertolt Brecht in his work journal, is still wanting in current research.

93 Dant and Gilloch, "Pictures of the Past," 9.

tions."[94] Such a combination of sources and materials is also characteristic of Sebald's works.[95] Although Sebald greatly admires the work of Alexander Kluge, placing a special emphasis on him in *Luftkrieg und Literatur*, Sebald's fiction must be held distinct this form of documentary literature, for which Kluge was a pioneering force. Nevertheless, the connection between Sebald and Kluge has been made with particular attention to the way both incorporate images into their texts. While the variation in the text-image relationship in Sebald's works resists reduction to a single principle, the following comment by Kluge regarding his use of images could easily apply to Sebald as well. Kluge states, "Das Prinzip, nach dem ich Bilder verwende, ist nicht das der Abbildungen, dass ich etwas unterstütze, sondern dass ich einen Kontrast bilde. Dass ich Raum gewinne. Dass ich Zeit gewinne"[96] [The principle according to which I use images is not that of direct representations, that I support something through the images, rather that I create a contrast. That I gain space. That I gain time]. Moreover, Kluge and Sebald both use images in such a way as to demand the reader's engagement, as Mark M. Anderson has argued,

> Challenging the reader to believe in and simultaneously doubt the authenticity of their images, Kluge and Sebald ultimately question the notion that the world and its representations can be divided into entirely separate categories of truth and fiction, into factual 'documents' and aesthetic constructs. There is no 'pure' historical document.[97]

Sebald's individual approach to history distinguishes itself by adding invented subjects and by creating documents – such as journal or diary entries – which are then cited by characters or even documented in the form of a photograph inserted in the text.

Looking across Sebald's œuvre, one finds similar types of photographs: family snapshots, personal portraits, architectural structures, as well as landscapes and cityscapes, where individuals are strikingly absent. One also finds photographs of coincidental *objets trouvés*, ranging from the mundane, such as a restaurant receipt, to the significant, such as a page from a passport. The images used by Sebald are predominantly, though not exclusively, photographs. Interspersed in his narratives are reproductions of classic paintings, schematic

---

94 Ibid.

95 Sebald's technique could be considered a "montage" in the sense that Didi-Huberman develops in *Images in Spite of All* (2008).

96 Thomas von Steinaecker, "'Im Grunde bin ich Ikonoklast.' Ein Gespräch mit Alexander Kluge über die Abbildungen in seinen Texten," *Kultur & Gespenster* 1 (2006) 28–34, here 32.

97 Mark M. Anderson, "Documents, Photography, Postmemory: Alexander Kluge, W.G. Sebald, and the German Family," *Photography in Fiction*, eds. Silke Horstkotte and Nancy Pedri, special issue of *Poetics Today* 29.1 (2008) 129–151, here 150.

maps, pages from journals, diaries, and other books. Sebald had a great collection of found images, including old photographs and postcards,[98] and his statement that he "had always collected 'stray photographs' because 'there's a lot of memory in them'"[99] is cited so often that it is taken at face value rather than considered critically. I would like to briefly problematize this statement, for Sebald's use of images demonstrates that the "memory" in the photographs is not necessarily that of the referent but that of the viewer. Sebald's works demonstrate the imaginary potential in images, and his prose is composed in such a way to incorporate such *objets trouvés*, inviting the reader to join him in his process of deciphering their meaning. His narratives guide our reading of the images, yet nothing is ever clear; a degree of ambiguity always persists. This ambiguity that resists interpretation is compounded by a more literal ambiguity elicited by the qualitative fuzziness of the photographs themselves. Robin Kinross points to the particular tension between the provisional quality of the images and carefully-wrought precision of the verbal narratives in Sebald's works, "It is like a collection of working images that a writer might gather as an aid; except that Sebald has decided to include them in his book, to intersperse them in his (by contrast) highly considered prose."[100] Sebald acknowledged having manipulated some of the images he used in order to increase the inextricability of text and image:

> I write up to these pictures and I write out of them also, so they are really part of the text and not illustrations and hence, if they were produced in a much better form, which would be technically very easy to do nowadays, then they would ruin the text. They must not stand out; they must be of the same leaden grain as the rest.[101]

Sebald's position on photography thus provides clear answers to Ludwig Wittgenstein's provocative questions, "Ist eine unscharfe Photographie überhaupt ein Bild eines Menschen? Ja, kann man ein unscharfes Bild immer mit Vorteil durch ein scharfes ersetzen? Ist das unscharfe nicht oft gerade das, was wir

---

98 Renate Just, "Stille Katastrophen," *W.G. Sebald*, ed. Franz Loquai (Eggingen: Ed. Isele, 1997) 25–30, here 30.

99 Sebald with Maya Jaggi, "Recovered Memories. The Guardian Profile" *Guardian* (September 22, 2001). http://www.guardian.co.uk/education/2001/dec/21/artsandhumanities.higheredu cation [accessed: June 22, 2013]

100 Robin Kinross, "Judging a Book by its Material Embodiment: A German-English Example," *Unjustified Texts* (London: Hyphen Press, 2002) 186–199, here 195.

101 Sebald in Christopher Bigsby, "W.G. Sebald," *Writers in Conversation with Christopher Bigsby. Volume Two* (Norwich: Arthur Miller Centre for American Studies, 2001) 139–165, here 155.

brauchen?"[102] ["Is an indistinct photograph a picture of a person at all? Is it even always an advantage to replace an indistinct picture by a sharp one? Isn't the indistinct one often exactly what we need?"[103]]. Considering what Sebald means and implies with the term "Bild" can further elucidate the connection between images and memory in his works. Take for example his use of the word "Vernichtungsbilder" in the first lecture given in Zurich.[104] One can glean from the context that Sebald is implying a mental *image* or a memory that is not necessarily gained by direct physical and mental experience. Such "Schmerzens-spuren" (*A* 24) ["marks of pain" (*AE* 14)], images that we produce in our heads based on what we have been told and independent of what we visually perceive and intellectually process, are essential to both Sebald's concept of history and his poetics. According to this idea, images can develop in a narrative and in the mental processing or imagining of the story.

The visual images in Sebald's works are inextricable from the written narrative, yet they simultaneously point to the fundamental differences between the two media. According to Sebald, "A picture, being visual information, can be contemplated, it does not have to be decoded in time. You can just sit and see it, and the ideal reader for me would be a reader who doesn't read the text but sees it, who lifts it out of the perennial wasting which occurs in time."[105] Several of Sebald's professional readers have met his ideal, demonstrating how to also become viewers.[106]

---

102 Ludwig Wittgenstein, *Philosophische Untersuchungen*. Kritisch-genetische Edition, ed. Joachim Schulte. In Zusammenarbeit mit Heikki Nyman, Eike von Savigny und Georg Henrik von Wright (Frankfurt am Main: Suhrkamp, 2001) 790.

103 Ludwig Wittgenstein, *Philosophical Investigations*, trans. G.E.M. Anscombe (Oxford: Basil Blackwell, 1968) 34.

104 W.G. Sebald, unpublished manuscript, A: Sebald, Sammlung: Luftkrieg und Literatur, Mappe 2, Deutsches Literaturarchiv Marbach.

105 Sebald in Bigsby, 156.

106 Cf. Jakob Lothe, "Narrative, Memory, and Visual Image: W.G. Sebald's *Luftkrieg und Literatur* and *Austerlitz*," *After Testimony. The Ethics and Aesthetics of Holocaust Narrative for the Future*, eds. Jakob Lothe, Susan Rubin Suleiman, and James Phelan (Columbus: The Ohio State University Press, 2012) 221–246, here 222. To counter or at least problematize the strict dichotomy between 'reading' visual as opposed to written texts, one can look to Sabine Gross, *Lese-Zeichen. Kognition, Medium und Materialität im Leseprozeß* (Darmstadt: Wissenschaftliche Buchgesellschaft, 1994). Silke Horstkotte cites how Gross' study breaks down the common assumption that reading is a linear process, stating, "Auf der Basis neurobiologischer Forschungsergebnisse argumentiert Gross überzeugend, die Flexibilität der Augenbewegungen bei der Textlektüre sei dem Betrachten eines Bildes durchaus vergleichbar" [on the basis of neuro-biological research, Gross convincingly argues that the flexibility of eye movements while reading are comparable to those made when observing an image]. Silke Horstkotte, *Nachbilder. Fotografie und Gedächtnis in der deutschen Gegenwartsliteratur* (Cologne; Weimar; Vienna: Böhlau, 2009) 52.

Dora Osborne, for example, sees in his images both points of narrative resistance and visual representations of "something that in fact covers over what cannot be shown."[107] In addition to serving as 'evidence' – gesturing towards an authenticating function but also often undermining this possibility for authentication   images can provide "a very condensed account or a shorthand cipher."[108] Sebald describes this economy or efficiency of the photograph, "Sometimes these pictures contain very dense information which it would take you a long time to get across in writing."[109] In Sebald's funding applications for an unrealized film project on the life of Ludwig Wittgenstein, titled "L E B E N Ws" [L I F E of W], Sebald emphasized the visual aspect of this project and the differences between the two media, "Dem Text beigegeben ist dokumentarisches/fotografisches Material, über das Fragen wie Wahrheitssuche/Erfindung, Anwesenheit/Abwesenheit, Ruhe des Bildes/Dynamik des Textes ins Spiel gebracht werden"[110] [The text is supplemented with documentary/photographic material that brings certain questions into play: the search for truth/invention, presence/absence, the calmness of the image/the dynamic motion of the text]. Richard Weihe traces how the photocopied images integrated into Sebald's film script as film stills later become the "*story stills*" of *Austerlitz*, stating, "In der ursprünglichen 'Skizze einer möglichen Szenenreihe' haben die beigefügten Fotos den Status von Standbildern (*film stills*) eines nicht-realisierten Films; in *Austerlitz* sind die Fotos gleichsam Standbilder einer realisierten Lebensgeschichte – *story stills*"[111] [In the original 'sketch of a possible series of scenes', the included photos had the status of film stills from an unrealized film; in *Austerlitz* these photos are quasi film stills from a realized life story – story stills]. This idea of a "story still" can be very helpful in conceptualizing the way in which

---

107 Dora Osborne, *Traces of Trauma in W. G. Sebald and Christoph Ransmayr* (Oxford: Legenda, 2013) 130. Osborne's evocative readings of the visual material in both *Die Ausgewanderten* and *Austerlitz* operate on multiple levels: she examines the referent, draws out possible modes of signification, and considers image placement within the text and among the chain of associations suggested by Sebald. See for example her reading of the photograph of wind anemones in *Austerlitz* (137–138).
108 Sebald in Bigsby, 154.
109 Ibid. Here Sebald gives the example of the photograph of the Jewish family in Bavarian dress included in *Die Ausgewanderten*, stating further, "That early twentieth-century photograph of a Jewish family assimilated in this particular, almost farcical way to the Bavarian folk tradition says more than you could tell in a whole essay about the processes of assimilation and acculturation."
110 Richard Weihe cites from Sebald's funding applications that are included in his estate now held at the Deutsches Literaturarchiv Marbach. Richard Weihe, "Wittgensteins Augen. W. G. Sebalds Film-Szenario 'Leben Ws,'" *fair. Zeitung für Kunst und Ästhetik* Nr. 07/IV (2009) 11–12, here 11.
111 Weihe, "Wittgensteins Augen," 11.

Sebald uses images in his texts: they interrupt one's reading and force one to *look* at the text, or, "die Lektüre wird zur Bildbetrachtung" [the act of reading becomes one of looking at images], as Weihe later states.[112] This is only applicable at one stage of the reading, however. It is important to consider the placement of the images in the text, something that goes beyond the scope of Weihe's concise article. The images not only interrupt the first reading, but they also require retrospective reconsideration, since they often appear before the reader has the full context.[113]

Sebald's unique use of photographs and photographic reproductions of other documents, such as pages from a diary or a passport, raise questions of authenticity in his narrative form and in literary representations altogether. Not only must we consider how language works but also how images aid or confound our quest for understanding. Just as the photographs as such raise the question of authenticity, or of their relationship to reality, they also require human intervention and interpretation, in order to reveal their significance and to invest them with meaning, as Siegfried Kracauer has suggested.[114] There is an indisputable power of the image, as far as testimony of the Holocaust is concerned. Many of the photographs of concentration camps or of victims have achieved symbolic, even iconic status. Similar to the metonymic power of "Auschwitz" mentioned above, this symbolic or iconic status of Holocaust photographs can, however, inhibit narration precisely where it is needed. Arguing in a similar vein, Klaus Berghahn has described how an aerial photograph of Auschwitz, taken by the American reconnaissance in 1944, hardly says anything about the extermination camps, other than the fact that they existed. He writes,

> Auch eine Luftaufnahme von Auschwitz, von der amerikanischen Aufklärung im Jahre 1944 aufgenommen, sagt kaum etwas über das Vernichtungslager aus, außer daß es existierte. Die tragische Ironie dieser Aufnahme kommt erst durch die Beschriftung zum Vorschein; denn Auschwitz war für die indifferente Luftaufklärung militärisch uninteressant – nicht die Krematorien von Auschwitz, sondern das nahegelegene Buna-Werk wurde bombardiert. Das Beispiel zeigt, daß auch photographische Dokumente bloß stumme Zeugen sind, die erst durch Kommentierung zu sprechen beginnen.[115]

---

112 Ibid.

113 One could cite various instances, for example when the narrator cites Austerlitz indicating "dieses Treppenhaus" (*A* 219) ["this stairway" (*AE* 149)] after the reader has already seen the photograph (*A* 211) [(*AE* 144)].

114 Siegfried Kracauer, "Die Photographie [1927]," *Aufsätze 1927–1931*, vol. 5.2, *Schriften*, ed. Inka Mülder-Bach (Frankfurt am Main: Suhrkamp, 1990) 83–98, here 83.

115 Klaus Berghahn, "Ringelblums Milchkanne. Über Möglichkeiten und Grenzen der dokumentarischen Repräsentation des Holocaust," *Kulturelle Repräsentationen des Holocaust in Deutschland und den Vereinigten Staaten*, eds. Klaus L. Berghahn, Jürgen Fohrmann, and Helmut J. Schneider (New York: Peter Lang, 2002) 147–166, here 162.

[The tragic irony of these images only becomes apparent through their captions; for Auschwitz was uninteresting from a military perspective – not the crematoria of Auschwitz, but rather the nearby Buna-Works were bombed. This example shows how even photographic documents are mute witnesses that only begin to speak through the process of commentary.]

In evoking the implicit barrier between a photograph and the reality depicted, the echo of Bertolt Brecht can clearly be heard: "Eine Fotografie der Kruppwerke oder der AEG ergibt beinahe nichts über diese Institute. Die eigentliche Realität ist in die Funktionale gerutscht"[116] ["A photograph of the Krupp Works or of A.E.G. yields nearly nothing about these institutions. Actual reality has slipped into the functional"[117]]. He prefaces this statement as follows: "Die Lage wird dadurch so kompliziert, daß weniger denn je eine einfache 'Wiedergabe der Realität' etwas über die Realität aussagt" ["The situation thereby becomes so complicated that a simple 'representation of reality' says something about reality less than ever before"].[118] Brecht formulates a triple axiom for understanding the ontological status of the photograph: it can never be considered equal to the thing photographed; such a representation gives no information about the material reality pictured; and such a representation is always just that: a representation and not 'reality' itself. Brecht's statement could be understood as a modern-day translation of René Magritte's famous painting, *La trahison des images* (1928–29), transferring the same idea from the medium of painting to that of photography. The text – "Ceci n'est pas une pipe" – inscribed in the painting, above which the painted pipe hovers, tells the viewer how to read the painting: this is not a pipe, but really a painting of a pipe. This text-image constellation of Magritte's painting demands a critical and differentiated reflection from the viewer on the nature of images. Barthes makes the direct connection to Magritte, when he discusses the difference between painting and photography: "By nature, the Photograph [...] has something tautological about it: a pipe, here, is always and intractably a pipe."[119] Sontag also reminds us of the difference between painting and photography, which could be applied here to our understanding of Magritte's pipe. She writes, "No one takes an easel painting to be in any sense co-substantial with its subject; it only represents or refers."[120]

---

116 Brecht, "Dreigroschenprozeß," 469.

117 Bertolt Brecht, "The Three Penny Trial: A Sociological Experiment," trans., Lance W. Garmer, *German Essays on Film*, eds. Richard McCormick and Alison Guenther-Pal (New York: Continuum, 2004) 111–132, here 117.

118 Ibid.

119 Barthes, *Camera lucida*, 5.

120 Susan Sontag, *On Photography* (New York: Farrar, Straus and Giroux, 1973, 1974, 1977) 155.

Moving beyond Magritte's painting of a pipe, Brecht makes clear that representing reality is not the same as making a statement about this reality; a photograph does not necessarily give any information about the social reality pictured. While Brecht demands an interpretation of the socio-economic context, Sebald emphasizes both the historical and material context that often remains hidden in photographs. Predating Brecht and not referring to an actual photograph but reproductions of photographs in illustrated magazines, Kracauer writes, "Die Abbilder sind also grundsätzlich Zeichen, die an das Original erinnern mögen, das zu erkennen wäre"[121] [The images are fundamentally signs that remind one of the original of the recognizable thing]. This semiotics of representation, the understanding of photographs as signs that refer to reality while keeping in mind their ontological status as signs and not as that reality to which they refer, is a key principle of Sebald's use of images.

Photography's deceptively authentic mirroring of reality has from its inception evoked suspicion and reproach, as exemplified in Baudelaire's infamous scathing critique outlined above. The limits and possibilities of this medium were tested and explored soon after or almost parallel to its invention, illustrating that the interest in photography was not limited to a vision of an artistic medium that could more directly and immediately record an imprint of reality. Anderson writes of the "inherent epistemological instability of the medium" of photography and notes that photographs' "manipulability has been part of their identity since their invention in the nineteenth century and a source of controversy ever since."[122] One could thus argue that artistic representation as an imitation of nature ("Nachahmung der Natur") was thus not the ultimate goal of human imagination and artistic creation.[123] The inherent power of photographs, as can be seen across Sebald's works, is the memory they contain; but this potential for witnessing also reinforces the necessity of a human voice to both make this testimony audible and to interpret it. Photographs indeed provide evidence or documentation of the past in general and atrocity in particular. Yet they complicate and at times paralyze the endeavor of writing; revealing that this process of representation – the translation of a historical event or personal experience into arbitrary signs – is by no means a natural or fluid one.

---

121 Kracauer, "Die Photographie [1927]," 93.
122 Anderson, "Documents, Photography, Postmemory," 148.
123 Cf. Blumenberg, "'Nachahmung der Natur.'" An exhibition at the Metropolitan Museum of Art in New York City in 2005 showcased "surreal" and "phantasmagoric" photographs from the late nineteenth century, illustrating how experimentation with and manipulation of this new medium began almost immediately after its invention. See Michael Kimmelman, "Ghosts in the Lens, Tricks in the Darkroom," *The New York Times* (September 30, 2005).

Sebald's texts vividly demonstrate that the life of the photograph and the lives in the photographs are not as stable or static as Barthes asserts in *Camera Lucida*, "When we define the Photograph as a motionless image, this does not mean only that the figures it represents do not move; it means that they do not *emerge*, do not *leave*: they are anesthetized and fastened down, like butterflies."[124] The photographs in Sebald's texts become dynamic or "emerge," to speak with Barthes, insofar as Sebald removes them from their original context to (re)animate the figures captured within them via narration. In this way, we see that photographs have more of an authenticating than a documenting function when they are invested with new meaning within a new context. A paradigmatic example of this is the photograph of a butterfly cabinet integrated into *Austerlitz* that serves to reinforce the description of Andromeda Lodge as a natural history museum replete with cabinet upon cabinet of curiosities from nature. While there are neither indications nor captions that point to the 'original' source of this image in *Austerlitz*, we can identify the image as a photograph of Vladimir Nabokov's butterfly collection in St. Petersburg, if we look to Sebald's other works. This image was already reproduced in the Swiss illustrated literary magazine *Du* to accompany an essay by Sebald on Nabokov.[125] Unlike the photographs in Sebald's fictional works, this image, as it is included in his essay, is captioned: "Im zoologischen Museum in St. Petersburg. Foto Arwed Messmer" [In the Zoological Museum in St. Petersburg. Photograph by Arwed Messmer]. Although moths and butterflies play an important role in *Austerlitz*, the writer Nabokov is neither named nor represented in this text as he is in Sebald's other works.[126] Situated in the new context of *Austerlitz*, and according to the intratextual reality of the text, we attribute a new meaning to the image, reading it as a depiction of Austerlitz's

---

124 Barthes, *Camera Lucida*, 57.

125 W. G. Sebald, "Traumtexturen," *Du. Die Zeitschrift der Kultur* 6 [*Vladimir Nabokov. Das Leben erfinden*] (1996) 22–25, here 23. This article is also reprinted in *Campo Santo* albeit without the photograph. Sebald, "Traumtexturen. Kleine Anmerkung zu Nabokov," (*CS* 184–192).

126 A photograph of Nabokov holding a butterfly net occupies nearly an entire page in *Die Ausgewanderten* (*DA* 27) [(*E* 16)] and is referenced directly on the preceding page. In describing Dr. Henry Selwyn's slides, the narrator remarks that Selwyn resembles Nabokov in one of the images. "Eine der Aufnahmen glich bis in Einzelheiten einem in den Bergen oberhalb von Gstaad gemachten Foto von Nabokov, das ich ein paar Tage zuvor aus einer Schweizer Zeitschrift ausgeschnitten hatte" (*DA* 26) ["One of the shots resembled, even in detail, a photograph of Nabokov in the mountains above Gstaad that I had clipped from a Swiss magazine a few days before"(*E* 16)]. In an uncanny coincidence with this scene in *Die Ausgewanderten* and almost as if it were an intertextual prolepsis, this photograph of Nabokov is also included in the chronic of his life and work. See Marina Rumjanceva, "Chronik von Leben und Werk," *Du* 6 (1996) 84–91, here 90.

school friend Gerald's Great Uncle Alphonso's butterfly collection at Andromeda Lodge. In this way, the image serves to illustrate the text, but it goes beyond this. The image gains a more complex dimension and a (self-)referential playfulness when coupled with the knowledge of its 'original' context.

When integrating images into his texts, Sebald does not follow one single consistent aesthetic strategy but rather demonstrates a more playful poetics of concordance and dissonance. The relationship between the text and its images is not a static one, but rather it shifts and changes as we read. At times the relationship between the two media is complementary or illustrative, at other times dissonant and even contradictory. Images can both reveal and conceal, authenticate and deceive. Sometimes the images anticipate the text, and at other times they must be retrospectively considered. Pointing to how the text actually illustrates the images, Liliane Louvel identifies an "anachrony" that is particular to the text-image relationship in Sebald's texts. She states,

> Morphologically, text and photograph appear simultaneously and thus belong to the primary type, in the mode of 'interreference.' But semantically and chronologically, their relation is of the secondary type in that they belong to two different times. The printed text precedes the image as a rule in the Sebaldian text, but the image refers to an earlier diegetic time. It chronologically *precedes* the text, although it appears *after* its own deictic textual designation or its short ekphrasis. So it is the text that 'illustrates' the photograph and not the other way around, as one might morphologically expect.[127]

Images may also be narrated but remain visually absent from the text. Two prominent examples of this construction occur at the end of both *Die Ausgewanderten* and *Austerlitz*, and in both cases the reader has the possibility of searching out the photographic referent of the ekphrastic narration. Perhaps the most oft-cited example is the last narrated image in *Die Ausgewanderten* that depicts three women weaving and knotting a carpet.[128] The last sentence of this text speculates on their names, "Roza, Luisa und Lea oder Nona, Decuma und Morta, die Töchter der Nacht, mit Spindel und Faden und Schere" (*DA* 355) ["Roza, Luisa and Lea, or Nona, Decuma and Morta, the daughters of night, with spindle, scissors and

---

127 Liliane Louvel, "Photography as Critical Idiom and Intermedial Criticism," *Photography in Fiction*, eds. Silke Horstkotte and Nancy Pedri, special issue of *Poetics Today* 29.1 (2008) 31–48, here pp. 38–39.

128 The image that Sebald narrates was one taken by Walter Genewein, the famous photographer of the Łodz ghetto. Carol Jacobs obtained permission from the Jewish Museum in Frankfurt to reproduce this image, which was part of an exhibit and included in the catalog *"Unser einziger Weg ist Arbeit." Das Getto Łódź 1940–1944* (Vienna: Jüdisches Museum Frankfurt am Main and Löcker Verlag, 1990). Cf. Carol Jacobs, "What does it Mean to Count? W.G. Sebald's *The Emigrants*," *MLN* 119.5 (2004) 905–929, here 923.

thread" (*E* 237)], alluding to the mythological fates and lending this image an allegorical status. In contrast to the detailed description of this image, the visual absence of the photograph points to the principle of Sebald's oblique representation of the past: Sebald denies the reader a direct and potentially voyeuristic gaze into the eyes of these women, who most likely did not survive the Holocaust. One could, however, also entertain an additional interpretation or rather a more practical explanation for the absence of this image: it would have been highly unlikely for Sebald to incorporate this image in his text without any citation or without obtaining the rights, and such an explicit citation, caption, or connection to the original source also goes against Sebald's desired and practiced poetics. Sebald's use of ekphrasis thus provides a further opportunity to consider the discursive difference between the visual and the textual and the relationship between an image, imagining, and imagination.

In relation to the text the images can be self-reflexive and even ironic. An elongated image of a painting of the Battle of Marengo is inserted into the narrative and framed above and below by the text, "auf welchem [dem riesigen Leichenfeld] er sich nunmehr befand, mit sich allein[129] wie ein Untergehender" (*SG* 22), this last clause doubling as a caption to the image. The verticality of this image is reproduced in the English translation, however the text does not frame the image nor does it form a caption around it. The English translation reads, "the vast field of the dead on which he was now standing, alone with himself, like one meeting his doom" (*V* 18).[130] In addition to situating the photographs within the body of the text so that a caption or emblematic structure is formed in relation to the image, the image can even stand in for the text. In an example from *Schwindel.Gefühle*, the word "eyes" is replaced by a visual representation of Stendhal's eyes (*SG* 15). The English translation of this passage does not reproduce this play between the textual and visual sign systems (*V* 11). Considering these variations on the text-image relationship, multiple levels of analysis must be made: that is to say *intratextually*: the relationship of the image to the 'story' (how the image does or does not correspond to the narrated text and how the image is placed within the text to form a caption or not); *extratextually*: the relationship of the images to an extratextual reality (how the status of an image, in particular a photograph, as 'document' points to a broader, more fundamental question of literature's relationship to 'truth' and 'reality'); and *intertextually*: the images and text in relation to other texts, be they literary or documentary.

---

129 The image is inserted at this point to interrupt the flow of the narrative text.
130 The formatting of this image differs further in the first German edition of the book, insofar as it is elongated further, spread over two pages.

An outline of the complex layering of intra-, inter-, and extratextual reality in Sebald's works will further elucidate this discussion of the relationship between reality and representations. Bringing reality and fiction together in a way that goes beyond a fictionalized biography, Sebald creates composite characters, such as Max Aurach in *Die Ausgewanderten* and the eponymous protagonist of *Austerlitz*. The fourth "Ausgewanderte" [emigrant] Max Aurach, is based on two people – Sebald's former landlord and the German painter Frank Auerbach – both of whom lived in exile in England.[131] Auerbach expressed his discontent with Sebald's literary 'adaptation' of his life and in particular with the name Aurach, which he saw as too closely linked to his own. For this reason, the character's name was changed to "Max Ferber" in the English translation, and to further prevent a direct association between the fictional figure and the real person, a reproduction of one of Auerbach's paintings as well as a photograph of his eye that are included in the German edition have been removed in the English edition (*DA* 240, 265). Thomas Honickel's documentary "W. G. Sebald. Der Ausgewanderte" includes an interview with Peter Jordan, Sebald's landlord in England, who also served as a basis for the Aurach character. In recounting his family's history to Honickel – his rescue on a "Kindertransport," his exile in England, and the deportation and execution of his parents – Jordan refers to photographs, one of which also appears in *Die Ausgewanderten* (*DA* 278; *E* 186). Creating an interesting intertextual overlap of extratextual individual history, Jordan tells his story again in Dörte Franke's documentary on "Stolpersteine" [stumbling blocks], the collective memorial conceptualized by the artist Gunter Demnig as a way to commemorate the victims of the Holocaust and to bring their names back into public consciousness.[132] Jordan's story provides a case study for Franke's film and is actually recounted in greater detail here than in Honickel's film. Demnig's project reminds passers-by of the victims as *individuals* rather than as anonymous masses, which can be connected both to Sebald's concept of history and to his way of commemorating individuals in a literary form.

---

131 Cf. Klaus Gasseleder, "Erkundungen zum Prätext der Luisa-Lanzberg-Geschichte aus W. G. Sebalds *Die Ausgewanderten*. Ein Bericht," *Sebald. Lektüren*, eds. Marcel Atze and Franz Loquai (Eggingen: Ed. Isele, 2005) 157–175, here especially 160–162. See also Carole Angier, "Wer ist W. G. Sebald? Ein Besuch beim Autor der *Ausgewanderten*," *W. G. Sebald*, ed. Franz Loquai (Eggingen: Ed. Isele, 1997) 50.

132 See *Stolperstein*, directed by Dörte Franke (Germany, 2008, 76 minutes). Each "Stolperstein" lists an individual's name, dates of birth and, where possible, death, as well as the place of deportation or death. The stones are laid in the sidewalk in front of the individual's last place of voluntary residence. Demnig has laid "Stolpersteine" in over 500 cities in Germany and several other countries across Europe. http://www.stolpersteine.com/ [accessed: June 22, 2013]

Sebald's use of real biographies in his literary texts has been scrutinized and criticized as an unethical appropriation of another's life story, and in the case of *Austerlitz* it is perhaps the most extreme.[133] The character of Austerlitz presents another example of a "composite," loosely based on two living individuals: a historian and colleague of Sebald's and Susi Bechhöfer, who along with her twin sister were brought to Britain on a "Kindertransport."[134] After having read *Austerlitz* in English translation, Bechhöfer became angered at what she saw as a direct copying of some of the most important details of her life story, and she contacted the publisher both through a lawyer and personally, in an attempt to have her own biography referenced as a source of the text. Sebald's publisher asked for her understanding of the author's right to "artistic license" ("dichterische Freiheit").[135] The overlap between Bechhöfer's biography and the fictional figure of Austerlitz is limited but in part significant: like Bechhöfer, Austerlitz is rescued from Nazi Germany via a "Kindertransport" and adopted by a religious, childless couple who make a point of hiding his past from him. Furthermore, mirroring the way in which Bechhöfer is first confronted with her hidden past, Austerlitz also learns from a teacher that he must write his 'real' name on the final school exams. The fact that Bechhöfer and her twin sister arrived in London on May 18, 1939, five years to the day before Sebald's birth, is just one of many coincidences that could form a web of connections between the past and the present and blur the boundaries between intra- and extratextual reality. Whereas Sebald makes note of such coincidences of dates or names both explicitly in *Luftkrieg und Literatur* (*LuL* 84) and *Logis in einem Landhaus* as well as implicitly in *Austerlitz* (*A* 421), it is interesting that he did not find a way to weave this into Austerlitz's biography. Then again, this is perhaps an indication that he did not want his own biography, nor Austerlitz's, to overlap too closely with Bechhöfer's. The major difference between the two biographies is that Austerlitz suffered no physical or sexual abuse, as Bechhöfer did. These similarities on the level of the *histoire* make the difference in *discours* all the more stark. The striking difference between

---

133 After the publication of *Austerlitz*, Rebekka Göpfert noticed the similarities between the fictional figure of Austerlitz and Susi Bechhöfer. Through the mediation of Göpfert, Bechhöfer contacted Sebald, and they corresponded briefly. Sebald acknowledged that Bechhöfer's biography was indeed one of his models for the character of Austerlitz, as he states in the *Spiegel* interview. Cf. Rebekka Göpfert, "Susi Bechhöfer fragt zurück. W. G. Sebald lieh sich für *Austerlitz* ihre Biographie," *Frankfurter Rundschau* Nr. 63 (Saturday, March 15, 2003) 10.

134 Cf. Sebald's comments in Martin Doerry and Volker Hage, "'Ich fürchte das Melodramatische.'" *Der Spiegel* 11 (March 12, 2001) 228.

135 Bechhöfer had planned on asking Sebald that he acknowledge explicitly her role in the creation of his literary figure, but after his sudden death this was no longer possible.

Bechhöfer's memoir and Sebald's fiction goes beyond a difference in genre and illustrates both the uniqueness of Sebald's form and the quality of his writing.[136] While Bechhöfer's story repeatedly mentions her "dark and hidden past,"[137] referring to the abuse she suffered, "das Dunkel" (*A* 39 among other instances) ["the darkness" (*AE* 24)] in *Austerlitz* does not have a clear signified, thereby preserving a polyvalence in its vagueness. As discussed above in chapter two, Sebald's lectures on poetics formulate his concern with literary representations of the Allied air raids as a concern with language. This concern holds true for literary representations of the Holocaust as well, and encompasses the following questions: How do we write about the past? How, if it is at all ethically possible, do we speak for the victims? How can we commemorate the victims? Sebald's literary works are an attempt at realizing this uncompromising ideal of creating a new language that does not rely on clichés.

A salient feature of Sebald's works is the great topographical detail provided in the descriptions of cities and landscapes and accounts of casual walks and significant journeys. As outlined in the introduction, there is a tendency and desire to map the routes in Sebald's texts, in part out of curiosity about the trajectories themselves and in part out of the desire to determine how accurate the descriptions are, that is, if and how directly fiction 'matches' extratextual reality. For example, one can trace the walk made by Austerlitz and the narrator from his home on Alderney Street to St. Clement's Hospital and the Tower Hamlets cemetery, a distance of just one mile but over thirty pages when measured in the time of narration (*Erzählzeit*). In addition to these impulses to map the text, one may also be drawn to look up names and places that are mentioned in the text. Although it feels like a bad scholarly practice, a Google search is sometimes revealing. For instance, the Czech ophthalmologist, Zdeněk Gregor, whom the narrator consults in London due to persistent eye pain and his near complete loss of sight in his right eye, appears to have an extratextual source, an actual Zdenek Gregor who was an ophthalmic surgeon at Moorfields Eye Hospital.[138]

To further illuminate the intratextual and extratextual connections in Sebald's works, one can also consider his sources, which will also provide insight

---

136 See Jeremy Josephs with Susi Bechhöfer, *Rosa's Child. The True Story of One Woman's Quest for a Lost Mother and a Vanished Past* (London; New York: I.B. Tauris Publishers, 1996).

137 Josephs with Bechhöfer, *Rosa's Child*, 39.

138 This information can be found online, via a Google search for "Zdenek Gregor": http://www.moorfields-private.co.uk/Consultants/zdenekjgregor He is now retired but formerly had his private practice within The London Clinic, located indeed on Harley Street, as the narrator states in *Austerlitz*. http://www.drfosterhealth.co.uk/hospital-guide/hospital/private/London-Clinic,-The-10123.aspx [Both sites accessed: June 22, 2013]

into how he is writing. A newspaper article from *The Independent* is an indisputable source for the passage in *Austerlitz* that presents the veterinary medicine museum in Maisons-Alfort, which contains some of the over three thousand specimens prepared by Honoré Fragonard.[139] Austerlitz recounts to the narrator how he often spent Sundays, during his first time in Paris in the late 1950s, wandering through the Paris suburbs and taking hundreds of photographs, which he refers to as his "Banlieu-Ansichten" (*A* 376) ["*banlieu*-photographs" (*AE* 265, italics Bell)]; curiously none of these photographs are reproduced in the text. One of the Parisian suburbs Austerlitz explores is Maisons-Alfort, where the veterinary museum of anatomical curiosities is located. As if to substantiate his visit to the museum, Austerlitz hands the entrance ticket stub to the narrator, which he still carries in his wallet:

> Das Billett, das er mir für zwanzig Francs verkaufte, habe ich immer in meiner Brieftasche behalten, sagte Austerlitz, und reichte es mir, nachdem er es hervorgeholt hatte, über das Bistrotischchen, an dem wir saßen, als hätte es damit eine besondere Bewandtnis (*A* 377).
> [I still have the twenty-franc ticket he sold me in my wallet, said Austerlitz, and taking it out he handed it to me over the table of the bistro where we were sitting as if there were something very special about it (*AE* 265).]

To reinforce this act of providing proof, the ticket stub is integrated into the text at the beginning of Austerlitz's account (*A* 377) [(*AE* 265)]. This ticket stub, along with the *Independent* article, is among the Sebald's materials now located as part of his literary estate housed at the Deutsches Literaturarchiv in Marbach, Germany. The ticket stub has been visibly altered: the date of entry, most likely the year [19]**99**, was changed with white-out to correspond to the date Austerlitz must have visited the museum [19]**59**. In examining such changes, we as readers are able to reconstruct how Sebald constructs his text and creates his fiction: he transforms extratextual material into intratextual evidence. Attention to the

---

139 The article on which Sebald bases this passage – one could even argue that Sebald practically plagiarizes it – is Taras Grescoe, "Skeleton in the cupboard," *Independent on Sunday* (August 25, 1996) 46, 48. This article from the *Independent* can be found in the materials Sebald collected alongside his handwritten manuscript for *Austerlitz*. A: Sebald, DLA Marbach. Considering Sebald's heavy reliance on this article, it is curious that he only marks four passages in the physical paper article, and these marked passages in the article do not actually appear in his text. One could conjecture that Sebald was most likely intrigued by the *Independent* article enough to visit the museum himself and later write this into his text. Austerlitz describes Fragonard as an agnostic who did not believe in the "Unsterblichkeit der Seele" ["immortality of the soul"] and how he must have spent "Tag und Nacht über den Tod gebeugt" ["all the hours of his days and nights intent upon death"] in efforts to preserve these bodies, "am ewigen Leben zu sichern" ["secure [...] eternal life"] (*A* 380) [(*AE* 268)].

chronology of the text is necessary to differentiate or tease apart these layers. Comparing the descriptions in *Austerlitz* with those in the *Independent* reveals that Sebald more or less copied from the newspaper article and in a sense already had a source for this passage. One could therefore argue that Sebald did not need to travel to France to acquire knowledge of this physical place for his text. In light of this possibility, the images in the passage – the ticket stub and the photograph of one of Fragonard's specimens – would then seem to serve an authenticating function, not only for what is recounted on the intratextual level, but also of the author's extratextual experience and presence at the museum. Considering all of these pieces together, we are confronted with a textual palimpsest that brings together reading, imagination, curiosity, and travel. This palimpsest of meaning and experience and the inextricable layers of intra- and extratextual reality contribute to what one could term the aura of Sebald's texts, which evokes fascination among his readers. It is interesting to note that Sebald was not only conscious of this practice but also aiming at it. David Lambert and Robert McGill collected "writing tips" that Sebald provided them in one of his creative writing courses at the University of East Anglia. One of the maxims they list states explicitly, "It's very good that you write through another text, a foil, so that you write out of it and make your work a palimpsest. You don't have to declare it or tell where it's from."[140]

These above examples – "composite" characters, the *Independent* article on the veterinary museum as an intertext, and the use of an extratextual object as intratextual evidence – reveal how Sebald's works go beyond a fictionalization of reality. One final example shall reinforce this and further illustrate the particular way in which Sebald employs a strategy of intertextuality. Several points of connection – in structure, theme, and detail – exist between Sebald's *Austerlitz* and Saul Friedländer's memoir *When Memory Comes*.[141] The structure of *Austerlitz* owes much to Friedländer's memoir insofar as it is a similarly nonlinear narrative composed of memories and "meta-memories," that is, comments on memory in

---

140 David Lambert and Robert McGill, "Writing Tips: The Collected 'Maxims' [of W. G. Sebald]," *Five Dials* 5 (2009) 8–9, here 9. Another example of such an intra-, inter-, and extratextual palimpsest is found in the last scene of *Austerlitz*, which is discussed in further detail in chapter four.

141 Saul Friedländer, trans. Helen R. Lane, *When Memory Comes* (New York: Farrar, Straus, and Giroux, 1979). [Translated from the French, *Quand vient le souvenir* (Paris: Éditions du Seuil, 1978).] These points of connection can be made without consulting Sebald's copy of the German translation of Friedländer's memoir. However, Sebald's underlining, markings, and notes in the margins – which include explicit mention of "Aust" [= Austerlitz] – reveal that this text indeed served as one of the "pre-texts" to *Austerlitz*. Saul Friedländer, *Wenn die Erinnerung kommt* (Munich: C. H. Beck, 1998 [1978]). W. G. Sebald Nachlaß: Teilbibliothek, DLA Marbach.

general and childhood memory in particular. Friedländer's memoir not only recounts the process of coming back to his personal memories, but it also describes his coming to writing and the difficulties of both written and verbal expression. Friedländer describes the chasm that exists in his sense of self, a chasm created by the experience of exile, "The first ten years of my life, the memories of my childhood, were to disappear, for there was no possible synthesis between the person I had been and the one I was to become."[142] Friedländer and Sebald and by extension Sebald's narrators share similar concerns about the inadequacy of memory, their difficulties in bringing feelings into words, and the importance of giving a voice to documents and photographs. Of the letters and photographs he possesses, Friedländer writes, "For the others, these traces will soon no longer mean anything. I must write, then. Writing retraces the contours of the past with a possibly less ephemeral stroke than the others, it does at least preserve a presence [...]."[143] One of Friedländer's particular concerns is the effect his memoir will actually have; he wonders whether his struggle to write about his past will have a wider resonance, not an insignificant concern for a historian. He asks,

> And what are the values that I myself can transmit? Can experience as personal, as contra-dictory as mine rouse an echo here, in even the most indirect way? I am not sure. But must I then limit myself to the neutral indifference of the technician, or alternatively, pretend that I have roots, play at normality, and return to clear thoughts, those which help one to live and, perhaps, to die? Isn't the way out for me to attach myself to the necessary order, the inescapable simplification forced upon one by the passage of time and one's vision of history, to adopt the gaze of the historian?[144]

Taking into account the affinities between Friedländer's memoir and Sebald's *Austerlitz*, it then appears as though Friedländer's memoir indeed had a direct impact on Sebald. Not only *Austerlitz* but Sebald's new form of literary historio-graphy could be seen as a positive answer to Friedländer's rhetorical question of whether personal experience can rouse an echo.

Several significant details overlap between Sebald's fictional figure of Aus-terlitz and the historian Friedländer: both were born in Prague in 1934 and with the rise of the Nazis, their families were separated; while the child was brought

---

142 Friedländer, *When Memory Comes*, 80. Sebald marks the beginning of this sentence ["Meine ersten zehn Lebensjahre, die Erinnerungen an meine Kindheit mußten verschwinden, denn zwischen dem, was ich gewesen war, und dem, was ich werden sollte, war keine Synthese möglich"] in his copy of Friedländer, *Wenn die Erinnerung kommt*, 84, W.G. Sebald Nachlaß: Teilbibliothek, DLA Marbach.
143 Friedländer, *When Memory Comes*, 134–135.
144 Ibid., 144.

to safety in exile, the parents were deported. Furthermore, there are traces of Friedländer's childhood nanny, Vlasta, in the figure of Věra, but Sebald reverses the way the two reunite. While Austerlitz finds Věra after having sought out his childhood residence, it was Vlasta who, after having read a newspaper article about his book, contacts Friedländer upon his return to Prague. Věra and Austerlitz walk through Prague, much in the way that Friedländer recounts his rediscovery of Prague with Vlasta: "We walked about Prague – for hours. I asked her to retrace with me the route we had taken on our walks together in my childhood."[145] Vlasta appears as Friedländer remembers her, and when he revisits his childhood house, "[e]verything was in the right place, so to speak: every door, every wall, every corner."[146] Friedländer retraces the path his parents took, trying to escape the Nazis, via France into Switzerland, a search that is echoed in *Austerlitz* both in the way that Austerlitz retraces the journey he took on the "Kindertransport," and his search to find out what became of his parents. Friedländer's research into his past is ultimately a confrontation with history that forces him into a "strange paralysis,"[147] which is also echoed in the several instances of paralysis experienced by Austerlitz during his search for his identity. Moreover, this paralysis could be seen as a result in the problem of forming verbal and written accounts of the past, "It took me a long, long time to find the way back to my own past. I could not banish the memory of events themselves, but if I tried to speak of them or pick up a pen to describe them, I immediately found myself in the grip of a strange paralysis."[148] Sebald, like Friedländer recounts events that are distinct, geographically and chronologically, from the Holocaust, yet which can be read as metaphors for the problem of representation or expression. In short, the theme of the Holocaust, the problem of its representation is ever present, even in its apparent absence.

Friedländer's memoir could also been seen as a source of historical information for Sebald's *Austerlitz*, for the descriptions of the Nazis rolling into Prague and the details of the so-called "grand rafle" in Paris, for example. Friedländer writes,

---

145 Ibid., 32.
146 Ibid., 32–33. Sebald marks this entire passage in his copy of Friedländer, *Wenn die Erinnerung kommt*, 36–37, W.G. Sebald Nachlaß: Teilbibliothek, DLA Marbach.
147 Ibid., 102.
148 Ibid. The German translation formulates this paralysis as, "wie gelähmt," and Sebald marks this sentence in the margin. Friedländer, *Wenn die Erinnerung kommt*, 108, W.G. Sebald Nachlaß: Teilbibliothek, DLA Marbach.

On July 16, 1942, the great roundup began in Paris; nearly thirteen thousand foreign Jews, among them four thousand children, were herded into the Vélodrome d'Hiver. Adolf Eichmann let it be known that beginning on July 20 there would be sufficient space for children in the convoys destined to leave for the East before the end of August.[149]

Austerlitz's account of the "grand rafle" is marked by his imagination of the event, and he does not name his sources for the images he develops. He attempts to imagine his father, and he imagines things that he cannot even be certain happened, such as his father writing letters that never arrive in Prague. He wonders if his father was already interned at Drancy after the first "Pariser Razzia" in August 1941, which he describes as the action of the French gendarmerie rounding up 13,000 Jewish citizens (*A* 366) [(*AE* 257)], or perhaps later in July of the following year.[150] Austerlitz describes to the narrator how he thought he saw – "Ich glaubte manchmal [...] zu sehen" (*A* 366) ["I sometimes thought I saw" (*AE* 257)] – police wagons driving through city, taking people to the Vélodrome d'Hiver. In one and the same sentence, his imagination transitions into perception, and he "saw" images and his father – "*sah* Bilder von ihrer Reise durch das Großdeutsche Reich, *sah* den Vater [...] aufrecht und ruhig, unter all diesen angstvollen Leuten" (*A* 366, my emphasis) ["I pictured their journey through the Greater German Reich, I *saw* my father [...] calm and upright among all those frightened people" (*AE* 257, my emphasis)]. At the same time, Austerlitz also entertains the possibility, and he even has the impression – "es war mir [...] als sei" (*A* 367) ["I felt [...] as if" (*AE* 257)] – that his father is still in Paris, awaiting the right moment to make his identity be known.[151] Sebald does not mark or highlight the account of the "grand rafle" in his copy of Friedländer's memoir, but the connections between his text and Friedländer's in this instance are unmistakable. This makes an important point about the limits of the "Spurensuche," or search for traces among the volumes in Sebald's library. One must be attentive to possible intertextual connections but also aware that not every connection is to be substantiated with one of Sebald's pencil marks.

The different layers of reality in Sebald's texts and the larger problem of literature's relationship to reality is further embodied in the similarities between Sebald the author and his nameless first-person narrators. Moreover, the way the ambiguities of this relationship are often smoothed out from a critical or analytical perspective is also revealing. On the one hand, there is a certain

---

149 Friedländer, *When Memory Comes*, 70–71.
150 The reader must complete the information and identify the year as 1942.
151 Such moments and ideas are connected to particular places, and this possibility of his father still being present in Paris also connects to the theory of time developed in *Austerlitz* and described in more detail in chapter four.

tendency in Sebald scholarship to collapse the person and author W.G. Sebald with his anonymous, albeit autobiographically inflected, narrators.[152] On the other hand, there are critics who explicitly avoid equating Sebald with his narrators. Sigrid Löffler, for example, most clearly asserts that Sebald's narrator is a construction and not to be confused with Sebald the author: "Das Erzähler-Ich [ist] mit W.G. Sebald *nicht* identisch. Es ist eine Kunstfigur, ein narratives Ich."[153] Going beyond this assertion, Michael Niehaus and Markus Weber provide detailed narratological analyses that argue the importance of this distinction.[154] Related to the conflation of Sebald with his narrators is the problem of his extratextual identity, which is "in danger of becoming less a writer than a phenomenon,"[155] as Martin Swales has asserted with regard to the "industry" of secondary literature on Sebald. Jens Mühling's differentiation between Sebald the person and Sebald the author points exactly to this problem.[156] Some scholars attempt to solve the problem by simply putting quotation marks around Sebald's name, which only provides the illusion of a distinction between Sebald and his narrators, ultimately allowing for a degree of semantic slippage. For example, Eric Santner subsumes all of Sebald's narrators under one "central narrator figure, 'W.G. Sebald.'"[157] John Zilcosky also puts the narrator "Sebald" in quotation marks. Referring to *Schwindel.Gefühle*, Zilcosky writes, "reading Sebald is like 'Sebald' [meaning the narrator] reading."[158] Maya Jaggi writes, "As in all his fiction, Sebald's narrator is one 'WG Sebald,' who lives in Norfolk, comes from the German village of 'W,' and has a companion, 'Clara.'"[159] These

---

152 Some critics are more forthright in their equation of Sebald with his narrators than others. See for example Elinor Shaffer, "W.G. Sebald's Photographic Narrative," *The Anatomist of Melancholy. Essays in Memory of W.G. Sebald*, ed. Rüdiger Görner (Munich: iudicium, 2003) 56.

153 Sigrid Löffler, "'Melancholie ist eine Form des Widerstands.' Über das Saturnische bei W.G. Sebald und seine Aufhebung in der Schrift," *Text + Kritik* 158/4 (2003) 103–111, here 107.

154 See essays by Michael Niehaus, "W.G. Sebalds sentimentalische Dichtung," *W.G. Sebald. Politische Archäologie und melancholische Bastelei*, eds. Michael Niehaus and Claudia Öhlschläger [*Philologische Studien und Quellen* 196] (Berlin: Schmidt, 2006) 173–187. See also Markus Weber, "Bilder erzählen den Erzähler: Zur Bedeutung der Abbildungen für die Herausbildung von Erzählerrollen in den Werken W.G. Sebalds," *Mémoire. Transferts. Images./Erinnerung. Übertragungen. Bilder*, ed. Ruth Vogel-Klein, *Recherches germaniques* Hors Série 2 (2005) 25–45.

155 Martin Swales, Review of *W.G. Sebald. History – Memory – Trauma* (Berlin and New York: de Gruyter, 2006), *Arbitrium* 26.1 (2008) 128–130, here 128.

156 Jens Mühling, "The Permanent Exile of W.G. Sebald," *Pretext* 7 (2003) 15–26, here 15.

157 Eric L. Santner, *On Creaturely Life* (Chicago and London: University of Chicago Press, 2006) 49.

158 John Zilcosky, "Sebald's Uncanny Travels," *W.G. Sebald: A Critical Companion*, eds. J.J. Long and Anne Whitehead (Seattle: University of Washington Press, 2004) 102–120, here 118.

159 Jaggi, "Recovered Memories."

are problematic generalizations, however, since such details are neither explicit nor consistent across all of Sebald's works. The relationship between Sebald and his narrators is certainly not as clear as presented here, rather this ambiguous relationship can serve as a paradigmatic example for the way in which one must pay particular attention to distinguish between intratextual and extratextual realities in Sebald's works. A clear advisory not to confuse or confound the author Sebald with his narrators is expressed by Sebald himself:

> 'There is always the desire to find out how one is made up, to get to those layers that are out of sight; but I would find it hard to write anything confessional. I prefer to look at the trajectories of the other lives that cross one's own trajectory – do it by proxy rather than expose oneself in public.'[160]

Furthermore, Sebald also stresses the "symbolic significance" of "W." and "S." when explaining why he abbreviates the names Wertach and Sonthofen, the villages where he grew up, in his literary texts. This explanation parallels why we should be wary of reading the narrators as his alter egos. Sebald explains, "These two places have more of a symbolic significance than anything. I wanted to avoid the trap of them being identified and the text being seen as a realistic and faithful portrayal of these places, when in the texts they are in fact imaginary locations."[161]

In the unpublished first lecture of his Zurich lectures on poetics given in 1997, Sebald read among other passages a lengthy section from the fourth and final part of *Schwindel.Gefühle*, "Il ritorno in patria." Indicative of the necessary distinction between Sebald the author and his nameless first-person narrators, Sebald prefaces his reading of this passage by referring to the *narrator's* experiences rather than his own experiences.[162] Further reinforcing the argument that Sebald's works are not novels but rather a new genre that is more difficult to classify, Sebald refers to *Schwindel.Gefühle* as a "Prosabuch" in this same passage. This is the longest section of the book, and can be seen as a complement to the second section "All'estero." Both second and fourth sections are told from the

---

160 Sebald quoted in James Atlas, "W. G. Sebald: A Profile," *Paris Review* 41 (1999) 278–295, here 291. This idea of one's life as a "trajectory," implying movement and direction, while at the same time denying a certain sense of individual initiative or control over that direction, coincides with the strong role apparent coincidence plays in *Austerlitz* and additionally in both Austerlitz's and the narrator's frequent inability to rationally explain events, occurrences, and feelings.

161 W.G. Sebald, "W.G. Sebald," Christopher Bigsby, *Writers in Conversation with Christopher Bigsby. Volume Two* (Norwich [U.K.]: Arthur Miller Centre for American Studies, 2001) 139–165, here 141.

162 Cf. A: Sebald, Sammlung: Luftkrieg und Literatur, Mappe 2, DLA Marbach.

perspective of an unnamed, first-person narrator. One can indeed draw certain biographical connections between the unnamed narrator and the author Sebald, and there are even pictorial hints as well: the narrator includes a reproduction of his passport in the body of the text when recounting how he lost his passport during this trip to Italy. The photograph and name listed on the passport are clearly those of the real person W. G. Sebald. However, the black mark through the photograph both invalidates the passport from a legal standpoint and furthermore discourages the reader from making a direct connection between the person depicted in the image, the extratextual author, and the narrator; or from collapsing the border or boundary between reality and fiction.[163] This act is characteristic of Sebald's works – there are other instances in *Die Ausgewanderten* and *Die Ringe des Saturn* where Sebald includes photographs of himself – and provides an example of the sort of "swindle" or "deception" alluded to by the German title *Schwindel.Gefühle* that gets elided in its English translation as *Vertigo*.

Challenging the association of photography with authenticating an extratextual reality and the notion of photographs as a visual *aide-mémoire*, photographs or, more broadly, images in Sebald's texts activate the imagination of both the characters and the readers and provide an impetus for narrative. Photography, of course, can be considered a "mimetic" art, insofar as it is linked to an ontological reality, as established by Barthes in his *Camera lucida* and Sontag in her book *On Photography*. Sontag recounts how photographs have been seen as the "most realistic, therefore facile, of the mimetic arts,"[164] but she also works against this illusion of photography as a direct (i.e., 'accurate,' objective) representation of reality by reiterating the importance of angle and perspective, and that, in short, a photograph is never neutral, for there is always already interpretation implicit in the composition and act of taking a photograph. Sebald's works demonstrate the potential of literary discourse to both process and perform the interdiscursive transfer from experience to representation via semioticization, ultimately revealing *mimesis* to be more than mere imitation. His works present not just a representation of something ontologically prior to the text but rather something that comes into being only with(in) the text. Sebald's *Austerlitz* in particular is a text that works against a simplistic understanding of mimesis as imitation or direct reflection by presenting photographs that actually prove more deceptive than revealing. The closer Austerlitz examines photographs and film stills, the more obscured his vision becomes and the further away he feels from the refer-

---

163 Cf. Martin Klebes, "Infinite Journey: From Kafka to Sebald," *W. G. Sebald. A Critical Companion*, eds. J.J. Long and Anne Whitehead (Seattle, WA: University of Washington Press, 2004) 123–139, here 131.
164 Sontag, *On Photography*, 51.

ents. It has been stated that Sebald's narratives are a "renovation of the novel form" in the way that they reveal "the mendacity or mystery [....] of visual images."[165] I would agree and push this point further by saying that Sebald's fiction lays claim to a certain kind of truth only possible through literature or in the literary discourse. Plato, who occasionally viewed poets as liars and called for their banishment from the Republic, would shudder at such an assertion. The potentiality of fiction contrasted with the limitations of the pictorial discourse in Sebald's writing reveals an aesthetic transformation of reality and a rewriting of history – German history and the Holocaust in particular – through both individual memory and imagination. Read against the backdrop of the theorists of photography (Kracauer, Brecht, Benjamin, Barthes, and Sontag, for example), one gains an appreciation for the theoretically informed use of photographs that Sebald is making. He is not only integrating images but also reflecting on this action within the literary discourse, thematizing the acts of seeing, remembering, and knowing.

Literature as Historiography and Visual History

As Jan Gerstner has asserted, "Die Erinnerung ans 20. Jahrhundert kommt auch in der Literatur kaum noch ohne Fotos aus."[166] A turn toward the visual is not limited to literature, of course. One can observe a similar shift in history as well. One could even adapt the title of Benjamin's "Kunstwerk" essay to correspond to current concerns in history, that is, the question of "Geschichtsschreibung im

---

165 Russell J. A. Kilbourn, "Architecture and Cinema: The Representation of Memory in W. G. Sebald's *Austerlitz*" *W. G. Sebald: A Critical Companion* eds. J. J. Long and Anne Whitehead (Seattle, WA: University of Washington Press, 2004) 140–154, here 152.

166 Jan Gerstner, "Nach der Erinnerung. Silke Horstkotte erschließt in 'Nachbilder' den Komplex von 'Fotografie und Gedächtnis in der deutschen Gegenwartsliteratur,'" *literaturkritik.de* http://www.literaturkritik.de/public/rezension.php?rez_id=13333 [accessed: June 22, 2013]. Gerstner's apt observation holds true for literary texts that incorporate images, like Sebald's works, as well as a novel like Bernhard Schlink's *Der Vorleser*, for example. The latter makes an explicit connection between memory and images and by extension imagination. The protagonist Michael Berg refers to his "innere Leinwand" ["inner screen"] onto which he projects images of his lover Hanna as he remembers her, images that also become confused with what he imagines of her past as a concentration camp guard, which is based on what he hears during her trial. Memory, contrary to its presentation in Sebald's works, is never questioned by Schlink's protagonist. The details recalled and recounted, moreover, contribute to the realism of the novel and serve to establish the reliability of Michael as a narrator. Bernhard Schlink, *Der Vorleser* (Zurich: Diogenes, 1995) 61.

Zeitalter der photographischen Reproduzierbarkeit" ["Historiography in the era of photographic reproduction"]. Photographic technology was used to a great extent during World War II, for instance; aerial photography documented the topography and architecture of a city and gave insight into the demography as well. Such photography was an essential means for military reconnaissance and strategy. While photographing the concentration and extermination camps was prohibited, photography nevertheless played an important role in the camps. There were even two photography laboratories at Auschwitz.[167] Despite what seems to be an immediate and inextricable connection between photography and history, the concept of "visual history" is a relatively recent development.[168] Identifying the wide scope of the "pictorial turn" and its influence on the discipline of history, Gerhard Paul asserts the historian's need for "eine Schule des Sehens und der kritisch-ikonografischen Interpretation"[169] [a lesson in looking and critical-iconographic interpretation]. As Paul writes in the introduction to this collection of essays by historians,

> Letztlich geht es darum, Bilder über ihre zeichenhafte Abbildhaftigkeit hinaus als Medien zu untersuchen, die Sehweisen konditionieren, Wahrnehmungsmuster prägen, historische Deutungsweisen transportieren und ästhetische Beziehung historischer Subjekte zu ihrer sozialen und politischen Wirklichkeit organisieren.[170]
>
> [Ultimately we are investigating how images go beyond their value as representative signs and function as a medium that conditions how we see, that influences our patterns of perceptions, that transports historical forms of meaning and that organizes the aesthetic relationship between historical subjects into social and political reality.]

The influence of images on (re)forming memory has been established in the significant work of social psychologist Harald Welzer, whose studies have shown the correspondence between individual memory and film scenes and narratives:

> 'Der Erinnernde importiert die Bilder in sein eigenes Erleben,' erklärt Welzer. Der Forscher hat Dutzende Interviews mit Zeitzeugen, deren Kindern und Enkeln geführt und fand in ihren Berichten Sequenzen von Filmen wie 'Die Brücke,' 'Das Boot' oder 'Des Teufels

---

167 See Didi-Huberman, *Images in Spite of All*, in particular the chapter "Against All Unimaginable," 19–29 and his footnotes 23, 30, 32, 188–189.

168 Gerhard Paul traces historians' interest in visual materials as well as the influence of such materials on the discipline and practice of history as having started approximately twenty years ago. Gerhard Paul, "Von der historischen Bildkunde zur Visual History. Eine Einführung," *Visual History. Ein Studienbuch*, ed. Gerhard Paul (Göttingen: Vandenhoeck & Ruprecht, 2006) 7–36, here 7.

169 Paul, "Einführung," 7.

170 Ibid., 25.

General' nahtlos eingebaut. 'Sie werden verwoben mit den autobiografischen Erfahrungen, aber auch mit Träumen, Phantasien, Erzählungen, Romanen. Und weil wir nicht über einen inneren Lügendetektor verfügen, schwören die Leute Stein und Bein, dass es so gewesen ist und nicht anders.'[171]

['The one who remembers imports images into his own experiences,' explains Welzer. The researcher conducted dozens of interviews with contemporary witnesses, their children and grandchildren and found that they seamlessly integrated sequences from films like 'Die Brücke' (*The Bridge*), 'Das Boot' (*The Boat*) or 'Des Teufels General' (*The Devil's General*) into their reports. 'These sequences are woven together with autobiographical experiences, but also with dreams, fantasies, stories, novels. And because we aren't equipped with a built-in lie detector, these people swore to high heaven that what they remembered happened like that and not differently.']

Photographs and films thus have the power to form and (re)form individual memories as well as to ultimately revise and even falsify what is held as factual knowledge of history. As Rafaela von Bredow writes, "Fotos und Filme können die eigene Erinnerung komplett fälschen. Sie füllen Lücken, überlagern tatsächlich Geschehenes mit Bildern aus Szenen, denen der Zeitzeuge in Wahrheit nie beigewohnt hat, die vielleicht sogar nie wirklich passiert sind"[172] [Photos and films can falsify one's own memory. They fill in gaps and superimpose images and scenes, which the person did not actually witness at the time and which perhaps never actually occurred, onto actual events]. Von Bredow also points to the problem of basing historical films on documentary footage: "Die Filmemacher bedienen sich aus dem Bildinventar und der Ästhetik des Nazi-Regimes selbst"[173] [The filmmaker uses the inventory of images and aesthetic of the Nazi Regime]. She again refers to Welzer on this problem, "'Man interpretiert heute noch das Dritte Reich nach dem Bild, das es von sich selbst geschaffen hat'"[174] [Still today one interprets the Third Reich according to the image that it made of itself].

This adds an additional problematic layer to Austerlitz's attempts to find his mother in the film clip made of the Theresienstadt Ghetto. As Jakob Lothe notes, this "documentary" film material creates a tension in *Austerlitz*:

> Accentuating the novel's ethical dimension, Sebald's incorporation of the documentary into the fiction of *Austerlitz* testifies to a powerful concern on his part not just with the relations

---

171 Harald Welzer quoted in Rafaela von Bredow, "Bilder machen Geschichte," *Der Spiegel* (September 18, 2006) 164. See Welzer's study, published as Harald Welzer, Sabine Moller, and Karoline Tschuggnall, eds., *'Opa war kein Nazi.' Nationalsozialismus und Holocaust im Familiengedächtnis* (Frankfurt: Fischer, 2002). See also Horstkotte, *Nachbilder*, 25–26.
172 Von Bredow, "Bilder machen Geschichte," 164.
173 Ibid.
174 Ibid.

between history and fiction but also with the relations between truth and falsity: the documentary has a historical existence but its purpose was not to fictionalize but to lie, whereas Sebald's narrative is fictional but its purpose is to capture truths that the documentary either denies or neglects. Indeed, the Nazi film does not really merit the term 'documentary,' even if, as Sebald demonstrates, documentary evidence of some sort may be obtained from it through an oppositional reading.[175]

This recognition of the role that images play in conditioning both how we see and the patterns of our perception, is something that Sebald's literary texts repeatedly demonstrate. Sebald's works ultimately demand that we move the discussion away from images as documents of the past.

The turn toward the visual in both literature and history is certainly linked to questions of memory, but the problem of representation forms the basis. The illusion of reality that is inherent in every photograph and the deceptive closeness and immediacy to the photographed subject magnify the problem of historiography and make writing the history of World War II and the Holocaust all the more problematic. Sebald's works combine verbal and visual elements in a provocative way, but it is the operations made by the reader to negotiate between these media and to process the various forms and interrelationships that establish his texts as rich fields of exploration. His body of work, in particular the role of the visual, reflects what is at stake in these recent discussions of "visual history." A peculiar aspect in *Austerlitz* is that the photographs (as well as other objects) are often presented as having the capacity of memory. It is as if these photographs possess the memories that the individual has forgotten or repressed. The individual seeks out these memories in the photograph and attempts to "read," or interpret, their past from the image. For instance, two photographs mysteriously resurface while Austerlitz visits with Věra; they were contained in one of the many small volumes of Balzac, a detail among others noticed and described by Austerlitz when he first enters her apartment, as if to foreshadow the later reappearance of the photographs. Of these photographs, Věra states,

> Man habe den Eindruck, sagte sie, es rühre sich etwas in ihnen, als vernehme man kleine Verzweiflungsseufzer, gémissements de désespoir, so sagte sie, sagte Austerlitz, als hätten die Bilder selbst ein Gedächtnis und erinnerten sich an uns, daran, wie wir, die Überlebenden, und diejenigen, die nicht mehr unter uns weilen, vordem gewesen sind (A 266).
>
> [One has the impression, she said, of something stirring in them, as if one caught small sighs of despair, *gémissements de désespoir* was her expression, said Austerlitz, as if the pictures had a memory of their own and remembered us, remembered the roles that we, the survivors, and those no longer among us had played in our former lives (AE 182–183, emphasis Bell)].

---

175 Lothe, "Narrative, Memory, and Visual Image," 239.

Austerlitz attempts to remember himself in the photograph he sees before him, an object he refrains from even touching at first. The photograph forms the cover image of most editions of *Austerlitz*, and it is provided for the reader's further consideration within the text as well, taking up the bottom half of one page. Austerlitz recognizes his characteristically slanting hairline in the boy in the image, yet all other feeling seem to be erased inside of him, "doch sonst war alles in mir ausgelöscht von einem überwältigenden Gefühl der Vergangenheit" (*A* 267) ["all memory was extinguished in me by an overwhelming sense of the long years that had passed" (*AE* 184)]. In studying the photo again and again in later years, "ohne je den geringsten Anhalt zu finden," (*A* 268) ["without once finding the slightest clue,"] Austerlitz recalls how he,

> immer fühlte ich mich dabei durchdrungen von dem forschenden Blick des Pagen, der gekommen war, sein Teil zurückzufordern und der nun im Morgengrauen auf dem leeren Feld darauf wartete, daß ich den Handschuh aufhebe und das ihm bevorstehende Unglück abwenden würde (*A* 268).
>
> [always felt the piercing, inquiring gaze of the page boy who had come to demand his dues, who was waiting in the gray light of dawn on the empty field for me to accept the challenge and avert the misfortune lying ahead of him (*AE* 184).]

Not only do such photographs possess a memory of their own, a memory that often eludes even the subjects of the photographs, but they also make demands.[176] Their silence drives their viewers to search out their past, confront it, and live to tell it: to ultimately become the witness to the photograph and give voice to the memory contained in it. Sebald's works show us the complex role of photographs not so much to document the past but to serve as a testimony to the past. The further ethical dimension of Sebald's literary historiography is the responsibility placed on the readers to continue this memory process through investigation, interrogation, and narration of the past. The debate around the Holocaust's representability becomes all the more problematic when we consider the proliferation of images and the fact that certain images have attained an iconic status. While we may have these visual representations, the physical and temporal distance from the experience of the events themselves forces us to consider our cognitive and emotional means of processing these images. Seeing,

---

176 Sebald similarly describes his reaction to looking at old photographs in an interview with Christian Scholz in 1997: "Immer ist mir dabei aufgefallen, daß von diesen Bildern ein ungeheurer Appell ausgeht; eine Forderung an den Beschauer, zu erzählen oder sich vorzustellen, was man, von diesen Bildern ausgehend, erzählen könnte" (*G* 165). [When looking at old photographs, I have always had the impression that a formidable plea comes forth from these images; a demand on the viewer to recount or to imagine what one could recount by starting from these images.]

remembering, and imagining are three processes that become blurred in our efforts to understand and engage with the past.

Coda

The discussion around the controversial photographs from the Abu Ghraib prison in Iraq reveals the continued importance of such questions as the photograph's status as document and the close connection among photography, writing, and memory that have been developed above. Philip Gourevitch and Errol Morris' detailed portrait of Sabrina Harman, a member of the Military Police in part responsible for the now infamous photographs from Abu Ghraib, reveals her actions not only *behind* but even more significantly *in* the photographs.[177] The motivation behind taking the photographs, as Harman told Gourevitch and Morris, attests to the documentary quality of photographs, their status as indisputable evidence, but also to photography's ability to serve as a confirmation of reality: "'If I come up to you and I'm like, "Hey this is going on," you probably wouldn't believe me unless I had something to show you,' she said. 'So if I say, "Hey this is going on. Look, I have proof," you can't deny it, I guess.'"[178] While aiding Harman as a coping mechanism, her letters home function in a similar way to the photographs: they serve as a form of documentation. Harman told Gourevitch and Morris,

> 'Maybe writing home was a release, to help me forget about what was happening,' she said. Then, moments later, she said, 'I put everything down on paper that I was thinking. And if it weren't for those letters, I don't think I could ever tell you anything that went on. That's the only way I can remember things, is letters and photos.' The remarks sound contradictory, but Harman seemed to conceive of memory as an external storage device. By downloading her impressions to a document, she could clear them from her mind and transform reality into an artifact.[179]

Harman's remarks are not as contradictory as Gourevitch and Morris so easily state. In her earlier statements, it is clear that Harman was struggling with the reality of the prison, and photography provides her with a way of documenting this for herself and for others. The letters, although they may aid in momentary

---

177 She is repeatedly shown smiling and giving a 'thumb's up,' even when leaning over a corpse. Philip Gourevitch and Errol Morris, "Annals of War. Exposure. The Woman Behind the Camera at Abu Ghraib," *The New Yorker* (March 24, 2008) 44–57, here 47. See also Philip Gourevitch and Errol Morris, *Standard Operating Procedure* (New York: Penguin, 2008).
178 Harman quoted in Gourevitch and Morris, "Exposure," 51–52.
179 Ibid., 54.

repression by facilitating a form of catharsis, they, too, are forms of documentation. The photographs from Abu Ghraib demonstrate the multiple ways in which a photograph functions and the multiple ways we can read them. While serving as an *aide-mémoire* for the photographer, the photographs, once dispersed worldwide in print and online, became representative of the contradictions and hypocrisy of the United States' "war on terror." Gourevitch and Morris provide a differentiated reading of the various photographs that came out of Abu Ghraib, revealing "the power of an image does not necessarily lie in what it depicts."[180] They describe "the quality of pornography" of unambiguous photographs that depict death and nudity and leave "little to the imagination" versus the particular photograph of the man "hooded, caped, and wired on his box," which has become "the icon of Abu Ghraib and possibly the most recognized emblem of the war on terror after the World Trade towers."[181] The development from analog to digital photography may demand new considerations based on technical changes, yet, as we have seen, touch-ups, manipulation, and experimentation are not phenomena of the twentieth and twenty-first centuries. It seems that this change in medium has not issued forth a paradigm shift in how we consider the operation of photography. Yet, the theoretical considerations initiated by Kracauer, Benjamin, and Brecht and developed further by Barthes, Sontag, and Didi-Huberman have gained renewed relevance as we continue to negotiate questions of documentation, authenticity, deception, imagination, and memory in our evaluation of history, literature, and current political events.

---

180 Ibid., 57.
181 Ibid.

Chapter 4
Chronology and Coincidence in the Narrative Cosmos

Outlining the Narrative Frame: From Flow to Tableau

Susan Sontag's 1979 essay on Walter Benjamin, "Under the Sign of Saturn," offers various points of connection to Sebald's literary and scholarly works.[1] She begins her essay by describing several photographs of Benjamin: one taken in 1927, one of him in the Bibliothèque nationale in Paris in 1937, and one of him taken in front of Brecht's house in Denmark in 1938.[2] Memory, as Sontag develops in her reading of Benjamin, stages the past, "turns the flow of events into tableaux."[3] This key passage in the essay outlines Sontag's notion that memory collapses time,[4] which also provides a useful way for conceptualizing how time is presented in Sebald's works. Memory is, of course, one of the unifying themes across Sebald's œuvre and will be discussed in further detail in chapter five. One of the characteristic aspects of his writing is the emphasis on the co-presence of various points of time within one physical space – be it geographic, architectural, or narrative space – rather than on a chronological ordering, which creates the effect of a tableau rather than flow similar to that which Sontag identifies in Benjamin. However, this is not to say that there is an absence of chronology or 'order' in Sebald's works. That is, a specific chronology is necessary to make the diegesis both possible and comprehensible. At the same time, Sebald's texts often withhold indicators of time and space, and his manuscripts even reveal a purposeful erasing of such chronological traces to create a disjointed, non-linear narrative progression.

In this chapter I build upon my previous analyses of historiography and representation to outline Sebald's unique theory of time that allows for the simultaneity of past, present, and future.[5] It is necessary to examine such con-

---

1 Susan Sontag, "Under the Sign of Saturn," *Under the Sign of Saturn* (New York: Farrar, Straus and Giroux, 1980) 107–134.
2 The way Sebald outlines several photographs of Robert Walser in his essay "Le promeneur solitaire" echoes Sontag's psychologizing gaze of Benjamin. Moreover, Sebald's essay is similar to Sontag's in both form and style. See chapter two for a discussion of this essay (*Logis* 127–168/ *PC* 117–154).
3 Sontag, "Under the Sign of Saturn," 116.
4 Ibid., 115.
5 The effect of such a concept of time on his characters' perception and memory will be explored further in chapter five.

cepts as time and space since they define a fundamental framework for approaching reality. Moreover, since literature of the twentieth century can in part be characterized by its emphasis on "Räumlichkeit als Dimension ihres Mediums und ihrer Darstellungsverfahren"[6] [spatiality as both dimension of its medium and of its representational process], I consider the interrelationship of time and space in Sebald's works both thematically and from a narratological perspective. Building upon Claudia Öhlschläger's useful differentiation of two models that operate simultaneously in Sebald's works – a vertical model of archaeological layers and a horizontal model of connected networks[7] – my analyses draw out the implications of the archaeological perspective and the various networks of connections in Sebald's works.

Austerlitz in particular illustrates the tension between co-presence and chronological progression, thus I will first outline this text's narrative framework as my later considerations of perception, language, memory, and imagination all relate back to their formulation within literary discourse. Sebald repeatedly noted down the chronology of both the *histoire* and *discours* of this work – presumably for the first time in the inside back cover of his copy of Claude Simon's *Le jardin des plantes*[8] and on various handwritten sheets accompanying the manuscript – in order to keep the story lines and layers of the text straight. This chronology is invisible to the reader at first glance, that is, the first time one reads the text; it can only be established or reconstructed in retrospect. A closer examination of the text will make this clear.

Austerlitz is a framed narrative, yet the borders of this frame prove to be very porous, as the clear differentiation continually dissolves between the two perspectives of the nameless first-person narrator and the main character Austerlitz.

---

6 Inka Mülder-Bach, "Einleitung [Section III. Literarische Räume]," *Topographien der Literatur. Deutsche Literatur im transnationalen Kontext.* DFG-Symposium 2004, eds. Hartmut Böhme, Inka Mülder-Bach, Bernhard Siegert, and Horst Wenzel (Stuttgart: Metzler, 2005) 403–407, here p. 406.

7 Cf. Claudia Öhlschläger, "'Die Bahn des korsischen Kometen.' Zur Dimension 'Napoleon' in W. G. Sebalds literarischem Netzwerk," *Topographien der Literatur. Deutsche Literatur im transnationalen Kontext.* DFG-Symposium 2004, eds. Hartmut Böhme, Inka Mülder-Bach, Bernhard Siegert, and Horst Wenzel (Stuttgart: Metzler, 2005) 536–558.

8 Claude Simon, *Le jardin des plantes* (Paris: Les Éditions de Minuit, 1997), W.G. Sebald Nachlaß: Teilbibliothek, DLA Marbach. For the connections between Simon's novel and Sebald's *Die Ausgewanderten* and*Austerlitz*, see Antje Tennstedt, *Annäherungen an die Vergangenheit bei Claude Simon und W.G. Sebald* (Am Beispiel von *Le Jardin des Plantes, Die Ausgewanderten* und *Austerlitz*) (Freiburg im Breisgau: Rombach, 2007). The back cover of Simon's book with Sebald's notes is reproduced in Muriel Pic, *W.G. Sebald – L'image papillon – suivi de W.G. Sebald: L'art de voler* (Paris: Les Presses du Réel, 2009) 53.

Austerlitz's narration is blurred even further by the dreams and memories he recounts as well as by his recollections of stories heard from other individuals. The multiplicity of voices creates a multi-layered narrative that spans close to sixty years and ranges geographically across Belgium, Czechoslovakia, Germany, France, and England. By writing one individual's search for his identity and his past – in particular the fate of his mother – and his efforts to recover his lost and repressed memories, Sebald situates an individual's story within a greater political and collective past.

As Sebald approaches the larger history of the Holocaust via individual experience, his narrator recedes into the background, only to resurface again with an exaggerated attention brought to the distance between him and his sources. The similarities – almost to a point of merging – between the narrator and Austerlitz are rooted in the structure and style of the narrative.[9] While it has been asserted that "[m]ost of the time, we cannot be sure who is speaking,"[10] a narratological analysis reveals the contrary to be true, making clear the basic structure and traceable framework in *Austerlitz*. The narrator recounts his meetings and discussions with Austerlitz, and further layers of narration are added when Austerlitz recounts his discussions with other individuals: Gerald's uncle Alphonso in Wales, Austerlitz's former nanny Věra Rysonová in Prague, his friend Marie de Verneuil in Paris, or his librarian acquaintance named Henri Lemoine at the Bibliothèque nationale, among others. The recollection of dreams and nightmares Austerlitz has had or accounts of texts he has read build further layers of narration much like the reported speech of other figures. The narrator periodically interrupts his account with such markers as: "Vielleicht, hat Věra gesagt, sagte Austerlitz, wäre es anders gewesen" (*A* 296) ["Perhaps, Vera surmised, said Austerlitz, it would have been different" (*AE* 205)] or "Kannst du mir nicht sagen, sagte sie, sagte Austerlitz" (*A* 311)

---

9 Marianne Hirsch aptly identifies the testimonial structure of Sebald's *Austerlitz*, and Jakob Lothe describes the way "the frame narrator and via him the reader are placed into that role [of listener in testimony] here." See Marianne Hirsch, *The Generation of Postmemory. Writing and Visual Culture After the Holocaust* (New York: Columbia University Press, 2012) 40 and Jakob Lothe, "Narrative, Memory, and Visual Image: W.G. Sebald's *Luftkrieg und Literatur* and *Austerlitz*," *After Testimony. The Ethics and Aesthetics of Holocaust Narrative for the Future*, eds. Jakob Lothe, Susan Rubin Suleiman, and James Phelan (Columbus: The Ohio State University Press, 2012) 221–246, here 243. Chapter five expands on the notion of testimony with regard to memory in Sebald's works.

10 Bernhard Malkmus, "'All of them Signs and Characters from the Type-Case of Forgotten Things' – Intermedia Configurations of History in W.G. Sebald," *Memory Traces. 1989 and the Question of German Cultural Identity*, ed. Silke Arnold-de Simine (New York: Peter Lang, 2005) 211–244, here 232–233.

["Can't you tell me the reason, she asked, said Austerlitz" (*AE* 215)] or "Manch-mal, sagte Lemoine, sagte Austerlitz" (*A* 406) ["Sometimes, so Lemoine told me, said Austerlitz" (*AE* 287)].[11] This twice-mediated representation – the narrator recounting what Austerlitz recounted to him, which is often based on what was told to him by someone else – thus creates a two-fold distance, not unlike Plato's description of the artist's imitation of the world of 'ideas' as twice removed from 'reality.'

Despite the multiple layers and twice, often thrice-mediated narration, the reader never truly loses orientation, for the various strands of Austerlitz's story can be traced and clearly delineated; the encounters and discussions between Austerlitz and the narrator can almost always be situated in very specific temporal and spatial terms even if these times and locations are given belatedly. What Sebald himself has referred to as "periscopic" narration – a term he used to characterize the narrative style of Thomas Bernhard as a narration "um ein, zwei Ecken"[12] [around one, two corners] – can also be seen analogously in the complex layering of time and space in his own prose works. The distinction and often significant disjuncture between the time of narration (*Erzählzeit*) and the narrated time (*erzählte Zeit*), and by extension the place of narration and the narrated place, characterizes and complicates these multiple layers. This emphasized distance from a 'source' challenges the reductive notion of literature as a reflection of reality while also making clear that history is not accessibly without mediation and a certain degree of fiction.

Austerlitz begins with the first-person narrator's recollections of his travels from England to Belgium during the second half of the 1960s. The place and time of the main narrative frame remains uncertain, that is, we are never able to establish with absolute certainty from where or at what time the narrator tells, i.e., reconstructs the final story of Austerlitz's life. We can, however, determine that the time of the frame is after their last meeting in September 1997. There are also distinct points in the narrative where the narrator reveals that he has taken notes on his encounters with Austerlitz, such as after their coincidental meeting in the Bar of the Great Eastern Hotel. In this instance, the narrator recalls staying

---

11 Irene Kacandes convincingly notes how frequently Sebald's characters "point to oral transmission" and how "the inquits sound like poetic refrains." Cf. Irene Kacandes, "'When facts are scarce': Authenticating Strategies in Writing by Children of Survivors," *After Testimony. The Ethics and Aesthetics of Holocaust Narrative for the Future*, eds. Jakob Lothe, Susan Rubin Suleiman, and James Phelan (Columbus: The Ohio State University Press, 2012) 179–197, here 195.
12 Martin Doerry and Volker Hage, "'Ich fürchte das Melodramatische,'" Interview in *Der Spiegel* (March 12, 2001) 228–234, here 233. Sebald similarly refers to Bernhard's narrative strategy as a basis for his own construction in an interview with Sven Boedecker in 1993 (*G* 108).

awake until three in the morning, using only the wan light cast from a street lamp, "um in Stichworten und unverbundenen Sätzen soviel als möglich aufzuschreiben von dem, was Austerlitz den Abend hindurch mir erzählt hatte" (*A* 146) ["writing down, in the form of notes and disconnected sentences, as much as possible of what Austerlitz had told me that evening" (*AE* 97)]. Such instances remind the reader of the constructedness of the narrative and also reveal how precarious the truth value of the narrative must be. There is a repetition of deictic elements in the narrative frame: "Selbst *jetzt*, wo ich mich mühe, mich zu erinnern" (*A* 38, my emphasis in all of the following quotes in this passage) ["Even *now*, when I try to remember them" (*AE* 24)]; "das kommt mir *jetzt* beim Schreiben zum erstenmal seit jener Zeit wieder in den Sinn [...] so erinnere ich mich *jetzt*, dachte ich damals" [" – and *now*, in writing this, I do remember that such an idea occurred to me at that time – " (*AE* 24)[13]]; "Und *jetzt* indem ich dies niederschreibe" (*A* 60) ["As I write this I once again see" (*AE* 38)]. Yet these deictic elements frustrate our desire to specify the time and place of the narrative frame. Despite the repetition of "jetzt," we cannot unequivocally identify this moment in time. Sebald further plays with the reader's desire to situate the narrative within a particular temporal context in how he withholds time markers to preserve a sense of vagueness. For example, it is not until page forty-four that the narrator specifies the time and year that he and Austerlitz met, "an jenem Junimorgen des Jahres 1967" (*A* 44) ["that June day in 1967" (*AE* 27)].

In a prolepsis,[14] the narrator provides the reader with a context for his later account of Austerlitz's story and thereby explicitly reveals this text to be both a construction and a reconstruction from memory by acknowledging its material sources, the photographs in particular. In recalling his first sight of Austerlitz in the Antwerp Centraal Station, the narrator describes how Austerlitz

> machte mehrere Aufnahmen von den inzwischen ganz verdunkelten Spiegeln, die ich jedoch unter den vielen Hunderten mir von ihm bald nach unserer Wiederbegegnung im Winter 1996 überantworteten und größtenteils unsortierten Bildern bisher noch nicht habe auffinden können (*A* 15).[15]

---

13 This statement is set off by "m" dashes in the English translation by Anthea Bell. Bell also breaks up the original German sentence, starting a new sentence with "I also recollect *now* [...]" (*AE* 24).

14 Gérard Genette, *Figures III* (Paris: Éditions du Seuil, 1972) 105–114. Basing their terminology in large part on Genette, Martinez and Scheffel discuss the term "zukunftsgewisse Prolepse" to indicate a narrative act that discloses information about a future event. See Matias Martinez and Michael Scheffel, *Einführung in die Erzähltheorie* (Munich: Verlag C.H. Beck, 2000) 33–37.

15 Even before the narrator has approached Austerlitz, he describes how he observes this curious figure taking photographs, which he would later come to possess. In contrast to how

[took several pictures of the mirrors, which were now quite dark, but so far I have been unable to find them among the many hundreds of pictures, most of them unsorted, that he entrusted to me soon after we met again in the winter of 1996 (*AE* 7).]

By acknowledging his possession of the photographs and how Austerlitz will later give them to him, the narrator reveals that he is responsible for their placement within the text.[16] The fact that we are from the outset confronted with the problem of missing photographs – the narrator cannot find those that Austerlitz took on the day they met in Antwerp – inscribes a fundamental sense of uncertainty, of the uncanny even, indicating that the reader will not be on stable ground throughout the text. Moreover, it is probably not a coincidence that the missing photographs are of darkened mirrors, "ganz verdunkelten Spiegeln" (*A* 15). Reflections and darkness are repeated motifs in Sebald's works that implicitly and explicitly thematize the problem, impossibility even, of approaching and representing both present and past realities.

Plotting the Text: Simultaneity and Co-Presence of Past, Present, and Future

While Sebald may present an explicit critique of Cartesian rationalism in both *Die Ringe des Saturn*[17] and *Austerlitz*, systems of order are present throughout his works and are most apparent in the visual reproductions of maps and diagrams.

Austerlitz tends to avoid naming others, the narrator announces Austerlitz by name before the reader knows anything else about him: "Eine der in der *Salle des pas perdus* wartenden Personen war Austerlitz" (*A* 14) ["One of the people waiting in the *Salle des pas perdus* was Austerlitz" (*AE* 7)].

16 This comment also reveals that the narrator and Austerlitz will develop a relationship of trust. *Austerlitz* is, of course, a creation of the author W.G. Sebald, as established in chapter three's delineation of the different levels of 'reality.' Furthermore, Sebald the author makes his presence known, i.e., underlines the construction of the literary text, precisely through the integration of visual material and the use of literary techniques such as alliteration and listing.

17 Austerlitz also refers to the "cartesische[r] Gesamtplan der Nationalbibliothek" (*A* 398) ["the Cartesian overall plan of the Bibliothèque Nationale" (*AE* 251)] in his harsh critique of how hostile the new library is to readers and researchers. Despite this Cartesian critique, Helmut Lethen argues that Sebald's "altmeisterliche[] Prosa" [prose in the style of the old masters] actually "cartesianisiert" [imposes a Cartesian framework] on the aspect of perception in his works. Cf. Helmut Lethen, "Sebalds Raster: Überlegungen zur ontologischen Unruhe in Sebalds *Die Ringe des Saturn*," *W.G. Sebald. Politische Archäologie und melancholische Bastelei*, eds. Michael Niehaus and Claudia Öhlschläger (Berlin: Schmidt, 2006) [*Philologische Studien und Quellen* 196] 13–30, here 21.

Such schematic presentations of established knowledge serve as a means of orientation, out of which new knowledge can be created. These visual representations actually run counter to the narrative "dis-order" of Sebald's texts. The reading experience of his works is marked by a desire to establish a sense of order among the various voices, levels, times, and places of narration, not to mention between the text, the images, and extratextual reality, as discussed in the previous chapter. One way in which to understand the stories Sebald tells is to bring an order to his texts, to plot the essential elements of the narrative: time and space. "For geography and chronology are the two eyes of history," after all, as Vico tells us.[18] The digital projects and blogs discussed at the beginning of this book illustrate this desire for order in their attempts to visualize, map, reorder, and even reproduce the narrative of Sebald's texts. Richard T. Gray's narratological analysis of *Die Ringe des Saturn* has outlined the text's analogous rings of narration and illuminated how these layers remain "distinct and identifiable" yet "laminated onto each other."[19] Sebald's "segues," as Gray terms these "creative linkages that stitch together these diverse fragments into a coherent textual whole," also form "points of transition" and "points of cohesion in an otherwise disjointed text."[20] In response to Uwe Pralle's suggestion that his works be characterized as "literarische Archäologien" (*G* 259) [literary archaeologies], as if he were working "an einer Art Universalgeschichte der Katastrophen" (ibid.) [on a sort of universal history of catastrophes], Sebald describes the central structural conceit of *Die Ringe des Saturn* as the concentric circles that move outwards, the outer circles always determining the inner ones (cf. *G* 259–260).

The particular concept of time put forth in Sebald's works and the complex layering of the narrative challenge our attempts to establish an order while simultaneously drawing us further into his texts. Non-linear, coexisting time has serious implications for Sebald's characters and is compounded by their own awareness of two opposing possibilities: an abyss of amnesiac repression and a traumatic, ceaseless repetition.[21] This concept of time is itself rooted in experiences of trauma, which Sebald first alludes to in an essay on Jean Améry.

---

18 Giambattista Vico, trans. David Marsh, "Book I: Establishing Principles," *New Science. Principles of the New Science Concerning the Common Nature of Nations* (New York: Penguin, 1999) 12.

19 Richard T. Gray, "Sebald's Segues: Performing Narrative Contingency in *The Rings of Saturn*," *The Germanic Review* 84.1 (2009) 26–58, here 28.

20 Ibid., 26, 27.

21 While this temporal concept is particularly prominent in *Austerlitz*, it can also be traced in Sebald's earlier works.

Here he states, "Für die Opfer der Verfolgung aber ist der rote Faden der Zeit zerrissen, Hintergrund und Vordergrund verschwimmen ineinander, die logische Absicherung im Dasein ist suspendiert. Die Erfahrung des Terrors bewirkt die Dislokation auch in der Zeit, der abstraktesten Heimat der Menschen" (LS 153–154). ["For the victims of persecution, however, the thread of chronological time is broken, background and foreground merge, the victim's logical means of support in his existence are suspended. The experience of terror also dislocates time, that most abstract of all humanity's homes" (*NH* 150).] In the last section of *Die Ausgewanderten*, the narrator recounts Max Aurach's suspicion of time, "aber die Zeit, so fuhr er fort, ist ein unzuverlässiger Maßstab, ja, sie ist nichts als das Rumoren der Seele. Es gibt weder eine Vergangenheit noch eine Zukunft" (*DA* 270) ["but time, [Ferber] went on, is an unreliable way of gauging these things, indeed it is nothing but a disquiet of the soul. There is neither a past nor a future" (*E* 181)]. The permeable boundaries between a past, present, and future are echoed by Austerlitz in his suspicion as to whether we can actually understand the laws that determine "die Wiederkunft der Vergangenheit" (*A* 269) ["the return of the past" (*AE* 185)]. He moreover pushes further this notion of uncertain temporal borders to assert his sense that there is no time at all, which would in turn mean that the living and the dead co-exist in the same space. The narrator recounts how Austerlitz describes this sense to him,

> doch ist es mir immer mehr, als gäbe es überhaupt keine Zeit, sondern nur verschiedene, nach einer höheren Stereometrie ineinander verschachtelte Räume, zwischen denen die Lebendigen und die Toten, je nachdem es ihnen zumute ist, hin und her gehen können, und je länger ich es bedenke, desto mehr kommt mir vor, daß wir, die wir uns noch am Leben befinden, in den Augen der Toten irreale und nur manchmal, unter bestimmten Lichtverhältnissen und atmosphärischen Bedingungen sichtbar werdende Wesen sind (*A* 269).
>
> [but I feel more and more as if time did not exist at all, only various spaces interlocking according to the rules of a higher form of stereometry, between which the living and the dead can move back and forth as they like, and the longer I think about it the more it seems to me that we who are still alive are unreal in the eyes of the dead, that only occasionally, in certain lights and atmospheric conditions, do we appear in their field of vision (*AE* 185).]

At an earlier point in their discussions, Austerlitz lays out for the narrator how he not only imagines but actually perceives the continuous plane of time and space, for which models can be found in nature. At the Barmouth Bay in Wales, for example, which he recalls in great detail – "daran erinnere ich mich genau" (*A* 143) ["I remember this well" (*AE* 95)] – Austerlitz experienced a vision that gave him "so etwas wie ein Gefühl für die Ewigkeit" (*A* 143) ["something like a sense of eternity" (*AE* 95)] in the dissolving borders of space:

In einem perlgrauen Dunst lösten sämtliche Formen und Farben sich auf; es gab keine Kontraste, keine Abstufungen mehr, nur noch fließende, vom Licht durchpulste Übergänge, ein einziges Verschwimmen, aus dem nur die allerflüchtigsten Erscheinungen noch auftauchten [...] (A 143).

[All forms and colors were dissolved in a pearl-gray haze; there were no contrasts, no shading anymore, only flowing transitions with the light throbbing through them, a single blur from which only the most fleeting of visions emerged [...] (AE 95).]

This way of perceiving without contrast – without being able to distinguish between different elements, between light and dark – is analogous to Austerlitz's idea of time and his sense of the past, present, and future all being on the same plane, which is formulated in the key scene of the book. Austerlitz experiences the continuous plane of time and space in a moment of anagnorisis, when he is confronted with his own long-repressed past: in the Ladies' Waiting Room of the Liverpool Street Station, he literally encounters himself as a little boy, decades prior upon his arrival in London after having traveled from Prague on a so-called "Kindertransport." Making up the key scene of the book, the narrator recounts Austerlitz's experience of time collapsing around him within the waiting room:

Tatsächlich hatte ich das Gefühl, sagte Austerlitz, als enthalte der Wartesaal, in dessen Mitte ich wie ein Geblendeter stand, alle Stunden meiner Vergangenheit, all meine von jeher unterdrückten, ausgelöschten Ängste und Wünsche, als sei das schwarzweiße Rautenmuster der Steinplatten zu meinen Füßen das Feld für das Endspiel meines Lebens, als erstreckte es sich über die gesamte Ebene der Zeit (A 200–201).

[In fact I felt, said Austerlitz, that the waiting room where I stood as if dazzled contained all the hours of my past life, all the suppressed and extinguished fears and wishes I had ever entertained, as if the black and white diamond pattern of the stone slabs beneath my feet were the board on which the endgame would be played, and it covered the entire plane of time (AE 136).]

Austerlitz characterizes his vision in the Ladies' Waiting Room as one of both imprisonment and liberation; the room appears to him as simultaneously in ruins and reconstruction. The imagery of this scene calls to mind both Hubert Robert's imaginary ruins ("Vue Imaginaire" of 1796) and Giovanni Battista Piranesi's imaginary prisons ("Carceri D'Invenzione" of 1745).[22]

---

22 Austerlitz's experiences in boarding school at Stower Grange were marked by a similar tension between liberation and imprisonment. His description of the Ladies' Waiting Room as simultaneously in ruins and in the process of reconstruction also echoes his vision of an ideal landscape, which he developed during these years at Stower Grange. He recounts the way he began conceptualizing space as not being determined or limited by geographical distances or defined by historical relationships, but rather in an ideal landscape in the form of a continuous panorama: "Nach und nach entstand so in meinem Kopf eine Art idealer Landschaft, in der die

The coexistence of past, present, and future and Austerlitz's extreme notion of nonexistent time, although often described in a figurative way, is not to be understood in a strictly metaphorical sense. The narrator reveals the very literal way in which Austerlitz's perceives and experiences time, when he states, "Wäre mir damals schon recht aufgegangen, daß es für Austerlitz Augenblicke gab ohne Anfang und Ende und daß ihm andererseits sein ganzes Leben bisweilen wie ein blinder Punkt ohne jede Dauer erschien, ich hätte wohl besser gewußt zu warten" (*A* 173) ["Had I realized at the time that for Austerlitz certain moments had no beginning or end, while on the other hand his whole life had sometimes seemed to him a blank point without duration, I would probably have waited more patiently" (*AE* 117)]. In his attempts to grasp the feeling of passing time or past time, Austerlitz likens time to a current, but he nevertheless cannot deny how time affects him in a deeply physical way. He describes this sensation to the narrator as follows,

Wenn ich beispielsweise irgendwo auf meinen Wegen durch die Stadt in einen jener stillen Höfe hineinblicke, in denen sich über Jahrzehnte nichts verändert hat, spüre ich beinahe körperlich, wie sich die Strömung der Zeit im Gravitationsfeld der vergessenen Dinge verlangsamt. Alle Momente unseres Lebens scheinen mir dann in einem einzigen Raum beisammen, ganz als existierten die zukünftigen Ereignisse bereits und harrten nur darauf, daß wir uns endlich in ihnen einfinden, so wie wir uns, einer einmal angenommenen Einladung folgend, zu einer bestimmten Stunde einfinden in einem bestimmten Haus. Und wäre es nicht denkbar, fuhr Austerlitz fort, daß wir auch in der Vergangenheit, in dem, was schon gewesen und größtenteils ausgelöscht ist, Verabredungen haben und dort Orte und Personen aufsuchen müssen, die quasi jenseits der Zeit, in einem Zusammenhang stehen mit uns? (*A* 367)

[For instance, if I am walking through the city and look into one of those quiet courtyards where nothing has changed for decades, I feel, almost physically, the current of time slowing down in the gravitational field of oblivion. It seems to me then as if all the moments of our life occupy the same space, as if future events already existed and were only waiting for us to find our way to them at last, just as when we have accepted an invitation we duly arrive in a certain house at a given time. And might it not be, continued Austerlitz, that we also have appointments to keep in the past, in what has gone before and is for the most part extinguished, and must go there in search of places and people who have some connection with us on the far side of time, so to speak? (*AE* 257–258)]

---

arabische Wüste, das Reich der Azteken, der antarktische Kontinent, die Schneealpen, die Nordwestpassage, der Kongostrom und die Halbinsel Krim in einem einzigen Panorama beieinander waren, bevölkert mit sämtlichen dazugehörigen Gestalten" (*A* 93). ["My mind thus gradually created a kind of ideal landscape in which the Arabian desert, the realm of the Aztecs, the continent of Antarctica, the snow-covered Alps, the North-West Passage, the River Congo, and the Crimean peninsula formed a single panorama, populated by all the figures proper to those places" (*AE* 61).]

Austerlitz further connects his non-linear sense and his profound suspicion of time with the need to reconceptualize history:

> Eine Uhr ist mir immer wie etwas Lachhaftes vorgekommen, wie etwas von Grund auf Verlogenes, vielleicht weil ich mich, aus einem mir selber nie verständlichen inneren Antrieb heraus, gegen die Macht der Zeit stets gesträubt und von dem sogenannten Zeitgeschehen mich ausgeschlossen habe, in der Hoffnung, wie ich heute denke, sagte Austerlitz, daß die Zeit nicht verging, nicht vergangen sei, daß ich hinter sie zurücklaufen könne, daß dort alles so wäre wie vordem oder, genauer gesagt, daß sämtliche Zeitmomente gleichzeitig nebeneinander existierten, beziehungsweise daß nichts von dem, was die Geschichte erzählt, wahr wäre, das Geschehene noch gar nicht geschehen ist, sondern eben erst geschieht, in dem Augenblick, in dem wir an es denken, was natürlich andererseits den trostlosen Prospekt eröffne eines immerwährenden Elends und einer niemals zu Ende gehenden Pein (*A* 151–152).[23]
>
> [A clock has always struck me as something ridiculous, a thoroughly mendacious object, perhaps because I have always resisted the power of time out of some internal compulsion which I myself have never understood, keeping myself apart from so-called current events in the hope, as I now think, said Austerlitz, that time will not pass away, has not passed away, that I can turn back and go behind it, and there I shall find everything as it once was, or more precisely I shall find that all moments of time have co-existed simultaneously, in which case none of what history tells us would be true, past events have not yet occurred but are waiting to do so at the moment when we think of them, although that, of course, opens up the bleak prospect of everlasting misery and neverending anguish (*AE* 101).]

Austerlitz cannot rationally explain his antagonistic relationship to time, his constant efforts to both resist the "Macht der Zeit" (*A* 152) ["power of time" (*AE* 101)] and to close himself off to the passing of time. He describes rather the way he is moved by an incomprehensible drive – "aus einem mir selber nie verständlichen inneren Antrieb heraus" (*A* 152) ["out of some internal compulsion which I myself have never understood" (*AE* 101)] – which marks a separation between the body and the mind. The absence of rational explanation and the presence of such alogical connections can both be located in the space between sensate perception and cognition, a space that can be bridged by imagination.

The implications of an ever present past in general and a continuously repeating event in particular is first exemplified in Austerlitz's description of his reaction to Lucas van Valckenborch's painting of the frozen Schelde river. Recalling this painted representation of the Schelde while simultaneously looking out

---

23 After this long discourse on time, given in the Greenwich observatory, and in light of Austerlitz's deep suspicion of time, it is ironic that the narrator asserts what time it is when they leave: "Es war gegen halb vier Uhr nachmittags" (*A* 152) ["It was around three-thirty in the afternoon" (*AE* 101)]. This marking of the time, a rather rare occurrence in *Austerlitz*, parallels the "gegen elf Uhr" (*A* 147) ["around eleven" (*AE* 98)], with which this passage began. Taken together, the two assertions of time mark the beginning and end of this passage on time.

at the actual river, Sebald emphasizes the inextricability of memory and imagination. Illustrating the effect of this painting on him and how it has become engrained in his memory, Austerlitz in fact does not need to see the painting in order to be moved by it: just the thought of the painting or the sight of the actual river evokes the following reaction:

> Wenn ich nun dort hinausschaue und an dieses Gemälde und seine winzigen Figuren denke, dann kommt es mir vor, als sei der von Lucas van Valckenborch dargestellte Augenblick niemals vergangen, als sei die kanariengelbe Dame gerade jetzt erst gestürzt oder in Ohnmacht gesunken, die schwarze Samthaube eben erst seitwärts von ihrem Kopf weggerollt, als geschähe das kleine, von den meisten Betrachtern gewiß übersehene Unglück immer wieder von neuem, als höre es nie mehr auf und als sei es durch nichts und von niemandem mehr gutzumachen (*A* 24).
>
> [Looking at the river now, thinking of that painting and its tiny figures, said Austerlitz, I feel as if the moment depicted by Lucas van Valckenborch had never come to an end, as if the canary-yellow lady had only just fallen over or swooned, as if the black velvet hood had only this moment dropped away from her head, as if the little accident, which no doubt goes unnoticed by most viewers, were always happening over and over again, and nothing and no one could ever remedy it (*AE* 13–14).]

In a similar scene, that brings together a mise-en-abyme of representations, Austerlitz and the narrator walk through Greenwich Park while discussing artistic renderings of the park, beginning first with paintings, then moving to engravings made after the paintings, and lastly memories of such representations. In a prolepsis that introduces us to his former history teacher André Hilary, Austerlitz recalls a panorama of Greenwich Park that he saw in one of the abandoned country houses that he visited with Hilary. This scene, like the description of Valckenborch's painting that captures the eternal repetition of an accident, does not necessarily bring the narrative forward but rather demonstrates the sense of "tableau" that is characteristic of Sebald's works. In this way, *Austerlitz* not only thematically discusses the co-presence of time but also structurally demonstrates this co-presence.

Eric Homberger describes Sebald as a "connoisseur of the isolation of an area which has been left largely untouched,"[24] and Austerlitz can be seen as the embodiment of this perspective, especially in his sense of isolation that turns into alienation when trying to write or when exploring the town of Terezín in an attempt to find traces of his mother's fate. Here, while trying to overcome the separation he feels from his lost mother Agáta, he only experiences an oppressive sense of isolation in the emptiness of the city that surrounds him. This isolation

---

24 Eric Homberger, "W. G. Sebald. German Writer Shaped by the 'Forgetfulness' of his Fellow Countrymen after the Second World War," *The Guardian* (December 17, 2001).

is reflected visually in the composition of ten photos – interspersed within the narrative – that dominate a span of twelve pages. Amidst this isolation, Austerlitz is confronted with the past he all along has been trying to avoid. In his wanderings throughout the city, he finds himself outside of the Ghetto Museum, which he had overlooked upon his arrival (*A* 285) [(*AE* 197)]. Inside the museum, Austerlitz is overwhelmed by the photographs and descriptions. He recounts to the narrator how he was "wie geblendet von den Dokumenten" (*A* 286) ["blinded by the documentation (*AE* 198)]. Although both mesmerizing and overwhelming, the historical information presented in the Ghetto Museum nevertheless provides a basis for Austerlitz's intense epiphany outside of the museum. He recounts what he read on one panel, "daß Mitte Dezember 1942, zu dem Zeitpunkt also, zu dem Agáta nach Terezín gekommen ist, in dem Ghetto, auf einer bebauten Grundfläche von höchstens einem Quadratkilometer, an die sechzigtausend Personen zusammengesperrt gewesen sind" (*A* 289) ["that in the middle of December 1942, and thus at the very time when Agáta came to Terezín, some sixty thousand people were shut up together in the ghetto, a built-up area of one square kilometer at the most" (*AE* 200)].[25] The idea of sixty thousand people imprisoned within the narrow confines of the ghetto stands in stark contrast to the deserted city center of Terezín, but this description enables us to better imagine Austerlitz's epiphany,

> wenig später […] schien es mir auf einmal mit der größten Deutlichkeit so, als wären sie nicht fortgebracht worden, sondern lebten, nach wie vor, dichtgedrängt in den Häusern, in den Souterrains und auf den Dachböden, als gingen sie pausenlos die Stiegen auf und ab, schauten bei den Fenstern heraus, bewegten sich in großer Zahl durch die Straßen und Gassen und erfüllten sogar in stummer Versammlung den gesamten, grau von dem feinen Regen schraffierten Raum der Luft (*A* 289).
>
> [and a little later, when I was out in the deserted town square again, it suddenly seemed to me, with the greatest clarity, that they had never been taken away after all, but were still living crammed into those buildings and basements and attics, as if they were incessantly going up and down the stairs, looking out of the windows, moving in vast numbers through the streets and alleys, and even, a silent assembly, filling the entire space occupied by the air, hatched with gray as it was by the fine rain (*AE* 200).]

In contrast to his feeling of blindness experienced in the Ghetto Museum, when Austerlitz is back in the empty streets of Terezín he imagines – in a momentary flash of clarity – that his mother and the others in the Theresienstadt ghetto were in fact not taken away but continue to occupy the spaces around him. Here we

---

25 Austerlitz will later refer back to this comment, creating one of the examples of the intratextual cross-referencing that occurs across the text.

see how the permeability or absence of borders between past and present makes it possible for Austerlitz and his mother to coexist in both time and space. In short, it is through imagination that the past remains ever present.

Drawing Parallels: Narrative Dis/Conjuncture and Intratextual Cross-References

The disjuncture between the chronology of the story (*histoire*) and the narrative progression (*discours*) is the main way in which *Austerlitz* does not follow the conventions of a traditional novel. Due to this narrative disjuncture, conventions such as foreshadowing are impeded, but connections can nevertheless be drawn across the text. One can delineate implicit parallels and explicit intratextual cross-references, which create a narrative conjuncture that inextricably binds the stories of the narrator and Austerlitz together. While this oscillation between disjuncture and conjuncture in the narrative creates a sense of uncertainty, images can serve a stabilizing function and both theories of memory and discussions of time – although ultimately questioned – provide frameworks in which to situate the experiences represented in the text.

When the narrator arrives at Austerlitz's home on Alderney Street, one of the rare instances in which their meeting is pre-arranged, he describes the sparsely furnished house: there are no curtains or carpets, the walls are painted a dark matte-gray, and the table is glazed a matte-gray as well. Visually echoing the shades of gray of the walls and furniture are the photographs the narrator observes lying on the table:

> Es waren Aufnahmen darunter, die ich, sozusagen, schon kannte,[26] Aufnahmen von leeren belgischen Landstrichen, von Bahnhöfen und Métroviadukten in Paris, vom Palmenhaus im Jardin des Plantes, von verschiedenen Nachtfaltern und Motten, von kunstvoll gebauten Taubenhäusern, von Gerald Fitzpatrick auf dem Flugfeld in der Nähe von Quy[27] und von einer Anzahl schwerer Türen und Tore[28] (*A* 175).

---

26 The narrator already "knows" several of these photographs for various reasons, namely because he was there while Austerlitz took the photographs or because he slowly has come to know Austerlitz's taste in photographic objects or because he has heard the stories "behind" the photographs. Likewise the readers will connect this reference to empty Belgian landscapes to the images inserted at the beginning of the text (*A* 34) [(*AE* 20)].

27 This serves as a delayed caption for the photograph (*A* 172) [(*AE* 116)].

28 Like the photographs of Paris train stations that will appear later in the text (*A* 410–411, 413) [(*AE* 290–291, 293)], similar images of doors and gateways are included in the passage on Theresienstadt (*A* 276–279) [(*AE* 190–193)], hence these comments by the narrator serve as verbal prolepses to a visual presence in the text.

[Some of the pictures were already familiar to me, so to speak: pictures of empty Belgian landscapes, stations and Métro viaducts in Paris, the palm house in the Jardin des Plantes, various moths and other night-flying insects, ornate dovecotes, Gerald Fitzpatrick on the airfield near Quy, and a number of heavy doors and gateways (*AE* 118–119).]

Austerlitz explains to the narrator that he moves the images around, like in a game of solitaire but more "in eine aus Familienähnlichkeiten sich ergebende Ordnung" (*A* 176) ["in an order depending on their family resemblances" (*AE* 119)]. The way in which Austerlitz orders his photographs presents a model for approaching the work itself: we are not to impose a pre-existing schema upon Sebald's text, but rather we should examine the possible connections and explore the potential for underlying yet mutable networks.

Besides the coincidental encounters between the narrator and Austerlitz that simultaneously defy reason and make the story possible, several coincidences of sensation, appearance, and place can also be observed. Plagued by persistent eye pain, the narrator visits an ophthalmologist in London, noting that he is Czech. He describes how overheated the doctor's waiting room is, which one may later recall when Austerlitz visits the State Archive in Prague. Tereza Ambrosová, the woman working at the archive, "eine blasse, beinahe transparente Frau" (*A* 214–215) ["a pale woman of almost transparent appearance" (*AE* 146)], who can in turn be connected to Austerlitz's later descriptions of other similarly transparent women, namely Věra and Otylie.[29] The doctor's technical assistant wears a white turban much like the one that characterizes the mysterious man sweeping the Liverpool Street Station, whom Austerlitz follows into the long-forgotten Ladies' Waiting Room in the key scene of the book. The scene in the ophthalmologist's office moreover directly precedes the fourth coincidental meeting between the narrator and Austerlitz, which is significant for the fact that this is when Austerlitz first begins to tell the story of how he came to search for his true identity and to trace his origins. Rather than viewing such connections as motifs, as certain scholars have done,[30] I would argue that they create a sense of order, unsystematic as it may be. Such coincidences forge a connection between Austerlitz and the narrator, and the reader is able to identify parallels between their stories.[31] Such

---

29 This recollection and repetition illustrates how memory collapses time, much in the way that Benjamin described, according to Sontag's reading of Benjamin cited above.

30 Eric L. Santner, for example, emphasizes the repeated "motifs" of desert scenes and ashes. Eric L. Santner, *On Creaturely Life. Rilke, Benjamin, Sebald* (Chicago and London: The University of Chicago Press, 2006).

31 In addition to coincidence, connections that are un/alogical seem to lead Austerlitz and the narrator through life; one thinks of the "Überblendung" (*A* 13) ["a curious confusion" (*AE* 6)] that the narrator experiences when he recalls either the Nocturama or the Antwerp Centraal Station.

connections create a text that is a cohesive whole yet contribute to the text's blurred chronology and the reader's sense of uncertainty.

These connections and parallels created through coincidence further contribute to the complex layering of Sebald's narratives outlined in chapter three. At the beginning of the text, the narrator recalls his various coincidental encounters with Austerlitz in Belgium during the late 1960s, which Austerlitz later referred to as their "Antwerpener Konversationen" (*A* 16) ["Antwerp conversations" (*AE* 8)]. Up until their third coincidental encounter, which occurs on the steps of the Palace of Justice in Brussels, the narrator is meticulous in describing the situations in which they meet, although his narration is often marked by a tension between specific details and a delay of information. After recounting this third coincidental encounter, the narrator formulates a general recollection of their subsequent meetings, briefly unsettling the reader and leaving one to wonder if the following meetings that are described are *all* of the times they met or just those that the narrator chooses to emphasize. In any case, the significance of those meetings that the narrator recounts becomes clear, such as the time he happens upon Austerlitz on the Zeebrugge promenade on a November afternoon. They walk together, hardly taking notice as they cross the border from Belgium into the Netherlands, then finding their way to the Billardcafé in Terneuzen, where they sit awaiting the departure of their ferry over the English Channel. It is on this night crossing – as if protected by the darkness or as if it were inappropriate to disclose anything personal in the bright light of day – and only in passing comments that the narrator and Austerlitz exchange certain personal details. Here the narrator explicitly states that they spoke in French since their first meetings in Antwerp, because neither knew of the other's background, nor was it possible to talk of oneself, "Da es mit Austerlitz so gut wie unmöglich war, von sich selber beziehungsweise über seine Person zu reden, und da also keiner vom anderen wußte, woher er stammte" (*A* 50) ["As it was almost impossible to talk to him about anything personal, and as neither one of us knew where the other came from" (*AE* 31)]. After crossing the political border from Belgium to the Netherlands and while in transit across another political and geographical border from the Netherlands to England over the Channel, the narrator and Austerlitz cross a metaphorical border to an increased level of personal intimacy, and they also cross a linguistic border from French to English. It is moreover through the narrator's description of their language use that Austerlitz's character develops

---

See Bettina Mosbach, "Superimposition as a Narrative Strategy in *Austerlitz*," *Searching for Sebald. Photography After W. G. Sebald*, ed. Lise Patt (Los Angeles: Institute for Cultural Inquiry and ICI Press, 2007) 390–411.

more depth and a personal dimension. The narrator recalls having been uncertain of his French, believing Austerlitz to be a native speaker, perhaps also basing this assumption on Austerlitz's name. When they switch to English – "das für mich praktikablere Englisch" ["English, in which I was better versed" (*AE* 32)] – a hidden insecurity in Austerlitz becomes apparent, manifesting itself "in gelegentlichen Stotteranfällen, bei denen er das abgewetzte Brillenfutteral, das er stets in seiner linken Hand hielt, so fest umklammerte, daß man das Weiße sehen konnte unter der Haut seiner Knöchel" (*A* 50) ["in a slight speech impediment and occasional fits of stammering, during which he clutched the worn spectacle case he always held in his left hand so tightly that you could see the white of his knuckles beneath the skin" (*AE* 32)]. The narrator's comment that English is "praktikabler" [more convenient] for him is not a full disclosure, however. Only later will it become clear that he is a native German. In addition to marking a new level of acquaintance between the narrator and Austerlitz, the ferry crossing over the Channel coincides with end of the first section of the book; this break is also marked graphically by an asterisk.[32] The next section begins with the narrator's recollections of his frequent encounters with Austerlitz at his workplace in Bloomsbury, not far from the British Museum. These meetings become more regular and occur over an unspecified period of time – "In den nachfolgenden Jahren" (*A* 51) ["in the years that followed" (*AE* 32)] – as the narrator simply states.

Once one knows the entire story of Austerlitz's search for his past, a dramatic irony arises in the aforementioned scene. In Terneuzen, Austerlitz is in fact not far from Hoek van Holland, from where he departed as part of the "Kindertransport" some thirty years earlier. It will be another thirty years before Austerlitz becomes aware of the geographical significance, consciously and purposely setting out to retrace the journey he made as a young boy. Interestingly, Austerlitz "arrives" in Hoek van Holland – in his thoughts, that is – even before he knows for a fact that he passed through there as a boy. Upon his first venture outside after having been in a state of paralysis, which was brought on by the anagnorisis of seeing himself as a boy in the Ladies' Waiting Room of the Liverpool Street Station, Austerlitz has a second revelation when he overhears voices on the radio recounting their journey from Vienna to Harwich via Hoek van Holland. The certainty of this recognition stands in contrast to the air of uncertainty that persists throughout the text. Austerlitz recalls how he knew, "*jenseits jeden Zweifels*, daß diese Erinnerungsbruchstücke auch in mein eigenes

---

32 There are a total of four section breaks marked by an asterisk in *Austerlitz* (*A* 50, 173, 362, 409).

Leben gehörten" (*A* 208, my emphasis) ["only then did I know *beyond any doubt* that these fragments of memory were part of my own life as well" (*AE* 141, my emphasis)]. So certain is he of his place on this trajectory that his response to the antique shop owner's concerned question, "Are you allright?" is that his thoughts were elsewhere, "in Hoek van Holland, as a matter of fact" (*A* 209) ["in the Hook of Holland as a matter of fact" (*AE* 142)].

Some of the details Austerlitz slowly reveals to the narrator include growing up in Wales with his adoptive parents the Elias' and his years in school at Stower Grange. The emotional connection Austerlitz feels to his adoptive parents is almost non-existent, which is underlined by their cold and ascetic home. The father, a preacher, as well as the mother reveal next to nothing about themselves to their son. The first and only comment that Austerlitz's adoptive father makes concerning his own background is of the drowned community of Llanwddyn.[33] The intensity with which Austerlitz sees this drowned community is not merely figurative, based in a young boy's imagination, but rather is an early indication of his sense of a permeable border between the worlds occupied by the living and the dead. Austerlitz's adoptive father Elias in fact chastises him for his wild imagination, thus Austerlitz seeks refuge with Evan, the village shoemaker who has a reputation of being a "Geisterseher" [visionary/seer of ghosts]. By contrasting Elias' and Evan's views of death and the dead, Austerlitz implicitly reveals the influence Evan had on this conceptualization of the permeable border between, coexistence even, of the living and the dead, which further relates to the temporal coexistence of the present and the past.[34] According to Evan, "mehr als ein solches Seidentuch trenne uns nicht von der nächsten

---

33 After the flood in the fall of 1888, Elias' father's house among the other buildings and properties of the community of Llanwddyn now lie at the bottom of the Vyrnwy reservoir (*A* 78) [(*AE* 51)]. "In diesem einen Augenblick auf der Staumauer von Vyrnwy, in dem er, aus Vorsatz oder aus Unachtsamkeit, mich hineinsehen ließ in das Innere seiner Predigerbrust, fühlte ich so sehr mit ihm, daß er, der Gerechte, mir wie der einzige Überlebende der Flutkatastrophe von Llanwddyn erschien, während ich die anderen alle, seine Eltern, seine Geschwister, seine Anverwandten, die Nachbarsleute und die übrigen Dorfbewohner, drunten in der Tiefe noch wähnte, wo sie weiterhin in ihren Häusern saßen und auf der Gasse herumgingen, aber ohne sprechen zu können und mit viel zu weit offenen Augen" (*A* 79–80) ["At this one moment on the Vyrnwy dam when, intentionally or unintentionally, he allowed me a glimpse into his clerical heart, I felt for him so much that he, the righteous man, seemed to me like the only survivor of the deluge which had destroyed Llanwddyn, while I imagined all the others – his parents, his brothers and sisters, his relations, their neighbors, all the other villagers – still down in the depths, sitting in their houses and walking along the road, but unable to speak and with their eyes opened far too wide" (*AE* 51–52)].

34 While Elias connects sickness and death with being tested, just punishment, and guilt, Evan tells of the dead, "die das Los zur Unzeit getroffen hat," (*A* 82) ["who had been struck down by

Welt" (*A* 84) ["nothing but a piece of silk like that separates us from the next world" (*AE* 54)], and one just needs an eye for the dead. At first glance, they appear like normal people, "aber wenn man sie genauer anschaute, verwischten sich ihre Gesichter oder flackerten ein wenig an den Rändern" (*A* 83) ["but when you looked more closely their faces would blur or flicker slightly at the edges" (*AE* 54)]. They are also a bit smaller than they were during their lifetime, "denn die Erfahrung des Todes, behauptete Evan, verkürzt uns [...]" (*A* 83) ["for the experience of death, said Evan, diminishes us, just as a piece of linen shrinks when you first wash it" (*AE* 54)]. Austerlitz's imagination of the Llanwddyn residents' sub-aquatic existence is intensified all the more through the photographs contained in an album that Elias shows him. The visual power of this album as it is ingrained in Austerlitz's memory relates to the idea of traumatic repetition illustrated by the van Valckenborch painting, insofar as the drowned are present every time Austerlitz thinks of them. Austerlitz later obtains these few photographs along with Elias' Calvinist calendar in a situation that parallels how the narrator came into possession of Austerlitz's photographs (*A* 15) [(*AE* 7)], formulated in a narrative gesture that explains the provenance of the images and their inclusion in the text.[35] The intensity with which Austerlitz regards the photographs combined with his imagination result in a contact and an intimacy that transcends the borders of time and space. He feels as if he were living with them at the bottom of the lake,[36] and he imagines sharing this sub-aquatic existence with the drowned while at the same time sharing the space above water, seeing the drowned move on the street or in the field. Later in the text when Austerlitz muses on how little we know about the return of the past,

---

fate untimely" (*AE* 54)], and how, feeling cheated that fate took them too soon, they try to return to life (*A* 83) [(*AE* 54)].

35 "diese paar wenigen Photographien, die später zusammen mit dem calvinistischen Kalender in meinen Besitz gekommen sind [...]" (*A* 80–81) ["these few photographs, which came into my own possession only much later along with the Calvinist calendar" (*AE* 52)]. The Calvinist calendar is mentioned previously (*A* 73–74) [(*AE* 47)].

36 "Nachts vor dem Einschlafen in meinem kalten Zimmer war es mir oft, als sei auch ich untergegangen in dem dunklen Wasser, als müßte ich, nicht anders als die armen Seelen von Vyrnwy, die Augen weit offen halten, um hoch über mir einen schwachen Lichtschein zu sehen und das von den Wellen gebrochene Spiegelbild des steinernen Turms, der so furchterregend für sich allein an dem bewaldeten Ufer steht" (*A* 82) ["At night, before I fell asleep in my cold room, I often felt as if I too had been submerged in that dark water, and like the poor souls of Vyrnwy must keep my eyes wide open to catch a faint glimmer of light far above me, and see the reflection, broken by ripples, of the stone tower standing in such fearsome isolation on the wooded bank" (*AE* 52–53)].

he offers the complementary perspective to these sensations and suppositions he had as a boy:

> je länger ich es bedenke, desto mehr kommt mir vor, daß wir, die wir uns noch am Leben befinden, in den Augen der Toten irreale und nur manchmal, unter bestimmten Lichtverhältnissen und atmosphärischen Bedingungen sichtbar werdende Wesen sind (*A* 269).
>
> [the longer I think about it the more it seems to me that we who are still alive are unreal in the eyes of the dead, that only occasionally, in certain lights and atmospheric conditions, do we appear in their field of vision (*AE* 185).]

Reading Balzac's *Le Colonel Chabert* "reinforces" (*AE* 283) the suspicion he has long entertained, "daß die Grenze zwischen dem Tod und dem Leben durchlässiger ist, als wir gemeinhin glauben" (*A* 401) ["that the border between life and death is less impermeable than we commonly think" (*AE* 283)].[37]

Intratextual cross-referencing can be both explicit – such as Austerlitz referring back to a previous comment, "wie ich schon gesagt habe" (*A* 143) ["as I mentioned before" (*AE* 95)] – and implicit – such as when Austerlitz makes connections or analogies based on previous stories. One finds an example of such implicit cross-referencing when Austerlitz likens Toby, the dog at Andromeda Lodge, to the dog held by the little girl of Vyrnwy, whose photograph so deeply impressed him (*A* 144 [*AE* 96], photograph *A* 81 [*AE* 53]). In a scene that reinforces coexistence across time – the simultaneity of past, present, and future – Austerlitz imagines the presence of those imprisoned in the Theresienstadt ghetto; he first imagined this when visiting Terezín and later recalls this scene to the narrator with the explicit intratextual cross-reference: "wie ich wohl schon einmal sagte, sagte Austerlitz" (*A* 339) ["as I think I have mentioned before" (*AE* 236)].[38] Based on Sebald's handwritten manuscript, one could conjecture that the explicit intratextual cross-references were not part of the original conception of the text. It appears as if Sebald, while rereading and revising his manuscript, discovers his own implicit cross-

---

37 Ruth Vogel-Klein has elucidated the Balzac passage above and focused on the French intertexts of Sebald's works. See her articles: "Rückkehr und Gegen-Zeitigkeit. Totengedenken bei W.G. Sebald," *Mémoire. Transferts. Images./Erinnerung. Übertragungen. Bilder*, ed. Ruth Vogel-Klein, *Recherches germaniques* Hors Série 2 (2005) 99–115, in particular 111–115. See also Ruth Vogel-Klein, "Französische Intertexte in W.G. Sebalds *Austerlitz*," *W.G. Sebald. Intertextualität und Topographie*, eds. Irene Heidelberger-Leonard and Mireille Tabah (Berlin: LIT Verlag, 2008) 73–92.

38 This reference is inserted in the longest sentence in the book, where Austerlitz recounts his reading of H.G. Adler's historical, sociological, and psychological account of Theresienstadt. For further connections between Sebald and H.G. Adler, see Lynn L. Wolff, "H.G. Adler and W.G. Sebald: From History and Literature to Literary Historiography," Special Issue: H.G. Adler, eds. Rüdiger Görner and Klaus L. Berghahn, *Monatshefte* 103.2 (2011) 257–275.

referencing and then decides to insert direct cross-references to make such connections explicit.[39]

Intratextual connections, if not necessarily implicit or explicit cross-references, are found throughout the book. For example, in the lengthy description Austerlitz provides of his plans for "bau- und zivilisationsgeschichtlichen Untersuchungen" (*A* 178) ["investigations into the history of architecture and civilization" (*AE* 120)], he names some of the themes he considered including, such as: "Hygiene und Assanierung, Architektur des Strafvollzugs, profane Tempelbauten, Wasserheilkunst, zoologische Gärten, Abreise und Ankunft, Licht und Schatten, Dampf und Gas und ähnliches mehr" (*A* 178) ["hygiene and sanitation, the architecture of the penal system, secular temples, hydrotherapy, zoological gardens, departure and arrival, light and shade, steam and gas, and so forth" (*AE* 121)]. These themes are in fact present over the course of the entire book, written into scenes such as those at the Breendonk Fortress and the Palace of Justice in Brussels ["Architektur des Strafvollzugs"/"architecture of the penal system"], the Great Eastern Hotel ["profane Tempelbauten"/"secular temples"], Marienbad ["Wasserheilkunst"/"hydrotherapy"], the Nocturama and the Jardin des Plantes ["zoologische Gärten"/"zoological gardens"], or in the constant description of light and shadow ["Licht und Schatten"/"light and shade"], as well as the importance of travel ["Abreise und Ankunft"/"departure and arrival"], train travel especially ["Dampf"/"steam"]. Recalling the structure of the text – the narrator is recounting what Austerlitz has told him – the above instances of intratextual connections and cross-references are ultimately put in place by the narrator, and, of course, structured in this way by the author himself.

Revealing Changes: Additions and Subtractions in the *Austerlitz* Manuscript

When comparing Sebald's handwritten manuscript to the published version of *Austerlitz*, one can observe the following types of changes: name changes, experimentation with word choice, the insertion of additional information that aids the reader, and the omission of details in order to obscure the chronology of the text. While names (*signifiers*) may change or even be exchanged among characters, the characters (*signified*) themselves essentially remain the same. One sees Sebald experimenting with a certain set of names for the significant female figures in

---

39 In the handwritten manuscript, one finds that the remark "wie ich sagte" was perhaps an afterthought, since it was obviously inserted at a later time of writing. A: Sebald, DLA Marbach.

Austerlitz's life, such as his birth mother Agáta (Sophia, Adela, Auralia, Alma, Amalia), his adoptive mother Gwendolyn (Grace), and Gerald's mother Adela (Adelaïde, Frances, Sophia), who in a way is a second adoptive mother to Austerlitz.[40] The change in Austerlitz's female companion from an Italian woman named Alma Martini (who at a point is also referred to as Cecilia), to a French woman named Marie de Verneuil has wider repercussions on the story beyond a simple name change, that is, significant portions of the text are then cut out and aspects of the visit to Marienbad are altered. Other name changes include: Tereza Ambrosová, the woman who helps Austerlitz at the State Archive in Prague, is first referred to as Eliša Ambrožova [unnumbered manuscript pages between numbered manuscript pages M 291–292]; Stela Ryžanová becomes Věra Ryšanová [M 302]; and Emilie Cerf becomes Amélie Cerf [unnumbered manuscript page]. The shoemaker Evan is at times also referred to as Hughie, and the name of the neighbor Saly Bleyberg is changed to Saly Horowitz in the manuscript [M 334]. Like these shifting names in the handwritten manuscript, one can also trace Sebald's experimentation with certain formulations, most significantly with how to linguistically express one's relationship to the past, more precisely how to express the recollection of memories.[41] The passage that includes André Hilary's lesson on the Battle of Austerlitz is particularly revealing of Sebald's various attempts at finding the right formulation for Austerlitz's memory of this scene. In the manuscript Sebald crosses out the following formulations – "~~daß mir dann~~"; "~~so weiß   so weiß ich~~"; "~~so verstehe ich~~"; "~~dann scheint mir~~"; "~~dann kommt mir auch wieder~~" – before arriving at "dann erinnere ich mich auch." One finds both additions and omissions that could be seen as aiding the reader, such as the reduction of complicated and lengthy adjectival constructions. The narrator's side comments, such as "sagte Austerlitz" ["said Austerlitz"] in effect help the reader identify the narrative voice. Such indicators actually appear more often in the printed text than in the manuscript, and one finds multiple instances of this later insertion in the manuscript.[42]

Most interesting, however, are the changes that further challenge the reader, such as the reduction of specificity, be it through explicit omissions of details or altered expressions of time. While one may be able to quantify the encounters (between the narrator and Austerlitz or between Austerlitz and Věra) based on the handwritten manuscript, such details are eliminated in the printed text. The same

---

40 References to the handwritten manuscript will henceforth be cited as "M" with the page number. A: Sebald, DLA Marbach.

41 A: Sebald, DLA Marbach.

42 A: Sebald, DLA Marbach. (M 81, 144, 444, 445, 451, etc., and on unnumbered manuscript pages).

is true for the specification of the year, the time of year, or the time of day, most of which are omitted in the printed text.[43] Sebald reduces specificity by explicitly cutting out the indication of time and place: "Dergleichen apokryphe Geschichten erzählte mir Austerlitz mit besonderer Vorliebe, auch bei unseren späteren – ~~sechs oder sieben, glaube ich, sind es gewesen~~ – belgischen Begegnungen, von denen ich mit einiger Zuverlässigkeit nur noch erinnere" (M 60); "& wieder zurückzugehen ~~nach Norwich~~ / auf die Insel" (M 67) [Bell's English translation counteracts this by making explicit "the United Kingdom" (AE 34).]. Further comparisons between the manuscript and the printed text reveal the following alterations and eliminations, which also reduce specificity: "erst viel später, [ich glaube] bei einem anderen russischen Schriftsteller [sagte Aust]..." (M 125–127) versus "später in einem anderen Buch" (A 95) ["only much later and in another book" (AE 63)]; "an diesem 11. April 1993" (M 417) versus "an diesem fahlen Aprilmorgen" (A 319) ["on this pallid April morning" (AE 221)]; "Maimorgen [...] wo wir denn gewiß vier oder fünf Stunden" (unnumbered manuscript page) versus "Morgen [...] wo wir dann lange" (A 373) ["where we sat for a long time" (AE 262)]. Sebald further reduces specificity by changing the expression of time: "genau wie im Ausgang des 18. Jahrhunderts" (M 208) versus "genau so, wie es vor hundertfünfzig Jahren" (A 157) ["exactly as it must have been a hundred and fifty years before" (AE 105)]; "in den Jahren zwischen 1943 & 1945" (unnumbered manuscript page) versus "in den Jahren ab 1942" (A 408) ["in the years from 1942" (AE 288)]; and crossing out "dritten" and writing in "vorläufig letzten Besuch" (M 389/390). Sebald also eliminates the source of the poem Austerlitz thinks to himself in the ophthalmologist's waiting room: "eine Zeile durch den Kopf von Stephen Watts, der, seit er zurückgekehrt ist in die Hauptstadt aus seinem mehrjährigen Exil auf der Ha{llig} Kiss, in Shadwell, nahe dem Ufer des Themse lebt & dessen Verse für mich zu den sch{önen} & genauesten zählen, die ich kenne" (M 75); and an explicit statement about the photographs of the doors and gateways in Terezín in the handwritten manuscript is not included in the printed text.[44]

Besides the reduction of specificity, there are frequent cases of deliberate vagueness in the narration. After leaving the Greenwich Observatory, in which Austerlitz gives his disquisition on time, he and the narrator stand outside for a "gewisse Zeitlang" (A 152) ["for a while" (AE 102)]. The narrator's auditory and visual senses seem to become dull as dusk falls around them. This is reflected

---

43 The following examples of the reduction of specificity between handwritten manuscript and printed text are taken from the *Austerlitz* manuscript, A: Sebald, DLA Marbach. Sebald's strikethroughs are reproduced here; and his insertions are reproduced in square brackets.
44 Cf. M 370 with A 276/280.

in a degree of vagueness in his descriptions of what they hear and intensified in his further resistance to make direct references to objects that he could identify.

> Man hörte in der Ferne das dumpfe Mahlen der Stadt und in der Höhe das Dröhnen der großen Maschinen, die in Abständen von kaum mehr als einer Minute sehr niedrig und unglaublich langsam, wie es mir erschien, aus dem Nordosten über Greenwich hereinschwebten und westwärts nach Heathrow hinaus wieder verschwanden (*A* 152).
>
> [Far away, we could hear the hollow grinding of the city, and the air was full of the drone of the great planes flying low and as it seemed to me incredibly slowly over Greenwich from the northeast, at intervals of scarcely more than a minute, and then disappearing again westwards towards Heathrow (*AE* 102).][45]

The narrator emphasizes his own subjective perception of time – "wie es mir erschien" ["as it seemed to me"] – further unsettling the reader by employing a curious simile to anthropomorphize the planes, "Wie fremde Ungetüme, die abends zu ihren Schlafplätzen heimkehren, hingen sie mit starr von ihren Leibern abstehenden Flügeln über uns in der dunkler werdenden Luft" (*A* 152–153) ["Like strange monsters going home to their dens to sleep in the evening, they hovered above us in the darkening air, rigid wings extended from their bodies" (*AE* 102)].

The most significant difference between the manuscript and the printed book lies in what can be broadly termed the text's chronology, referring to both the chronology of the *histoire* and the sequence of the *discours*. Changes have been made in the sequence of events and the places in which parts of the story are told. Moreover, Sebald systematically erases chronological traces, that is, he eliminates markers that specify time and duration from the final version of the text. *Austerlitz* ends more or less where it began, at the Breendonk Fortress, but this time the narrator does not enter the fortress, choosing rather to sit just outside of it. The original numbering and handwriting of the manuscript lead one to surmise that this final scene was written at an early stage in the text's genesis. It appears to be a continuation of the beginning of *Austerlitz* in which the narrator recounts Claude Simon's account of "die fragmentarische Lebensgeschichte" (*A* 42) ["the fragmentary tale" (*AE* 26)] of the Italian painter Gastone Novelli in his novel *Le Jardin des Plantes*.[46] In what becomes the final scene of the book, the narrator sits at the

---

45 Bell's translation makes both the planes and the sound their flying more explicit, as compared with Sebald's vague descriptions of machines that float in.

46 One can also discern different stages of the text based on the different paper and pen used as well as differences in Sebald's handwriting. In general, one can conjecture that Sebald's handwritten manuscripts represent an already advanced stage of conceptualization and formulation. Of his writing process that incorporates documentary material, Sebald states in an interview with Sven Boedecker from 1993, "Der Vorgang ist eine ziemlich komplizierte Destillationsarbeit

Fortress of Breendonk in Belgium, reading from Dan Jacobson's memoir *Heshel's Kingdom*,[47] a book that Austerlitz gave to the narrator before they part ways for the last time.[48] While the narrator does not name the title of the book until the very last sentence, he repeatedly cites the author's name and reports from his reading in a form of directed speech that echoes the way he reports what Austerlitz recounted to him during their meetings.[49] Jacobson's memoir details his search for traces of his relatives, a search which leads him to find "überall nur die Zeichen der Vernichtung" (*A* 420) ["only signs everywhere of the annihilation" (*AE* 297)]. The inactive diamond mine of Kimberley, South Africa serves as Jacobson's metaphor for the chasm between life and death: ["auf der einen Seite das selbstverständliche Leben, auf der anderen sein unausdenkbares Gegenteil" (*A* 420)] ["only this dividing line, with ordinary life on one side and its unimaginable opposite on the other" (*AE* 297)]. In the final scene of *Austerlitz*, the narrator's physical position vis-à-vis the fortress parallels what he reads in Jacobson's memoir: In choosing not to physically reenter the fortress, but by reading Jacobson's book, the narrator of *Austerlitz* both insists on this insurmountable threshold between life and death while also finding a way to traverse it, to dissolve the barrier to the past.

In a complex operation, the simultaneously mediated and immediate experience of reading, we find a way to cross over this insurmountable gap. Jacobson's memoir provides a detailed account of the ring of fortresses built by the Russians around the city of Kaunas, Lithuania at the end of the nineteenth century.[50] Jacobson reports that all of these fortresses proved to be useless to the Russians, but some fell into German hands in 1941, including Fort IX, where more than 30,000 died during a period of three years.[51] The narrator of *Austerlitz* recounts, "Bis in den

---

gewesen: Ich brauche ungefähr zwanzig Seiten, um eine herauszuarbeiten" (*G* 108) [The process was a rather complicated work of distillation: I need about twenty pages in order to arrive at one].

47 See Dan Jacobson, *Heshel's Kingdom* (London, New York: Penguin, 1999).

48 Uwe Schütte points to the actual impossibility of this, since Jacobson's book was first published in 1998, whereas *Austerlitz* and the narrator last meet in 1997. Cf. Uwe Schütte, *W. G. Sebald. Einführung in Leben und Werk* (Göttingen: Vandenhoeck & Ruprecht, 2011) 218, footnote 28.

49 The narrator reports, "schreibt Jacobson" (*A* 420) ["Jacobson writes" (*AE* 297)], "ist Jacobsons Bild" (*A* 420) ["was Jacobson's image" (*AE* 297)], "findet Jacobson" (*A* 420) ["Jacobson finds" (*AE* 297)], "berichtet Jacobson" (*A* 420) ["Jacobson tells us" (*AE* 297)]; "schreibt Jacobson" (*A* 420) ["writes Jacobson" (*AE* 298)], "so Jacobson" (*A* 420) ["says Jacobson" (*AE* 298)], "schreibt Jacobson" (*A* 421) ["writes Jacobson" (*AE* 298)].

50 Kaunas is also, incidentally, the city where the parents of Peter Jordan were executed. See Honickel's documentary, *W. G. Sebald. Der Ausgewanderte* as well as Dörte Franke's documentary *Stolperstein*.

51 Sebald's account reproduces parts of Jacobson's text almost verbatim (in German translation of course) (*A* 418–421). "[The Germans] used the forts as headquarters, torture chambers and

Mai 1944 hinein, als der Krieg längst verloren war, kamen Transporte aus dem Westen nach Kaunas. Die letzten Nachrichten der in die Verliese der Festung Gesperrten bezeugen es" (*A* 421) ["Transports from the west kept coming to Kaunas until May 1944, when the war had long since been lost, as the last messages from those locked in the dungeons of the fortress bear witness" (*AE* 298)]. The narrator lists some of these last traces and testaments written on the walls of the fort, based on Jacobson's text, but Sebald inscribes a biographical emphasis by choosing to end his account with the name "Max Stern, Paris, 18.5.44"[52] (*A* 421) ["Max Stern, Paris, 18.5.44" (*AE* 298)].[53] Sebald in a sense finds "himself" in the "Max Stern 18.5.44" of Jacobson's book. The distance between the past and the present is collapsed, as Sebald reads the coincidence of his birth and the death of the individual indicated by the name inscribed in the wall, which has in turn been reinscribed in Jacobson's book and reinscribed again in the last lines of *Austerlitz*. In this way, we find the redemptive potential of literature or what Sebald sees as literature's attempt at restitution: the possibilities to draw connections across time and space and the possibilities to rewrite memoirs as literature in order to ultimately keep writing history and to keep witnessing to the past.

That Sebald chooses to end his text with this scene makes us consider the following points. It offers a conclusion to the story without a complete resolution. More broadly, one can read this last scene at the Breendonk Fortress as the text's major statement: not only of its attempt at restitution but also of the challenges that face such attempts in the first place. The challenge of representing the Holocaust is central to Sebald's works, but it is not his sole concern. Rather the broader challenge of representing another individual's life and the respectful commemoration of the victims of history without drifting into illegitimate identification. Inextricable from these questions is also Sebald's interest in his particular subject position in relation to the atrocities of the twentieth century, having been born at the end of World War II and raised in relative innocence. We can read the closing passage as a statement about the insurmountable distance between life

---

places of mass slaughter. Of the three, Fort IX had the most horrific reputation – which is to say only that more innocent people, the overwhelming majority of them Jews, were killed there than at the other sites in and near the city." One striking omission is that Sebald leaves out "the overwhelming majority of Jews." Jacobson, *Heshel's Kingdom*, 159.

52 Sebald was known to his friends and colleagues in England as "Max" and his date of birth was May 18, 1944.

53 Jacobson's list reads: "'Nous sommes neuf cents Français,' one of them had cut into the plaster, anonymously enough. Also, among many others, were 'Lob, Marcel, Mai 1944'; 'Wechsler, Abram, de Limoges – Paris, 18.5.44'; 'Max Stern, Paris, 18.5.44'; 'Herskovits L'Anvers de Monaco via Drancy Paris, Kaunas.'" Jacobson, *Heshel's Kingdom*, 161.

and death, between the present and the past, and the double necessity of attempting to bridge the gap and also respecting this distance. Faced with the challenge of representing another's life, the only thing one is left with in this case is the inward glance, the representation of oneself, however fraught this endeavor may also be. In this way, Sebald's works remain located between genres: between biography and autobiography and between historiography and literature.

Uncovering the Past: Restitution through Literary Archaeology

"So also kehren sie wieder, die Toten" (*DA* 36). ["And so they are ever returning to us, the dead" (*E* 23).] This is perhaps one of the most oft-cited passages of Sebald's works. In its brevity, this sentence from *Die Ausgewanderten* both embodies a poetic gravitas and encapsulates a complicated physical and metaphysical worldview developed across Sebald's œuvre that easily finds connections in the extra-literary world. A collection of sculptures that were put on display by the Nazis as examples of "degenerate art" were unearthed in Berlin, revealing how the past is indeed ever returning.[54] This archaeological and art historical discovery was made while digging out a new path for Berlin's underground rail, further demonstrating how life sometimes imitates art. In *Austerlitz*, two significant and explicit instances of the architectural erasure of history occur close to train stations: the Liverpool Street Station in London and the Gare d'Austerlitz in Paris. By chance, Austerlitz discovers that the Liverpool Street Station was built over Bedlam, a hospital for the insane. Prior to this knowledge, however, Austerlitz recalls feeling "dieses andauernde Ziehen in mir, eine Art Herzweh, das, wie ich zu ahnen begann, verursacht wurde von dem Sog der verflossenen Zeit" (*A* 190) ["that constant wrenching inside me, a kind of heartache which, as I was beginning to sense, was caused by the vortex of past time" (*AE* 129)]. After learning of the history buried below the station, Austerlitz attempts, obsessively, to imagine the structure and the people that occupied the asylum, and wonders

> ob das Leid und die Schmerzen, die sich dort über die Jahrhunderte angesammelt haben, je wirklich vergangen sind, ob wir sie nicht heute noch, wie ich bisweilen an einem kalten Zug um die Stirn zu spüren glaubte, auf unseren Wegen durch die Hallen und über die Treppen durchqueren (*A* 191).
>
> [whether the pain and suffering accumulated on this site over the centuries had ever really ebbed away, or whether they might not still, as I sometimes thought when I felt a cold breath of air on my forehead, be sensed as we passed through them (*AE* 129–130).]

---

54 Cf. Michael Kimmelman, "Art Survivors of Hitler's War," *The New York Times* (December 1, 2010) A1.

The surface of the Liverpool Street Station, had it not been dug up during construction, would not have revealed what was below. In spite of such covering up of the past that is part of the inevitable "natural" development of a city, Austerlitz himself embodies the continued presence of the past through his physical sensations.

Similar to the Liverpool Street Station, the construction of the new Bibliothè-que nationale in Paris has covered up a part of history,[55] but in this case it is a history that is very close to Austerlitz's own personal past. Significantly, it is not through archaeological digging that this past is revealed, but rather through individual memory. In his discussions with Henri Lemoine, Austerlitz learns that the site on which the new national library was built served as a collection point for the confiscated possessions of the deported Jews of Paris. The scene in which Lemoine recounts this history to Austerlitz also demonstrates the impressive effect of Sebald's masterful use of understatement. Lemoine describes all those who took part in the emptying of some 40,000 apartments, "ein Heer von nicht weniger als fünfzehnhundert Packarbeitern" (*A* 407) ["an army of no fewer than 1500 removal men" (*AE* 288)] were involved in the "bis ins letzte durchorganisier-ten Enteignungs- und Weiterverwertungsprogramm" (*A* 407) ["highly organized program of expropriation and reutilization" (*AE* 288)], such as "die Finanz- und Steuerbehörden, die Einwohner- und Katasterämter, die Banken und Versiche-rungsagenturen, die Polizei, die Transportfirmen, die Hauseigentümer und Haus-besorger" (*A* 407) ["the financial and fiscal authorities, the residents' and prop-erty registries, the banks and insurance agencies, the police, the transport firms, the landlords and caretakers of the apartment buildings" (*AE* 288)] and those who appraised the possessions, "Mehr als fünfhundert Kunsthistoriker, Antiquitäten-händler, Restaurateure, Tischler, Uhrmacher, Kürschner und Couturièren [...] die bewacht wurden von einem Kontingent Soldaten aus Hinterindien" (*A* 408) ["over five hundred art historians, antique dealers, restorers, joiners, clockmakers, furriers, and couturiers," all "guarded by a contingent of Indochinese soldiers" (*AE* 289)]. In this series of involved parties, the often-voiced claim "no one knew," though not explicitly stated, echoes in the bitter reproach stated by Lemoine: they "hätten zweifellos gewußt" (*A* 407) ["must undoubtedly have known" (*AE* 288)]. This then becomes exactly where individual memory is needed – as opposed to the artificial, institutional memory created and preserved by such a construction

---

55 For a meticulous and illuminating discussion of this passage, see James L. Cowan, "Sebald's *Austerlitz* and the Great Library. A Documentary Study," *W.G. Sebald. Schreiben ex patria/ Expatriate Writing*, ed. Gerhard Fischer (Amsterdam; New York: Rodopi, 2009) 193–212; James L. Cowan, "Sebald's *Austerlitz* and the Great Library. History, Fiction, Memory. Parts I and II," *Monatshefte* 102.1 (2010) 51–81 and 102.2 (2010) 192–207.

as the Bibliothèque nationale – for it is absolutely essential in preserving the knowledge of this past when all physical traces have been erased. Without individual memory, the history of the site on which the Bibliothèque nationale was built would remain literally buried.

This climactic scene induces a sense of vertigo through the contrast between the high place of narration, from the eighteenth floor of the southeast tower with a sprawling view of Paris, and the depth of the invisible history, buried under the immediate area around the library. The insertion of a photograph, taken apparently from inside one of the library's four towers, presumably from the eighteenth floor, where Austerlitz and Lemoine stand, adds a further layer to consider. The photograph as a two-dimensional image reminds us of the surface of 'reality,' or the architectural landscape that reveals nothing of the past. Sebald's characters are frustrated again and again in their search for historical truth or personal memory as they view photograph after photograph or read and study various sorts of historical documentation. The photograph of the new Bibliothèque natio-nale, inserted within the text just prior to Lemoine's account of this buried history, creates a mise-en-abyme of this problem: the photograph, as a surface that reveals nothing of 'reality,' parallels the surface of the city that reveals nothing of the past.[56] It is Lemoine's narration that reveals what lies underneath the surface of the city. His account reveals the history that architecture has covered up, a history that would remain hidden and invisible without personal memory and without the continued efforts to preserve this past within collective memory. The insertion of a photograph mirrors this invisibility, adding yet an-other surface that hides the past, while simultaneously providing a deceptive 'reflection' of reality. To reiterate what was established in the previous chapter, *Austerlitz* is a text working against an understanding of mimesis as imitation and direct reflection insofar as images indicate precisely this need for narration.

In repeatedly pointing to the architectural erasure of history and subse-quently memory, it is of course ironic that architectural history should serve Austerlitz as a "ersatzweises, kompensatorisches Gedächtnis" (A 206) ["substitute or compensatory memory" (*AE* 140)]. Furthermore one could also conceive of architectural reconstruction as a form of historical fiction.[57] Whereas architecture covers up even in its attempts to reconstruct, in literature a multi-layering of time and space is possible. *Austerlitz* presents a harsh critique of the architectural

---

56 See previous discussion of Brecht in chapter three.

57 The debate around reconstruction, of the Dresden Frauenkirche for example, raises questions of authenticity and fiction in architectural terms. See for example Peter Bürger, "Die Echtheit der alten Steine. Deutschland streitet über den Wiederaufbau historischer Gebäude," *Neue Zürcher Zeitung* (January 7, 2009) 25.

erasure of history, implicitly affirming the strength of the literary discourse to reveal multiple layers of time and space simultaneously. This difference lies not only on the level of content or form – what differentiates the poet from the historian, according to Aristotle, is not that one writes in verse and the other in prose, or that literature shows *what could be* while historiography recounts *what was* – but more significantly in the way in which literature is produced. This emphasis on the process of creation recalls Hans Blumenberg's distinction – an adaptation and transformation of Spinoza – between nature as a product (*natura naturata*) and nature as a producing principle (*natura naturans*), which can be extended to our understanding of art as reflection of the external world within the artform versus art as creation.[58]

In Sebald's attempts to forge a new form of historiography, he explores other forms of representation from the natural world. Hence the repeated emphasis on evolution, geology, and archaeology, all of which are in a way outside of human control and can therefore stand in contrast to official forms of historiography. Evolution represents a development in time that is beyond what one person can experience in his lifetime or even what an entire genera- tion can experience. The slow and natural process of evolution encompasses not only the development of human or animal species but also the natural world and as far as the cosmos can reach. Sebald transfers this form of evolutionary development to architectural structures, describing buildings and entire cityscapes as if they too were examples of this natural phenomenon of evolution. He writes at the end of *Austerlitz*,

> Manchmal, sagte Lemoine, sagte Austerlitz, sei es ihm, als spüre er hier heroben die Strömung der Zeit um seine Schläfen und seine Stirn, doch wahrscheinlich, setzte er hinzu, ist das nur ein Reflex des Bewußtseins, das sich im Laufe der Jahre in meinem Kopf ausgebildet hat von den verschiedenen Schichten, die dort drunten auf dem Grund der Stadt übereinandergewachsen sind (*A* 406–407).
>
> [Sometimes, so Lemoine told me, said Austerlitz, he felt the current of time streaming round his temples and brow when he was up here, but perhaps he added, that is only a reflex of the awareness formed in my mind over the years of the various layers which have been superimposed on each other to form the carapace of the city (*AE* 287–288).]

The way in which Sebald describes cities and urban structures in natural terms, as if they were the result of natural outgrowths and overgrowths or as if they continue to develop beyond human control even after the initial human interven-

---

58 Hans Blumenberg, "'Nachahmung der Natur.' Zur Vorgeschichte der Idee des schöpferischen Menschen," *Wirklichkeiten in denen wir leben. Aufsätze und eine Rede* (Stuttgart: Reclam, 1993) 55–103, here 55.

tion, corresponds to his search for alternative forms of representing both the past and the presence of the past.

Sebald's texts reveal that cruelty has not been controlled or tamed through culture and that destruction remains a constant over time. Therefore it is not surprising that he marked the following passage in a volume of Elias Canetti's writings,

> Ich gäbe viel darum, wenn ich mir die historische Betrachtung der Welt wieder abgewöhnen könnte. Erbärmlich ist diese Abteilung nach Jahren und ihre Rückerstreckung ins Leben der Tiere und Pflanzen, als es von uns noch nicht belastet war. Die Krone der menschlichen Zwingherrschaft ist die Zählung der Jahre; die niederdrückendste aller Sagen die von einer Erschaffung der Welt für uns.[59]
>
> [I would give a lot to be able to break the habit of viewing the world in historical terms. Wretched is this division according to years and this extension backwards toward the life of plants and animals, a time when we had not yet contaminated life. The crown of human oppression is the counting of years; the most oppressive of all myths is that of a creation of the world for us.]

In addition to marking this passage in the margin, Sebald also writes "Geschichte & Naturgeschichte" [history & natural history] above this paragraph. His literary texts transport this worldview that recognizes connections between (human) history and natural history but at the same time challenges a historical view of the world as presented in standard chronological forms.[60] Despite his representation of humanity's potential for cruelty and violence, Sebald is able to counterbalance this with a search for meaning and order. Rather than representing a simple form of cultural pessimism, he is driven to make things conceivable, *begreifbar*, through literature and the development of the imagination. Sebald searches for and draws out connections between varied, even disparate events, often using his biography as a starting point or point of orientation. For this reason, he emphasizes coincidence and even invents coincidence. He notes the terrible discrepancy between his life, in particular the safety of his childhood in southern Germany, and the simultaneous fate of those who were being deported to Auschwitz or driven to death on one of the so-called death marches. Despite the geographical

---

59 Elias Canetti, *Alle vergeudete Verehrung. Aufzeichnungen 1949–1960*. Reihe Hanser 50 (Munich: Hanser, 1970) 23. W.G. Sebald Nachlaß: Teilbibliothek, DLA Marbach.

60 Ignasi Ribó has described Sebald's worldview as one of "cosmological ontology," with which he is referring to ancient thinkers, like Lucretius and his *Of the Nature of Things*, more precisely the "Epicurean conception of history and nature as a permanent process of creation and destruction, which is not guided by reason or divinity." Ignasi Ribó, "The One-Winged Angel. History and Memory in the Literary Discourse of W. G. Sebald," *Orbis Litterarum* 64.3 (2009) 222–262, here 225.

distance that separates these experiences, they are united across time. The non-linear progression of *Austerlitz*, which to a certain degree is a form of reverse chronology, presents a challenge to the reader while also reflecting the fact that meaning and sense can only be ascribed to experiences and events retrospectively. Meaning, like memory, is made in the present.

Chapter 5
Witness and Testimony in Literary Memory

This chapter builds upon the preceding analyses of historiography and visuality to further investigate the role of memory and imagination in accessing and representing the past. More precisely, I examine how these operations are explored via their formulation within literary discourse, further elucidating the complex relationship between art and reality and revealing that Sebald's concept of history is not to be reduced to an overriding metaphysics. This investigation offers a critical reconsideration of theories of memory and structures of testimony, which underline the possibilities and specific achievement of literature in the post-Holocaust context. The concepts of witnessing and testimony – along with the fact that the definitions and implications of these concepts continue to evolve – are essential to considerations of historical as well as artistic representations of the Holocaust. The volume *After Testimony. The Ethics and Aesthetics of Holocaust Narrative for the Future*, for example, points precisely to the temporal and relational dimensions of these considerations. The temporal dimension implies the concern with the historical cusp on which we are currently located: that is, we are approaching the time when no new "first-person accounts by Holocaust survivors" will be available.[1] The relational dimension implied by "*after* testimony" points to the variety of artistic forms that are modeled after or created in homage to eyewitness testimony. This volume moreover makes a clear case for specifically artistic – as opposed other discursive – forms when confronting the representation of the Holocaust, underscoring the narrative dimension in such artistic forms of testimony. As the editors state, "Narrative, whether fictional or nonfictional, whether in print, paint, or pixels, has the capacity to offer us explanations about our experiences that often elude other modes such as expository descriptions, abstract arguments, or statistical analyses [...]."[2]

---

1 Jakob Lothe, Susan Rubin Suleiman, and James Phelan, "Introduction: 'After' Testimony: Holocaust Representation and Narrative Theory," *After Testimony. The Ethics and Aesthetics of Holocaust Narrative for the Future*, eds. Jakob Lothe, Susan Rubin Suleiman, and James Phelan (Columbus: The Ohio State University Press, 2012) 1–19, here 2.

2 Ibid., 8. Stefan Gunther also points to the powerful contribution of artistic forms in the constitution of collective memory. He aptly states, "literature and art, far from being the falsifying agents destroying a putatively objective historical discourse, actually constitute the conduits of collective processes of memory." Stefan Gunther, "The Holocaust as the Still Point of the World in W.G. Sebald's *The Emigrants*," *W.G. Sebald. History – Memory – Trauma*, eds. Scott Denham and Mark McCulloh (Berlin: de Gruyter, 2006) 279–290, here 281.

Such considerations can be linked to Shoshana Felman and Dori Laub's groundbreaking work on testimony that reveals the power of literature to contain truths about the past – "truths that are unspoken – or unspeakable – and that are yet inscribed in texts."[3] They also point to the dynamic process involved in coming to an understanding of the trauma of the Holocaust, that is, how acts of careful reading enable us to become witnesses to this past. When Felman and Laub invoke "unspeakable" truths, this is not in the sense of an ethical prohibition or epistemological impossibility but rather refers to the challenge such truths present to conceptual forms of articulation. Throughout the course of my analyses of Sebald's works, I have aimed to show how literature has the ability to respond to these challenges of representation and how the texts we label, if not dismiss, as 'literary' make a contribution to the historical record that cannot be made in any other way. These explorations of how historical truth is rendered through a literary form reveal how literature, to speak with Felman and Laub, "becomes a witness, and perhaps the only witness, to the crisis within history which precisely cannot be articulated, witnessed in the given categories of history itself."[4] Moreover, this present investigation, positioned in relation to Felman and Laub, aims at a broader historical perspective, starting from but moving beyond the paradigmatic atrocity of the twentieth century, to describe "how art inscribes (artistically bears witness to) *what we do not yet know of our lived historical relation to events of our times.*"[5] It is therefore significant that Felman and Laub's explorations do not pursue definite answers but rather "new *enabling questions.*"[6] As developed in the previous chapters, the true achievement of literary discourse is neither the direct representation of reality nor the transmission of knowledge, rather it is the way literary texts engage us to formulate new questions, to consider both what is presented and how it is formulated. Out of this dynamic process of engagement with literature – an imaginative as well as aesthetic engagement – it becomes possible to develop an ethical as well as emotional connection to the past.

Based on the above considerations, it is possible to challenge the rhetoric of the 'unimaginable' or 'unspeakable,' claims of unrepresentability which demonstrate an unwillingness to critically engage with the past. In his exploration of the concept of "witnessness" – a neologism to represent "the state, condition or

---

3 Shoshana Felman and Dori Laub, *Testimony. Crises of Witnessing in Literature, Psychoanalysis, and History* (New York and London: Routledge, 1992) xiii.
4 Ibid., xviii.
5 Ibid., xx, emphasis SF and DL.
6 Ibid., xvi, emphasis SF and DL.

potential for being a witness"[7] – Robert Harvey builds upon Georges Didi-Huberman's considerations of the ethics and aesthetics of imagining to ultimately make the claim that an empathetic form of witnessing can take place through the act of reading. Harvey states, "Reading enables those of us who have never been victims of crime to nonetheless become witnesses by proxy. To read is, therefore, to empathize, and consequently, the imagination must be at least as important for our potential for witnessing as reason."[8] Witnessness, then, like reason and imagination, is an essential human capacity; it "dwells within us and lends us contour even before logical connectors between our senses and our intellect set the standards for reasonable life."[9] In his performative and provocative study of what it means to be a witness and how this relates to an ethically responsible means of living together with victims of the past as well as with our contemporaries, Harvey repeatedly comes to the defense of Didi-Huberman after Claude Lanzmann discredited his analysis of the four clandestine photographs that were taken in Auschwitz in an act of both resistance and witnessing. By describing Lanzmann's "indictment against Didi-Huberman" as "frivolous or, simply, insane," Harvey essentially takes away Lanzmann's right to both speak and be heard.[10] For someone so concerned with the possibilities of both witnessing by proxy and attaining a universal ethics, this accusation is not only aporetic but also a disservice to Harvey's own aims. This incomprehensible interjection notwithstanding, Harvey's meditations on witnessing and witnessness provide a useful point of reference for the considerations of memory and imagination that follow. For, as Harvey states, "If the endless lesson of *Auschwitz* has taught us anything, it is that if any remnant of ethical behavior can sustain itself when humanity threatens itself with its own annihilation, it is to our unflagging capacity for imagination."[11] And it is through imagination and our "imaginativeness" that we can achieve "a glimmer of empathetic recognition" of others.[12]

---

7 Robert Harvey, *Witnessness: Beckett, Dante, Levi and the Foundations of Responsibility* (London; New York: Continuum, 2010) x.

8 Ibid., xi. In a similar vein, Dora Osborne sees the potential for the reader of Sebald's texts to take on a role as witness, while acknowledging the inherent challenge to this act, "By looking at the images we adopt the position of witness, but are always trying to view events that are irrevocably past." Dora Osborne, *Traces of Trauma in W.G. Sebald and Christoph Ransmayr* (Oxford: Legenda, 2013) 131.

9 Harvey, *Witnessness*, 11.

10 Ibid., 103.

11 Ibid., 138, emphasis RH. Harvey uses italics to mark the metonymical sense in which he uses the word Auschwitz (referring to "the destruction of the European Jews"). Cf. ibid., 1.

12 Ibid.

Post-Postmemory: Discourses, Concepts, and Modes of Memory

Sebald's works explore individual, collective, and cultural memory. His narrators will often turn to their own memories and past experiences as a way to approach the memories of others. In exploring the past of fictional figures, Sebald is able to reveal a larger political and collective past; and by giving voice to individual memory, his works counterbalance institutional forms of memory. Similar to the critique of official forms of historiography formulated in his works, Sebald's texts also present official forms of memorialization, i.e., national memorial sites, in a critical light. Various modes of describing memory thus arise, and connections can be made between memory, narrative, and imagination when conceptualizing the dynamic process of how memory is formed. Memory appears on the one hand as a tool to be used and practiced, yet on the other there are memories that resist recollection, only to resurface and recede again outside of the individual's control. Memory is tied to or located in both objects and places, and, as Aleida Assmann has argued, "[...] bestimmte Orte [bilden] eine Kontaktzone zwischen Gegenwart und Vergangenheit" [certain places create a contact zone between the present and the past].[13] Objects that possess memory contain a degree of what Harvey calls "witnessness," referring to the *quality* of bearing witness as opposed to the act itself. Places and spaces of memory – where memories are collected, exchanged, or reactivated – lend Sebald's texts a structural coherence. Assmann describes libraries, museums, and archives as an "immobile" part of cultural memory that requires our mobility to experience this "Qualität des Gedächtnisses" [quality of memory].[14] Sebald's wandering narrators and characters exemplify such mobility. Memory is experienced in an intensely sensual way, and related to this is the attempt to describe memory in physical terms, which in turn is ultimately connected to the difficulty in writing that the narrators and figures often have. By inscribing meaning in coincidental encounters or experiences that elude rational comprehension, Sebald's literary form offers a distanced – "oblique" and "tangential"[15] – approach to history via the individual while also showing how personal memory, individual identity even, becomes accessible via investigations of architectural, institutional, and historical structures. This dedication to individual history and singular cases is the only way to gain empathetic access to the past (cf. *G* 242).

---

13 Aleida Assmann, *Der lange Schatten der Vergangenheit. Erinnerungskultur und Geschichtspolitik* (Munich: C.H. Beck, 2006) 218.
14 Cf. Ibid., 217.
15 Cf. Jean-Pierre Rondas' 2001 interview with Sebald (*G* 216).

The particular form of memory based in imagination, evoked by or resulting in an emotional connection to a past that one has not experienced firsthand is how Marianne Hirsch describes her concept of "postmemory." She writes,

> In my reading, postmemory is distinguished from memory by generational distance and from history by deep personal connection. Postmemory is a powerful and very particular form of memory precisely because its connection to its object or source is mediated not through recollection but through an imaginative investment and creation.[16]

As this theory was developed specifically in relation to the experiences of children of Holocaust survivors, it has proven very productive when brought to bear on literary works, in particular those of the so-called second and third generations. Several scholars have written on Sebald's works as manifestations of this phenomenon of postmemory.[17] As explicitly asserted in *Luftkrieg und Literatur*, Sebald sees his own memory as being affected by the memories of others. Similarly, in his essay on the nineteenth-century author Eduard Mörike, Sebald writes,

> Liegen die Schrecken der Revolution für den jungen Mörike schon in einer legendären Vorvergangenheit, so waren die Schlußakte der napoleonischen Ära, die Schlachten von Leipzig und Waterloo, von denen er als Kind viel gehört haben muß, *gewiß Teil seiner eigenen Erinnerung* (*Logis* 78, my emphasis).
> [If, for the young Mörike, the terrors of the Revolution have already receded into a legendary and distant past, the closing acts of the Napoleonic era – the battles of Leipzig and Waterloo, which as a child he must have heard a great deal about – *surely formed part of his own memories* (PC 70, my emphasis).]

Implicitly Sebald's works reveal how events of the past can become part of one's own memory in the sense that they affect one emotionally. While informed by

---

16 Marianne Hirsch, *Family Frames. Photography, Narrative, and Postmemory* (Cambridge, MA. and London, England: Harvard University Press, 1997) 22.
17 J.J. Long, "History, Narrative, and Photography in W.G. Sebald's *Die Ausgewanderten*," *Modern Language Review* 98.1 (2003) 117–137; Mark M. Anderson, "Documents, Photography, Postmemory: Alexander Kluge, W.G. Sebald, and the German Family," *Photography in Fiction*, eds. Silke Horstkotte and Nancy Pedri, special issue of *Poetics Today* 29.1 (2008) 129–151; Murray Baumgarten, "'Not Knowing What I Should Think:' The Landscape of Postmemory in W.G. Sebald's *The Emigrants*," *Partial Answers: Journal of Literature and the History of Ideas* 5.2 (2007) 267–287; Richard Crownshaw, "Reconsidering Postmemory: Photography, the Archive, and Post-Holocaust Memory in W.G. Sebald's *Austerlitz*," *Mosaic: A Journal for the Interdisciplinary Study of Literature* 37.4 (2004) 215–236; Silke Horstkotte, "Fotografie, Gedächtnis, Postmemory. Bildzitate in der deutschen Erinnerungsliteratur," *Lesen ist wie Sehen. Intermediale Zitate in Bild und Text*, eds. Silke Horstkotte and Karin Leonhard (Cologne; Weimar; Vienna: Böhlau, 2006) 177–195.

discussions of cultural memory, as Aleida and Jan Assmann distinguish it from communicative and collective memory, as well as Hirsch's concept of "postmemory," my analysis of memory here does not attempt to fit Sebald's complex literary texts into the mold of any existing theory. Rather, my concern is first and foremost with the way Sebald depicts memory's suspect and unreliable nature and how this is closely related to one's access to the past and one's own identity or relation to this past. Furthermore, I suggest reconsidering the concept of postmemory in order to think of the "post" not only in a temporal sense but also in a positional one. By casting a critical gaze on this concept, we find that it overlaps considerably with the operation an author goes through when writing a work of fictional literature.

In her book *The Generation of Postmemory. Writing and Visual Culture After the Holocaust*, Hirsch returns to her concept of postmemory, keeping the essential definition intact – that of a generational distance but emotional connection to the past – but differentiating further *forms* that postmemory can take: as an action, object or attribute, relationship or structure. That is, Hirsch considers postmemorial viewing,[18] postmemory as a "process of transmission,"[19] and postmemorial working through.[20] She discusses postmemorial viewers and subjects,[21] how past traumatic events can continue to have an effect on an individual in the present.[22] Hirsch suggests moving away from postmemory as an *"identity* position"[23] and gestures toward loosening the ontological foundation of this concept. While acknowledging "affiliative" forms of postmemory, i.e., similar structures of transmission that occur outside of families with direct connections to a traumatic past,[24] the family and familial connections nevertheless maintain a privileged status in her book. This becomes clear when she declares her central argument and the goal of postmemorial work:

---

18 Marianne Hirsch, *The Generation of Postmemory. Writing and Visual Culture After the Holocaust* (New York: Columbia University Press, 2012) 59.

19 Ibid., 89.

20 Ibid., 122.

21 Ibid., 220.

22 Here, Hirsch discusses postmemory as both "a *structure* of inter- and transgenerational return of traumatic knowledge and embodied experience" and "a *consequence* of traumatic recall but (unlike posttraumatic stress disorder) at a generational remove." Ibid., 6, italics in quotes are from MH unless otherwise indicated.

23 Ibid., 35.

24 Hirsch differentiates between *"familial* and *'affiliative'* postmemory," the former referring to vertical transmission within a family from parents to children while the latter refers to a horizontal transmission among contemporaries. Cf. ibid., 36.

> Postmemorial work [...] strives to *reactivate* and *re embody* more distant political and cultural memorial structures by reinvesting them with resonant individual and familial forms of mediation and aesthetic expression. In these ways, less directly affected participants can become engaged in the generation of postmemory that can persist even after all participants and even their familial descendants are gone.[25]

In acknowledging other forms of transmission beyond those that are intergenerational and beyond the specific historical trauma of the Holocaust, Hirsch attempts to broaden the discussion to include "transnational"[26] and "transgenerational memory work,"[27] invoking notions of contiguity, intersection, and connection. She furthermore sharpens the focus of her analysis by using a feminist lens, provoked in large part by the absence of women witnesses in Claude Lanzmann's *Shoah*. Feminism and memory studies prove to be complementary approaches, for both aim to research and write recuperative, alternative histories: "As a form of counter-history, 'memory' offered a means to account for the power structures animating forgetting, oblivion, and erasure and thus to engage in acts of repair and redress," as Hirsch states.[28] In addition to redefining how we understand memory, Hirsch also calls for a reconsideration of the archive; for example, her reflections on personal photographs and albums as archival material challenge the notion of the archive as an institutional body that aids in the documentation of official forms of history. Affinities thus exist between the postmemorial archival practices that Hirsch describes and Sebald's form of literary historiography as an attempt at restitution. Hirsch characterizes such aesthetic and ethical practices as follows, "In a consciously reparative move, they assemble collections that function as correctives and additions, rather than as counters, to the historical archive, attempting to undo the ruptures caused by war and genocide."[29] In line with Hirsch, my considerations have been very much concerned with the way literary discourse formulates supplementary stories to offer an alternative and reparative form of history. However, I find Hirsch's emphasis on familial lines of connection to the past – "the family as a privileged site of memorial transmission"[30] – a severe limitation.[31] To

---

25 Ibid., 33.

26 Ibid., 247.

27 Ibid., 20.

28 Cf. ibid., 15–16. As in her first book on postmemory, Hirsch emphasizes the significant role photography plays in postmemorial work.

29 Ibid., 228.

30 Hirsch's position aligns with Aleida Assmann's schema of memory that identifies social memory as one form of communicative memory, where "the family is a privileged site of memorial transmission." Ibid., 32.

31 Later in her study, Hirsch takes up the notion of "heteropathic" memory from Kaja Silverman, who has borrowed it from Max Scheler, to argue that, "Postmemory is a form of heteropathic

counter this position, I would argue that literature provides an insight into the past – it can evoke a postmemorial relationship – precisely for those with no such familial connections or for those who may have such a connection but where communication (about the past) is not fostered or may be impossible. Moreover, literary discourse has an inherent ability and possibility to "reactivate" and "re-embody" the past in ways that engage those who are not directly affected by what is represented. As can be seen in Sebald's works, a significant form of transmission takes place between his narrators and characters – be they of Jewish descent or not – independent of familial or group relations.

Testimonial Structure: Making Sense of the Past by Making Meaning in the Present

Solitary figures populate Sebald's works, but their explorations of both nature and history make it impossible for these individuals to ever be completely alone. His nameless wandering narrators come into contact with others via personal encounters as well as intellectual and textual investigations. Such encounters form the basis of the testimonial structure of his works, and at the same time this testimonial dimension demands a certain narratorial distance created by Sebald's characteristic form of mediated narration. In considering testimony and trauma as both themes and literary structures in Sebald's works, Christina Szentivanyi describes the form of "fictional testimony" developed in the "Paul Bereyter" story of *Die Ausgewanderten*, a form that is rooted in Sebald's previous considerations of Jean Améry and Primo Levi, a form that "commemorates exemplary life-histories without claiming impossible historic objectivity or the sort of empathic understanding that the narrator refers to as 'wrongful trespass.'"[32] A similar form of "fictional testimony" can be found in *Austerlitz*, where the most significant relationship is the one between the narrator and the eponymous figure. Although there are affinities between the two men and instances where they seem to overlap both narratologically and thematically, the relationship is imbalanced insofar as it is Austerlitz who talks and the narrator who listens. This quantitative imbalance, in the sense that

---

memory in which the self and the other are more closely connected through familial or group relation – through an understanding of what it means to be Jewish or of African descent, for example." Cf. Hirsch, *The Generation of Postmemory*, 85, 86. Here again, we can point to the familial connection as an unnecessary limitation within the concept of postmemory.

32 Christina M. E. Szentivanyi, "W. G. Sebald and Structures of Testimony and Trauma: There are Spots of Mist that No Eye can Dispel," *W. G. Sebald. History – Memory – Trauma*, eds. Scott Denham and Mark McCulloh (Berlin: de Gruyter, 2006) 351–363, here 355.

Austerlitz's story as well as the narrator's telling of this story take precedence, is not to be understood in a hierarchical sense or as a value judgment, for the narrator's capacity to listen and by extension to relay Austerlitz's story is essential to the testimonial structure of the work. That is, for testimony to take place there must be a listener.[33] As Dori Laub states, the listener is "the blank screen on which the event comes to be inscribed for the first time"[34]; the testimonial process requires "a bonding, the intimate and total presence of an *other* – in the position of one who hears. Testimonies are not monologues; they cannot take place in solitude. The witnesses are talking *to somebody*: to somebody they have been waiting for for a long time."[35] Directly indicating such a testimonial structure, Austerlitz tells the narrator that he was just thinking back on their past meetings in Belgium nearly twenty years prior and had come to the realization, "daß er bald für seine Geschichte, hinter die er erst in den letzten Jahren gekommen sei, einen Zuhörer finden müsse, ähnlich wie ich es seinerzeit gewesen sei in Antwerpen, Liège und Zeebrugge" (*A* 68) ["he must find someone to whom he could relate his own story, a story which he had learned only in the last years and for which he needed the kind of listener I had once been in Antwerp, Liège, and Zeebrugge" (*AE* 43–44)].[36] Jakob Lothe identifies Austerlitz's "moral obligation" to search out his own past as well

---

33 Marianne Hirsch points to "the testimonial structure of listener and witness separated by relative proximity and distance to the events of the war" in both Art Spiegelman's *Maus* and Sebald's *Austerlitz*. See Marianne Hirsch, *The Generation of Postmemory. Writing and Visual Culture After the Holocaust* (New York: Columbia University Press, 2012) 40. Relying on Felman and Laub's exploration of testimony and emphasis on the role of the listener, Jakob Lothe also points to the testimonial structure of *Austerlitz*. See Jakob Lothe, "Narrative, Memory, and Visual Image: W.G. Sebald's *Luftkrieg und Literatur* und *Austerlitz*," *After Testimony. The Ethics and Aesthetics of Holocaust Narrative for the Future*, eds. Jakob Lothe, Susan Rubin Suleiman, and James Phelan (Columbus: The Ohio State University Press, 2012) 221–246.

34 Laub, *Testimony. Crises of Witnessing*, 57. Laub further outlines three "distinct levels of witnessing in relation to the Holocaust experience: the level of being a witness to oneself with the experience; the level of being a witness to the testimonies of others; and the level of being a witness to the process of witnessing itself" (75). Irene Kacandes' differentiated "circuits of witnessing" provides a fruitful model to consider the testimonial structure in literary texts and the relationship between characters, narrators, and readers. See Irene Kacandes, "Testimony: Talk as Witnessing," *Talk Fiction. Literature and the Talk Explosion* (Lincoln and London: University of Nebraska Press, 2001) 89–140.

35 Laub, *Testimony. Crises of Witnessing*, 70–71.

36 Although the narrator's detailed description of persistent eye problems established a rationale for his being in London, this coincidental encounter in the Salon Bar of the Great Eastern Hotel has an air of magic, as if Austerlitz conjured the narrator's presence.

the text's "ethical thrust" embodied by the narrator, who fulfills "a kind of moral duty" in serving as a witness to Austerlitz's story.[37]

The testimonial structure of *Austerlitz* is both delayed and doubled through the complex construction of the narrative, that is, not only does Austerlitz need the narrator as his listener, but the narrator also needs someone as his reader. Paralleling the mise-en-abyme effect of the text-image-constellation, the testimonial structure has further layers beyond the relationship between Austerlitz and the narrator and the narrator and the reader. After arriving at the State Archive in Prague, Austerlitz tells one of the employees, Tereza Ambrosová, his story or what he assumes his past to be and why he has come to the archive: to find the addresses of those with the same name as his. It is in the act of telling this to the archive employee that Austerlitz begins to recognize his years of repression. He recalls to the narrator,

> Frau Ambrosová [...] hörte mir, ihren Kopf ein wenig zur Seite geneigt, auf das aufmerksamste zu, als ich, zum erstenmal überhaupt jemandem auseinanderzusetzen begann, daß mir aufgrund verschiedener Umstände meine Herkunft verborgen geblieben war, daß ich es aus anderen Gründen stets unterlassen hätte, Nachforschungen über meine Person anzustellen, jetzt aber infolge einer Reihe von bedeutsamen Vorfällen zu der Überzeugung gelangt sei oder zumindest die Vermutung hege, im Alter von viereinhalb Jahren, in den Monaten unmittelbar vor dem Ausbruch des Krieges, die Stadt Prag verlassen zu haben mit einem der damals von hier abgehenden, sogenannten Kindertransporte und deshalb in das Archiv gekommen sei in der Hoffnung, die in der Zeit zwischen 1934 und 1939 in Prag wohnhaften Personen meines Namens, bei denen es gewiß nicht um allzu viele sich handle, mit ihren Anschriften aus den Registern heraussuchen zu können (*A* 216).
>
> [Mrs Ambrosová [...] listened attentively with her head tilted slightly to one side as, for the first time in my life, I began explaining to someone else that because of certain circumstances my origins had been unknown to me, and that for other reasons I had never inquired into them, but now felt compelled, because of a series of coincidental events, to conclude or at least to conjecture that I had left Prague at the age of four and a half, in the months just before the war broke out, on one of the so-called children's transports departing from the city at the time, and I had therefore come to consult the archives in the hope that people of my surname living here between 1934 and 1939, who could not have been very numerous, might be found in the registers, with details of their address (*AE* 147).]

Austerlitz explictly remarks to the narrator that this is the first time he has every told his story, and this is futhermore the first time that the "Kindertransport" [children's transport] has been named explicitly in the text. Austerlitz recalls how, while telling his story to Ambrosová, he began to panic and stuttered as he struggled to find his words (*A* 216–217) [(*AE* 147–148)]. Austerlitz's difficulty in

---

37 Lothe, "Narrative, Memory, and Visual Image," 242.

confronting the past and accessing his own memories is in one way transferred to language, making his attempts to formulate this repressed past near impossible. However, such difficulties in speech are not reflected directly in the narration; his discomfort and stuttering, for example, only become evident in retrospect after his lengthy and complicated recollection, presented in this nearly page-long sentence. In another way, such discomfort and difficulty in articulation are reinforced in the language of the text on the level of syntax. That is, the disjointed syntax, in particular the distance between definite article and noun, challenges easy and immediate comprehension. Austerlitz's description of how his senses were heightened in the State Archive, his acute awareness of the overheated room and intense acoustic impressions, starkly contrasts the previous suppression of his senses, the numbing blindness and deafness that enabled him to repress his past.

After Austerlitz receives a list of addresses where individuals with his name lived between 1934–1939, he describes his (re-)discovery of the city, the effortless return of memories and the awakening of his long suppressed senses, "als eröffnete sich mir, nicht durch die Anstrengung des Nachdenkens, sondern durch meine so lange betäubt gewesenen und jetzt wiedererwachenden Sinne, die Erinnerung" (*A* 220) ["memories were revealing themselves to me not by means of any mental effort but through my senses, so long numbed and now coming back to life" (*AE* 150)]. Explicitly referring the deliberate repression of his past, Austerlitz recalls to the narrator how, walking through the streets of Prague, he rediscovered the places of his childhood, "von dem, soweit ich zurückdenken konnte, jede Spur in meinem Gedächtnis ausgelöscht war" (*A* 220) ["every trace of which had been expunged from my memory for as long as I could recollect" (*AE* 150)]. After walking through the streets, in and out of courtyards, gazing up at buildings and through windows, Austerlitz cannot be certain of his recognitions. Until, that is, he comes upon a half-relief set in plaster above an arch, "das vor einem gestirnten, seegrünen Hintergrund einen blaufarbenen Hund zeigte mit einem Zweig im Maul, den er, wie ich, bis in die Haarwurzeln erschauernd, erahnte, herbeigebracht hatte aus meiner Vergangenheit" (*A* 221) ["the cast was no more than a square foot in size, and showed, set against a spangled sea-green background, a blue dog carrying a small branch in its mouth, which I could tell, by the prickling of my scalp, it had brought back out of my past" (*AE* 151)]. This arch is above the entrance of the building in which he spent the first four and a half years of his life before being sent by his mother to England on one of the "children's transports." Austerlitz proceeds to describe the various architectural details and decorations, "lauter Buchstaben und Zeichen aus dem Setzkasten der vergessenen Dinge" (*A* 222) ["all of them signs and characters from the type case of forgotten things" (*AE* 151)], and according to this metaphor, these objects form the text of his memory. This array of details is so dizzying that Austerlitz must rest on a staircase and lean his head against a wall, where he sits, possibly the length of an hour, before finally ringing the bell of one of the apartments. The inquiry into his family's name at the archive has led him to this apartment. Upon entering the apartment, which appears as it did sixty years prior, Austerlitz's entire life unravels before him, as he describes the "gesamte Zeit meines Lebens, die sich jetzt in mir überstürzte" (*A* 224) ["my entire life, which was now unraveling headlong before me" (*AE* 153)]. While only four and a half years, this period of time during his childhood in Prague forms the core of his identity that he has long repressed.

The next journey Austerlitz makes, retracing the trajectory from Prague to London via Germany, is no less painful than the first flight on the "Kindertransport," as Austerlitz recounts to the narrator. In looking back from the present moment upon this journey, the passage of time has not alleviated his pain; rather, he experiences a further loss of control when his own experiences and memories – "Erinnerungen, die auftauchen und wieder versinken" (*A* 327) ["memories resurfacing and then sinking out of sight again" (*AE* 226)] – blend together with what he has read and seen as well as with "schmerzhaften blinden Stellen" (*A* 327) ["distressing blank spots" (*AE* 226)]. Austerlitz further describes to the narrator, while they walk through Tower Hamlets Cemetery near his house in London, how, within the first weeks after his return from Prague, he spent his days in this cemetery. While wandering among the graves, committing the names as well as birth and death dates of the dead to memory, Austerlitz managed to find momentary peace of mind. As if in an effort to maintain this calm, he even brought parts of the cemetery home with him: pebbles, ivy leaves, a stone rose, and even a broken off hand from one of the stone angels (*A* 330/ *AE* 228). A photograph of grave stones, a handless stone angel prominently in the foreground, precedes this description in the German edition (*A* 329) and 'mirrors' the text in the English translation (*AE* 229). Reason and rationality are of no help to Austerlitz when dealing with the repercussions of his repression:

> Es nutzte mir offenbar wenig, daß ich die Quellen meiner Verstörung entdeckt hatte, mich selber, über all die vergangenen Jahre hinweg, mit größter Deutlichkeit sehen konnte als das von seinem vertrauten Leben von einem Tag auf den anderen abgesonderte Kind: die Vernunft kam nicht an gegen das seit jeher von mir unterdrückte und jetzt gewaltsam aus mir hervorbrechende Gefühl des Verstoßen- und Ausgelöschtseins (*A* 330).
>
> [It was obviously of little use that I had discovered the sources of my distress and, looking back over all the past years, could now see myself with the utmost clarity as that child suddenly cast out of his familiar surroundings: reason was powerless against the sense of rejection and annihilation which I had always suppressed, and which was now breaking through the walls of its confinement (*AE* 228).]

In the following sections, I will explore how Austerlitz confronts his repressed passed and slowly excavates his own personal history. In recounting this story and the process of memory and remembering that takes place, the narrator bears witness to Austerlitz's quest to re-establish his own identity. It is through Sebald's particular form of literary historiography, as exemplified in *Austerlitz*, that we as readers form an empathetic investment in the text and thereby witness the formation of literary knowledge of the past.

Memory's Attributes: Visuality, Physicality, Materiality, Uncertainty

Building upon the discussion in chapter three of what qualifies as an image for Sebald, we find examples in *Austerlitz* where images operate independently of the sense of sight and are thus more closely connected to imagination than memory. It is thus possible to conjure images independently of both memory and experiences, that is, without a basis in sensate perception. Therefore, imagination must be conceptualized as an independent faculty. When recalling his visit to Terezín, Austerlitz describes the after-effects as follows,

> Aber gleich, ob ich die Augen weit offen hielt oder geschlossen, die ganze Nacht hindurch *sah* ich *Bilder* aus Terezín und aus dem Ghettomuseum, die Ziegel der Festungsmauern, das Schaufenster des Bazars, die endlosen Namenslisten, einen ledernen Reisekoffer mit einem Doppelaufkleber der Hotels Bristol in Salzburg und Wien [...] (*A* 291, my emphasis).
> [But whether I kept my eyes wide open or closed, all through the night I *saw pictures* from Terezín and the Ghetto Museum, the bricks of the fortification walls, the display window of the Bazaar, the endless lists of names, a leather suitcase bearing a double sticker from the Hotels Bristol in Salzburg and Vienna [...] (*AE* 201–202, my emphasis).]

During his visit to the Ghetto Museum, the information challenged his ability to understand the events of the past; the documentation lead to simultaneous comprehension and incomprehension: "Das alles begriff ich nun und begriff es auch nicht, denn jede Einzelheit, die sich mir, dem, wie ich fürchtete, aus eigener Schuld unwissend Gewesenen, eröffnete auf meinem Weg durch das Museum, aus einem Raum in den nächsten und wieder zurück, überstieg bei weitem mein Fassungsvermögen" (*A* 287). ["I understood it all now, yet I did not understand it, for every detail that was revealed to me as I went through the museum from room to room and back again, ignorant as I feared I had been through my own fault, far exceeded my comprehension" (*AE* 199).] Austerlitz's progression through the museum, moving from room to room, parallels his effort to go back further in the past, to establish his own memories. Although that which is depicted in the museum cannot correspond to his own personal memories, the documentation, and in particular the objects he saw – such as the suitcases that belonged to those "aus Prag und aus Pilsen, Würzburg und Wien, Kufstein und Karlsbad" (*A* 287) ["from Prague and Pilsen, Würzburg and Vienna, Kufstein and Karlsbad" (*AE* 199)] – nevertheless make such an impression on him that he is able to see them again later as images in his mind. The use of alliteration here reveals the way that literature can make sense or give order to an incomprehensible event.

Austerlitz recalls further to the narrator the images that he *saw* through the night, both with his eyes opened and closed, including "die versperrten Tore, die ich photographiert hatte" (*A* 291) ["the closed gates I had photographed" (*AE* 202)]. The reader will already be familiar with these images, recalling the opening scene of the book, in which the narrator mentions photographs of heavy doors and gates among the images that Austerlitz passes on to him. This sense of familiarity – which we could tentatively term an intratextual memory, a memory established within the text – is reinforced by the visual prolepsis just prior to Austerlitz's recollection, that is, the series of photographs of these doors included in the preceding section of the text (*A* 276–279) [(*AE* 190–193)]. Reversing the ontological referent inherent to photography, this use of photography serves to testify to the intratextual reality. These doors are thus presented three times in the text: first by the narrator in the opening scene of the book, second in a visual form that is also accompanied by Austerlitz's verbal reference to them almost in the form of a caption, and third when Austerlitz sees the doors again in his mind. Christoph Eggers argues that Sebald's "poetics of photography" makes a "poetics of memory" possible, insofar as the images provide the reader with the opportunity to pause, reflect, compare, and thereby remember.[38] The type of "Erinnerungsarbeit" [memory work] that Sebald's works initiate, according to Eggers, occurs within the reader's imagination in the act of developing images in our minds.[39] To talk of "memory work" here must however always be placed in relation to the imaginative process that starts from and occurs within the literary work. Sebald's texts certainly contribute to memory work in the sense that they both commemorate and reanimate the past, yet by expanding the concept of memory – as Hirsch's concept of postmemory encourages us to do – we risk leveling the complexity of Sebald's works in particular and dissolving the specific achievement of literary discourse more broadly.

---

38 Cf. Christoph Eggers, *Das Dunkel durchdringen, das uns umgibt. Die Fotografie im Werk von W. G. Sebald* (Frankfurt am Main: Peter Lang, 2011) 59.
39 Cf. ibid., 55.

The last image that Austerlitz recalls to the narrator is of "die Schatten Agátas und Věras, wie sie den bepackten Rodelschlitten durch das Schneetreiben zogen zu dem Messegelände von Holešovice hinaus" (*A* 291) ["the two forlorn figures of Agáta and Vera pulling the laden toboggan through the driving snow to the Trade Fair building at Holešovice" (*AE* 202)]. This last 'image' that Austerlitz *sees* is actually an image conjured up in his imagination, not based in any personal experience but rather based on what Věra has recounted to him. 'Seeing,' as it is presented here, is not limited to the process of sensate perception. Rather, it is possible to transition between seeing and imagining, i.e., one can imagine based on the knowledge of an event and ultimately 'see' the past. We can trace this possibility back to Immanuel Kant's definition of imagination as the faculty of perception without the presence of an object. Or, to speak with Robert Harvey, "sight and its consequence, insight, can always be supplemented by the force of the imagination – Kant's *Einbildungskraft*."[40] Imagination, according to Kant, can be either *productive* – preceding experience; pure perception in space and time – or *reproductive* – recalling to mind a previous empirical perception; perception linked with the concept of the object thus becomes empirical cognition, or experience. While "productive," Kant does not see the faculty of imagination as "creative," for he does not see the possibility of producing new sense impressions that never before occurred in our senses.[41] Memory, as Kant defines it, is the "faculty of visualizing the past intentionally."[42] In transitioning from imagining to seeing and finally telling, Austerlitz demonstrates his ability to bear witness to this past event via his emotional investment in Věra's account. The empathy the reader develops while following the narrator's account of Austerlitz's story carries forth this act of bearing witness.

Noticeable in Sebald's works – *Die Ausgewanderten* and *Austerlitz* in particular – is the attempt to describe memory in physical terms by describing the body's visceral response to both involuntary memories and the efforts to call up a past image. Rather than shrouding such experiences in metaphor, Sebald seems to prefer more literal, very physical descriptions. This is reflected in the postscript in Great-Uncle Adelwarth's agenda, which reads, "Die Erinnerung [...] kommt mir oft vor wie eine Art von Dummheit. Sie macht einen schweren, schwindligen Kopf, als blickte man nicht zurück durch die Fluchten der Zeit, sondern aus großer Höhe auf

---

40 Harvey, *Witnessness*, 7–8.

41 Immanuel Kant, *Anthropology. From a Pragmatic Point of View*, trans. Victor Lyle Dowdell, ed. Hans H. Rudnick (Carbondale and Edwardsville: Southern Illinois University Press; London and Amsterdam: Feffer & Simons, Inc., 1978) 56 [167].

42 Kant, *Anthropology*, 73 [182].

die Erde hinab von einem jener Türme, die sich im Himmel verlieren" (*DA* 215) ["Memory [...] often strikes me as a kind of dumbness. It makes one's head heavy and giddy, as if one were not looking back down the receding perspectives of time but rather down on the earth from a great height, from one of those towers whose tops are lost to view in the clouds" (*E* 145)]. This physical description of memory, in particular the perspective from a great height, is revisited, revised, and reformulated in *Die Ringe des Saturn*, when the narrator describes the perspective of historical representation.[43] A heightened awareness of physical surroundings and acute sensations immediately precede significant moments in *Austerlitz*, almost as if to signal these moments of connection or revelation to the reader. Once memories are reactivated, Austerlitz experiences them as if they were physical spaces he could enter, "hinter denen und in denen sich viel weiter noch zurückreichende Dinge verbargen, immer das eine im anderen verschachtelt, gerade so wie die labyrinthischen Gewölbe, die ich in dem staubgrauen Licht zu erkennen glaubte, sich fortsetzen in unendlicher Folge" (*A* 200) ["behind and within which many things much further back in the past seemed to lie, all interlocking like the labyrinthine vaults I saw in the dusty gray light, and which seemed to go on and on for ever" (*AE* 136).] In this scene in the Ladies' Waiting Room, Austerlitz has the feeling that all moments of his past life were contained within this physical space. The way in which deictic elements, like "here" and "now," are connected to memories reinforces the perspective that memory is always situated and defined in the present.[44]

Not only is memory experienced in an intensely physical manner, but a general focus on the body and physicality is also found in *Austerlitz*. Similar to the narrator's eye pain and sudden blindness, Austerlitz experiences a literal paralysis of his thought processes and emotions, all of which is linked to his repression of the past. He describes his nearly three-week-long "Geistesabwesenheit, die zwar nicht die Körperfunktionen, aber sämtliche Denkvorgänge und Gefühlsregungen lahmgelegt hatte" (*A* 332) ["mental absence which, though it did not impair the bodily functions, paralyzed all thought processes and emotions" (*AE* 230)]. Just as a chain of coincidences brings Austerlitz to the Ladies' Waiting Room of the Liverpool Street Station, an ambiguous force kept Austerlitz from searching out his origins earlier. In this way, his repression could be seen as involuntary and outside his control. When confronting his years of repression for

---

43 See the discussion in chapter one.
44 Aleida Assmann underscores the dominant perspective in memory studies, namely that history and the past in general are human constructs, developed according to what is needed and possible in our present time. Cf. Assmann, *Der lange Schatten der Vergangenheit*, 16.

the first time by trying to bring his assumptions about his uncertain past into words, Austerlitz falls into a panic and has difficulty speaking.[45]

The explicit statement of memory's failure and the "unreality" in attempts to recount the past are first formulated in *Die Ringe des Saturn* and then revisited and further developed in *Austerlitz*. The narrator in *Die Ringe des Saturn* evokes our suspicion when he asserts "Aber in Wirklichkeit erinnert man sich natürlich nicht" (*RS* 211) ["But in reality, of course, memory fails us" (*RoS* 177)]. Remarkably, the transmission of Michael Hamburger's memories by the narrator occurs before he has even met Hamburger. In other words, he has gained his knowledge of Hamburger through the process of reading Hamburger's own memoirs. In describing the moments before they meet, the narrator reflects on how his own story – his "Irrgänge[] auf der Heide" ["wanderings on the heath"] – and how these wanderings, "die mir jetzt, da ich von ihnen erzählte, unwillkürlich den Charakter des bloß Erfundenen anzunehmen schienen" (*RS* 216) ["in the telling, assumed an air of unreality" (*RoS* 181)]. This passage makes clear both the degree of invention in memory and the distance between an experience on the one hand and the materialization of that experience by way of its translation into a narrative text on the other. Such succinct comments, as this one in *Die Ringe des Saturn*, often made as if in passing or as if to undercut the detailed consideration just given, underline Sebald's principle of simultaneously thematizing and problematizing narration – narration not only as story-telling but also as story-making – all while remaining within the narrative process.

The link between memory and material traces, or the material basis for activating the memory (much in the same way that the other senses operate), is a further particularity of Sebald's narratives. However, one finds memory conceptualized in a similar manner in current discussions as well. For instance, the materiality of memory, or how memory is tied to objects, became clear with an absolute literalness after the collapse of the historical archive in Cologne in March 2009. This loss of material has been equated with a loss of memory.[46] Revisiting the key scene of *Austerlitz*, his anagnorisis in the Ladies' Waiting Room of the Liverpool Street Station, we see not only the play between perception and reality as established through scientific observation but also the role that objects play in constituting or reactivating memory. Here, Austerlitz observes rays of light that travel in "gegen die Gesetze der Physik verstoßende Bahnen" (*A* 198) ["trajectories which violated

---

45 The way in which repression manifests itself as a crisis of language is developed below.

46 Cf. *Bergen, Ordnen, Restaurieren. Der Wiederaufbau des Historischen Archivs der Stadt Köln*, publication of the Historisches Archiv Amt für Presse- und Öffentlichkeitsarbeit (Cologne: Barz & Beienburg, 2012). See also Johannes Nitschmann, "Eine Stadt verliert ihr Gedächtnis," *Berliner Zeitung* (5. March 2009) 2.

the laws of physics" (*AE* 135)], and the dimensions of the room make him dizzy, "als setzte er [der Innenraum] in der unwahrscheinlichsten perspektivischen Verkür- zung unendlich sich fort und beugte sich zugleich, wie das nur in einem derartigen falschen Universum möglich war, in sich selber zurück" (*A* 199) ["as if the room where I stood were expanding, going on forever and ever in an improbably fore- shortened perspective, at the same time turning back into itself in a way possible only in such a deranged universe" (*AE* 135)]. What Austerlitz first describes as a false universe, based on the physical impossibility of what he perceives, in the end turns out to be the truest place he has ever been. That is, the Ladies' Waiting Room, although it evokes an altered state of perception, not only contains all the moments of his past – "alle Stunden meiner Vergangenheit" (*A* 200) ["all the hours of my past life" (*AE* 136)] – but also reveals the truth of who he is, initiating a process of self- recognition and the reactivation of his long-repressed memories.[47] In the "Halb- dämmer" (*A* 201) ["gloomy light" (*AE* 137)] he sees a couple, a preacher and his wife, who have come to pick up a little boy with a backpack. He then recognizes himself through this backpack; this object calls up and forms a memory that he has long repressed, providing him with sudden certainty that he came to England more than half a century earlier. Austerlitz is at first unable to describe his reaction to this moment of recognition and the process of memory that ensues.

> Den Zustand, in den ich darüber geriet, sagte Austerlitz, weiß ich, wie so vieles, nicht genau zu beschreiben; es war ein Reißen, das ich in mir verspürte, und Scham und Kummer, oder ganz etwas anderes, worüber man nicht reden kann, weil dafür die Worte fehlen, so wie mir die Worte damals gefehlt haben, als die zwei fremden Leute auf mich zutraten, deren Sprache ich nicht verstand (*A* 201–202).
>
> [As so often, said Austerlitz, I cannot give any precise description of the state of mind this realization induced; I felt something rending within me, and a sense of shame and sorrow, or perhaps something quite different, something inexpressible because we have no words for it, just as I had no words all those years ago when the two strangers came over to me speaking a language I did not understand (*AE* 137).]

It is not that Austerlitz does not know what happened at that moment, nor is it merely the problem of translating from his mother tongue into the unknown language of his adoptive parents. Rather, he does not know how to put his experience into words, which is clearly a problem of representation that in itself challenges Wittgenstein's notion that thinking only occurs in language. Similar to the rending he experiences here, it was a sensation of "Ziehen" [pulling] that

---

47 Austerlitz also recalls that he becomes conscious, through "eine dumpfe Benommenheit" (*A* 202) ["through my dull bemusement" (*AE* 137)], of the destruction he suffered from the "Verlassensein" (*A* 202) ["desolation" (*AE* 137)], which echoes his description of the Ladies' Waiting Room as a "Verlies" (*A* 198) ["dungeon" (*AE* 135)].

brought him to this room in the train station, formerly unknown to him. The concrete terms in which Austerlitz's revelation and sudden flashes of memory are described here are remarkable. He does not imagine or remember himself as a boy, having arrived in London from Prague, but he literally *sees* himself there: "ich *sah* auch den Knaben" (*A* 201, my emphasis) ["I also *saw* the boy" (*AE* 137, my emphasis)]. The reader shares this sense of vertigo, as the entire plane of time expands, containing both the present and the past. One may also wonder if it is really Austerlitz who sees himself in the past or if it is as he conjectured earlier that the dead, or even his former self, who see him in this present moment.[48]

In a further instance of how certain objects possess memory or at least incite the memory process, Austerlitz recalls a cast-iron column in the Pilsen train station that he came upon while retracing the journey he made from Prague to London via Germany on the so-called "Kindertransport."[49] Upon arrival in Pilsen, Austerlitz photographs the cast-iron column that "einen Reflex des Wiedererkennens ausgelöst hatte in mir" (*A* 319) ["had touched some chord of recognition in me" (*AE* 221)]. He explains,

> Was mich beunruhigte bei ihrem Anblick war jedoch nicht die Frage, ob sich die von einem leberfarbenen Schorf überzogenen komplizierten Formen des Kapitells tatsächlich meinem Gedächtnis eingeprägt hatten, als ich seinerzeit, im Sommer 1939, mit dem Kindertransport durch Pilsen gekommen war, sondern die an sich unsinnige Vorstellung, daß diese durch die Verschuppung ihrer Oberfläche gewissermaßen ans Lebendige heranreichende gußeiserne Säule sich erinnerte an mich und, wenn man so sagen kann, sagte Austerlitz, Zeugnis ablegte von dem, was ich selbst nicht mehr wußte (*A* 319–320)
>
> [What made me uneasy at the sight of it, however, was not the question whether the complex form of the capital, now covered with a puce-tinged encrustation, had really

---

[48] See discussion in chapter four of the permeable borders between past and present, which enables the living and dead to coexist.

[49] In an article on Art Spiegelman's *Maus* and Sebald's *Austerlitz*, Marianne Hirsch reiterates her definition of postmemory and exemplifies how it operates in these two texts, highlighting in particular the strong connection that memory has to objects: "For them [the narrator and the protagonist], the past is located in objects, images, and documents, in fragments and traces barely noticeable in the layered train stations, streets, and official and private buildings of the European cities in which they meet and talk." Marianne Hirsch, "The Generation of Postmemory," *Photography in Fiction*, eds. Silke Horstkotte and Nancy Pedri, special issue of *Poetics Today* 29.1 (2008) 103–128, here 119. In her book, *The Generation of Postmemory*, Hirsch also uses this example to illustrate the difference between familial and affiliative postmemory: "And, as a German, [the narrator] also shows how the lines of affiliation can cross the divide between victim and perpetrator memory and postmemory." Hirsch, *The Generation of Postmemory*, 41. Hirsch's implied alignment of the German narrator with the 'perpetrators' is indeed problematic.

impressed itself on my mind when I passed through Pilsen with the children's transport in the summer of 1939, but the idea, ridiculous in itself, that this cast-iron column, which with its scaly surface seemed almost to approach the nature of a living being, might remember me and was, if I may so put it, said Austerlitz, a witness to what I could no longer recollect for myself (*AE* 221).]

Objects become memory-retaining beings with the power to bear witness to a long-repressed past, as Austerlitz experiences here. Similar to the way in which the objects of the Antikos Bazar in Terezín have outlived their owners, Sebald identifies "das autonome Dasein der Dinge" (*Logis* 173) ["the autonomous life of things" (*PC* 158)] with regard to the objects depicted by Jan Peter Tripp in the form of a still life. The description that follows applies just as well to the status of objects as carriers of history that one finds in these above mentioned passages in *Austerlitz*. Sebald writes in this essay on Tripp, "Da die Dinge uns (im Prinzip) überdauern, wissen sie mehr von uns als wir über sie; sie tragen die Erfahrungen, die sie mit uns gemacht haben, in sich und *sind* – tatsächlich – das vor uns aufgeschlagene Buch unserer Geschichte" (*Logis* 173) ["Since (in theory) things outlast us, they know more about us than we do about them; they bear their experience of us within them and *are* – in a literal sense – the book of our history lying open before us" (*PC* 159)]. Or, as Sebald expressed in an interview with Jean-Pierre Rondas in 2001, "Für mich sind die Dinge Mahnmale, wenn man das so sagen kann. In den Objekten ist so was wie stumme, sprachlose Geschichte kondensiert. Für mich wäre es also wichtig, diese Geschichte dieser Objekte zu erzählen" (*G* 214–215) [For me, objects are memorials, if one can say this. There is a mute, speechless history that condenses in objects. For me it is important to tell this history of these objects].

In addition to memory being connected to or located in objects, memory is also reactivated and preserved in the act of telling (i.e., in narration). In his book *Imagining the Holocaust*, which considers various textual forms within the broad category of Holocaust literature, Daniel Schwarz highlights how memory of the experiences are themselves "mediated by hunger, fear, and physical and psychological abuse beyond our imagination,"[50] thus affecting the possibility of representation. Schwarz furthermore presents memory as dependent upon narration for its formation, which he describes in metaphorical terms,

> But memory distorts even as it records, seeks narrative patterning in its sense-making, and depends often on a repetition compulsion that wears tracks in the mind for subsequent sense impressions to follow. Memory breaks a trail, and in its iteration that complex path of

---

50 Daniel Schwarz, *Imagining the Holocaust* (New York: St. Martin's Press, 1999) 11.

> understanding and misunderstanding deepens. Memory relies upon narrative to shape
> inchoate form and make that path into a road.[51]

Since memory eludes a distinct physical location, such a metaphoric description of memory formation is perhaps the only way to approach a definition of memory or to describe this process. An illustration of what Schwarz describes as the narrative formation of memory can be found when Věra recounts how Austerlitz would narrate to her the scenes of daily life that he observed through the kitchen window: "diese und andere Bilder mehr, sagte Austerlitz, reihten sich nun eines an das nächste, und so tief versunken und verschlossen sie in mir gewesen sind, so leuchtend kamen sie mir während des Hinausschauens aus dem Fenster nun wieder in den Sinn" (*A* 229) ["these and other images, said Austerlitz, ranged themselves side by side, so that deeply buried and locked away within me as they had been, they now came luminously back to my mind as I looked out that window" (*AE* 156)]. Thus it is another person's narrative of his own childhood that calls up and rearranges past images in his mind, providing him with the ability to (re)create his own memory of the past. Memories, images that once were repressed to the point of nonexistence in his mind, are now present and readily accessible, as Austerlitz states: "Ich konnte mir mit der kleinsten Willensbewegung alles vorstellen [...] und jetzt noch spüre ich, sagte Austerlitz, oder spüre erst wieder, wie es war" (*A* 230) ["With only the slightest effort of will I could conjure it all up...and I can still feel, said Austerlitz, or perhaps it is only now that I feel again" (*AE* 157)].

This (re)activation of long-repressed memories does not follow in every instance, however. In fact, memories often resist or elude Austerlitz's attempts to gain access to them. Even with the aid of Věra, who recounts in great detail his departure on the children's transport, Austerlitz falls short in his efforts to think back and remember this moment. He is as unable to bring back these images from the past, "Aber weder Agáta, noch Věra, noch ich selber kamen aus der Vergangenheit hervor" (*A* 316) ["But neither Agáta nor Vera nor I myself emerged from the past" (*AE* 218–219)]. Fragments from this past seem to resurface, only to recede again: "Manchmal schien es, als ob sich die Schleier teilen wollten [...], doch sowie ich eines dieser Fragmente festhalten oder, wenn man so sagen kann, schärfer einstellen wollte, verschwand es in der über mir sich drehenden Leere (*A* 316) ["Sometimes it seemed as if the veil would part [...], but as soon as I tried to hold one of these fragments fast, or get it into better focus, as it were, it disappeared into the emptiness revolving over my head" (*AE* 219)].

---

51 Ibid.

It becomes apparent that memory does not function as a storage room, into which one can go and pick up an object at will, what Aleida Assmann would refer to as the process of "Speichern": the form of memory that is "ein mechanisches Verfahren der Einlagerung und Rückholung" [a mechanical process of storage and retrieval].[52] Rather, memories resurface as if by their own will and without the concerted effort of the individual, what Assmann describes as the uncontrollable process of "Erinnern."[53] This can be seen when Austerlitz visits the theater where his mother performed, describing how the stage "war wie ein erloschenes Auge" (*A* 235) ["was like a blind eye" (*AE* 160)]. He continues,

> Und je angestrengter ich versuchte, von ihrem Erscheinen wenigstens eine Ahnung noch in mir zu finden, desto mehr dünkte es mich, als verengte sich der Theaterraum, als sei ich selber geschrumpft und säße als Däumling eingesperrt im Inneren eines Futterals oder einer mit Samt ausgepolsterten Schatulle (*A* 235).
>
> [And the harder I tried to conjure up at least some faint recollection of her appearance, the more the theater seemed to be shrinking, as if I myself had shrunk to the stature of a little Tom Thumb enclosed in a sort of velvet-lined casket[54] (*AE* 160–161).]

Only through an outside force, someone's movement on the stage, "begannen sich die Schatten zu regen" (*A* 236) ["the shadows begin to move" (*AE* 161)], and details arise in Austerlitz's mind of an orchestra, conductor, and musicians, the sound of voices and music. He then sees "in dem hellen Lichtstreif zwischen dem Bretterboden und dem Saum des Vorhangs einen himmelblauen, mit Silberflitter bestickten Schuh zu erblicken" (*A* 236) ["in the bright strip of light between the wooden floorboards and the hem of the curtain, I caught sight of a sky-blue shoe embroidered with silver sequins" (*AE* 161)]. Later, after asking Věra about his mother's past roles and costumes, she confirms that Agáta had indeed worn such shoes in one of her performances, a confirmation that produces an intense physical reaction in Austerlitz, or so he thinks, "da meinte ich, es zerspringe etwas in meinem Gehirn" (*A* 236) ["I felt as if something were shattering inside my brain" (*AE* 161)]. It is not in the moment in the theater but rather Věra's confirma-

---

52 Aleida Assmann, "Speichern oder Erinnern? Das kulturelle Gedächtnis zwischen Archiv und Kanon," *Kakanien Revisted*, January 31, 2006, 1–8, here 1, http://www.kakanien.ac.at/beitr/theorie/AAssmann1.pdf [accessed: June 22, 2013]. While memory does not function as a storehouse for Austerlitz, the narrator uses this metaphor in recounting his reading of Claude Simon's *Le Jardin des Plantes*; he describes how the author "von neuem in das Magazin seiner Erinnerungen hinabsteigt" (*A* 42) ["descends once more into the storehouse of his memories" (*AE* 26)].
53 Ibid. After delineating these two forms of memory, Assmann acknowledges that this clear separation is not entirely appropriate to the complexity of memory. Cf. ibid., 2.
54 For the German "Schatulle," "jewel case" might be better than "casket" in English.

tion that enables Austerlitz to make sense of this "involuntary memory," bringing with it an intense physical reaction. Similarly, Austerlitz has no memory of his family's trip to Marienbad in 1938, which Věra reminds him of during their conversations in her apartment. The memories he does have, however, are of a trip he took there with Marie de Verneuil in 1972, during which "unfaßbare Gefühle" (*A* 312) ["incomprehensible feelings" (*AE* 216)] weighed down upon him. Here, it was only with a "blinde Angst" (*A* 298) ["blind terror" (*AE* 206)] that he could entertain the idea of this being the better turn in his life. The sense and sensations Austerlitz experienced during this trip with Marie de Verneuil, could tentatively be called an unconscious or unrecognized memory of the vacation with his parents, one of the last times they were together as a family. Here it becomes clear that there is more to a memory then a distinguishable image; memories also include feelings that resist comprehension, elude visualization, and escape immediate connections. The basis for the intense physical experience of memory in *Austerlitz* is established by the narrator himself. After visiting the Fortress of Breendonk, the narrator's recollections of this experience lead him to reflect on both the nature of memory and the human capacity for memory. He describes his efforts to recall the past,

> Selbst jetzt, wo ich mich mühe, mich zu erinnern [...] löst sich das Dunkel nicht auf, sondern verdichtet sich bei dem Gedanken, wie wenig wir festhalten können, was alles und wie viel ständig in Vergessenheit gerät, mit jedem ausgelöschten Leben, wie die Welt sich sozusagen von selber ausleert, indem die Geschichten, die an den ungezählten Orten und Gegenständen haften, welche selbst keine Fähigkeit zur Erinnerung haben, von niemandem je gehört, aufgezeichnet oder weitererzählt werden [...] (*A* 39).
>
> [Even now, when I try to remember [...] the darkness does not lift but becomes yet heavier as I think how little we can hold in mind, how everything is constantly lapsing into oblivion with every extinguished life, how the world is, as it were, draining itself, in that the history of countless places and objects which themselves have no power of memory is never heard, never described or passed on (*AE* 24).]

This passage gains broader significance after we have gained knowledge of the history of objects, places, and people that Austerlitz will pass on to the narrator. The importance of communicative memory to preserve the history and histories of places and objects is incontrovertible when one considers the several instances in which Austerlitz (or Austerlitz through the stories of others) uncovers and thus preserves knowledge of the past that risks being lost and forgotten.

In addition to the complex layering of the narrative outlined in chapter four, the depiction of memory's suspect and unreliable nature, which is closely related to one's access to the past and one's own identity, creates a unique atmosphere of indeterminacy in *Austerlitz*. The many brief but intense flashes of epiphany often coupled with actual physical reactions heighten the feeling of the uncanny in this work. Austerlitz describes the prickling of his scalp or a sensation of shattering in his brain, as if these physical sensations were signs or signals of his memory at work, even before he is rationally able to explain a connection between what he sees and remembers. Here memory as recognition of what Austerlitz once knew – in his former life, that is, his childhood in Prague – hearkens back to Plato's concept of anamnesis.[55] Moreover, the years of repression that annihilated Austerlitz's memories of his past are further emphasized when contrasted with his moments of lucid recollection, where he lists in great detail things that he has seen in museums or read in books.

> J'entendis, ou crus entendre, so zitierte Austerlitz aus dem Gedächtnis, indem er durch die Fenster der Brasserie hinausblickte auf den Boulevard Auguste Blanqui, des gémissements poussés par le monde des cadavres au milieu duquel je gisais. Et quoique la mémoire de ces moments soit bien ténébreuse, quoique mes souvenirs soient bien confus, malgré les impressions de souffrances encore plus profondes que je devais éprouver et qui ont brouillé mes idées, il y a des nuits où je crois encore entendre ces soupirs étouffés (*A* 400–401).
>
> [*J'entendis, ou crus entendre*, Austerlitz quoted from memory, looking out of the brasserie window at the boulevard Auguste Blanqui, *des gémissements poussés par le monde des cadavres au milieu duquel je gisais. Et quoique la mémoire de ces moments soit bien ténébreuse, quoique mes souvenirs soient bien confus, malgré les impressions de souffrances encoure plus profondes que je devais éprouver et qui on brouillé mes idées, il y a des nuits où je crois encore entendre ces soupirs étouffés* (*AE* 283, italics Bell)].

This passage that Austerlitz quotes from Balzac's *Le Colonel Chabert* thematizes the uncertainty of memory that permeates the entire text and also recalls Věra's curious expression of the "gémissements de désespoir" (*A* 266) ["*gémissements de désespoir*" (*AE* 182, italics Bell)], which she imagines coming forth from the photographs found by chance between the pages of one of the small Balzac volumes. However, the *histoire* recounted here is undercut through the *discours* in which it is told: the uncertainty of memory is thematized within a detailed citation, recited from memory.

The confusion of sensate experience with conceptual knowledge is rooted in the problem of memory. In addition to Austerlitz's uncertainty, the narrator expresses his own reservations about memory and perception with such qualifying statements as, "wie es mir schien" (*A* 9) ["as it seemed to me" (*AE* 3)], "Ich weiß nicht mehr genau" (*A* 10) ["I cannot now recall" (*AE* 4)], "glaube ich" (*A* 12) ["I believe" (*AE* 5)], "wie ich gesehen haben müsste" (*A* 21) ["as I must have

---

55 According to Plato's definition of anamnesis, every act of cognition is an act of the soul remembering having been part of the world of ideas, which is also the realm of truth and, for Plato, reality. In this sense, every act of cognition is thus an act of remembering.

noticed" (*AE* 12)], "wie ich mich zu erinnern glaube" (*A* 40) ["(as I think I remember)" (*AE* 25; parentheses added by Bell)]. All of these expressions uttered by the narrator at the outset of *Austerlitz* establish a tone of uncertainty and apprehension in the retelling of the story that unfolds before us. Throughout the rest of the text, Austerlitz mirrors this uncertainty in his recollections of the past: "Ich weiß jetzt nicht mehr" (*A* 56) ["I no longer know" (*AE* 35)], "glaube ich" (*A* 63) ["I believe" (*AE* 40)], "das weiß ich nicht mehr genau" (*A* 98) ["I don't remember exactly how" (*AE* 65)],[56] "wie ich mich vielleicht erinnerte" (*A* 231) ["as I might perhaps remember" (*AE* 158)]. This last example illustrates a doubling of the problem of memory – Austerlitz cannot remember if he remembered at an early time – a doubling that makes memories even more elusive. Austerlitz also experiences the inability to remember despite concerted efforts to recall, such as when he stares endlessly at the photograph of himself as a boy, which serves as the cover image for most editions of this work. Such uncertainty leads him to make assumptions qualified with: "kann nur mutmaßen" (*A* 202) ["I can only guess" (*AE* 137)], "vielleicht" (*A* 202) ["perhaps" (*AE* 137)], "möglicherweise" (*A* 202) ["perhaps" (*AE* 138); additional "perhaps" added in English (*AE* 138)], "Auch kann ich nicht mehr sagen" (*A* 202) ["I myself cannot say" (*AE* 138)]. In contrast to the countless expressions of uncertainty in *Austerlitz* and the scrupulous questioning of memory that plagues the narrators of all of Sebald's fictional works, it is striking how the voice of Sebald's 1999 poem "Marienbader Elegie" ["Marienbad Elegy"] begins with a confident assertion – "Ich kann mir vorstellen" (*Ü* 79) ["I can see" (*ALW* 126)].[57]

At several points in his narration, Austerlitz makes what seem to be side comments that underline the difference between appearance and reality, a disjuncture that reinforces a sense of epistemological uncertainty in the text, which further underscores the uncertainty of memory. The difference between seeing and comprehending (i.e., the process of understanding) is perhaps most marked in the text when Austerlitz recounts his experience of viewing an excerpt from the Nazi propaganda film, "Der Führer schenkt den Juden eine Stadt,"[58] in which he hoped to catch a glimpse of his mother. His hope for the film is a hope to both see and know the reality of the past: "so würde ich vielleicht *sehen* oder *erahnen* können, *wie es in Wirklichkeit war*, und einmal ums andere malte ich mir

---

56 Ironically this expression directly follows a long and detailed description.

57 This poem was previously published: W.G. Sebald, "Marienbader Elegie," *Neue Zürcher Zeitung* Nr. 256 (13. November 1999) 50.

58 Although a detailed genesis of this film has already been provided, based on Austerlitz's reading of H.G. Adler, Austerlitz only names the film after having received a copy of it (*A* 352 [*AE* 246]).

aus, daß ich Agáta, eine im Vergleich zu mir junge Frau, ohne jeden Zweifel erkannte" (*A* 350, my emphasis) ["I might perhaps be able to *see* or *gain some inkling* of *what it was really like*, and then I imagined recognizing Agáta, beyond any possibility of doubt" (*AE* 245, my emphasis)]. To compensate what he does not find in the film – a glimpse of his mother with the unequivocal recognition of her identity – Austerlitz imagines further scenes and almost convinces himself of their effect on him, "bis [Agáta] zuletzt, wie ich zu spüren meinte, aus dem Film herausgetreten und in mich übergangen war" (*A* 350) ["at last I thought I could sense her stepping out of the frame and passing over into me" (*AE* 245)]. Here it becomes evident that a re-union with his mother can only take place in the space of Austerlitz's imagination. Austerlitz provides detail after detail from the film, but acknowledges that he cannot process (let alone perceive) what he saw: "Aber nichts von all diesen Bildern ging mir zunächst in den Kopf, sondern sie flimmerten mir bloß vor den Augen in einer Art von kontinuierlicher Irritation" (*A* 352) ["At first I could get none of these images into my head; they merely flickered before my eyes as the source of continual irritation or vexation" (*AE* 246)]. The medium of film – the moving images – presents a further challenge: "Die Unmöglichkeit, genauer in die gewissermaßen im Aufscheinen schon vergehenden Bilder hineinblicken zu können" (*A* 352) ["In the end the impossibility of seeing anything more closely in the pictures, which seemed to dissolve even as they appeared" (*AE* 246)]. Furthermore, Austerlitz is frustrated by the fact that the copy he has is incomplete, a fragment of only about fourteen minutes long. In an effort to get closer to the reality captured in the film, he has a slow-motion copy made, which draws out the fourteen minutes into a full hour. In this slow-motion version, he is able to see things and persons that had not been visible before, but the manipulation also has a strange effect, changing both appearances and sounds. The "Verwandlung" (*A* 353) ["transformation" (*AE* 247)] in sound is the most uncanny ("unheimlich") aspect: the lively polka music playing in the background becomes a funeral march, and the spoken commentary is completely lost; one can only hear "ein bedrohliches Grollen" (*A* 357) ["a menacing growl" (*AE* 250)]. The way in which Austerlitz has the film slowed down so that he can focus on the details is similar to his close reading process that leads him to get lost in footnotes.[59] In a sense, the film's surface and condition become magnified, in particular the damaged places in the film material. This focus on the medium itself ultimately brings Austerlitz further away from the content of the film.

---

59 See *A* 370–371 [(*AE* 260)].

The feeling of uncertainty that marks the beginning of *Austerlitz* and which continues throughout the book has direct links to the instability and suspect nature of memory, but this needs to be differentiated from the sense of incomprehensibility that also dominates the text. Incomprehensibility could be seen as a broader problem that encompasses both memory and perception as well as the uncertainty of both conceptual knowledge and sensate experiences. Austerlitz is driven by feelings and forces that are not always fully understandable or explicable. The narrator relays what Austerlitz told him of his grand plans to write a multi-volume architectural history and how he could not be sure why he was driven to take on such a task, "Weshalb er auf ein derart weites Feld sich begeben hatte, sagte Austerlitz, wisse er nicht" (*A* 52) ["Why he had embarked on such a wide field, said Austerlitz, he did not know" (*AE* 33)]. The existence of the drive is incontestable, although it is not completely understandable. What is certain behind this drive is Austerlitz's interest in networks,

> Richtig sei jedoch auch, daß er bis heute einem ihm selber nicht recht verständlichen Antrieb gehorche, der irgendwo mit einer früh schon in ihm sich bemerkbar machenden Faszination mit der Idee eines Netzwerks, beispielsweise mit dem gesamten System der Eisenbahnen, verbunden sei (*A* 52–53).
>
> [But then again, it was also true that he was still obeying an impulse which he himself, to this day, did not really understand, but which was somehow linked to his early fascination with the idea of a network such as that of the entire railway system (*AE* 33).]

Even though Austerlitz is rationally conscious of this fascination, which he refers to as his "Bahnhofsmanie" (*A* 53) ["obsession with railway trains" (*AE* 34)]; when he is physically in the train stations of Paris, he is seized by incomprehensible feelings, a situation that he describes as being caught "in die gefährlichsten, ihm ganz und gar unbegreiflichen Gefühlsströmungen" (*A* 53) ["in the grip of dangerous and entirely incomprehensible currents of emotion" (*AE* 33–34)]. This incomprehensibility of feelings of course has to do with his repressed past, of which he is at this point not yet fully conscious. The implication is that comprehension is only possible with full or at least more complete knowledge.

In dealing with such questions of memory as they connect to a greater history, the narrator of *Die Ausgewanderten* is keenly aware of how problematic his search for clues, information, and stories of the particular individual in question is, not to mention the presentation of these memories or this history. In essence, the problem of knowing another person and the problem of writing this individual's personal history are ever-present for Sebald and his narrators. After attempting to imagine the second emigrant's death, down to the minutest detail of Paul Bereyter most likely taking off his glasses and placing them onto the stones before lying down on the railroad tracks, the narrator comes to the following conclusion:

> Solche Versuche der Vergegenwärtigung brachten mich jedoch, wie ich mir eingestehen mußte, dem Paul nicht näher, höchstens augenblicksweise, in gewissen Ausuferungen des Gefühls, wie sie mir unzulässig erscheinen und zu deren Vermeidung ich jetzt aufgeschrieben habe, was ich von Paul Bereyter weiß und im Verlauf meiner Erkundungen über ihn in Erfahrung bringen konnte (*DA* 44–45).
>
> [Such endeavors to imagine his life and death did not, as I had to admit, bring me any closer to Paul, except at best for brief emotional moments of the kind that seemed presumptuous to me. It is in order to avoid this sort of wrongful trespass that I have written down what I know of Paul Bereyter (*E* 29).]

Here we see the importance of not only documentation but also narrativization for approaching an understanding of the past: the succinct but significant "in Erfahrung bringen" that is curiously left out of the English translation. Sebald's extreme understatement can almost be read as an "un-statement." This is true for the unspoken anti-Semitism felt by the first "emigrant," Dr. Selwyn, as well as the mass murder of the Jews in the Holocaust, which is implicitly present throughout all four stories that make up *Die Ausgewanderten* but never described in explicit detail. By focusing on the minutiae of experience, the details of what might have been *seen*, and withholding an assumption of what might have been *felt*, Sebald creates an apparent absence which points precisely to the problem of representing such atrocity.

Memory's Opposites: Repression and the Crisis of Language

Any discussion of memory must also consider forgetting – they are inextricably linked and enable each other[60] – and may further involve both repression and oblivion. Sebald's texts present no exception. Rather than a faculty that functions automatically, memory is presented as both a tool and ability that needs to be cultivated and practiced. In recognizing his own repression, Austerlitz further reveals how remembering is something that one must be conscious of not doing. He describes this process of recognition to the narrator as follows,

> Ich merkte jetzt, wie wenig Übung ich in der Erinnerung hatte und wie sehr ich, im Gegenteil, immer bemüht gewesen sein mußte, mich an möglichst gar nichts zu erinnern und allem aus dem Weg zu gehen, was sich auf die eine oder andere Weise auf meine mir unbekannte Herkunft bezog (*A* 205).

---

60 Cf. Assmann, "Speichern oder Erinnern?" 1.

[I realized then, he said, how little practice I had in using my memory, and conversely how hard I must always have tried to recollect as little as possible, avoiding everything which related in any way to my unknown past (*AE* 139).]

He further elucidates his own strategies of repression, the ways he avoided contact with the present, and how he

verfeinerte mehr und mehr meine Abwehrreaktionen und bildete eine Art von Quarantäne-und Immunsystem aus, durch das ich gefeit war gegen alles, was in irgendeinem, sei es noch so entfernten Zusammenhang stand mit der Vorgeschichte meiner auf immer engerem Raum sich erhaltenden Person (*A* 205–206).

[was always refining my defensive reactions, creating a kind of quarantine or immune system which, as I maintained my existence in a smaller and smaller space, protected me from anything that could be connected in any way, however distant, with my own early history (*AE* 140)].

Austerlitz acknowledges how his "kompensatorische Gedächtnis" (*A* 206) ["compensatory memory" (*AE* 140)] – the architectural knowledge he has amassed over the years – has at the same time enabled the repression of his past and is ultimately a form of unconscious censorship of his thoughts, "Selbstzensur meines Denkens" (*A* 206) ["self-censorship of my mind" (*AE* 140)]. He realizes that he was able to numb himself and deny his senses, "offenbar fähig, mich blind zu stellen und taub" (*A* 206) ["clearly capable of closing my eyes and ears to it" (*AE* 140)]. This repression, censorship, and denial of his senses lead unavoidably to paralysis: his inability to speak, his insomnia and night wandering, his hallucinations, and his ultimate breakdowns. The way in which Austerlitz expresses his limited knowledge of World War II, the concentration camp system, and the persecution of the Jews without directly naming these historical events[61] is revealing not only of his repression mechanisms but also of the link between coexistent time and history. Not wanting to name these events would correspond to his not wanting to make them 'real,' that is, naming them or even just thinking of them would call them back into existence, according to his concept of time, as outlined above in chapter four.

One of the central aspects of memory that Aleida Assmann points to is a process of translation,

---

61 "So wußte ich, so unvorstellbar mir dies heute selber ist, nichts von der Eroberung Europas durch die Deutschen, von dem Sklavenstaat, den sie aufgerichtet hatten, und nichts von der Verfolgung, der ich entgangen war, oder wenn ich etwas wußte, so war es nicht mehr, als ein Ladenmädchen weiß beispielsweise von der Pest oder der Cholera" (*A* 205). ["Inconceivable as it seems to me today, I knew nothing about the conquest of Europe by the Germans and the slave state they set up, and nothing about the persecution I had escaped, or at least, what I did know was not much more than a salesgirl in a shop, for instance, knows about the plague or cholera" (*AE* 139).]

[...] d[ie] permanente[] Umkodierung von Vorbewusstem in Bewusstes, von Sinnlichem in Sprachliches und Bildliches, von Bildern und Sprache in Schriftliches usw. Anders als das materielle Konservieren in Bibliotheken, Magazinen und Archiven vollzieht sich lebendiges Erinnern stets im Prozess solcher Übersetzungen. Ja, wir können geradezu sagen: *erinnern ist übersetzen*, und damit bleiben Erinnerungen zugleich in plastischer Bewegung.[62]

[[...] the constant coding anew from that which precedes consciousness into something conscious, from sensate experiences into something linguistic and visual, from images and language into something written, etc. Living memory, as opposed to the material conservation in libraries, storage houses, and archives, always takes place in such processes of translation. Yes, we could even say that *to remember is to translate*, and in this way memories remain in constant movement. They retain a plasticity.]

Assmann further specifies that such 'translations' of memories always already encompass change, displacement, and deferral.[63] In addition to being inherently fragmentary, memories are both imprecise and variable in comparison to historical documents, for example. However, inconsistencies and 'errors' in memories can in fact be the details that have the potential to bear witness to trauma, as Dori Laub has convincingly shown.[64] In his illuminating discussion of an 'inaccurate' testimony – from a historical perspective – given by an Auschwitz survivor, Laub reveals the necessity for rethinking how we define knowledge. 'Knowledge' in testimony, according to Laub, is "not simply a factual given that is reproduced and replicated by the testifier, but a genuine advent, an event in its own right."[65] Sebald's fictional works are similarly an event in which a particular form of literary knowledge of the past comes into being, a process upon which the text moreover reflects. For example, *Die Ringe des Saturn* describes the irreconcilable chasm between the act of writing and the meaning of that which one wants to describe, be it a person, an event, experience, or emotion. The narrator recalls how Stanley Kerry recounted that, "eine der Hauptschwierigkeiten beim Schreiben darin bestehe, mit der Spitze des Schreibgeräts einzig und allein an das zu schreibende Wort zu denken und darüber das, was man beschreiben wolle, restlos zu vergessen" (*RS* 222) ["one of the chief difficulties of writing consisted in thinking, with the tip of the pen, solely of the word to be written, whilst banishing from one's mind the reality of what one intends to describe" (*RoS* 186)]. Sebald's *Austerlitz* further reflects on the way in which literature can bring forth knowledge of the past insofar as the text brings together the idea of memory as a process with the writing process, including its inherent problems and difficulties. Reminiscent

---

62 Assmann, *Der lange Schatten der Vergangenheit*, 124, emphasis AA.
63 Cf. 288.
64 Cf. Laub, *Testimony. Crises of Witnessing*, in particular 59–63.
65 Ibid., 62.

of Lord Chandos' crisis of language described by Hugo von Hofmannsthal,[66] Austerlitz describes the arduous process of writing and ultimate dissatisfaction with his results. He states,

> Jetzt aber war mir das Schreiben so schwer geworden, daß ich oft einen ganzen Tag brauchte für einen einzigen Satz, und kaum daß ich einen solchen mit äußerster Anstrengung ausgesonnenen Satz niedergeschrieben hatte, zeigte sich die peinliche Unwahrheit meiner Konstruktionen und die Unangemessenheit sämtlicher von mir verwendeten Wörter (*A* 180).
>
> [But now I found writing such hard going that it often took me a whole day to compose a single sentence, and no sooner had I thought such a sentence out, with the greatest effort, and written it down, that I saw the awkward falsity of my constructions and the inadequacy of all the words I had employed (*AE* 122).]

Not only does the task of writing prove arduous, but the signs themselves – the individual words and their meanings – hinder the actual physical process of writing. Austerlitz continues,

> Hie und da geschah es noch, daß sich ein Gedankengang in meinem Kopf abzeichnete in schöner Klarheit, doch wußte ich schon, indem dies geschah, daß ich außerstande war, ihn festzuhalten, denn sowie ich nur den Bleistift ergriff, schrumpften die unendlichen Möglichkeiten der Sprache, der ich mich früher doch getrost überlassen konnte, zu einem Sammelsurium der abgeschmacktesten Phrasen zusammen. Keine Wendung im Satz, die sich dann nicht als eine jämmerliche Krücke erwies, kein Wort, das nicht ausgehöhlt klang und verlogen (*A* 181).
>
> [Now and then a train of thought did succeed in emerging with wonderful clarity inside my head, but I knew even as it formed that I was in no position to record it, for as soon as I so much as picked up my pencil the endless possibilities of language, to which I could once safely abandon myself, became a conglomeration of the most inane phrases. There was not an expression in the sentence but it proved to be a miserable crutch, not a word but it sounded false and hollow (*AE* 122–123).]

All of language, the "gesamte Gliederwerk der Sprache" (*AE* 183) ["entire structure of language" (*A* 124)], is described by Austerlitz as "eingehüllt in einen undurchdringlichen Nebel" (*A* 183) ["enveloped in impenetrable fog" (*AE* 124)]. He describes his loss of orientation in writing and in language – his intellectual staple – down to its base components: the arbitrary signs, which themselves even lose profile. He states, "Nirgends sah ich mehr einen Zusammenhang, die Sätze lösten sich auf in lauter einzelne Worte, die Worte in eine willkürliche Folge von

---

66 Even before the publication of *Austerlitz*, Susan Sontag alludes to "the passionate bleakness of Sebald's voice" and roots it in a "German genealogy," which includes among others "the Hofmannsthal of *The Lord Chandos Letter*." Susan Sontag, "A Mind in Mourning," *Times Literary Supplement* (February 25, 2000) 3–4, here 4.

Buchstaben, die Buchstaben in zerbrochene Zeichen" (*A* 184) ["I could see no connections anymore, the sentences resolved themselves into a series of separate words, the words into random sets of letters, the letters into disjointed signs" (*AE* 124)]. Austerlitz eventually links his suspicion and fundamental mistrust of language to his absolute isolation, the lack of any real connections to those around him. Moreover, his isolation and alienation are accompanied by fainting spells, complete memory loss, and eventual hospitalization. The famous irony of Hofmannsthal's *Letter of Lord Chandos* is preserved here in the figurative language rich in metaphors and similes that Austerlitz employs to express the elusiveness of linguistic meaning. Austerlitz attempts to overcome his "Schreibkrise" [crisis of writing] by burying his piles of papers and notes in the compost heap in his backyard. In the handwritten manuscript, Sebald originally had Austerlitz burning these papers, the process of which and the result – the fire and ashes – are described in great detail. This is a noteworthy change from the manuscript to the printed text, for it also reveals a further intertextual connection that Sebald ultimately decides to eliminate. In an article in *The Paris Review* of 1967, Vladimir Nabokov recalls being plagued by writer's block and self-doubt while working on *Lolita* and how he even wanted to take the first chapter out into the garden and put it into the basket used for burning paper.[67]

The crisis of language described in *Austerlitz* is however not a mere intertextual rehashing of the ideas expressed by Hofmannsthal one hundred years prior.[68] The shortcomings and purported failure of language that characterized one of the core issues of modernity gain new dimension when considered after the Holocaust. This focus on, or one might even call it an obsession with, the question of representation can be connected specifically with the Holocaust's representability but relates as well to the representation of history in general. Although the impossibility of representation – of something being either too

---

67 Sebald underlines this comment in his Nabokov edition ["[...] ich, von Schreibproblemen und Selbstzweifeln bedrängt, die erstem Kapitel von *Lolita* zum Papierverbrennungskorb in unserem Garten tragen wollte."] Vladimir Nabokov, "The Paris Review (1967)," *Deutliche Worte. Interviews – Leserbriefe – Aufsätze* vol. 20 *Gesammelte Werke*, ed. Dieter E. Zimmer (Reinbek bei Hamburg: Rowohlt, 1993 [1970]) 167, W.G. Sebald Nachlaß: Teilbibliothek, DLA Marbach. Since Nabokov's life and works serve as a frequent source of intertextuality, perhaps Sebald changed this scene in order to avoid the direct connection to Nabokov.

68 In an article from 1978 on Hugo von Hofmannsthal's play *Der Turm*, Sebald accuses Germanistik scholars of having interpreted the letter of Lord Chandos "bis zum Überdruß" [ad nauseam], and he moreover claims that it is difficult to bring scholarship away from its fetishes. While Sebald does not take up the Chandos letter in a scholarly way, it appears as though he were not immune to this fetish, considering the essential role this intertextual reference plays in *Austerlitz*. W.G. Sebald, "Das Wort unter der Zunge." *Literatur & Kritik* 125 (1978) 294–303, here 296.

beautiful or too horrific for words – is a trope that can be traced back to the Middle Ages, this trope must be reconsidered after the Holocaust. Sebald's works reconceptualize memory as more of a process than as something one possesses. One could even argue that Sebald is creating a dynamic poetics of memory in order to deconstruct the notion that memory is a thing to be possessed in a subject-object relationship with the individual.[69] Though the concerns voiced by Hofmannsthal continue to persist – in particular the difficulty in approaching 'reality' through writing, 'reality' seen as always eluding any objective, logical, systematic, or semiotic grasp[70] – the problem of modernity is reformulated in the works of Sebald to take into account the effects of new media, in relationship to the already problematic endeavor of representing the Holocaust.

"He wrote me: I will have spent my life trying to understand the function of remembering, which is not the opposite of forgetting, but rather its lining. We do not remember, we rewrite memory much as history is rewritten."[71] These words, spoken by the narrator in Chris Marker's filmic essay *Sans soleil*, could have been voiced just as easily by one of Sebald's narrators. Marker's film deals with time, memory, history, and narration, as well as how these concerns are culturally determined. Both the thematic aspects and the film's narration offer up myriad points of connection to Sebald's œuvre.[72] The nameless narrator, and by extension the filmmaker Marker, recalls the images he has filmed and how: "They have substituted themselves for my memory. They are my memory. I wonder how people remember things who don't film, don't photograph, don't tape. How has mankind managed to remember?"[73] Film images that both substitute and create memory can be related to Austerlitz's form of "compensatory memory," which he built up over his many years of architectural research. Both the images in Sebald's text as well as the texts themselves function as a form of memory (as we saw in the example of the doors in Terezín). Photographs, moreover, quite literally serve

---

69 Bernhard Malkmus points out how "Benjamin's concept of memory as medium of, rather than instrument for, the exploration of the past," can be helpful in approaching Sebald's poetics of memory. Bernhard Malkmus, "'All of them Signs and Characters from the Type-Case of Forgotten Things' – Intermedia Configurations of History in W.G. Sebald," *Memory Traces. 1989 and the Question of German Cultural Identity*, ed. Silke Arnold-de Simine (New York: Peter Lang, 2005) 211–244, here 215.

70 Cf. Paul Hansom, *Literary Modernism and Photography* (Westport, CT; London: Praeger, 2002) xiv.

71 Text of *Sans soleil*, film by Chris Marker; France 1982; 16 mm, 100 min. http://www.marker text.com/sans_soleil.htm [accessed June 22, 2013].

72 The film's narration, for instance, could be described as periscopic much in the way that Sebald, with reference to Thomas Bernhard, uses this term to describe his own narration.

73 Marker, *Sans soleil*, http://www.markertext.com/sans_soleil.htm.

a compensatory function insofar as they help Austerlitz reconstruct experiences that have been erased from his memory after his fits of fainting and ultimate breakdowns. Austerlitz recalls to the narrator, "Erst als ich die an jenem Septembersonntag in Maisons-Alfort aufgenommenen Photographien entwickelte, gelang es mir, anhand dieser Bilder und geleitet von den geduldigen Fragen, die Marie mir stellte, meine verschütteten Erlebnisse zu rekonstruieren" (*A* 381) ["Only when I developed the photographs I had taken that Sunday in September at Maisons-Alfort was I able, with their aid and guided by Marie's patient questioning, to reconstruct my buried experiences" (*AE* 268)]. Rather than replacing a memory, literature has the power to *create* memory based on historical knowledge that is infused with imagination. Ultimately, the "compensatory" aspect of memory, as it is explored through the testimonial structure of the text, reveals it to be not only a form of substitution but also one of *restitution*.

Chapter 6
Translation as Metaphor and Conservative Innovation

The opening passage of Elias Canetti's "Die Rufe der Blinden" ["The Cries of the Blind"] exemplifies the central concern of all the vignettes that make up *Die Stimmen von Marrakesch* (1967) [*The Voices of Marrakesh* (1978)]: the inherent difficulty in translating sensate perception and emotional reaction into cognitive reflection and linguistic expression. Canetti writes,

> Ich versuche, etwas zu berichten, und sobald ich verstumme, merke ich, daß ich noch gar nichts gesagt habe. Eine wunderbar leuchtende, schwerflüssige Substanz bleibt in mir zurück und spottet der Worte. Ist es die Sprache, die ich dort nicht verstand, und die sich nun allmählich in mir übersetzen muß? Da waren Ereignisse, Bilder, Laute, deren Sinn erst in einem *entsteht*; die durch Worte weder aufgenommen noch beschnitten wurden; die jenseits von Worten, tiefer und mehrdeutiger sind als diese.[1]
>
> [Here I am, trying to give an account of something, and as soon as I pause I realize that I have not yet said anything at all. A marvellously luminous, viscid substance is left behind in me, defying words. Is it the language I did not understand there, and that must now gradually find its translation in me? There were incidents, images, sounds, the meaning of which is only now emerging; that words neither recorded nor edited; that are beyond words, deeper and more equivocal than words.]

Canetti intentionally refuses to learn the languages he hears in Marrakesh, in order to remain a foreign outsider; he nevertheless experiences and can describe a process of translation that takes place "jenseits von Worten" ["beyond words"]. A core strand of my investigation of Sebald's works can be subsumed under the broad question of 'translation' – translation as both a challenge and a process of creation – as Canetti so beautifully describes in the passage cited above.

The word *translation*, from the Latin *trans-ferre* – cf. the German *über-setzen* – refers etymologically to a process of 'carrying across', either from one set of sign-systems (*langue*) to another or from a 'mute' experience to a semiotic expression, and like the Greek *meta-pherein*, *trans-ferre* is itself a metaphor. Indeed, many discussions of translation are by nature metaphorical, since we both approach translation in metaphorical terms and use the word 'translation' as a metaphor to describe a variety of transfers: linguistic, historical, cultural, medial. Although all

---

1 Canetti, Elias, *Die Stimmen von Marrakesch. Aufzeichnungen nach einer Reise*, (Munich: Hanser, 1967) 21. [*The Voices of Marrakesh. A Record of a Visit*, trans. J.A. Underwood (New York: Seabury Press, 1978) 23.]

processes of translation are, to a certain extent, metaphoric, we are nevertheless too often prompted to draw a clear line between 'metaphoric' and 'literal' translations. In light of Canetti's perception of just how much of the translation process eludes rational explanation, escapes materialization in a linguistic form, or occurs beyond words, we must (re)consider whether language is absolutely necessary to our thought processes. That is, we need to examine how thinking can occur outside of articulation in a sign system. The translation of literary texts provides fertile ground for discussions of cultural translation and the productive tension between experience and language that Canetti identifies. These reflections form the starting point for this chapter, as it will identify multiple levels of translation in Sebald's work and elucidate the different challenges these levels pose to 'translation.'

Textual Translation

"China Marks, Dark Porcelains and Marbled Beauties, Scarce Silver-lines or Burnished Brass, Green Foresters and Green Adelas, White Plumes, Light Arches, Old Ladies and Ghost Moths [...]" (*AE* 91). Even if the reader does not understand these names, they immediately initiate a chain of associations, with the alliteration alone activating one's imagination, revealing the distinct connotative force of Anthea Bell's translation of *Austerlitz*. This is accentuated by her comments on the process of translating Sebald, especially with regard to the above list of different varieties of moths. Because Bell did not have the exact English equivalents of the vernacular German names used by Sebald when describing late night moth-watching, she sent Sebald a list of moth names from which he could choose appropriate 'equivalents' for the original German list that included: "Porzellan- und Pergamentspinner", "spanische Fahnen und schwarze Ordensbänder, Messing- und Ypsiloneulen, Wolfsmilch- und Fledermausschwärmer, Jungfernkinder und alte Damen, Totenköpfe und Geistermotten [...]" (*A* 136). Bell recalls Sebald's response to her inquiry as follows.

> Max thought that we didn't necessarily have to enumerate exactly the same moths in English as in German; it was the general effect he wanted. [...] He decided to leave out the Death's-Head Hawk-moth entirely, feeling that it sounded too sinister in English, more so than the German *Totenkopf*.[2]

---

2 Which is odd since the notorious *SS Totenkopf-Division* not only had a very bad record of atrocities in Eastern Europe, but also provided the staff for concentration camps. Anthea Bell,

The vast array of flora and fauna, not to mention the other technical terms that fill Sebald's texts, raise similar problems to the above list of moths. But since moths are akin to butterflies, which serve as a common metaphor for transformation and translation,[3] it is a rather Sebaldian coincidence that this discussion of types of moths should reveal an essential question of translation: that of equivalence.

Bell's translation, which sought to approximate Sebald's meaning in terms of "general effect" without using an exact or 'literal' equivalent[4], illustrates the various levels at which a translator has to work and the varying units with which he has to engage. Beyond such discrete linguistic units as words, such elements as sounds, phrases, tone, and even what one could call "atmosphere" are also important. In a discussion of what can be *found* rather than lost in translation, the author Michael Cunningham has written, "Language in fiction is made up of equal parts meaning and music."[5] This combination of meaning and music or "force," as Cunningham later calls it, poses a particular challenge to the translator that has to be taken seriously, since readers will respond to both elements albeit often unconsciously. The complex constellation of elements with which a translator has to deal undermines the myth of a 'literal', 'direct', or 'word-for-word' translation by demonstrating how translation can never be x = x. Willis Barnstone writes, "Since sound and meaning are ingredients in the phonic-semantic code of every word, there can be no full lexical identity between languages or full synonymy in the same language."[6] Or, as Yoko Tawada has it, "Die Übersetzung ist nicht Abbild des Originals, sondern in ihr bekommt eine Bedeutung des Originals einen neuen Körper" ["The translation is not the (mirror) image of the original but the means by which one version of the original acquires

---

"On Translating W. G. Sebald" *The Anatomist of Melancholy. Essays in Memory of W. G. Sebald* ed. Rüdiger Görner (Munich: iudicium, 2003) 11–18, here 17.

3 Martin Klebes identifies butterflies as "the master metaphor for translation" and makes a further intertextual connection between Sebald and Vladimir Nabokov. Martin Klebes, "Infinite Journey: From Kafka to Sebald" *W. G. Sebald: A Critical Companion* eds. J.J. Long and Anne Whitehead (Seattle, WA: University of Washington Press, 2004) 123–139, here 134.

4 I use 'literal' tentatively, heeding Edith Grossman's warning that "fidelity should never be confused with literalness" since "literalism is a clumsy, unhelpful concept that radically skews and oversimplifies the complicated relationship between a translation and an original." Edith Grossman, "Translating Cervantes: Lecture by Edith Grossman," *Encuentros* 52 (2005) 1–11, here 3.

5 Michael Cunningham, "Found in Translation," *The New York Times* (October 3, 2010) WK10. Theoreticians of poetry (as opposed to prose fiction) have engaged with this problem since at least Baudelaire.

6 Willis Barnstone, *The Poetics of Translation. History, Theory, Practice* (New Haven and London: Yale University Press, 1993) 42.

a new body"].[7] Despite such challenges, translation is nevertheless possible, and with Sebald's works, the often curious differences between original and translation demand a closer look to discover what they signify.[8]

Patrick Charbonneau, Sebald's French translator, has not only illuminated such core questions in terms of the translation of the syntax, tone and rhythm of a text,[9] he has also, like Matthias Zucchi,[10] raised questions about the translation of such peculiar features of Sebald's works, as regionalisms, dialects and rare words. But Charbonneau has identified a further challenge: Sebald's own neologisms. When, for example, Charbonneau rendered "Lusitanischer Lorbeer" as "lauriers lusitaniens," Sebald willingly agreed to the translation, explaining that as such a tree was non-existent in Germany but well-known in England as the Portuguese Laurel or *prunus lusitanica*, he had had to invent a name in German.[11]

Just as invented terms are common in Sebald's prose, so his predilection for obscure words also challenges his translators to find an equivalent with the same or comparable connotative power. Thus, in *Austerlitz*, "das arsanische Grauen" (*A* 95) is a key phrase because it puzzles the reader in a particularly productive way, which I shall develop below. This formulation proved particularly perplexing for Ioanna Meïtani, one of Sebald's Greek translators, who explained that in a

---

7 Yoko Tawada, "Das Tor des Übersetzers oder Celan liest Japanisch," *Ansichten und Auskünfte zur deutschen Literatur nach 1945. Sonderband Text + Kritik* 9, ed. Heinz Ludwig Arnold (1995) 179–186, here 186.

8 After scrutinizing differences between the English and German texts, Mark McCulloh has even asserted that Sebald has "two distinct œuvres" because of the allegedly paradoxical "tendency in two different directions" of Hulse's translations. Mark R. McCulloh, "Introduction: Two Languages, Two Audiences: The Tandem Literary Œuvres of W. G. Sebald," *W. G. Sebald. History – Memory – Trauma*, eds. Scott Denham and Mark McCulloh (Berlin: de Gruyter, 2006) 7–20, here 7 and 13. McCulloh notes in particular the humor of the German text, evoked by the text-image relationship that does not carry over into English, and the matter-of-factness of the German text that Hulse makes more lyrical in English. The major difference between these two versions of Sebald's texts is, McCulloh argues, the "absence of any feature in English that corresponds to the subjunctive mood for indirect discourse, lending as it does a strong sense of the tentative, the uncertain." See ibid. 16.

9 Patrick Charbonneau, "Correspondence(s). Le traducteur et son auteur," *Mémoire. Transferts. Images./Erinnerung. Übertragungen. Bilder*, ed. Ruth Vogel-Klein, *Recherches germaniques* Hors Série 2 (2005) 193–210.

10 Matthias Zucchi, "Zur Kunstsprache W. G. Sebalds," *Verschiebebahnhöfe der Erinnerung: Zum Werk W. G. Sebalds*, eds. Sigurd Martin and Ingo Wintermeyer (Würzburg: Königshausen & Neumann, 2007) 163–181.

11 Charbonneau, "Correspondence(s)," 202. To illustrate Sebald's attention to detail, Charbonneau recounts how Sebald included a leaf of this particular tree in a letter discussing this passage in *Die Ausgewanderten*.

last-ditch effort to identify its source, she performed a Google search which simply resulted in links back to Sebald.[12] Bell translates the German as "arsanical horror" (*AE* 63), while Charbonneau uses "la terreur arsanique" and inexplicably refers the reader in a footnote to the Curé d'Ars (1786–1859).[13] Charbonneau provides further notes ("N.d.T.") at five points in his translation of *Austerlitz* and the editor provides one more ("N.d.E."). These may be informative, but collectively, they diminish the text's aura by reminding the reader that the text *is* a translation. More specifically, I would argue that the editorial note on the final page of the French translation goes too far when it footnotes "Max Stern, Paris, 18.5.44" and offers the explanation: "Date de naissance de W. G. Sebald, elle est aussi celle de l'arrivée au Neuvième Fort de Kaunas du convoi 73 avec lequel 878 Juifs de toutes nationalités ont été déportés à partir de Drancy"[14] [W. G. Sebald's date of birth, which is also the date on which convoy 73 arrived at the Ninth Fort of Kaunas; a convoy on which 878 Jews from various nations were deported from Drancy]. While the significance of the biographical coincidence of this quotation from Dan Jacobson's *Heshel's Kingdom* (1999) reveals the complex way in which Sebald weaves together intra-, inter-, and extratextual strands,[15] it is central to Sebald's poetics of engagement that such things remain implicit so as to engage the reader more intimately with the fictional text and lead him to a closer evaluation of the history (re)presented there. As Ignasi Ribó puts it, such documents and references "are not there to *show the past*, but to show what is *absent* from the representation of the past. They are part of a system that exploits the citational structure of historiography, not to represent history directly, as documentary fiction would tend to do, but *indirectly.*"[16]

Sebald's style, characterized by long sentences and frequent subordinating clauses, is often described, sometimes even reproachfully, as reminiscent of such nineteenth-century German authors as Johann Peter Hebel, Gottfried Keller, and Adalbert Stifter. Bell, however, contrasts Sebald's style appreciatively with "the short sentences and staccato effect" of other modern German works of

---

12 "W. G. Sebald: Im Geäst der Sätze," a presentation by Ioanna Meïtani and Iannis Kalifatidis at a conference entitled "Widerstand des (literarischen) Textes": Deutsch-Griechische/Griechisch-Deutsche Übersetzungspraxis. The conference was organized by the Fachbereich Philosophie und Geisteswissenschaften of the Freie Universität Berlin and held there at the Institut für Griechische und Lateinische Philologie on November 14, 2008.

13 W. G. Sebald, *Austerlitz*, trans. Patrick Charbonneau (Arles: Actes Sud, 2002) 78.

14 Ibid., 349.

15 See discussion in chapter four.

16 Ignasi Ribó, "The One-Winged Angel: History and Memory in the Literary Discourse of W. G. Sebald," *Orbis Litterarum* 64.3 (2009) 222–262, here 232, emphasis IR.

fiction.[17] She also highlights Sebald's deployment of relative clauses, subordinate clauses and participial constructions used adjectivally, on the grounds that they accelerate the reading and so compel the careful reader to return and reread. Even Sebald's translators, by necessity his most meticulous readers,[18] are not exempt from the effects of such acceleration: Charbonneau, for instance, demonstrates the effect that this deferral of meaning has on readers by admitting that it caused him to inadvertently omit a clause from his translation of *Schwindel.Gefühle*.[19] While Sebald's œuvre abounds in lengthy participial constructions, we need only to look again at the list of moths, for preceding it we read of "die Mannigfaltigkeit dieser sonst vor unseren Blicken verborgenen wirbellosen Wesen" (*A* 136) ["the endless variety of these invertebrate beings, which are usually hidden from our sight" (*AE* 91)]. Sebald's participial adjectives precede the German noun, often by a significant distance, and so delay considerably the reader's awareness of what is being described. But to translate such cases, the Anglophone translator has to start with the noun and then qualify it by adding on subordinate clauses, since similar syntactical constructions do not exist in English.[20] Literary scholars, too, have described the above delay-effect as characteristic of Sebald's style, with Richard Eldridge finding it "somewhat more natural in German than in English."[21] Indeed, Amir Eshel regards Sebald's "poetics of suspension," as central to his work and describes it as one that "suspends notions of chronology, succession, comprehension, and

---

17 Anthea Bell, "Translating W.G. Sebald's *Austerlitz*," *Linguist* 41.6 (2002) 162–163, here 163. Zucchi's analysis of Sebald's grammatical structures and particular word choice challenges the notion that his language and style are homogeneous across his texts, thus breaking down the sweeping generalization that his style is classical, epic, or in the nineteenth-century narrative tradition. See Zucchi, "Zur Kunstsprache W.G. Sebalds."

18 Referring to Willis Barnstone, Bell states that "translation is a 'particularly intensive form of reading.'" Bell, "On Translating W.G. Sebald," 8.

19 Charbonneau, "Correspondance(s)," 207. Charbonneau is referring to the passage in W.G. Sebald, *Vertiges*, trans. Patrick Charbonneau (Paris: Gallimard, 2003) 75.

20 A few examples from *Die Ringe des Saturn/The Rings of Saturn* show how the object of the German sentence is brought forward in the English translation: "eine mit Lichtern bestückte, chromglänzende amerikanische Limousine mit offenem Verdeck" (*RS* 101) becomes "an open-top American limousine studded with lights and gleaming with chrome" (*RoS* 82); "angesichts des unter den Blicken der Chirurgengilde ausgestreckt daliegenden Prosektursubjekts" (*RS* 102) becomes "I looked at the body being dissected under the eyes of the Guild of Surgeons" (*RoS* 82); and "der wohl um die Jahrhundertwende mitten in den Sand gesetzte Hotelpalast" (*RS* 106) becomes "the palatial hotel, built on the beach at the turn of the century" (*RoS* 85).

21 Richard Eldridge, "Literature as Material Figuration: Benjamin, Sebald, and Human Life in Time," *Visions of Value and Truth. Understanding Philosophy and Literature*, eds. Floora Ruokonen and Laura Werner *Acta Philosophica Fennica* 79 (2006) 13–29, here 20.

closure – a poetics that, rather than depicting and commenting on the historical event in time, constitutes an event, becomes the writing of a different, a literary time."[22]

To illustrate contrastively the above considerations, it is worth looking at the last passage of *Schwindel.Gefühle*, where Sebald uses uncharacteristically short sentences, some even lacking verbs. The narrator has been dozing in a train after reading excerpts from an edition of Samuel Pepys' Diary that was published in the fateful year of 1913,[23] in particular Pepys' account of the Great Fire of London (1666):

> Als ein fast vergangenes Echo kehrten sodann in diese atemlose Leere die Worte zurück – Fragmente aus dem Bericht über das große Feuer von London. Ich sah es wachsen mehr und mehr. Es war nicht hell, es war ein grausig blutig böses Lohen, vom Wind getrieben durch die ganze Stadt. Zu Hunderten die toten Tauben auf dem Pflaster, das Federkleid versengt. Ein Haufen Plünderer in Lincoln's Inn. Die Kirchen, Häuser, Holz und Mauersteine, alles brennt zugleich. Am Gottesacker die immergrünen Bäume fangen Feuer. Ein rasend kurzer Fackelbrand, ein Krachen, Funkenstieben und Erlöschen. Des Bischofs Braybrookes Grab ist aufgetan. Ist dies die letzte Stunde? Ein dumpfer, ungeheurer Schlag. Wie Wellen in der Luft. Das Pulverhaus fliegt auf. Wir fliehen auf das Wasser. Um uns der Widerschein, und vor dem tiefen Himmelsdunkel in einem Bogen hügelan die ausgezackte Feuerwand bald eine Meile breit. Und andern Tags ein stiller Aschenregen – westwärts, bis über Windsor Park hinaus. – 2013 – Ende (*SG* 298–299).
>
> [Into that breathless void, then, words returned to me as an echo that had almost faded away – fragments from the account of the Great Fire of London as recorded by Samuel Pepys. We saw the fire grow. It was not bright, it was a gruesome, evil, bloody flame, sweeping, before the wind, through all the City. Pigeons lay destroyed upon the pavements, in hundreds, their feathers singed and burned. A crowd of looters roams through Lincoln's Inn. The churches, houses, the woodwork and the building stones, ablaze at once. The churchyard yews ignited, each one a lighted torch, a shower of sparks now tumbling to the ground. And Bishop Braybrooke's grave is opened up, his body disinterred. Is this the end of time? A muffled, fearful, thudding sound, moving, like waves, throughout the air. The powder house exploded. We flee onto the water. The glare around us everywhere, and yonder, before the darkened skies, in one great arc the jagged wall of fire. And, the day after, a silent rain of ashes, westward, as far as Windsor Park (*V* 262–263).]

Though uncharacteristic of Sebald's style and syntax, the function of the abrupt sentences in this passage is clear. Echoing such Expressionist poems as Georg Heym's "Der Krieg" (1911) and "Die Dämonen der Städte" (1911), the syntax here enacts the elemental chaos and uncontrolled destruction of the conflagration in

---

22 Amir Eshel, "Against the Power of Time: The Poetics of Suspension in W. G. Sebald's *Austerlitz*," *New German Critique* 88 (2003) 71–96, here 74.
23 This date, as Martine Carré has shown, is no accident. Martine Carré, *W. G. Sebald. Le retour de l'auteur* (Lyon: Presses Universitaires de Lyon, 2008) 73.

a way that corresponds to the often abrupt sequencing of the dream recalled by the narrator.[24] In contrast to Sebald's German text, the English translation removes the portentous "2013 – end," lessens the immediacy of the experience by translating "diese" as "that" (line 1) and "ich" as "we" (line 3), and reminds the reader that he is dealing with a literary account (lines 2–3). The English version also weakens the sense of the conflagration as an aspect of impersonal, elemental violence by specifying "es" as "the fire" (line 3), inserting "before the" (line 4), naturalizing the ironically named "immergrünen Bäume" ["ever-green trees"] into "yews" (line 7), rendering "ungeheurer" [monstrous] as "fear-ful" (line 9) and replacing the stark and unspecific "aufgetan" by passive verbs which could be construed to mean that the Bishop's grave has been opened up by human agency *for the purpose of* disinterring his body (something that is not even mentioned in the German). The translation also brings the shorter sentences together (lines 9; 10–12) and fills in the missing or implied verb (lines 5; 9), actions which are untypical of German-into-English translations, where one is more often confronted with the need to break up long, compound sentences. One might make any number of conjectures as to why the translator has taken such liberties, but Hulse's drafts reveal that here, Sebald has overridden Hulse's translation by rewriting the entire passage,[25] possibly because of his growing dislike of anything expressionistic, by which he meant violent and apocalyptic.[26]

In another instance, in *Die Ringe des Saturn*, we have a scene much like others across Sebald's prose fiction: darkness has suddenly fallen, and the narrator stands at his hotel window looking out into a storm. Whereas in the German text, the narrator describes a pair of ducks being illuminated by a flash of lightning (*RS* 110), they become "a solitary mallard" in the English translation (*RoS* 89). This epiphanic moment is already highly stylized in the German original, and one might construe the change – 'transformation' even – as a willful mistranslation that has perhaps been made to capture Sebald's well-

---

24 See also Anja K. Johannsen, "'The Contrarieties that are in our Yearnings': Allegorical, Nostalgic and Transcendent Spaces in the Works of W.G. Sebald," *Journal of European Studies*, Special Issue: W.G. Sebald, ed. Richard Sheppard 41.3–4 (2011) 377–393.
25 Typescript with corrections. Hulse Papers, bMS Eng 1632, box 2, folder 11, 49. Harvard Houghton Library. I am very grateful to Michael Hulse for his permission to quote from his papers. I would also like to extend my thanks to both Peter Accardo and Roger E. Stoddard for their assistance with the Hulse Papers during my brief stay in Cambridge.
26 See Rob Burns and Wilfried van der Will, "The Calamitous Perspective of Modernity: Sebald's Negative Ontology," *Journal of European Studies*, Special Issue: W.G. Sebald, ed. Richard Sheppard 41.3–4 (2011) 341–358.

known melancholic tone.[27] But here again, Sebald's annotations reveal that it was not Hulse who enhanced the pathos of this passage by the change to "solitary mallard," but the author himself.[28] The stark differences between the German and English texts have often been asserted, but it is only through such examination of the translation manuscripts that one can gain authoritative insight into the dimensions of such discrepancies and the source of the related textual changes. From this privileged perspective one soon realizes that it is less a question of Sebald 'correcting' Hulse's translations and more a question of Sebald rewriting the original German text. Sebald admits in his correspondence with Hulse that, only after reviewing the translations, he has become aware of certain stylistic problems in his own texts. Such drastic changes, such as striking out and rewriting entire paragraphs may seem like an extreme intervention on the part of the author. At the same time, one must not forget that approximately ten years had elapsed between the original publication and the English translation. With this in mind, it may seem only natural that the author would have a new take on his text.

The tension between specificity and ambiguity in Sebald's writing presents further challenges, first to the translator and then to the reader who endeavors to make sense of the differences between original and translation. On the one hand, there is precision in the detailed lists and specialized terminology of Sebald's texts and on the other there is room for variation in the complex syntax that allows the components of lengthy descriptions and compound sentences to be shifted and shuffled almost at random. Several examples of this can be found in the changes Sebald made to Hulse's translation manuscripts: "dark and deep" becomes "deep and dark"; "from attic to cellar" becomes "from the cellar to the attic"[29]; "travel books and novels" becomes "novels and travel books"[30]; "with groans and death

---

27 Since the style and syntax of Sebald's German vary according to context and the tone of each individual work, his œuvre is by no means so monolithically melancholic as some critics claim. Ernestine Schlant, for example, describes melancholy as the "underlying and all-pervasive mood" of the four narratives of *Die Ausgewanderten/The Emigrants*. Ernestine Schlant, *The Language of Silence. West German Literature and the Holocaust* (New York, London: Routledge, 1999) 233. Charbonneau also refers to the specific tone "de 'mélancolie'" in Sebald's works. See Charbonneau, "Correspondance(s)," 208. Tone, even more than style, presents a challenge to all literary translation, for it cannot be easily located in discrete elements, such as word choice, but rather results from the relationship among elements of the text and is perhaps best described in more general terms as "feeling" or "atmosphere."

28 See Michael Hulse's translations of W.G. Sebald, bMS Eng 1632–1633. Harvard Houghton Library.

29 bMS Eng 1632, box 2, folder 6, section II, 6.

30 Ibid., section V, 4.

rattles" becomes "with death rattles and groans"[31]; "deposits and moraines" becomes "moraines and deposits"[32] and "stone and water" becomes "water and stone."[33] Once again, such alterations are not mere corrections of the translator's text but examples of the author re-ordering, re-phrasing and rewriting so that the English text sounds right. Sound was indeed very important to Sebald. After first expressing dissatisfaction with the "sonorité" [sonority/sound] of Charbonneau's translation of the last pages of *Schwindel.Gefühle*, Sebald then commented on the revised manuscript as follows. "'Ce n'est pas la même musique, mais c'est aussi une belle musique.'"[34] [It may not be the same music, but it is still a beautiful music.]

In one interview and one essay, Hulse has commented on the experience of translating Sebald's works.[35] What he has revealed about this working relationship and the process of exchanging drafts echoes comments that Bell and Charbonneau have made, yet there is divergence, too:

> I send my draft translations to Max for comment, since his English is exceptionally accomplished, and the suggestions and amendments he offers frequently astonish me by their dexterity. But equally frequently, when the effect is to add lexical weight to a sentence already sufficiently burdened by the melancholy of its insight, I feel the child of an author's dark single-mindedness raising the hairs on my neck, and I'm reminded of the gap which still yawns between us, no matter how many points of coincidence there may be in our understanding of cultures and histories.[36]

Furthermore, Hulse describes his efforts to keep his "mental distance" due to "a wary circuitousness" in Sebald's prose, and likens his work to that of a "surveyor carefully assessing every inch of the ground, knowing that the historical, cultural and psychological structure it will have to bear will be a weighty one."[37] Hulse's letters to Sebald that accompany his translation drafts substantiate this process of careful surveying and assessing. The pages of detailed queries reveal the intensity with which Hulse researched and critically reflected upon textual details in order to infuse his translation with corresponding allusions and connotations.[38]

---

31 Ibid., section V, 16.

32 Ibid., section VII, 6.

33 bMS Eng 1632, folder 7.1, *All'estero*, 16.

34 Sebald cited in Charbonneau, "Correspondance(s)," 210.

35 Michael Hulse with Jill Kitson, "Beyond Translation..." January 22, 2000. http://www.abc.net.au/rn/linguafranca/stories/2000/74464.htm [accessed: June 22, 2013]; Michael Hulse, "Englishing Max," *Saturn's Moons: A W. G. Sebald Handbook*, eds. Jo Catling and Richard Hibbitt (Oxford: Legenda, 2011) 192–205.

36 Hulse with Kitson, "Beyond Translation..." unpaginated.

37 Ibid.

38 See Hulse's papers at Harvard Houghton Library, and for select examples see Hulse, "Englishing Max."

Hulse and Sebald shared a sense of being "at home" in a foreign country as long as they still had their native language. Hulse states, "It's become second nature, when asked where I feel at home, to reply: in Germany, but in the English language. English is for me what Paris was for Hemingway, a movable feast: I can take it with me wherever I go."[39] Revealing his sensitivity to the complex relationship between nationality and language, and echoing Hulse's observations above, Sebald marked the following sentence in one of Canetti's books: "Zuhause fühle ich mich, wenn ich mit dem Bleistift in der Hand deutsche Wörter niederschreibe und alles um mich herum spricht Englisch"[40] [I feel at home when I take my pencil and write down German words while everyone around me is speaking English]. When interviewing Sebald, Christopher Bigsby suggested that the loss of the narrator's passport in *Schwindel. Gefühle* should be read metaphorically, as a token of Sebald's desire as a writer not to be limited to one particular society or national identity. Sebald, however, resisted this interpretation and, like Canetti, insisted on a particular devotion to one's origin, which, in his view, inscribes a quality of veracity to the work.[41]

Intermedial, Intratextual, and Intertextual Translation

Willis Barnstone defines the "double art" of translation as follows: on the one hand the translation of linguistic signs, but on the other the translation of a work's context, where source, background, canon, and tradition are components of this context.[42] Moreover, for Barnstone, "no art [...] is entirely self-sufficient and self-created," since authors belong to "the great river of tradition. No author invents a genre."[43] As an author and interviewee, Sebald made his use of sources conspicuous and so rejected the myth that an author begins with a blank page. He also lays bare the processes of translation that occur between sign systems by incorporating video stills, photographs, and reproductions of art

---

39 Hulse with Kitson, "Beyond Translation..." unpaginated.

40 Elias Canetti, *Alle vergeudete Verehrung. Aufzeichnungen 1949–1960*. Reihe Hanser 50 (Munich: Hanser, 1970) 122. W. G. Sebald Nachlaß: Teilbibliothek, Deutsches Literaturarchiv Marbach.

41 See "W. G. Sebald," Christopher Bigsby, *Writers in Conversation with Christopher Bigsby. Volume Two* (Norwich [U. K.]: Arthur Miller Centre for American Studies, 2001) 139–165, here 157. See also Mark M. Anderson, "A Childhood in the Allgäu: Wertach, 1944–1952," *Saturn's Moons: A W. G. Sebald Handbook*, eds. Jo Catling and Richard Hibbitt (Oxford: Legenda, 2011) 16–41.

42 Barnstone, *The Poetics of Translation*, 88. Barnstone also describes translation as a "double art" inasmuch as it involves collaboration between two artists: "To produce a translation the normal triad of author-text-receiver is doubled." Ibid. 13.

43 Ibid., 92.

works; by rewriting the biographies of writers (Stendhal, Joseph Conrad, Franz Kafka, Jean Améry), translators (Michael Hamburger), painters (Frank Auerbach) and scientists (Francis Bacon); and, ultimately, by retelling history (the Holocaust, silk trade, imperialism, colonialism). And while Sebald does not ever create a completely new genre, his 'hybrid' fiction certainly resists easy assimilation to pre-existing generic and sub-generic categories, not least because of his varied interests and sources. Moreover, by freely acknowledging the importance of other authors and literary traditions for his work, Sebald's incorporation of extratextual and intertextual references into his literary texts is not only an act of adaptation and reformulation, but also one of translation and transformation. But, it must be noted, in the particular act of incorporating visual images, Sebald tacitly points to the fundamental untranslatability of the different verbal and pictorial discourses that he is deploying. Paradoxically, this untranslatability proves to be productive since the tension between verbal text and visual image provokes a dialogue between the two media and encourages multiple readings.[44]

Translating Sebald's texts so as to preserve the text-image arrangement presents no small task to the translator, since Sebald, when supervising the production of the various German editions, took particular care of image placement. While the grainy, black and white images enhance the sense of the uncanny and the melancholy tone that both permeate Sebald's texts, the text-image constellations also lend his prose fiction a playfulness and sense of humor that can very easily get lost in translation. McCulloh notes, "Not all is poignant, melancholy, plangent, or grave when it comes to Sebald's pictures."[45] McCulloh observes a general tendency in Hulse's translations to favor "severity over playfulness" which affects "the cumulative tone of the English-language book."[46] In light of this observation it is worth again recalling the span of ten years that stand between the original publication of *Schwindel.Gefühle* and its English translation. In pointing to the differences and discrepancies in image placement between the German and English editions, Elinor Shaffer has suggested that the translation may actually "represent[] an experiment in creating a much more tenuous and floating relationship between text and image gener-

---

44 On 'untranslatability', see Barbara Cassin, general ed., *Vocabulaire européen des philosophies: Dictionnaire des Intraduisibles* (Paris: Éditions du Seuil/Le Robert, 2004).
45 Mark R. McCulloh, *Understanding W. G. Sebald* (Columbia: South Carolina University Press, 2003) 9. McCulloh offers as an example the image of the "Untergehender" (*SG* 22) [one who goes down, or as Hulse translates it, "one meeting his doom" (*V* 18)], noting the impossibility of effectively bringing over the playful dimension of both verbal and visual components of the text.
46 Ibid., 87.

ally;"[47] however, her first inclination – that the contrasts may simply be a case of "careless bookmaking" – is most likely closer to the truth. In his examination of the differences between the original publication of *Die Ringe des Saturn* in *Die andere Bibliothek* series and the English translation first published with Harvill, Robin Kinross notes a "more conventional approach" to the text-image relationship in the translation, counting up nineteen of the seventy-two images as having suffered a "change of status."[48]

Silke Horstkotte's essay of 2008 involves the most systematic study to date of the way Sebald's images are placed in his German works, showing how the photographs introduce a third, spatial dimension into the linear verbal narrative and how this 'photo-text topography' determines the texts' rhetoric, semantics, and reception.[49] Thus, she argues, since Sebald's visual images are neither simple supplements nor secondary illustrations, something crucial is lost if the translator ignores or alters the photo-textual arrangement. To elucidate the problem, Horstkotte cites the photograph of Uncle Ambros' diary in the third long story of *Die Ausgewanderten*. She points out that in the reproduction of the handwritten document, the word "Schwindelgefühle" is barely discernible, but that the narrative stops transcribing the diary just before it reaches this word. This intertextual allusion to *Schwindel.Gefühle* is, she argues, a "strong signal of the collection's fictionality," which most English-speaking readers will not receive because of the incomplete transcription and because the photograph has been shrunk to a fraction of its original size, thus precluding any comparison between the photographed entries and their citation in the narrative.[50] Horstkotte concludes that the translational choices "seem to indicate a reluctance to consider this books' photographs as fictional or textual (and therefore translatable) while at the same time not considering them as immutable objects either (witness the change of size and location)."[51] While Horstkotte's latter point is well-taken, the former is problematic, as it seems to go against what she argues throughout: since Sebald's images are fictional but occupy an autonomous position within the text, to collapse the status of the image with that of the text and claim that both can be

---

47 Elinor Shaffer, "W. G. Sebald's Photographic Narrative," *The Anatomist of Melancholy. Essays in Memory of W. G. Sebald*, ed. Rüdiger Görner (Munich: iudicium, 2003) 51–62, here 55.

48 Robin Kinross, "Judging a Book by its Material Embodiment: A German-English Example," *Unjustified Texts* (London: Hyphen Press, 2002) 186–199, here 195–196.

49 Silke Horstkotte, "Photo-Text Topographies: Photography and the Representation of Space in W. G. Sebald and Monika Maron," *Photography in Fiction*, eds. Silke Horstkotte and Nancy Pedri, special issue of *Poetics Today* 29.1 (2008) 49–78, here 49–50.

50 Ibid., 59.

51 Ibid., 60.

read and translated in the same way would erase the image's aesthetic specificity. Thus, both the translators and the editors of translations face a complex dilemma concerning the positioning of the images within the translated text. Unfortunately, too little information is available about the way in which this problem was resolved for *The Emigrants, The Rings of Saturn,* and *Vertigo.*

The intratextual translation between *histoire* and *discours* so provocatively implied by Sebald's works presents the translator with a further challenge, and in his discussion of *Die Ausgewanderten* Noam Elcott states:

> By the book's own logic, Dr. Selwyn's narration and Sebald's [sic!] conversations, indeed nearly everything verbal, transpire in English. And so, every now and again, an English name, an abrupt switch into English, or a photographic reproduction of an English text betrays the secret we dare not speak: Sebald's German narration is always already in translation.[52]

The same consideration applies to *Austerlitz,* albeit more strongly since it involves at times an even more complex case of intratextual translation. *Austerlitz*'s geographical range is impressive, extending from Czechoslovakia to England with stops in Belgium, Germany, France and Wales, and its characters' linguistic range is correspondingly vast. While the narrator of Sebald's text tells Austerlitz's story (*histoire*) to the reader in German (*discours*), the narrator's discussions with Austerlitz that constitute this story originally occurred in French and English. Further complicating this is the fact that Austerlitz's own story includes interactions with his former nanny Věra that must have occurred in both French and Czech and conversations with his librarian acquaintance Lemoine that must have occurred in French. Thus, rather than a mere compilation of stories, *Austerlitz* is a complex enmeshment of stories. The complexity is created through the stories, their constitution in a linguistic form, and their presentation and re-presentation in the mediated narration of the text. In recounting the various linguistic events that make up *Austerlitz* – both Austerlitz's story and the narrator's story of his own journeys and encounters with Austerlitz – Sebald brings together the two levels of *histoire* and *discours* in an inextricable relationship. That is to say, the *histoire* is already transferred to the level of *discours* insofar as Austerlitz's story is constituted in the act of his own narration, a narration that also incorporates the stories of others (e.g. Věra and Lemoine). Or, according to the more differentiated three-part relation that Karlheinz Stierle presents in his model of the constitution of a text ["Textkonstitutionsrelation"]: the "Geschehen" (i.e. pre-narrative events

---

52 Noam M. Elcott, "Tattered Snapshots and Castaway Tongues: An Essay at Layout and Translation in W. G. Sebald" *Germanic Review* 79.3 (2004) 203–223, here 209.

and experiences) provides the basis for the "Geschichte" (e.g. Austerlitz's story) which in turn provides the foundation for the "Text der Geschichte" (Sebald's *Austerlitz*).[53] Moreover, these levels are interrelated in time in such a way that is not visible on the level of the text but only when one teases apart the simultaneously synchronic and diachronic strands of the narration. These considerations reveal the three operations involved: first, the process of semioticization from extra-linguistic experience into language; second, the transfer of Austerlitz's semioticized experiences into a cohesive narration; and third, the translation of this narration from one language into the German of the original text. As a result, the issue of loss that is always at stake in any translation is here multiplied by both the various levels of the text and their interrelationship in time.

In exploring specific instances of intratextual translation, we find how Austerlitz's difficulties in confronting the past and accessing his memories are compounded by the fact that language often seems outside of his control. Thus, on his arrival in Prague, Austerlitz cannot speak Czech at the airport or in the State Archive, but after reaching Věra, whose name, incidentally, connotes 'truth,' he rediscovers key aspects of his childhood, including the ability to speak his mother tongue.[54] Significantly, during their meeting, Věra recalls feeling that Austerlitz is someone who understood her better than anyone else, even when he was a child and unable to speak, further reinforcing the idea that understanding may be located somewhere beyond words. And as a reciprocal index of the level of his new-found comfort with Věra, Austerlitz rapidly rediscovers his ability to speak Czech and later tells the narrator how he could now understand almost everything she said, "wie ein Tauber, dem durch ein Wunder das Gehör wiederaufging, [...] und wollte nurmehr die Augen schließen und ihren vielsilbig dahineilenden Wörtern lauschen in einem fort" (*A* 227) ["like a deaf man whose hearing has been miracu-

---

53 Karlheinz Stierle, "Geschehen, Geschichte, Text der Geschichte," *Geschichte: Ereignis und Erzählung*, eds. Reinhart Koselleck and Wolf-Dieter Stempel (*Poetik und Hermeneutik 5*) (Munich: Fink, 1973) 530–534, here 531.

54 Prior to any unequivocal knowledge that he came from Prague to Wales, Austerlitz nevertheless recalls remembering, or believes he can remember the loss, "the dying away," of this native tongue. In the Liverpool Street Station episode, he recounts, "letzthin bildete ich mir sogar ein, ich erahnte noch etwas vom Absterben der Muttersprache, von ihrem von Monat zu Monat leiser werdenden Rumoren, von dem ich denke, daß es eine Zeitlang zumindest noch in mir gewesen ist wie eine Art Scharren oder Pochen von etwas Eingesperrtem, das immer, wenn man auf es achthaben will, vor Schrecken stillhält und schweigt" (*A* 203) ["recently I have even thought that I could still apprehend the dying away of my native tongue, the faltering and fading sounds which I think lingered on in me at least for a while, like something shut up and scratching or knocking, something which, out of fear, stops its noise and falls silent whenever one tries to listen to it" (*AE* 138).]

lously restored, so that all I wanted to do was close my eyes and listen forever to her polysyllabic flood of words" (*AE* 155)]. Moreover, we also learn that during Austerlitz's childhood, he and Věra spoke French outside the house, whereas they used Czech while at home to speak of "häuslichere und kindlichere Dinge suzusagen" (*A* 227) ["more domestic and childish matters, as it were" (*AE* 155)]. And it is during this metalinguistic act of talking about language that Věra, "unwillkürlich, wie ich annehme" (*A* 227) ["quite involuntarily" (*AE* 155)] switches from one language to the other. In addition to the way in which feelings, experiences, and understanding often seem to be located somewhere beyond the language of the text, language itself also seems to elude the characters' volition, at times frustrating their attempts at expression and at others restoring forgotten fluency. Such considerations echo Canetti's reflections on his experiences "beyond language" in Marrakesh and challenge the central idea of Wittgenstein's *Tractatus* (5.6) that the limits of my language mean/indicate ("bedeuten") the limits of my world.[55]

Moving on to intertextual translation, we return to the lepidoptera with which this chapter began. Although these creatures occur as a leitmotif in all of Sebald's works of prose fiction, they also thematize the problem of intertextual translation that is so central to his œuvre. For example, in the final scene of *Schwindel.Gefühle*, the narrator describes the contrast between the soot-stained walls of Liverpool Street Station and the "Schmetterlingssträucher" growing out of them.[56] The narrator recalls seeing these bushes in bloom during the summer and, to his astonishment, a "Zitronenfalter" ["yellow brimstone butterfly"] flitting about from one purple flower to the other, "bald oben, bald unten, bald links, immer in Bewegung" (*SG* 284) ["first at the top, then at the bottom, now on the left, constantly moving" (*V* 260)]. This passage is revealing not only because it continues the butterfly/translation motif but also because it alludes intertextually to Kafka's fragment "Der Jäger Gracchus" (1917), posthumously titled by Max Brod. Kafka, whose influence on Sebald was decisive from the early 1970s, tells us that Gracchus can always be found flitting about purposelessly on an infinitely broad stairway that leads upwards, "bald oben bald unten, bald rechts bald links, immer in Bewegung" and then adds, "aus dem Jäger ist ein Schmetterling geworden. Lachen Sie nicht"[57] [the hunter has turned into a butterfly. Do not laugh]. In recognizing this quotation, a

---

55 Ludwig Wittgenstein, *Logisch-philosophische Abhandlung. Tractatus logico-philosophicus*, eds. Brian McGuinness and Joachim Schulte (Frankfurt am Main: Suhrkamp, 1989) 134.
56 Unlike "Lusitanischer Lorbeer," the name of this plant is both current in German and has an English vernacular equivalent: "buddleia" or "butterfly bush."
57 Franz Kafka, "Oktavheft B," *Kritische Ausgabe, Nachgelassene Schriften und Fragmente I (Schriften und Tagebücher)*, ed. Malcolm Pasley (Darmstadt: Wissenschaftliche Buchgesellschaft, 1993) 304–334, here 309; see also R.J.A. Kilbourn, "Kafka, Nabokov...Sebald: Intertextuality and

new, intertextual dimension opens up before our eyes – much like what happens during the metamorphosis of a butterfly – offering up an intertextual connection between this final passage of *Schwindel.Gefühle* and back to the book's third section where Kafka's Gracchus has already made his appearance.

Another example of Sebald's intertextual use of Kafka can be found in the final story of *Die Ausgewanderten/The Emigrants* when the narrator visits the painter Max Aurach/Ferber, who is lying in the hospital with pulmonary emphysema. Due to this illness he can barely speak, and when he does so, his voice sounds "wie das Geraschel vertrockneter Blätter im Wind" (*DA* 345–346) ["like the rustle of dry leaves in the wind" (*E* 231)]. This description evokes Kafka's story "Die Sorge des Hausvaters" ["The Worries of a Head of Household"] and its central "character," an uncategorizable being ["Wesen"] called Odradek, whose laugh is one "that one can bring forth only without lungs," sounding like "the rustling in fallen leaves" ["das Rascheln in gefallenen Blättern"].[58] Intertextuality abounds throughout Sebald's œuvre and is by no means limited to Kafka's works. It is, for example, now well established that Austerlitz's breakdown recalls the crisis of language undergone by Hofmannsthal's Lord Chandos (1902), and references to Nabokov are also central to Sebald's prose works, whether explicitly, as in *Die Ausgewanderten*, or implicitly, as in *Austerlitz*. Like the self-referential presence of 'Schwindelgefühle' in the visual peproduction of Uncle Ambros' diary, such instances of intertextuality not only point to Sebald's influences but create *ipso facto* a secondary web of meaning with nodes of connection that extend across his œuvre.

There are further connections between Sebald and Kafka that are not instances of intertextuality in a strict sense but rather examples of Kafka's influence on Sebald. Like Kafka, Sebald creates an atmosphere that can be described as uncanny, by presenting familiar and mundane experiences in a strange and almost horrifying way; and this particular atmosphere presents a further challenge to translation. A simple task, like the act of buying a cappuccino, turns into a surreal, almost nightmarish experience of life and death, replete with scenes reminiscent of those in Kafka's *The Trial*. Metaphor and simile aid in creating this

---

Narratives of Redemption in *Vertigo* and *The Emigrants*" *W.G. Sebald. History, Memory, Trauma* eds. Scott Denham and Mark McCulloh (Berlin; New York: de Gruyter, 2006) 33–63, here 52.

58 Franz Kafka, "Die Sorge des Hausvaters," *Kritische Ausgabe, Drucke zu Lebzeiten, Schriften und Tagebücher*, eds. Wolf Kittler, Hans-Gerd Koch, and Gerhard Neumann (Darmstadt: Wissenschaftliche Buchgesellschaft, 1994) 282–284, here 284. See also Michael Hofmann's translation where "in" becomes "of," making the cause of the sound more comprehensible and less in character with the elusive Odradek. Franz Kafka, "The Worries of a Head of Household," *Metamorphosis and Other Stories*, trans. Michael Hofmann (London: Penguin, 2007) 212.

strange and threatening atmosphere: the buffet is "eine Art feste Insel" (*SG* 76) ["a steadfast island" (*V* 66)] and the crowd of people, "d[as] andrängende[] Volk" (*SG* 77) ["the jostling masses" (*V* 67)], are described "wie ein Ährenfeld im Wind schwankende[] Menge der Menschen" (*SG* 76) ["swaying like a field of corn in the wind" (*V* 66)], and later appear to the narrator "wie ein weiter Kreis abgeschnittener Köpfe" (*SG* 78) ["like a circle of severed heads" (*V* 68)] and "mit sich selber beschäftigten Gespenster" (*SG* 79) ["circle of spectres" (*V* 68)]. The customers, "Bittsteller" (*SG* 77) ["supplicants" (*V* 67)], make requests that are described as "von den einander durchdringenden und sich überschlagenden Stimmen vorgebrachten Wünsche" (*SG* 77) ["pleas emerging from this crossfire of voices" (*V* 67)]. The cashiers, whom the narrator describes as "thronende[] Frauen" (*SG* 77) ["enthroned women" (*V* 66)], are "huldvoll und verächtlich zugleich" (*SG* 77) ["indulgent and at the same time disdainful" (*V* 67)]. The hectic "general commotion" (*V* 66) of the activity in the buffet is surrounded "von einem wahrhaft höllischen Lärm" (*SG* 76) ["an infernal upheaval" (*V* 66)], underlying which is an "allgemeine[] Panik" (*SG* 77) ["prevailing panic" (*V* 67)]. The elements of alienation and impenetrable bureaucratic structures that are constitutive of the Kafkaesque are also present in this scene. The narrator seems uncertain of the hierarchy ruling the buffet workers – "eine[] eigenartige[] Versammlung höherer Wesen" (*SG* 78) ["some strange company of higher beings sitting in judgment" (*V* 67)] – but what is certain is that there is a "dunkle[s] System" (*SG* 78) ["an obscure system" (*V* 67)] behind it all.[59]

---

59 The narrator in *Schwindel.Gefühle* has other hallucinations that create a further sense of vertigo, which is reinforced by descriptions of uncanny situations of strange coincidence. In one such instance he sees twin boys who resemble the young Franz Kafka while on a bus to Riva. He recounts the uncanny encounter, "Kurz vor der Abfahrt um fünf vor halb zwei stieg ein Junge von etwa fünfzehn Jahren ein, der auf die unheimlichste Weise, die man sich denken kann, den Bildern glich, die Kafka als heranwachsenden Schüler zeigen. Und als ob es damit nicht genug gewesen wäre, hatte er zudem noch einen Zwillingsbruder, der sich von ihm, soweit ich in meinem Entsetzen feststellen konnte, nicht im geringsten unterschied. Beide hatten sie den weit in die Stirn hereingehenden Haaransatz, dieselben dunklen Augen und dichten Brauen, dieselben großen, ungleichen und an den Läppchen festgewachsenen Ohren" (*SG* 101) ["Not long before the bus departed at twenty-five past, a boy of about fifteen climbed aboard who bore the most uncanny resemblance imaginable to pictures of Franz Kafka as an adolescent schoolboy. And as if that were not enough, he had a twin brother who, so far as I could tell in my perplexed state of mind, did not differ from him in the slightest. The hairlines of both boys began well down their foreheads, they had the same dark eyes and thick brows, the same large and unequal ears, with the lobes growing into the skin of the neck" (*V* 88).] The uncanniness of the situation, the fact that the narrator is confronted with not one but two Kafka look-a-likes, evokes a physical reaction, "ein Schwindelgefühl" (*SG* 101) ["a vertiginous feeling" (*V* 89)] that he likens to what he

Besides the structural importance of intertextuality for Sebald's texts, this literary technique also reveals how language works for his characters. In *Austerlitz*, for example, the disjointed syntax creates a textual uneasiness that runs parallel to the intangible uneasiness felt by *Austerlitz*'s characters, and out of this a highly paradoxical situation arises: like Kafka's Odradek, things can be simultaneously incomprehensible and self-evident. When discussing his adoptive mother Gwendolyn's "Pudermanie" (*A* 94) ["mania for powder" (*AE* 62)], Austerlitz recalls it in connection with the recollections of an unnamed Russian author whose grandmother suffered from a superficially similar mania.[60] Austerlitz describes how the powder used by his adoptive mother increasingly forms a layer throughout the entire house. At first, it was like freshly fallen snow, but then it became increasingly unpleasant, "etwas Ungutes" ["something bad"], for which Austerlitz could find no name until, much later in his life, he discovered the term "das arsanische Grauen" (*A* 95) ["arsanical horror" (*AE* 63)] in a completely different book. Although the origins of this phrase remain obscure to Austerlitz, he immediately intuits what it means to him in a way that is extra-, or even metalingual, and so connects the *signified* of his own childhood experience with a fitting, albeit unfamiliar *signifier*.

Austerlitz's own name – which his adoptive parents kept hidden from him throughout his youth in Wales – could also be considered an 'empty' signifier that, similar to "das arsanische Grauen," is later filled with connotations and associations. After the school director Penrith-Smith reveals his real name and hands it to him written on a piece of paper, Austerlitz is disconcerted that "ich mir unter dem Wort Austerlitz nicht das geringste vorstellen konnte" ["I could connect no ideas at all with the word *Austerlitz*" (*AE* 67, emphasis Bell)]. If his name had been Morgan or Jones, he could have related it "auf die Wirklichkeit" (*A* 102) ["to reality" (*AE* 67)]. He recalls having heard "Jacques" in a song but never "Austerlitz," and he is convinced that "außer mir niemand so heißt, weder in Wales noch auf den Britischen Inseln, noch sonst irgendwo auf der Welt" (*A* 102) ["from the first I was convinced that no one else bore the name, no one in Wales, or in the Isles, or anywhere else in the world" (*AE* 67)]. As a young school boy, Austerlitz seems to believe in language's ability to create both meaningful connections and a sense of reality, albeit in an almost magical way.

———

experienced as a child while traveling by car. Whereas the experience as a boy was physically provoked, the source of the narrator's current vertigo is strictly within his mind.

60 The reference is to one of Sebald's favorite books, Vladimir Nabokov's autobiography *Speak, Memory*, a heavily annotated copy of which is to be found in Sebald's library (Deutsches Literaturarchiv, Marbach). The anecdote occurs on the second page of chapter eight in Nabokov's text. Vladimir Nabokov, *Speak, Memory. An Autobiography Revisited* (London: Penguin, 1987) 121.

He recalls his teacher André Hilary's history lessons on the battle of Austerlitz, and how he felt "auf eine geheimnisvolle Weise verbunden zu sein mit der ruhmreichen Vergangenheit des französischen Volks" (*A* 110) ["linked in some mysterious way to the glorious past of the people of France" (*AE* 72)]. Austerlitz then qualifies his memory, leaving room for a degree of uncertainty regarding the power of language to create a definitive reality:

> Je öfter Hilary das Wort Austerlitz vor der Klasse aussprach, desto mehr wurde es mir zu meinem Namen, desto deutlicher *glaubte ich zu erkennen*, daß das, was ich zuerst als einen Schandfleck an mir empfunden hatte, sich verwandelte in einen Leuchtpunkt, der mir ständig vorschwebte, so vielversprechend wie die über dem Dezembernebel sich erhebende Sonne von Austerlitz selber (*A* 110, my emphasis).
>
> [The more often Hilary mentioned the word *Austerlitz* in front of the class, the more it really did become my own name, and the more clearly I thought I saw that what had at first seemed like an ignominious flaw was changing into a bright light always hovering before me, as promising as the sun of Austerlitz itself when it rose above the December mists (*AE* 72, emphasis Bell).]

It is curious that he does not immediately question why he has been called a different name up until this point. Had he made this connection, however, he would have had to immediately consider his true origins and question who and where his 'real' parents are. Thus, Austerlitz's repression persists even here without explicit mention.

The intertextuality of Sebald's texts is furthermore a form of translation that needs to be considered, because it reveals how closely memory and imagination are linked. In *Austerlitz*, for example, the protagonist transfers memories onto the various mother figures in his life such as Gerald's mother Adela,[61] who welcomes him into her home at Andromeda Lodge, a refuge that Austerlitz describes to the narrator in idyllic terms. But when, during a walk through Greenwich Park, Austerlitz describes seeing Adela again after accompanying Gerald down to Barmouth station, his memory has merged with one of Nabokov's descriptions of his mother:

> [...] es dämmerte bereits, sagte Austerlitz, und ein feiner Sprühregen hing, anscheinend ohne niederzusinken, in der Luft –, trat mir aus der nebligen Tiefe des Gartens Adela entgegen, in grünlichbraune Wollsachen gemummt, an deren hauchfein gekräuseltem Rand Millionen winziger Wassertropfen eine Art von silbrigem Glanz um sie bildeten (*A* 165).

---

61 Stephanie Bird reads Adela as a second "erotic mother" figure for Austerlitz. See Stephanie Bird, "'Er gab mir, was äußerst ungewöhnlich war, zum Abschied die Hand': Touch and Tact in W.G. Sebald's *Die Ausgewanderten* and *Austerlitz*," *Journal of European Studies*, Special Issue: W.G. Sebald, ed. Richard Sheppard 41.3–4 (2011) 359–375, in particular 362.

To which Nabokov's text bears striking similarities:

> Toward dinnertime, she could be seen emerging from the nebulous depths of a park alley, her small figure cloaked and hooded in greenish-brown wool, on which countless droplets of moisture made a kind of mist all around her.[62]

While Bell was not aware of this intertextual source, her translation nevertheless captures the features which the two passages have in common:

> When I returned – dusk was already falling, said Austerlitz, and fine rain hung suspended in the air, apparently without sinking to the ground – Adela came to meet me from the misty depths of the garden, muffled up in greenish-brown tweed with millions of tiny drops of water clinging to the fine fuzz of its outline and forming a kind of silvery radiance around her (*AE* 111).

Reconsidering Gerald's mother Adela after learning more about Austerlitz's birth mother Agáta, the reader can simultaneously connect and draw distinctions between the two women. For while Adela is preserved in Austerlitz's memory through her gestures, his mother is absent, and later when he finally recalls Agáta's gestures, one must question whether he is actually transposing memories of Adela onto her. So while this instance of intertextuality provides a re-inscription of memory through acts of association and imagination, it also adds to the sense of chronological disjuncture in *Austerlitz*. Rather than viewing such intertextual allusions and near quotations as clues that are waiting to be discovered and deciphered by the translator and/or reader, it is more fruitful to expand our understanding of intertextuality, adaptation even, to consider such reworkings of literary texts as illustrations of the process of translation in a metaphorical sense.

Metaphorical Translation

By metaphorical translation I mean the transfer from formless experience into language on which I touched at the beginning of this chapter and whose essence George Steiner captures by identifying the transfer that is necessary for all communication: "Translation is formally and pragmatically implicit in every act of communication, in the emission and reception of each and every mode of meaning, be it in the widest semiotic sense or in more specifically verbal ex-

---

62 Oddly enough, while Sebald's copy of *Speak, Memory* is heavily marked and annotated, this passage is not. Nabokov, *Speak, Memory*, 36.

changes."[63] Put another way, as the translator Edith Grossman does, citing Octavio Paz: "'learning to speak is learning to translate.'"[64] Furthermore, Grossman maintains that literature, as a particular form of writing and 'the most creative use of language', is always already a translation, "not the transmutation of the text into another language but the transformation and concretization of the content of the writer's imagination into literary artefact."[65]

The concept of metaphorical translation leads us to fundamental considerations of literary discourse, e.g. the question of representation: which is one of Sebald's primary concerns both as critic and as author and therefore one of the fundamental questions of this book. Sebald thematizes representation implicitly and problematizes it explicitly, whether it is historical (monuments, museum dioramas, paintings of famous battles etc.), biographical (the inserts of journals, letters, diaries etc.), or (auto)biographical (the juxtaposition of Sebald's nameless narrators with photographs of himself or members of his family). For Sebald, representation in general and writing in particular are forms of translation or, more precisely, aspects of a process of semioticization during which sensate experiences from an extralinguistic and extratextual reality are brought across into an intratextual one – that of literary language with all its various devices which is, according to Grossman, "a living bridge between two realms of discourse, two realms of experience, and two sets of readers."[66] To understand literature in such a way[67] means understanding *mimesis* not just as imitation but also creation.[68]

In discussing Claude Lanzmann's documentary film *Shoah* (1985),[69] James E. Young sets out to describe the translation process from experience and memory into language – what I called semioticization – but privileges film over language. Young writes,

---

63 George Steiner, *After Babel: Aspects of Language and Translation* (Oxford: Oxford University Press, 1992) xii.

64 Grossman, "Translating Cervantes," 6.

65 Ibid.

66 Ibid.

67 See Barnstone, *The Poetics of Translation*, 7–8.

68 See Hans Blumenberg, "'Nachahmung der Natur': Zur Vorgeschichte der Idee des schöpferischen Menschen," *Wirklichkeiten in denen wir leben. Aufsätze und eine Rede* (Stuttgart: Reclam, 1993) 55–103.

69 One of the few Holocaust films that Sebald appreciated. See Eleanor Wachtel, "Ghost Hunter," *The Emergence of Memory. Conversations with W. G. Sebald*, ed. Lynne Sharon Schwartz (New York: Seven Stories Press, 2007) 53 and Maya Jaggi, "Recovered Memories," *The Guardian* (Saturday Review Section) (September 22, 2001) 6–7, here 7.

> Having experienced events in Yiddish, or Polish, or German, survivors often find that English serves as much as mediation between themselves and experiences as it does as medium for their expression. In video and cinema[to]graphic testimonies, this on-camera simultaneous translation of events from memory into language and from one language into another is strikingly evident in ways *lost to literature.* Part of the video text here is precisely the visual record of this entry of memory into language, the search for the right words, and the simultaneous interpretation of events in this search for language.[70]

Like the interviewer in *Shoah,* Sebald's narrators are simultaneously translators and interpreters of the stories they tell. Sebald's complex narrative structure illustrates the translation process through the implicit and explicit code-switching performed by his characters during which events that were experienced in one language are translated literally and intratextually into another. Such processes of translation are fundamental to questions of representation and magnified when the object of representation is the Holocaust, one of the central concerns driving Sebald's literary production. But the above discussion of intratextual translation in Sebald's texts challenges Young's privileging of film over literature and demonstrates that the various levels of translation – from memory into language and from one language into another – not only occur but are also thematized and reflected upon within literary discourse. Furthermore, the tension in Sebald's texts between the semiotic symbiosis of the text-image relationship on the one hand and the irreducibility of both media on the other ultimately points to a metaphysical substratum of language that can be evoked through and even translated into literature.

Irony of/and Literary Innovation

The paradox of Sebald's "conservative" style makes possible the innovation of his fictional form. As stated above, Sebald is often compared to or even reproached for emulating nineteenth-century German realist authors. But such assertions are the result of a superficial encounter with Sebald's works. He incorporates innovative ideas on historiography, literary discourse, and perception in such a stylistically conservative and subtle manner that this has obviously eluded some critics. Rather than viewing tradition, nineteenth-century or any other, as a restriction placed on Sebald's style, I would like to evoke it in the sense used by T.S. Eliot,

---

70 James E. Young, *Writing and Rewriting the Holocaust. Narrative and the Consequences of Interpretation,* (Bloomington and Indianapolis: Indiana University Press, 1988) 160, my emphasis.

who writes, "[Tradition] cannot be inherited, and if you want it you must obtain it by great labour. It involves, in the first place, the historical sense," which Eliot goes on to describe as follows:

> the historical sense involves a perception, not only of the pastness of the past, but of its presence; the historical sense compels a man to write not merely with his own generation in his bones, but with a feeling that the whole of the literature of Europe from Homer and within it the whole of the literature of his own country has a simultaneous existence and composes a simultaneous order. This historical sense, which is a sense of the timeless as well as of the temporal and of the timeless and the temporal together, is what makes a writer traditional. And it is at the same time what makes a writer most acutely conscious of his place in time, of his contemporaneity.[71]

There is an almost uncanny resonance of Eliot's ideas in Sebald's writing and in particular in his concerns with history: not only the individual's relationship to specific historical events but rather an awareness and sensitivity to a broader notion of the past, the individual's recognition of his subject position in the present, and the way in which the past not only informs the present but is still present in different forms. Sebald has described the past as a sort of refuge but with the immediate recognition of the ambivalent implications of the notion that past pain of "calamitous episodes" is "no longer acute, it has been subdued."[72] Also confronting the reproach that his literary texts perpetuate a form of nostalgia or escapism, Sebald continues his thoughts in this interview with an ambiguous "it," which could refer to the past in general terms or the presence of the past in his works, as described above. Although never making explicit the referent of this "it," Sebald does make clear that he is referring to the specific concern and fascination with the past that dominates his literary works when he states, "It is to my mind an attempt to provide something like critical historiography, i.e. to see that it wasn't just the great events of the past that determine our lives."[73]

It is characteristic of Sebald's concept of fictional prose to bring various fields into dialogue, and often disparate ones such as the literary discourse and the natural sciences, for example, while at the same time questioning these various ways of knowing. This may be termed the ironic dimension of Sebald's work. This

---

71 T.S. Eliot, "Tradition and the Individual Talent," *The Sacred Wood. Essays on Poetry and Criticism* (New York: Barnes & Noble, 1960) 47–59, here 49.
72 W.G. Sebald and Gordon Turner (Interviewer: Michaël Zeeman), "Introduction and Transcript of an Interview Given by Max Sebald," *W.G. Sebald. History – Memory – Trauma*, eds. Scott Denham and Mark McCulloh (Berlin: de Gruyter, 2006) 21–29, here 23.
73 Ibid., 24.

irony is two-fold: first, in the sense of Romantic irony, Sebald is thematizing literary discourse within literary discourse. That is, these prose works go beyond a mere "meta"-literary critique by embodying Friedrich Schlegel's assertion that the theory of a novel must be written as a novel.[74] In Sebald's case there is also the thematization of historical representation in contrast to literary representation within his work, and this tension between historiography and literary discourse contributes to the echo of Romantic irony. Second, it is of course ironic in a colloquial sense that this literary scholar turns to his medium of study as the most effective expressions of his concerns. We might also want to consider Hayden White's consideration of irony as one of the four tropes he uses to classify "the deep structural forms of the historical imagination."[75] According to White, "Irony presupposes the occupation of a 'realistic' perspective on reality"; moreover, it "represents a stage of consciousness in which the problematical nature of language itself has become recognized."[76] The problematic nature of language is certainly recognized by Sebald, and he successfully transforms these concerns into the central questions raised by his literary works. Here, one may think of the frustrations expressed by his narrator in *Die Ausgewanderten* with the "questionable business of writing," or one may recall the crisis of writing and language experienced by Austerlitz, a crisis that also echoes the intellectual agony of Lord Chandos.

Irony occurs on several levels of Sebald's prose fiction. First, it serves an autoreferential function, pointing to the construction of the text itself. For instance, after Austerlitz's anagnorisis in the Liverpool Street Station, he is plagued by a dream that he describes as "ein böser, nichtendenwollender Traum, dessen Haupthandlung vielfach unterbrochen war von anderen Episoden" (*A* 204) ["a nightmarish, never-ending dream, with its main plot interrupted several times by other episodes" (*AE* 139)]. The irony here is that the description of the dream relates to and even parallels the structure of the text, i.e. the main plot is interrupted several times by other episodes. There is also irony on the level of word choice, such as when Věra recounts how Maximilian, in the summer of 1933, encountered people who had bought raspberry-colored swastika bonbons. The irony of these "Nazischleckereien" ["Nazi treats" (*AE* 167)] being described as "Geschmacklosigkeiten" (*A* 245) is lost in the English translation to "these vulgar sweets" (*AE* 168). In a strange premonition that

74 Cf. Friedrich Schlegel, "Brief über den Roman," *Kritische und theoretische Schriften* (Stuttgart: Reclam, 1997) 202–213, here 211.

75 Hayden White, *Metahistory. The Historical Imagination in Nineteenth Century Europe* (Baltimore: Johns Hopkins University Press, 1973) 31.

76 Ibid., 37.

is also a bitter irony and furthermore a foreshadowing of Austerlitz's stop in Nuremberg, his father Maximilian described to Věra what he witnessed there on the square outside of the Lorenzkirche. Věra tells Austerlitz how Maximilian recounted to her how the crooked housetops and people hanging out of the windows created a scene that resembled "einem hoffnungslos überfüllten Ghetto" (*A* 246) ["a hopelessly overcrowded ghetto" (*AE* 168)], and Hitler appeared to be "der Heilsbringer" (246) ["the long-awaited savior" (*AE* 168)]. What is later described as Austerlitz's spontaneous decision to jump out of the train in Nuremberg could thus be seen as actually having been foreshadowed by his father's experiences in this city during the Nazi's rise to power. Both the events of the past and his father's experiences appear to be inscribed in this physical location, forming a palimpsest of history and individual experience that physically draws Austerlitz in. Finally, while irony is not to be confused with humor, ironic moments and formulations can lend a lighter air to the weightier themes of Sebald's texts.[77] For instance, the diagnosis of his adoptive father's insanity comes, ironically, from a supposedly insane person, "einer der anderen Insassen, ein struppiges, eisgraues Männlein," (*A* 100) ["one of the other inmates, a gray little man with tangled hair" (*AE* 66)]. Austerlitz recounts how this fellow inmate of the Denbigh asylum "flüsterte mir hinter vorgehaltener Hand zu: he's not a full shilling, you know, was ich seltsamerweise damals, sagte Austerlitz, als eine beruhigende die ganze trostlose Lage für mich erträglich machende Diagnose empfand" (*A* 100) ["whispered behind his hand: He's not a full shilling you know – which at the time, curiously enough, said Austerlitz, I felt was a reassuring diagnosis and made the whole wretched situation tolerable" (*AE* 66)].

As set out in chapter two, Sebald's insistence on his status as a writer of prose as opposed to novelist contributes to the difficulty in categorizing his works according to traditional genre definitions. While Sebald dealt with poetry in his critical work more as an exception, he actually wrote poetry most of his adult life, starting already as a high school student and actively writing during his university years. *Über das Land und das Wasser/Across the Land and the Water*, a recently published selection of Sebald's poetry, adds another dimension to the picture of Sebald the author and underlines aspects of both his writing style and process. Several of Sebald's poems read like sketches for his

---

77 With secondary literature often focusing on Sebald's melancholy, this subtle humor has not yet been given proper attention. Arthur Lubow is one exception. He drew attention to the tension between Sebald's serious themes and subtle humor in the article published just before Sebald's death, "Preoccupied with Death, but Still Funny. W.G. Sebald Combines Memoir, Novel and Essay and Adds Photos," *The New York Times* (December 11, 2001) E1.

later prose works.[78] What later become developed stories, intricately connected
to and encapsulated within larger prose pieces, are contained here within a few
sparse lines of several poems.[79] We recognize scenes from *Schwindel.Gefühle*
and *Die Ausgewanderten*, but in drastically reduced forms. Poems like "Day
Return" and "New Jersey Journey" read almost as if they were skeletons of the
fleshed-out scenes in the longer prose works. The first and second strophes of
the second part of "Day Return" contain the narrator recounting his reading of
Samuel Pepys' diary about the great fire of London:

> Die untergehende Stadt im Rücken
> lese ich abends auf dem Heimweg
> den Bericht des Samuel Pepys
> über das große Feuer von London
>
> People taking to boats
> many pigeons killed
> panic on the river
> looting near Lincoln's Inn
> Bishop Baybrooke's corpse exposed
> fragments blown to Windsor Park (*Ü* 59)
>
> [The city sinks behind me
> as I head home in the evening
> reading Samuel Pepys's diary
> of the Great Fire of London
>
> People taking to boats
> many pigeons killed
> panic on the river
> looting near Lincoln's Inn
> Bishop Baybrooke's corpse exposed
> fragments blown to Windsor Park (*ALW* 95)]

Similar to this description, the very last part of *Schwindel.Gefühle*, as explicated
above, ends with the narrator recounting his reading of the diary, slowly fading
into sleep, and the nightmare/dream that melds what he has read with what he
imagines. The poem "New Jersey Journey" incorporates the account of the build-

---

78 Naming "Dr. K." and the "Jäger Gracchus" as examples, Meyer states how Sebald takes up
motifs and topoi from his early poems in his later prose works (*Ü* 108).

79 Hans Adler has elucidated a similar development in Günter Grass. See Hans Adler, "Günter
Grass, *Novemberland*," *Günter Grass: Ästhetik des Engagements*, eds. Hans Adler and Jost
Hermand (New York: Peter Lang, 1996) 93–109.

ing of the Augsburg Synagogue's copper cupola that Onkel Kasimir told to Tante Lina, which is subsequently recounted by her to the narrator (see *DA* 117–118).

> Schnaps trinkend
> erzählt er mir später
> von der Eroberung New Yorks
> Schnaps trinkend überlege ich
> die Verzweigungen unseres Unglücks
> und die Bedeutung des Bildes
> das ihn meinen Onkel
> als Spenglergesellen im 23erjahr
> auf dem neuen Kupferdach
> der Augsburger Synagoge zeigt
> was waren das für Zeiten (*Ü* 61-62)

> [Drinking schnapps
> he later tells me
> of the conquest of New York
> Drinking schnapps I consider
> the ramifications of our calamity
> and the meaning of the picture
> that shows him, my uncle
> as a tinsmith's assistant in '23
> on the new copper roof
> of the Augsburg synagogue
> those were the days (*ALW* 98)]

The poem continues with the narrator and uncle driving down to the seaside, which he describes as "menschenleer die hölzernen side-walks / verbarrikadierte Stehrestaurants" (*Ü* 62), calling to mind the deserted and dilapidated seaside town of Lowestoft that Sebald describes in *Die Ringe des Saturn*. At the end of the poem, the narrator's uncle, "vornübergebeugt in den Wind," takes a Polaroid snapshot of him on the beach. Readers of Sebald may be able to call up, as if in a mental slideshow, the photo of the narrator on the beach in *Die Ausgewanderten* (*DA* 130) [(*E* 89)], negating the question implied in the last two lines of the poem "Sterben wir wirklich / nur einmal" (*Ü* 62) ["Do we really die / only once" (*ALW* 99)]. Sebald alludes to this photograph again in his conversation with Bigsby, when describing how photographs can lend an "ironic quality." He states, "The writer says this is me on the seashore of New Jersey and you can't see anything on the photograph except some dark blot in a scarcely visible landscape."[80] It is not

---

80 Sebald in Bigsby, 154.

only the integration of photographs – memento mori on the one hand and a preservation of time on the other – that lend Sebald's works a dynamic aspect, but it is also this cross-referencing that makes out of Sebald's œuvre a web of connections with the potential to grow and change. Reading Sebald's poetry in tandem with his prose thus extends this web of connections and opens up the possibility for further reflections on his style and form.[81]

Translation as Context

Sebald's decision to remain for over thirty years in a country whose language and culture were not native to him manifests itself in his literary works both aesthetically and thematically. Although Sebald was fluent in English, the constant confrontation with issues of translation – linguistic and cultural – remains a strong presence in his literary works, reflections on writing, and even in the books that constitute his working library. Indeed, for Andreas Huyssen, translation is centrally important to Sebald's literary project, understanding "translation as the liminal space between past and present, between document and fiction, between human history and natural history, between the dead and the living."[82] Commenting on the thematic presence of translation in *Die Ringe des Saturn* specifically, McCulloh writes,

> Transformations and transmutations as such fascinate Sebald, whether manifested in the degradation of an orbiting moon to a vast collection of rings, or in the endlessly repetitive life cycle of the silkworm from egg to caterpillar to moth. The change of one object or creature into another can be brought on by annihilation due to blindly destructive forces or by equally mindless procreative instinctual drive.[83]

The problems raised by translation are particularly pertinent to the writings of an author like Sebald because of his highly nuanced use of language and deploy-

---

81 Since this posthumous volume of poetry was conceived as a "Leseausgabe" rather than a critical edition, close to one-third of the poems are not dated with certainty, but the poems are organized in an approximate chronological order. The two poems quoted above are part of the second section of the book, which Meyer suggests as having been written between 1981 and 1984. The possibility that the poems are even a retroactive reworking of the prose is not to be dismissed.

82 Andreas Huyssen, "Gray Zones of Remembrance," *A New History of German Literature*, ed. David Wellbery (Cambridge, MA: Belknap Press, 2004) 970–975, here 971.

83 McCulloh, *Understanding W. G. Sebald*, 68.

ment of complex image-text constellations in a 'factional' form that relies on intertextuality as well as interdiscursivity.

Despite the challenges his works present to a translator, Sebald's narratives nevertheless retain their aesthetic and political force, as Stanley Corngold asserts:

> [Sebald] is powerful in translation: he has found a transmissible narrative manner that exceeds its local value in German, dreamlike in its vividness and detail, yet coolly hypotactic and dense with historical fact. He renders real places precisely in a mood of universal uprootedness and sober appalledness, and his subject matter is vast: he re-dreams the nightmare of European ruin and its tributary, colonial ruin.[84]

The question of the English translations of Sebald's works is of particular concern, given his very positive reception in the Anglophone world and the continued interest to be found within English departments and Cultural Studies programs both in Britain and the USA. Thanks, probably, to the late Susan Sontag, who described *Die Ausgewanderten* as 'an astonishing masterpiece' after its translation into English, Sebald attained international status as one of the great German writers of the twentieth century. But it may also be the case, as Anne Fuchs has suggested, that his enormous success in the Anglophone world was due primarily to the quality of the English translations.[85] Not only the translation of Sebald's works, but Sebald's personal interest in translation – his extensive correspondence with his translators, his meticulous 'corrections' of and alterations to the translations which often led to the rewriting of entire passages, and his role in establishing and directing the British Centre for Literary Translation at the University of East Anglia – contributes to the uniqueness of his œuvre within Germany's post-war literature and within the broader category of twentieth- and twenty-first-century world literature.

---

84 Stanley Corngold, "Sebald's Tragedy," *Rethinking Tragedy*, ed. Rita Felski (Baltimore: The Johns Hopkins University Press, 2008) 218–240, here 220.
85 Anne Fuchs, *Die Schmerzensspuren der Geschichte. Zur Poetik der Erinnerung in W.G. Sebalds Prosa* (Cologne: Böhlau, 2004) 10.

Conclusion
Panoramic Outlook

It is not an epigraph with which Sebald begins his collection of four "long stories" but a photograph. To be more precise it is a photograph of a cemetery, empty of people, where an expansive tree looms at once ominously and protectively over the graves, some upright, most leaning at steep angles. Similar to this iconic beginning of *Die Ausgewanderten*, Sebald's first major prose work, *Schwindel. Gefühle*, also opens with an image – here it is a painting – prior to any text. The mountains that make up the background of the canvas and the masses of men and horses that populate the foreground form what could be seen as a prefiguration of the narrative to follow, that is, we are fist confronted with a visual representation of Napoleon's army attempting to cross the Alps. The textual description that follows directly below the image entices one to assume a direct, mutually illustrative relationship between text and image, one that will continue throughout the work. However, as one reads both of these works as well as Sebald's two other main prose works, *Die Ringe des Saturn* and *Austerlitz*, one finds the relationship between text and image to be anything but direct. Taken together, these text-image-constellations are vaguely reminiscent of an emblematic form, however such arrangements are more often than not *not* illustrative. The ultimate example of a text-image relationship that defiantly resists illustration can be found in *Unerzählt*, the collaborative project of Sebald and the artist Jan Peter Tripp. In her afterword to this posthumously published volume, Andrea Köhler explains that the goal was not for the texts and images to explain or illustrate each other but rather for them to enter into a conversation that allowed each to have its own room for expression ["erklärtes Ziel war, daß Text und Bild einander nicht erläutern oder gar illustrieren, sondern in ein Gespräch eintreten, das beiden den eigenen Echoraum läßt"[1]]. This joint project between Sebald and Tripp in particular – though the same can be argued for all of Sebald's texts that integrate images – underlines the fundamental difference between and irreducibility of each distinct medium. Lewis Hine's succinct statement summarizes this point, while also acknowledging the narrative value of photography: "If I could tell the story in words, I wouldn't need to lug a camera."[2]

---

1 Andrea Köhler, "Die Durchdringung des Dunkels," afterword to *Unerzählt* (Munich; Vienna: Hanser, 2003) 73.

2 Cited in Susan Sontag, *On Photography* (New York: Farrar, Straus and Giroux, 1977) 185.

I briefly revisit the text-image relationship for the way in which it echoes the broader concern of this book: the interaction yet irreducibility of distinct discourses and the resulting tension between creation and recreation, visualization and narrativization, imagination and memory. There is an ethical dimension inherent in Sebald's form of literary historiography that not only incorporates documents and information from apparent sources but also weaves in literary and autobiographical texts in an almost invisible manner. Mark M. Anderson points to this ethical impetus that drives Sebald to reveal his sources and to challenge the myth of the blank page.[3] Whether we consider the literaricity or the historicity of Sebald's works, questions of (re)construction and transformation demand our attention.

The starting point of this book was the desire to trace the sustained contact between historiography and literary discourse. To rein in such a broad topic, I plotted a trajectory that began with Aristotle's differentiation of two distinct discourses and ended with the discursive fusion that one finds in twentieth- and twenty-first-century fictional forms. By way of this diachronic view, the discursive difference between history and literature crystallizes as a constant, whether reinforced in narrative historiography of the eighteenth and nineteenth centuries or destabilized by the "linguistic turn" of structuralism and postmodernism. New literary forms emerge out of the consistent tension and constant exchange between history and literature, and Sebald's hybrid texts exemplify this. While a sense of the historical pervades his prose, Sebald insists on the legitimacy of the literary discourse, never subverting its independent status to make it the mere servant of history. While defending literature's autonomy, Sebald goes beyond this, troubling the fundamental distinction between literature and history as first defined by Aristotle in his *Poetics*. This discursive tension can be seen as the generator for Sebald's innovative form of fiction that eludes traditional genre distinctions. Drawing on sources from a variety of disciplines – architecture and archaeology in addition to literature and history – Sebald brings several genres and discourses into contact, and in this way his works retain the dialectic potential inherent in the relationship between literature and history. The new literary form that emerges across Sebald's œuvre thus reveals an intediscursive vision of literature and a transdiscursive ideal of "literary knowledge." In this way, Sebald's works serve as the vanishing point of this book: by forging a new discourse of literary historiography, a form which simultaneously critiques traditional forms of historiography while presenting a new type of historiography that

---

3 Cf. Mark M. Anderson, "'Loin, mais loin d'où?' Sur W.G. Sebald," *Critique. Revue générale des publications françaises et etrangères* Tome 58, Number 659 (2002) 252–262, here 259.

comes into being only in the literary mode, his texts reveal literature's privileged position for exploring, preserving, and understanding the past.

In exploring the particular tension between literature and history, I have drawn connections between Sebald's critical and fictional prose works to elucidate the immanent poetics of his new mode of literary historiography. The core areas of textual hybridity and interdiscursivity broadened the perspective beyond Sebald's particular fictional prose form to engage with the more fundamental discussion of the potential of the literary discourse to process, produce, and perform the interdiscursive transfer from experience to representation. The vanishing point of this book, then, can be located in this interdiscursive transfer out of which a type of aesthetic knowledge or form of literary (re)cognition can arise. Taking my cue from Sebald's works, in particular the non-linear progression and poetics of association, my circuitous attempt at approaching this vanishing point opens up both the possibility of reevaluating and also the potential for redefining how we understand knowledge and thinking.

Considering our present moment, one can diagnose both anxiety and anticipation in the way in which the Internet, or the "post-aesthetic space,"[4] as Hayden White has broadly termed it, is changing the way we communicate, experience the world, produce and transfer information, and thereby create knowledge. This is evident in current discussions around the subject of new media forms, from electronic devices in the realm of reading technology to instant messaging that uses only snapshots and videos. These developments have sparked discussions that on the one hand predict the death of physical books and images and on the other suggest that such new media may even lead to a renaissance of reading and photography. Independent of the form, what qualifies as a literary text and the value of literature seem to go unquestioned or even get lost in such popular debates, whereas what qualifies as knowledge presents itself as the more pressing issue. Although such discussions often confuse the difference between information and knowledge and assert newness and innovation from a very short-sighted perspective, they echo a longer tradition and an older constellation of concerns that I have been able to evoke and approach via the specific examination of Sebald's works.

In this "post-aesthetic space," we need more than ever the "historical sense" that T.S. Eliot describes or the "presence of the past," to speak with Sebald.[5]

---

4 Hayden White, "Commentary: 'With no particular place to go:' Literary History in the Age of the Global Picture," *New Literary History* 39.3 (2008) 727–745, here 728.
5 W.G. Sebald and Gordon Turner (Interviewer: Michaël Zeeman), "Introduction and Transcript of an Interview Given by Max Sebald,"*W.G. Sebald. History – Memory – Trauma*, eds. Scott Denham and Mark McCulloh (Berlin: de Gruyter, 2006) 21–29, here 23.

Sebald's works have shown how the literary discourse, in particular his new form of literature *as* historiography, is the privileged means by which such a perspective can be achieved. Moreover, his works provide the best answer to the question he posed at the opening of the Literaturhaus in Stuttgart: "what is literature good for?" Sebald's œuvre simultaneously raises and responds to ethical, epistemological, and aesthetic concerns, and it does so in an indirect manner that demands the reader's engagement and challenges trained responses. It is through our engagement with literary texts that we can attain a critical understanding of the past while reflecting upon both our relationship to the past and our present place in the world. Literature helps us to better understand what it means to be human, and such an understanding in turn helps us develop critical forms of empathy with which to approach the past and interact with the present world around us. While analyzing the different manifestations of textual hybridity and tracing the process of translation and transfer among multiple discourses, the literary discourse remained the focal point of this investigation in order to reinforce its unique role over time and to reassert its specificity within the humanities when currently other media are at the forefront of research. In exploring the borders of literature, it is possible to explore our own cognitive and imaginative horizons.

Bibliography of W. G. Sebald's Primary Works and of Works Cited

For the most complete bibliography of W. G. Sebald see the bibliographic survey in *Saturn's Moons. A W.G. Sebald Handbook*, eds. Jo Catling and Richard Hibbitt (Oxford: Legenda, 2011), which includes primary and secondary bibliographies, reviews of Sebald's works, an audio-visual bibliography, and an index to interviews with Sebald. Having co-authored the bibliography of secondary literature on Sebald in the *Handbook*,[1] the bibliography of secondary literature included here is limited to only those works cited within this book.

I. Primary Sources
II. Primary Texts of W. G. Sebald
    A. Fictional Prose and Poetry
    B. English Translations of Sebald's Works
    C. Works in Translation (cited in this book)
    D. Literary Criticism, Essays, Biographies, Translations
III. Secondary Literature on W. G. Sebald (cited in this book)
IV. W. G. Sebald-Related/-Inspired Films and Websites
V. Related Primary and Secondary Literature

I. Primary Sources

W. G. Sebald Nachlaß, Deutsches Literaturarchiv Marbach (DLA), A: Sebald [unpublished manuscripts and letters], G: Teilbibliothek [Sebald's library]. Copyright © The Estate of W. G. Sebald, used by permission of the Wylie Agency (UK) Limited.

Hulse Papers, bMS Eng 1632, Harvard Houghton Library, Cambridge, MA [Michael Hulse's correspondence with W. G. Sebald; Hulse's translation manuscripts of *Schwindel.Gefühle*, *Die Ausgewanderten*, and *Die Ringe des Saturn*]

---

1 See Jo Catling, Richard Hibbitt, and Lynn Wolff, "W.G. Sebald: Secondary Bibliography," *Saturn's Moons. A W.G. Sebald Handbook*, eds. Jo Catling and Richard Hibbitt (Oxford: Legenda, 2011) 495–543.

II. Primary Texts of W. G. Sebald

A. Fictional Prose and Poetry (listed in chronological order)

Sebald, Winfried Georg. "Panazee," "Analytische Sommerfrische," "Mithräisch," "Norfolk," "Stundenplan." *ZET. Das Zeichenheft für Literatur und Graphik* 3.10 (1974): 13.

——. "K.'s Auswanderung," "Mölkerbastei," "Elisabethanisch," "Unerschlossen." *ZET. Das Zeichenheft für Literatur und Graphik* 3.10 (1979): 18–19.

——. "Und blieb ich am äußersten Meer." *Manuskripte* Jg. 23, Heft 85 (1984): 23–27.

——. "Wie der Schnee auf den Alpen." *Manuskripte* Jg. 26, Heft 91 (1986): 26–31.

——. "Die dunckle Nacht fahrt aus." *Manuskripte* Jg. 27, Heft 95 (1987): 12–18.

——. "Die Kunst des Fliegens." *Träume. Literaturalmanach 1987.* Ed. Jochen Jung. Salzburg; Vienna: Residenz Verlag, 1987. 134–138.

——. *Nach der Natur. Ein Elementargedicht.* Photographien von Thomas Becker. Nördlingen: Greno, 1988.

——. "Berge oder das…" *Manuskripte* Jg. 28, Heft 99 (1988): 71–78.

——. "Verzehret das letzte selbst die Erinnerung nicht?" *Manuskripte* Jg. 28, Heft 100 (1988): 150–158.

——. *Schwindel. Gefühle.* Frankfurt a.M.: Eichborn, 1990. (Die Andere Bibliothek 63).

——. "Und manche Nebelflecken löset kein Auge auf." *Klagenfurter Texte. Ingeborg-Bachmann-Wettbewerb 1990.* Eds. Heinz Felsbach and Siegbert Metelko. Munich; Zurich: Piper, 1990. 111–137.

——. *Die Ausgewanderten. Vier lange Erzählungen.* Frankfurt a.M.: Eichborn, 1992. (Die Andere Bibliothek 93).

——. *Die Ringe des Saturn. Eine englische Wallfahrt.* Frankfurt a.M.: Eichborn, 1995. (Die Andere Bibliothek 130).

——. "Am 9. Juni 1904" and "Neunzig Jahre später." [printed with a postcard: "Gruss aus Badenweiler" and two photographs of a funeral procession] *Die Weltwoche* (June 1996): 30–31.

——. "Marienbader Elegie." *Neue Zürcher Zeitung.* Nr.265 (13. November 1999): 50.

——. *Austerlitz.* Munich; Vienna: Hanser, 2001.

——. *For Years Now. Poems.* Illustrated by Tess Jaray. London: Short Books, 2001.

——. *Gedichte. Akzente* 48 (2001): 112–121.

——. "Es heißt," "My eye," "Aus der Sammlung," "Im Notizbuch Turners," "Zu Sapios Zeit." *Manuskripte* Jg. 41, Heft 152 (2001): 68.

——. *Unerzählt.* Zusammen mit Jan Peter Tripp. 33 Texte und 33 Radierungen. Munich; Vienna: Hanser, 2003.

——. *Campo Santo.* Ed. Sven Meyer. Munich; Vienna: Hanser, 2003.

——. *Über das Land und das Wasser. Ausgewählte Gedichte 1964–2001.* Ed. Sven Meyer. Munich; Vienna: Hanser, 2008.

B. English Translation of Sebald's Works (listed in chronological order)

Sebald, W. G. *The Emigrants*. Trans. Michael Hulse. London: Harvill, 1996.

——. *Rings of Saturn*. Trans. Michael Hulse. London: Harvill, 1998.

——. *Vertigo*. Trans. Michael Hulse. London: Harvill, 2000.

——. *Austerlitz*. Trans. Anthea Bell. London: Hamish Hamilton, 2001.

——. *After Nature*. Trans. Michael Hamburger. London: Hamish Hamilton, 2002. [Part III published in *Mother Tongues. Non English-Language Poetry in England. Modern Poetry in Translation. New Series/No. 17*. Stephen Watts (Guest Editor). Strand, London: King's College London (2001): 248–250.]

——. "Dark Night Sallies Forth." Trans. Michael Hamburger. *The New Yorker* (June 17 & 24, 2002): 126.

——. "A Natural History of Destruction." Trans. Anthea Bell. *The New Yorker* (November 4, 2002): 66–77.

——. "Marienbad Elegy." Trans. Michael Hamburger. *Irish Pages* 1.2 (The Justice Issue) (2002/2003): 125–132.

——. *On the Natural History of Destruction*. Trans. Anthea Bell. New York: Random House, 2003.

——. "An Attempt at Restitution. A Memory of a German City." Trans. Anthea Bell. *The New Yorker* (December 20 & 27, 2004): 110–114.

——. *Unrecounted. 33 Poems*. Etchings by Jan Peter Tripp. Trans. Michael Hamburger. New York: New Directions, 2004.

——. *Campo Santo*. Ed. Sven Meyer. Trans. Anthea Bell. New York: Random House, 2005.

——. "Le Promeneur solitaire. A Remembrance of Robert Walser." Trans. Jo Catling. *The Tanners*, Robert Walser, trans. Susan Bernofsky. New York: New Directions, 2009. 1–36.

——. *Across the Land and the Water. Selected Poems, 1964–2001*. Ed. Sven Meyer. Trans. Iain Galbraith. London: Hamish Hamilton, 2011.

——. *A Place in the Country. On Gottfried Keller, Johann Peter Hebel, Robert Walser and Others*. Trans. Jo Catling. London: Hamish Hamilton, 2013.

C. Works in Translation (cited in this book)

Sebald, W. G. *Les Émigrants*. Trans. Patrick Charbonneau. Arles: Actes Sud, 1999.

——. *Austerlitz*. Trans. Patrick Charbonneau. Arles: Actes Sud, 2002.

——. *Vertiges*. Trans. Patrick Charbonneau. Paris: Gallimard, 2003.

D. Literary Criticism, Essays, Biographies, Translations

Evans, Richard J. *Sozialdemokratie und Frauenemanzipation im deutschen Kaiserreich*. Trans. W. G. Sebald. Berlin: J. H.W. Dietz, 1979.

Hulse, Michael. "An Botho Strauss in Berlin," "Raffles Hotel Singapur." Trans. W. G. Sebald. *Sprache im technischen Zeitalter* 33 Nr. 134 (1995): 162–164.

Sebald, W. G. "Adalbert Stifter." *Österreichische Porträts*. Ed. Jochen Jung. Vol. 1 (1985): 232–255.

——. "Alfred Döblin oder die politische Unzuverlässigkeit des bürgerlichen Literaten." *Interna-tionale Alfred Döblin-Kolloquien. Basel 1980, New York 1981, Freiburg i. Br. 1983.* Ed. Werner Stauffacher. Bern; Frankfurt; New York: Lang, 1986–88. 133–139.

——. "Die Alpen im Meer: ein Reisebild." *Literaturen* Heft 1 (2001): 30–33. [Also in· *Heine-Jahrbuch* (2001): 174–180. *Verleihung des Heine-Preises 2000 der Landeshauptstadt Düsseldorf an W. G. Sebald.* Ed. Kulturamt der Landeshauptstadt Düsseldorf.]

——. *Am deutschen Ozean.* Frankfurt am Main: DG-Bank 1995.

——. "Ansichten aus der Neuen Welt. Über Charles Sealsfield." *Unheimliche Heimat. Essays zur österreichischen Literatur.* Salzburg u.a.: Residenz-Verlag, 1991. 17–39, 179–181. [Also in: *Die Rampe* 1 (1988): 7–36; *Charles Sealsfield. Ralph Doughby's Esq. Brautfahrt.* Ed. Rolf Vollmann. Mit einem Essay von W. G. Sebald. Frankfurt am Main: Eichborn Verlag, 2006. 287–313.]

——. "The Art of Transformation. Herbert Achternbusch's Theatrical Mission." *A Radical Stage. Theatre in Germany in the 1970s and 1980s.* Ed. W. G. Sebald. Oxford; New York; Hamburg: Berg, 1988. 174–184.

——. "Ein Avantgardist in Reih und Glied. Kritische Überlegungen zum Verständnis des Drama-tikers Carl Sternheim und seiner Widersprüche." *Frankfurter Rundschau* Nr. 235 (October 10, 1970): V. Reprinted in: *Sebald. Lektüren.* Eds. Marcel Atze and Franz Loquai. Eggingen: Ed. Isele, 2005. 61–64.

——. "Beitrag W. G. Sebald: Schriftsteller und Essayist; Biographie." *Mörike-Preis der Stadt Fellbach 1991–2000. Ein Lesebuch.* Fellbach: Stadt Fellbach, 2000. 163–164.

——. *Die Beschreibung des Unglücks. Zur österreichischen Literatur von Stifter bis Handke.* Salzburg; Vienna: Residenz-Verlag 1985.

——. "Between the Devil and the Deep Blue Sea: Alfred Andersch; das Verschwinden in der Vorsehung." *Lettre international* Heft 20 (1993): 80–84.

——. "Bis an den Rand der Natur: Versuch über Stifter." *Die Beschreibung des Unglücks. Zur österreichischen Literatur von Stifter bis Handke.* Salzburg; Vienna: Residenz-Verlag, 1985. 15–37, 187–188. [Also in: *Die Rampe* 1 (1985): 7–35.]

——. *Carl Sternheim. Kritiker und Opfer der Wilhelminischen Ära.* Stuttgart; Berlin; Cologne; Mainz: Kohlhammer, 1969. (= *Sprache und Literatur* 58)

——. "Damals vor Graz: Randbemerkungen zum Thema Literatur & Heimat." *Trans-Garde. Die Literatur der 'Grazer Gruppe,' Forum Stadtpark und 'Manuskripte.'* Eds. Karl Bartsch und Gerhard Melzer. Graz: Droschl, 1990. 141–153. [Reprinted in: *Heimat im Wort. Die Proble-matik eines Begriffs im 19. und 20. Jahrhundert.* Ed. Rüdiger Görner. Munich: iudicium, 1992. 131–139.]

——. "Fremdheit, Integration und Krise. Über Peter Handkes Stück Kaspar." *Literatur und Kritik* 10 (1975): 152–158.

——. "Gedanken zu Elias Canetti." *Literatur und Kritik* 7 (1972): 280–285.

——. "Das Gesetz der Schande. Macht, Messianismus und Exil in Kafkas *Schloß*." *Unheimliche Heimat. Essays zur österreichischen Literatur.* Salzburg u.a.: Residenz-Verlag, 1991. 87–103, 186–187. [Also in: *Manuskripte* Jg. 25 Heft 89/90 (1985): 117–121.]

——. "Helle Bilder und dunkle: zur Dialektik der Eschatologie bei Stifter und Handke." *Die Beschreibung des Unglücks. Zur österreichischen Literatur von Stifter bis Handke.* Salzburg; Vienna: Residenz-Verlag, 1985. 165–86, 198–200. [Also in: *Manuskripte* Jg. 24 Heft 84 (1984): 58–64.]

——. "Ich möchte zu ihnen hinabsteigen und finde den Weg nicht. Zu den Romanen Jurek Beckers." *Sinn und Form* 62.2 (2010): 226–234.

——. "In a Completely Unknown Region: On Gerhard Roth's Novel *Landläufiger Tod.*" *Modern Austrian Literature* 40.4 (2007): 29–41.

——. "In einer wildfremden Gegend. Zu Gerhard Roths Romanwerk *Landläufiger Tod.*" *Unheimliche Heimat. Essays zur österreichischen Literatur.* Salzburg u.a.: Residenz-Verlag, 1991. 145–161, 191–192. [Also in: *Gerhard Roth. Materialien zu* Die Archive des Schweigens. Ed. Uwe Wittstock. Frankfurt am Main: Fischer, 1992. 164–179; *Manuskripte* Jg. 26 Heft 92 (1986): 52–56.]

——. "Jean Améry und Primo Levi." *Über Jean Améry.* Ed. Irene Heidelberger-Leonard. (Beiträge zur neueren Literaturgeschichte: Folge 3. 102) Heidelberg: Winter, 1990. 115–123.

——. "Jenseits der Grenze. Peter Handkes Erzählung *Die Wiederholung.*" *Unheimliche Heimat. Essays zur österreichischen Literatur.* Salzburg u.a.: Residenz-Verlag, 1991. 162–178, 192–194.

——. "Johann Bauer und Isidor Pollak, Kafka und Prag. Stuttgart 1971." *Literatur und Kritik* (1972): 421–422.

——. "Ein Kaddisch für Österreich. Über Joseph Roth." *Unheimliche Heimat. Essays zur österreichischen Literatur.* Salzburg u.a.: Residenz-Verlag, 1991. 104–117, 187–188.

——. "Eine kleine Traverse: Das poetische Werk Ernst Herbecks." *Die Beschreibung des Unglücks. Zur österreichischen Literatur von Stifter bis Handke.* Salzburg; Vienna: Residenz-Verlag 1985. 131–48, 196–97. [Also in: *Ernst Herbeck. Die Vergangenheit ist klar vorbei.* Eds. Carl Aigner und Leo Navratil. Vienna: Brandstätter; Krems: Kunsthalle Krems, 2002. 154–167.]

——. "Kleine Traverse. Über das poetische Werk des Alexander Herbrich [pseudonym for Ernst Herbeck]." *Manuskripte* Jg. 21 Heft 74 (1981): 35–41.

——. "Konstruktionen der Trauer: Zu Günter Grass *Tagebuch einer Schnecke* und Wolfgang Hildesheimer *Tynset.*" *Der Deutschunterricht* 35.5 (1983): 32–47.

——. "Die Kunst der Verwandlung: Achternbuschs theatralische Sendung." *Patterns of Change. German Drama and the European Tradition.* Ed. Dorothy James. New York: Lang, 1990. 297–306.

——. "Kurzer Versuch über System und Systemkritik bei Elias Canetti." *Études germaniques* 39 (1984): 268–275.

——. "Laudatio auf Wolfgang Schlüter." *Mörike-Preis der Stadt Fellbach 1991–2000: Ein Lesebuch.* Fellbach: Stadt Fellbach, 2000. 149–154.

——. "The Law of Ignominy. Authority, Messianism and Exile in the *Castle.*" *On Kafka. Semi-Centenary Perspectives.* Ed. Franz Kuna. London: Elek, 1976. 42–58.

——. "Leben Ws. Skizze einer möglichen Szenenreihe für einen nichtrealistischen Film." *Zeit und Bild: Frankfurter Rundschau am Wochenende* 94 (1989): ZB3.

——. "Le paysan de Vienne: Über Peter Altenberg." *Neue Rundschau* 100 Heft 1 (1989): 75–95.

——. "Liebste, Bilder sind schön...Kafka im Kino." *Weltwoche* Nr. 26 (June 26, 1997): 54–55.

——. "Literarische Pornographie? Zur 'Winterreise' Gerhard Roths." *Merkur* 38 (1984): 171–180.

——. *Logis in einem Landhaus: Über Gottfried Keller, Johann Peter Hebel, Robert Walser und andere.* Munich; Vienna: Hanser, 1998.

——. *Luftkrieg und Literatur. Mit einem Essay zu Alfred Andersch.* Munich; Vienna: Hanser, 1999.

——. "Die Mädchen aus der Feenwelt. Bemerkungen zu Liebe und Prostitution mit Bezügen zu Raimund, Schnitzler, Horvath." *Neophilologus* 67 (1983): 109–117.

——. "Der Mann mit dem Mantel: Gerhard Roths *Winterreise.*" *Die Beschreibung des Unglücks. Zur österreichischen Literatur von Stifter bis Handke.* Salzburg; Vienna: Residenz-Verlag, 1985. 149–64, 197–98.

——. "Mit den Augen des Nachtvogels: Über Jean Améry." *Études germaniques* 43 (1988): 313–327.

——. "Mord an den Vätern: Bemerkungen zu einigen Dramen der spätbürgerlichen Zeit." *Neophilologus. An International Journal of Modern and Mediaeval Language and Literature* 60 (1976): 432–441.

——. *Der Mythus der Zerstörung im Werk Döblins.* Stuttgart: Klett, 1980. (= *Literaturwissenschaft – Gesellschaftswissenschaft* 45).

——. "Peter Altenberg, le paysan de Vienne." *Unheimliche Heimat. Essays zur österreichischen Literatur.* Salzburg u.a.: Residenz-Verlag, 1991. 65–86, 183–186.

——. "Preußische Perversionen: Anmerkungen zum Thema Literatur und Gewalt, ausgehend vom Frühwerk Alfred Döblins." *Internationale Alfred Döblin-Kolloquien. Basel 1980, New York 1981, Freiburg i. Br. 1983.* Ed. Werner Stauffacher. Bern, Frankfurt, New York: Lang, 1986–88. 231–238.

——. ed. *A Radical Stage. Theatre in Germany in the 1970s and 1980s.* Oxford; New York, Hamburg: Berg, 1988.

——. "Rousseau auf der Île de Saint-Pierre." *Sinn und Form* 50.4 (1998): 499–513.

——. "Schock und Ästhetik. Zu den Romanen Döblins." *Orbis litterarum* 30 (1975): 241–250.

——. "Das Schrecknis der Liebe: Überlegungen zu Schnitzlers *Traumnovelle.*" *Merkur* 39 (1985): 120–131.

——. "Scomber scombrus oder die gemeine Makrele." *Centrales & Occasionelles.* Ed. Jan Peter Tripp. Offenburg: A. Reiff & Cie. KG, 2001. 40.

——. "Sternheims Narben (1970)." *Die Zeit* Nr. 35 (August 28, 1970): 46. Reprinted in: *Sebald. Lektüren.* Eds. Marcel Atze and Franz Loquai. Eggingen: Ed. Isele, 2005. 59–60.

——. "Summa scientiae: System und Systemkritik bei Elias Canetti." *Die Beschreibung des Unglücks. Zur österreichischen Literatur von Stifter bis Handke.* Salzburg; Vienna: Residenz-Verlag, 1985. 93–102, 193. [Also in: *Literatur und Kritik* 18 (1983): 398–404.]

——. "Thanatos. Zur Motivstruktur in Kafkas Schloss." *Literatur und Kritik* 7 (1972): 399–411.

——. "Thomas Bernhard (1931–1989)." *Vienna 1900. From Altenberg to Wittgenstein.* Eds. Edward Timms and Ritchie Robertson. Edinburgh: Edinburgh University Press, 1990. 215–216.

——. "Tiere, Menschen, Maschinen. Zu Kafkas Evolutionsgeschichten." *Literatur und Kritik* 201/202 (1986): 194–201.

——. "Traumtexturen." *Du* 661 (1996) 22–27.

——. "Überlebende als schreibende Subjekte. Jean Améry und Primo Levi, ein Gedenken." *Zeit und Bild: Frankfurter Rundschau am Wochenende* (January 28, 1989) ZB3.

——. "Una montagna bruna. Zum *Bergroman* Hermann Brochs." *Unheimliche Heimat. Essays zur österreichischen Literatur.* Salzburg u.a.: Residenz-Verlag, 1991. 118–130.

——. "Das unentdeckte Land. Zur Motivstruktur in Kafkas *Schloß.*" *Die Beschreibung des Unglücks. Zur österreichischen Literatur von Stifter bis Handke.* Salzburg; Vienna: Residenz-Verlag, 1985. 78–92, 191–92.

——. *Unheimliche Heimat. Essays zur österreichischen Literatur.* Salzburg u.a.: Residenz-Verlag, 1991.

——. "Unterm Spiegel des Wassers: Peter Handkes Erzählung von der Angst des Tormanns." *Austriaca* 9.16 (1983): 43–56. [Also in: *Die Beschreibung des Unglücks. Zur österreichischen Literatur von Stifter bis Handke.* Salzburg; Vienna: Residenz-Verlag, 1985. 115–130, 195–196.]

——. "Venezianisches Kryptogramm: Hofmannsthals *Andreas.*" *Die Beschreibung des Unglücks. Zur österreichischen Literatur von Stifter bis Handke.* Salzburg; Vienna: Residenz-Verlag, 1985. 61–77, 190–191.

——. "Venezianisches Kryptogramm: Hofmannsthals *Andreas.*" *Fin de siècle Vienna.* Eds. G. J. Carr and Eda Sagarra. Dublin: Trinity College, 1985. 143–160.

——. "Verlorenes Land. Jean Améry und Österreich." *Jean Améry. Text + Kritik 99.* Ed. Heinz Ludwig Arnold. Munich: Text + Kritik, 1988. 20–29. [Also in: *Unheimliche Heimat. Essays zur österreichischen Literatur.* Salzburg u.a.: Residenz-Verlag, 1991. 131–144, 189–191.]

——. [Antrittsrede] "Vorstellung neuer Mitglieder." *Jahrbuch. Deutsche Akademie für Sprache und Dichtung 1997.* Göttingen: Wallstein, 1998. 189–190.

——. "Walser im Urwald: Wege durch Zeit und Raum." *Du* 730 (2002): 53.

——. "'Was ich traure weiss ich nicht:' Kleinen Andenken an Mörike." *Mörike-Preis der Stadt Fellbach 1991–2000: Ein Lesebuch.* Fellbach: Stadt Fellbach, 2000. 137–147.

——. "Die weiße Adlerfeder am Kopf. Versuch über den Indianer Herbert Achternbusch." *Manuskripte* Jg. 23 Heft 79 (1983): 75–79.

——. "Die weiße Adlerfeder am Kopf: Versuch über Herbert Achternbusch." *Subjektivität, Innerlichkeit, Abkehr vom Politischen.* Eds. Keith Bullivant und Hans-Joachim Althof. Bonn: DAAD, 1986. 175–189.

——. "Westwärts – Ostwärts. Aporien deutschsprachiger Ghettogeschichten." *Literatur und Kritik* 233/234 (1989): 161–177. [Reprinted in: *Unheimliche Heimat. Essays zur österreichischen Literatur.* Salzburg u.a.: Residenz-Verlag, 1991. 40–64, 181–183.]

——. "Wo die Dunkelheit den Strick zuzieht. Einige Bemerkungen zum Werk Thomas Bernhards." *Literatur und Kritik* 151 (1981): 294–302. [Reprinted in: *Die Beschreibung des Unglücks. Zur österreichischen Literatur von Stifter bis Handke.* Salzburg; Vienna: Residenz-Verlag, 1985. 103–114, 194.]

——. "Das Wort unter der Zunge. Zu Hugo von Hofmannsthals Trauerspiel *Der Turm.*" *Literatur und Kritik* 121 (1978): 294–303.

——. "Die Zerknirschung des Herzens. Über Erinnerung und Grausamkeit im Werk von Peter Weiss." *Orbis litterarum* 41 (1986): 265–278.

——. "Zerstreute Reminiszenzen. Gedanken zur Eröffnung eines Stuttgarter Hauses." *Betrifft: Chotjewitz, Dorst, Hermann, Hoppe, Kehlmann, Klein, Kling, Kronauer, Mora, Ortheil, Oswald, Rakusa, Sebald, Walser, Zeh.* Eds. Florian Höllerer and Tim Schleider. Frankfurt am Main: Suhrkamp, 2004. 11–16.

——. "Zum Thema Messianismus im Werk Döblins." *Neophilologus* 59 (1975): 421–434.

——. "Die Zweideutigkeit der Toleranz. Anmerkungen zum Interesse der Aufklärung an der Emanzipation der Juden." *Der Deutschunterricht* 36.4 (1984): 27–47.

——. "Zwischen Geschichte und Naturgeschichte. Über die literarische Beschreibung totaler Zerstörung." *Campo Santo.* Ed. Sven Meyer. Munich; Vienna: Hanser, 2003. 69–100. [Also in *Orbis litterarum* 37 (1982): 345–366.]

——, Hellmuth Karasek, and Peter von Matt. "Carl Sternheim. Versuch eines Porträts. Ein Rundfunkgespräch (1971). Textfassung und Stellenkommentar von Marcel Atze." *Sebald. Lektüren.* Eds. Marcel Atze and Franz Loquai. Eggingen: Ed. Isele, 2005. 39–55.

——. and Theodor W. Adorno. "Briefwechsel (1967/1968)." *Sebald. Lektüren.* Eds. Marcel Atze and Franz Loquai. Eggingen: Ed. Isele, 2005. 12–16.

——. [u.a.] "Statement zur Österreichischen Literatur." *Manuskripte* Jg. 25 Heft 89/90 (1985): 229.

——. [Review of] Friedbert Aspetsberger, *Literarisches Leben im Austrofaschismus*. Königstein/ Ts: Verlag Anton Hain Meisenheim, 1980. Literatur in der Geschichte – Geschichte in der Literatur. Bd. 2. *Literatur und Kritik* 151 (1981): 483–484.

——. [Review of] Gerhard Kurz, *Traumschrecken. Kafkas literarische Existenzanalyse*. Stuttgart: Metzler, 1980. *Literatur und Kritik* 161/162 (1902). 98–100.

Sheppard, Richard, ed. *Die Schriften des Neuen Clubs 1908–1914*. Hildesheim: Gerstenberg, 1980 [Vol. 1], 1983 [Vol. 2]. ["Nachwort" translated by W. G. Sebald, 419–577.]

III. Secondary Literature on W. G. Sebald (cited in this book)

Albes, Claudia. "Between 'Surface Illusionism' and 'Awful Depth': Reflections on the Poetological and Generic Ambivalence of W. G. Sebald's *Logis in einem Landhaus*." *Journal of European Studies*, Special Issue: W. G. Sebald, ed. Richard Sheppard 41.3–4 (2011): 449–465.

The Anatomist of Melancholy. Essays in Memory of W. G. Sebald. Ed. Rüdiger Görner. Munich: iudicium, 2003.

Anderson, Mark M. "A Childhood in the Allgäu: Wertach, 1944–52." *Saturn's Moons: A W. G. Sebald Handbook*. Eds. Jo Catling and Richard Hibbitt. Oxford: Legenda, 2011. 16–41.

——. "Documents, Photography, Postmemory: Alexander Kluge, W. G. Sebald, and the German Family." *Photography in Fiction*. Eds. Silke Horstkotte and Nancy Pedri. Special issue of *Poetics Today* 29.1 (2008): 129–151.

——. "The Edge of Darkness: On W. G. Sebald." *October* 106 (2003): 102–21.

——. "'Loin, mais loin d'où?' Sur W. G. Sebald." *Critique. Revue générale des publications françaises et etrangères* Tome 58 Numero 659 (2002): 252–62.

Angier, Carole. "Wer ist W. G. Sebald? Ein Besuch beim Autor der *Ausgewanderten*." *W. G. Sebald*. Ed. Franz Loquai. Eggingen: Ed. Isele, 1997. 43–50.

Atlas, James. "W. G. Sebald. A Profile." *The Paris Review* 41.151 (1999): 278–298.

Atze, Marcel. "Casanova vor der Schwarzen Wand. Ein Beispiel intertextueller Repräsentanz des Holocaust in W. G. Sebalds *Austerlitz*." *Sebald. Lektüren*. Eds. Marcel Atze and Franz Loquai. Eggingen: Ed. Isele, 2005. 228–243.

——. "Die Gesetze von der Wiederkunft der Vergangenheit. W. G. Sebalds Lektüre des Gedächtnistheoretikers Maurice Halbwachs." *Sebald. Lektüren*. Eds. Marcel Atze and Franz Loquai. Eggingen: Ed. Isele, 2005. 195–211.

——. "Koinzidenz und Intertextualität. Der Einsatz von Prätexten in W. G. Sebalds Erzählung 'All'estero.'" *W. G. Sebald*. Ed. Franz Loquai. Eggingen: Ed. Isele, 1997. 151–175.

——. "'…und wer spricht über Dresden?' Der Luftkrieg als öffentliches und literarisches Thema in der Zeit des ersten Frankfurter Auschwitz-Prozesses 1963–1965." *Sebald. Lektüren*. Eds. Marcel Atze and Franz Loquai. Eggingen: Ed. Isele, 2005. 105–115.

——. "'…und wer spricht über Dresden?' Der Luftkrieg als öffentliches und literarisches Thema in der Zeit des ersten Frankfurter Auschwitz-Prozesses 1963–1965." *W. G. Sebald. Politische Archäologie und melancholische Bastelei*. Eds. Michael Niehaus and Claudia Öhlschläger. [*Philologische Studien und Quellen* 196] Berlin: Schmidt, 2006. 205–217.

——. "W. G. Sebald und H. G. Adler. Eine Begegnung in Texten." *Mémoire. Transferts. Images. / Erinnerung. Übertragungen. Bilder.* Ed. Ruth Vogel-Klein. *Recherches germaniques* Hors Série 2 (2005): 87–97.

"*Auf ungeheuer dünnem Eis.*" *Gespräche 1971 bis 2001.* Ed. Torsten Hoffmann. Frankfurt am Main: Fischer, 2011.

Baumgarten, Murray. "'Not Knowing What I Should Think:' The Landscape of Postmemory in W. G. Sebald's *The Emigrants.*" *Partial Answers: Journal of Literature and the History of Ideas* 5.2 (2007): 267–287.

Bell, Anthea. "On Translating W. G. Sebald." *The Anatomist of Melancholy. Essays in Memory of W. G. Sebald.* Ed. Rüdiger Görner. Munich: iudicium, 2003. 11–18.

——. "Translating W. G. Sebald's *Austerlitz.*" *Linguist* 41.6 (2002): 162–163.

Bere, Carol. "The Book of Memory: W. G. Sebald's *The Emigrants* and *Austerlitz.*" *Literary Review: An International Journal of Contemporary Writing* 46.1 (2002): 184–92.

Bigsby, Christopher. "W. G. Sebald." *Writers in Conversation with Christopher Bigsby. Volume Two.* Norwich [U. K.]: Arthur Miller Centre for American Studies, 2001. 139–165.

Bird, Stephanie. "'Er gab mir, was äußerst ungewöhnlich war, zum Abschied die Hand': Touch and Tact in W. G. Sebald's *Die Ausgewanderten* and *Austerlitz.*" *Journal of European Studies*, Special Issue: W. G. Sebald, ed. Richard Sheppard 41.3–4 (2011): 359–375.

Blackler, Deane. *Reading W. G. Sebald: Adventure and Disobedience.* Rochester, NY: Camden House, 2007.

Boehncke, Heiner. "Clair obscur: W. G. Sebalds Bilder." *W. G. Sebald. Text + Kritik* (2003): 43–62.

Braun, Michael. *Der zertrümmerte Orpheus. Über Dichtung.* Heidelberg: Wunderhorn, 2002.

Bülow, Ulrich von. "Sebalds Korsika-Projekt." *Wandernde Schatten. W. G. Sebalds Unterwelt.* Eds. Ulrich von Bülow, Heike Gfrereis, and Ellen Strittmatter. Marbach am Neckar: Deutsche Schillergesellschaft, 2008. 211–224.

Burns, Rob and Wilfried van der Will. "The Calamitous Perspective of Modernity: Sebald's Negative Ontology." *Journal of European Studies*, Special Issue: W. G. Sebald, ed. Richard Sheppard 41.3–4 (2011): 341–358.

Carré, Martine. *W. G. Sebald: Le retour de l'auteur.* Lyon: Presses universitaires de Lyon, 2008.

Catling, Jo. "Europäische Flânerien: W. G. Sebalds intertextuelle Wanderungen zwischen Melancholie und Ironie." *Gedächtnis und Widerstand: Festschrift für Irène Heidelberger-Leonard.* Eds. Mireille Tabah with Sylvia Weiler and Christian Poetini. Tübingen: Stauffenberg, 2009. 139–154.

——. "Silent Catastrophe. In Memoriam W. G. (Max) Sebald 1944–2001." http://www.new-books-in-german.com/features.html [Last accessed: April 21, 2007]

Ceuppens, Jan. "Im zerschundenen Papier herumgeisternde Gesichter. Fragen der Repräsentation bei W. G. Sebalds *Die Ausgewanderten.*" *Germanistische Mitteilungen* 55 (2002): 79–98.

——. "Tracing the Witness in W. G. Sebald." *W. G. Sebald and the Writing of History.* Eds. Anne Fuchs and J. J. Long. Würzburg: Königshausen & Neumann, 2007. 59–72.

Charbonneau, Patrick. "Correspondance(s): Le traducteur et son auteur." *Mémoire. Transferts. Images. / Erinnerung. Übertragungen. Bilder.* Ed. Ruth Vogel-Klein. *Recherches germaniques* Hors Série 2 (2005): 193–210.

Corngold, Stanley, "Sebald's Tragedy." *Rethinking Tragedy.* Ed. Rita Felski. Baltimore, MD: Johns Hopkins University Press, 2008. 218–240.

Cosgrove, Mary. "Sebald for our Time: The Politics of Melancholy and the Critique of Capitalism in his Work." *W. G. Sebald and the Writing of History*, eds. Anne Fuchs and J. J. Long. Würzburg: Königshausen & Neumann, 2007. 91–110.

Cowan, James L. "Sebald's *Austerlitz* and the Great Library: A Documentary Study." *W. G. Sebald: Schreiben ex patria / Expatriate Writing*. Ed. Gerhard Fischer. Amsterdam; New York: Rodopi, 2009. 193–212.

——. "Sebald's *Austerlitz* and the Great Library: History, Fiction, Memory. Part I." *Monatshefte* 102.1 (2010): 51–81.

——. "Sebald's *Austerlitz* and the Great Library: History, Fiction, Memory. Part II." *Monatshefte* 102.2 (2010): 192–207.

Craven, Peter, "W. G. Sebald: Anatomy of Faction." *HEAT* 13 (1999): 212–224.

Crownshaw, Richard. "Reconsidering Postmemory: Photography, the Archive, and Post-Holocaust Memory in W. G. Sebald's *Austerlitz*." *Mosaic: A Journal for the Interdisciplinary Study of Literature* 37.4 (2004): 215–236.

Daub, Adrian. "'Donner à voir:' The Logics of the Caption in W. G. Sebald's *Rings of Saturn* and Alexander Kluge's *Devil's Blind Spot*." *Searching for Sebald. Photography After W. G. Sebald*. Ed. Lise Patt. Los Angeles: Institute for Cultural Inquiry and ICI Press, 2007. 306–329.

Denham, Scott. "Die englischsprachige Sebald-Rezeption." *W. G. Sebald. Politische Archäologie und melancholische Bastelei*. Eds. Michael Niehaus and Claudia Öhlschläger. [*Philologische Studien und Quellen* 196] Berlin: Schmidt, 2006. 259–268.

——. "Foreword: The Sebald Phenomenon." *W. G. Sebald. History – Memory – Trauma*. Eds. Scott Denham and Mark McCulloh. Berlin: de Gruyter, 2006. 1–6.

Doerry, Martin and Volker Hage. "'Ich fürchte das Melodramatische.'" Interview in *Der Spiegel* (March 12, 2001): 228–234.

Duttlinger, Carolin. "A Lineage of Destruction? Rethinking Photography in *Luftkrieg und Literatur*." *W. G. Sebald and the Writing of History*. Eds. Anne Fuchs and J. J. Long. Würzburg: Königshausen & Neumann, 2007. 163–177.

——. "Traumatic Photographs: Remembrance and the Technical Media in W. G. Sebald's *Austerlitz*." *W. G. Sebald: A Critical Companion*. Eds. J. J. Long and Anne Whitehead. Seattle, WA: University of Washington Press, 2004. 155–171.

Eggers, Christoph. *Das Dunkel durchdringen, das uns umgibt. Die Fotografie im Werk von W. G. Sebald*. Frankfurt am Main: Peter Lang, 2011 [*Frankfurter Forschungen zur Kultur- und Sprachwissenschaft*, ed. Heiner Boehncke and Horst D. Schlosser, vol. 18].

Elcott, Noam M. "Tattered Snapshots and Castaway Tongues: An Essay at Layout and Translation with W. G. Sebald." *Germanic Review* 79.3 (2004): 203–23.

Eldridge, Richard. "Literature as Material Figuration: Benjamin, Sebald, and Human Life in Time." *Visions of Value and Truth. Understanding Philosophy and Literature*. Eds. Floora Ruokonen and Laura Werner. *Acta Philosophica Fennica* 79 (2006): 13–29.

The Emergence of Memory: Conversations with W. G. Sebald. Ed. Lynne Sharon Schwartz. New York; Melbourne; Toronto: Seven Stories Press, 2007. Translated as: *L'Archéologue de la mémoire: Conversations avec W. G. Sebald*. Trans. Patrick Charnonneau and Delphine Chartier. Arles: Actes Sud, 2009.

Eshel, Amir. "Against the Power of Time: The Poetics of Suspension in W. G. Sebald's *Austerlitz*." *New German Critique* 88.4 (2003): 71–96.

Far From Home. W. G. Sebald. Ed. Franz Loquai. Bamberg: Otto-Friedrich Universität, 1995.

Finch, Helen. "'Die irdische Erfüllung': Peter Handke's Poetic Landscapes and W. G. Sebald's Metaphysics of History." *W. G. Sebald and the Writing of History*. Eds. Anne Fuchs and J. J. Long. Würzburg: Königshausen & Neumann, 2007. 179–197.

Finke, Susanne. "W. G. Sebald, der fünfte Ausgewanderte." *W. G. Sebald*. Ed. Franz Loquai. Eggingen: Ed. Isele, 1997. 214–227.

Fischer, Gerhard. "Introduction: W. G. Sebald's Expatriate Experience and his Literary Beginnings." *W. G. Sebald: Schreiben ex patria / Expatriate Writing*. Ed. Gerhard Fischer. Amsterdam; New York: Rodopi, 2009. 15–26.

——. "Schreiben *ex patria*: W. G. Sebald und die Konstruktion einer literarischen Identität." *W. G. Sebald: Schreiben ex patria / Expatriate Writing*. Ed. Gerhard Fischer. Amsterdam; New York: Rodopi, 2009. 27–44.

Franklin, Ruth. "Sebald's Amateurs." *W. G. Sebald. History – Memory – Trauma*. Eds. Scott Denham and Mark McCulloh. Berlin: de Gruyter, 2006. 127–138.

Fuchs, Anne. '*Die Schmerzensspuren der Geschichte.*' Zur Poetik der Erinnerung in W. G. Sebalds Prosa. Cologne: Böhlau, 2004.

——. "A *Heimat* in Ruins and the Ruins as Heimat: W. G. Sebald's *Luftkrieg und Literatur*." *German Memory Contests. The Quest for Identity in Literature, Film, and Discourse since 1990*. Eds. Anne Fuchs, Mary Cosgrove, and Georg Grote. New York: Camden House, 2006. 287–302.

Furst, Lilian R. "Realism, Photography, and Degrees of Uncertainty." *W. G. Sebald. History – Memory – Trauma*. Eds. Scott Denham and Mark McCulloh. Berlin: de Gruyter, 2006. 219–229.

Gasseleder, Klaus. "Erkundungen zum Prätext der Luisa-Lanzberg-Geschichte aus W. G. Sebalds *Die Ausgewanderten*. Ein Bericht." *Sebald. Lektüren*. Eds. Marcel Atze and Franz Loquai. Eggingen: Ed. Isele, 2005. 157–175.

Gnam, Andrea. "Fotografie und Film in W. G. Sebalds Erzählung *Ambros Adelwarth* und seinem Roman *Austerlitz*." *Verschiebebahnhöfe der Erinnerung: Zum Werk W. G. Sebalds*. Eds. Sigurd Martin and Ingo Wintermeyer. Würzburg: Königshausen & Neumann, 2007. 27–47.

Gotterbarm, Mario. "Ich und der Luftkrieg. Sebalds erste Zürcher Vorlesung als Autofiktion." *Jahrbuch der deutschen Schillergesellschaft* 55 (2011): 324–345.

Gray, Richard T. "Sebald's Segues: Performing Narrative Contingency in *The Rings of Saturn*." *The Germanic Review* 84.1 (2009): 26–58.

Gunther, Stefan. "The Holocaust as the Still Point of the World in W. G. Sebald's *The Emigrants*." *W. G. Sebald. History – Memory – Trauma*. Eds. Scott Denham and Mark McCulloh. Berlin: de Gruyter, 2006. 279–290.

Hage, Volker. "Hitlers pyromanische Phantasien. W. G. Sebald." *Zeugen der Zerstörung. Die Literaten und der Luftkrieg. Essays und Gespräche*. Ed. Volker Hage. Frankfurt: S. Fischer, 2003. 259–279.

Hall, Katharina. "Jewish Memory in Exile: The Relation of W. G. Sebalds *Die Ausgewanderten* to the Tradition of the Yizkor Books." *Jews in German Literature since 1945: German-Jewish Literature?* Ed. Pól O'Dochartaigh. Amsterdam, Netherlands: Rodopi, 2000. 153–164.

Harris, Stefanie. "The Return of the Dead: Memory and Photography in W. G. Sebald's *Die Ausgewanderten*." *German Quarterly* 74.4 (2001): 379–91.

Heidelberger-Leonard, Irene. "Melancholie als Widerstand." *Akzente* 48.2 (2001): 122–30. [Also in: *Heine Jahrbuch 2001*. Stuttgart; Weimar: Metzler (2001): 181–190.]

Hirsch, Marianne. "The Generation of Postmemory." *Photography in Fiction*. Eds. Silke Horstkotte and Nancy Pedri. Special issue of *Poetics Today* 29.1 (2008): 103–128.

Hoffmann, Torsten. "Das Interview als Kunstwerk. Plädoyer für die Analyse von Schriftstellerinterviews am Beispiel W. G. Sebald." *Weimarer Beiträge* 55.2 (2009): 276–292.

Holdenried, Michaela. "Zeugen – Spuren – Erinnerung. Zum intertextuellen Resonanzraum von Grenzerfahrungen in der Literatur jüdischer Überlebender. Jean Améry und W. G. Sebald." *Autobiographisches Schreiben in der deutschsprachigen Gegenwartsliteratur 2. Grenzen der Fiktionalität und der Erinnerung*. Eds. Christoph Parry and Edgar Platen. Munich: iudicium, 2007. 74–85.

Homberger, Eric. "W. G. Sebald: German Writer Shaped by the Forgetfulness of his Fellow Countrymen after the Second World War." *The Guardian* (December 17, 2001): 20.

Horstkotte, Silke. "Fantastic Gaps: Photography Inserted into Narrative in W. G. Sebald's *Austerlitz*." *Science, Technology and the German Cultural Imagination*. Eds. Christian Emden and David Midgley [*Cultural History and Literary Imagination* 3] Berlin: Lang, 2005. 269–286.

——. "Fotografie, Gedächtnis, Postmemory. Bildzitate in der deutschen Erinnerungsliteratur." *Lesen ist wie Sehen. Intermediale Zitate in Bild und Text*. Eds. Silke Horstkotte and Karin Leonhard. Cologne; Weimar; Vienna: Böhlau, 2006. 177–195.

——. *Nachbilder. Fotografie und Gedächtnis in der deutschen Gegenwartsliteratur*. Cologne; Weimar; Vienna: Böhlau, 2009.

——. "Photo-Text Topographies: Photography and the Representation of Space in W. G. Sebald and Monika Maron." *Photography in Fiction*. Eds. Silke Horstkotte and Nancy Pedri. Special issue of *Poetics Today* 29.1 (2008): 49–78.

——. "Pictorial and Verbal Discourse in W. G. Sebald's *The Emigrants*." *Iowa Journal of Cultural Studies* 2 (2002): 33–50.

——. [Review of Ingo Wintermeyer and Sigurd Martin, eds. *Verschiebebahnhöfe der Erinnerung. Zum Werk W. G. Sebalds*. Würzburg: Königshausen & Neumann, 2007.] *Monatshefte* 100.3 (2008): 451–455, here 454.

Hünsche, Christina. *Textereignisse und Schlachtenbilder. Eine sebaldsche Poetik des Ereignisses*. Bielefeld: Aisthesis Verlag, 2012.

Hui, Barbara. "Mapping Historical Networks in *Die Ringe des Saturn*." *The Undiscover'd Country. W. G. Sebald and the Poetics of Travel*. Ed. Markus Zisselsberger. Rochester, NY: Camden House, 2010. 277–298.

Hulse, Michael with Jill Kitson. "Beyond Translation…" January 22, 2000. http://www.abc.net.au/rn/linguafranca/stories/2000/74464.htm [accessed: June 22, 2013]

Hulse, Michael. "Englishing Max." *Saturn's Moons: A W. G. Sebald Handbook*. Eds. Jo Catling and Richard Hibbitt. Oxford: Legenda, 2011. 192–205.

Hutchinson, Ben. *W. G. Sebald. Die dialektische Imagination*. Berlin: de Gruyter, 2009.

Huyssen, Andreas. "Gray Zones of Remembrance." *A New History of German Literature*. Eds. David Wellbery, Judith Ryan, Hans Ulrich Gumbrecht, Anton Kaes, Joseph Koerner, and Dorothea von Mücke. Cambridge: Harvard University Press, 2004. 970–975.

——. "Rewritings and New Beginnings: W. G. Sebald and the Literature on the Air War." *Present Pasts: Urban Palimpsests and the Politics of Memory*. Stanford, CA: Stanford University Press (2003): 138–157.

Jackman, Graham. "'Gebranntes Kind?' W. G. Sebald's 'Metaphysik der Geschichte.'" *German Life and Letters* 57.4 (2004): 456–471.

——. "Introduction." *German Life and Letters* 57.4 (2004): 343–353.

Jaggi, Maya. "Recovered Memories. The Guardian Profile." *Guardian* 22. September 2001. http://www.guardian.co.uk/education/2001/dec/21/artsandhumanities.highereducation [Last accessed: September 1, 2010.]

Jaray, Tess. "A Mystery and a Confession." *Irish Pages* 1.2 (The Justice Issue) (2002/2003): 137–139.

Jeutter, Ralf. "'Am Rand Der Finsternis:' The Jewish Experience in the Context of W. G. Sebald's Poetics." *Jews in German Literature since 1945: German-Jewish Literature?* Ed. Pól O'Dochartaigh. Amsterdam, Netherlands: Rodopi, 2000. 165–179.

Johannsen, Anja K. "'The Contrarieties that are in our Yearnings': Allegorical, Nostalgic and Transcendent Spaces in the Works of W. G. Sebald." *Journal of European Studies*, Special Issue: W. G. Sebald, ed. Richard Sheppard 41.3–4 (2011): 377–393.

Just, Renate. "Stille Katastrophen." *W. G. Sebald*. Ed. Franz Loquai. Eggingen: Ed. Isele, 1997. 25–30.

Kasper, Judith. "Intertextualitäten als Gedächtniskonstellationen im Zeichen der Vernichtung: Überlegungen zu W. G. Sebalds *Die Ausgewanderten*." *Wende des Erinnerns? Geschichtskonstruktionen in der deutschen Literatur nach 1989*. Eds. Barbara Beßlich, Katharina Grätz, Olaf Hildebrand. [*Philologische Studien und Quellen* 198] Berlin: Schmidt, 2006. 87–98.

Kilbourn, Russell J. A. "Architecture and Cinema: The Representation of Memory in W. G. Sebald's *Austerlitz*." *W. G. Sebald: A Critical Companion*. Eds. J. J. Long and Anne Whitehead. Seattle, WA: University of Washington Press, 2004. 140–154.

——. "'Catastrophe with Spectator:' Subjectivity, Intertextuality and the Representation of History in *Die Ringe des Saturn*." *W. G. Sebald and the Writing of History*. Eds. Anne Fuchs and J. J. Long. Würzburg: Königshausen & Neumann, 2007. 139–162.

——. "Kafka, Nabokov…Sebald: Intertextuality and Narratives of Redemption In *Vertigo* and *The Emigrants*." *W. G. Sebald. History – Memory – Trauma*. Eds. Scott Denham and Mark McCulloh. Berlin: de Gruyter, 2006. 33–63.

Kinross, Robin. "Judging a Book by its Material Embodiment: A German-English Example." *Unjustified Texts*. London: Hyphen Press, 2002. 186–199.

Klebes, Martin. "Infinite Journey: From Kafka to Sebald." *W. G. Sebald: A Critical Companion*. Eds. J. J. Long and Anne Whitehead. Seattle, WA: University of Washington Press, 2004. 123–139.

——. "No Exile: Crossing the Border with Sebald and Améry." *W. G. Sebald: Schreiben ex patria / Expatriate Writing*. Ed. Gerhard Fischer. Amsterdam; New York: Rodopi, 2009. 73–90.

——. "Sebald's Pathographies." *W. G. Sebald. History – Memory – Trauma*. Eds. Scott Denham and Mark McCulloh. Berlin: de Gruyter, 2006. 65–75.

Köhler, Andrea. "Die Durchdringung des Dunkels. W. G. Sebald and Jan Peter Tripp – ein letzter Blickwechsel." *Neue Zürcher Zeitung* 291 (December 14–15, 2002): 49–50. [Reprinted in W. G. Sebald. *Unerzählt*. Munich; Vienna: Hanser, 2003. 72–78.]

Körte, Mona and Toby Axelrod. "Bracelet, Hand Towel, Pocket Watch: Objects of the Last Moment in Memory and Narration." *Shofar: An Interdisciplinary Journal of Jewish Studies* 23.1 (2004): 109–120.

Lambert, David and Robert McGill. "Writing Tips: The Collected 'Maxims' [of W. G. Sebald]." *Five Dials* 5 (2009): 8–9.

Lethen, Helmut. "Sebalds Raster: Überlegungen zur ontologischen Unruhe in Sebalds *Die Ringe des Saturn*." *W. G. Sebald. Politische Archäologie und melancholische Bastelei*. Eds. Michael Niehaus and Claudia Öhlschläger. Berlin: Schmidt, 2006. [*Philologische Studien und Quellen* 196] 13–30.

Lennon, Patrick. "In the Weavers' Web: An Intertextual Approach to W. G. Sebald and Laurence Sterne." *W. G. Sebald. History – Memory – Trauma*. Eds. Scott Denham and Mark McCulloh. Berlin: de Gruyter, 2006. 91–104.

Löffler, Sigrid. "Kopfreisen in die Ferne. Ein Geheimtip: In Norwich, gar nicht hinter dem Mond, lebt und schreibt W. G. Max Sebald." *W. G. Sebald*. Ed. Franz Loquai. Eggingen: Ed. Isele, 1997. 32–36.

——. "'Melancholie ist eine Form des Widerstands:' Über das Saturnische bei W. G. Sebald und seine Aufhebung in der Schrift." *W. G. Sebald. Text + Kritik* (2003): 103–111.

──. "W. G. Sebald, der Ausgewanderte." *Kritiken, Portraits, Glossen.* Vienna, u.a.: Deuticke, 1995. 72–78.

──. "'Wildes Denken.' Gespräch mit W. G. Sebald." *W. G. Sebald.* Ed. Franz Loquai. Eggingen· Ed. Isele, 1997. 135–137.

Long, J. J. "Disziplin und Geständnis. Ansätze zu einer Foucaultschen Sebald-Lektüre." *W. G. Sebald. Politische Archäologie und melancholische Bastelei.* Eds. Michael Niehaus and Claudia Öhlschläger. [*Philologische Studien und Quellen* 196] Berlin: Schmidt, 2006. 219–239.

──. "History, Narrative, and Photography in W. G. Sebald's *Die Ausgewanderten.*" *Modern Language Review* 98.1 (2003): 117–137.

──. "W. G. Sebald: A Bibliographical Essay on Current Research." *W. G. Sebald and the Writing of History.* Eds. Anne Fuchs and J. J. Long. Würzburg: Königshausen & Neumann, 2007. 11–29.

──. *W. G. Sebald: Image, Archive, Modernity.* Edinburgh: Edinburgh University Press, 2007.

──. "W. G. Sebald's Miniature Histories." *W. G. Sebald and the Writing of History.* Eds. Anne Fuchs and J. J. Long. Würzburg: Königshausen & Neumann, 2007. 111–120.

Loquai, Franz. "Erinnerungskünstler im Beinhaus der Geschichte. Gedankenbrosamen zur Poetik W. G. Sebalds." *W. G. Sebald.* Ed. Franz Loquai. Eggingen: Ed. Isele, 1997. 257–267.

──. "Vom Beinhaus der Geschichte ins wiedergefundene Paradies: Zu Werk und Poetik W. G. Sebalds." *Sebald. Lektüren.* Eds. Marcel Atze and Franz Loquai. Eggingen: Ed. Isele, 2005. 244–256.

Louvel, Liliane. "Photography as Critical Idiom and Intermedial Criticism." *Photography in Fiction.* Eds. Silke Horstkotte and Nancy Pedri. Special Issue of *Poetics Today* 29.1 (2008): 31–48.

Lubow, Arthur. "Preoccupied with Death, but Still Funny. W. G. Sebald Combines Memoir, Novel and Essay and Adds Photos." *The New York Times* (December 11, 2001): E1.

Malkmus, Bernhard. "'All of them Signs and Characters from the Type-Case of Forgotten Things:' Intermedia Configurations of History in W. G. Sebald." *Memory Traces: 1989 and the Question of German Cultural Identity; Cultural History and Literary Imagination.* Ed. Silke Arnold-de Simine. Berlin, Germany: Lang, 2005. 211–244.

Masschelein, Anneleen. "Hand in Glove: Negative Indexicality in André Breton's *Nadja* and W. G. Sebald's *Austerlitz.*" *Searching for Sebald. Photography After W. G. Sebald.* Ed. Lise Patt. Los Angeles: Institute for Cultural Inquiry and ICI Press, 2007. 360–387.

McCulloh, Mark R. "Introduction: Two Languages, Two Audiences: The Tandem Literary Œuvres of W. G. Sebald." *W. G. Sebald. History – Memory – Trauma.* Eds. Scott Denham and Mark McCulloh. Berlin: de Gruyter, 2006. 7–20.

──. *Understanding W. G. Sebald.* Columbia, SC: University of South Carolina Press, 2003.

McKinney, Ronald H. "W. G. Sebald and 'the Questionable Business' of Post-Holocaust Writing." *Philosophy Today* 49.2 (2005): 115–126.

Medin, Daniel L. *Three Sons: Franz Kafka and the Fiction of J.M. Coetzee, Philip Roth and W. G. Sebald.* Evanston, IL: Northwestern University Press, 2010.

Menke, Timm. "W. G. Sebalds *Luftkrieg und Literatur* und die Folgen: Eine kritische Bestandaufnahme." *Bombs Away! Representing the Air War over Europe and Japan.* Eds. Wilfried Wilms and William Rasch. Amsterdam: Rodopi, 2006. 149–163.

Mémoire. Transferts. Images. / Erinnerung. Übertragungen. Bilder. Ed. Ruth Vogel-Klein. *Recherches germaniques* Hors série (2005).

Meyer, Sven. "Im Medium der Prosa. Essay und Erzählung bei W. G. Sebald." *Mémoire. Transferts. Images. / Erinnerung. Übertragungen. Bilder.* Ed. Ruth Vogel-Klein. *Recherches germaniques* Hors Série 2 (2005): 173–185.

Morris, Leslie. "How Jewish is it? W. G. Sebald and the Question of 'Jewish' Writing in Germany Today." *The New German Jewry and the European Context: The Return of the European Jewish Diaspora*. Ed. Y. Michal Bodemann. Houndmills [U.K.]; New York: Palgrave Macmillan, 2008. 111–128.

Mosbach, Bettina. *Figurationen der Katastrophe. Ästhetische Verfahren in W. G. Sebalds Die Ringe des Saturn und Austerlitz*. Bielefeld: Aisthesis Verlag, 2008.

——. "Superimposition as a Narrative Strategy in *Austerlitz*." *Searching for Sebald. Photography After W. G. Sebald*. Ed. Lise Patt. Los Angeles: Institute for Cultural Inquiry and ICI Press, 2007. 390–411.

—— and Nicolas Pethes. "Zugzwänge des Erzählens: Zur Relation von Oral History und Literatur am Beispiel W. G. Sebalds Roman *Austerlitz*." *Bios: Zeitschrift für Biographieforschung und Oral History* 21.1 (2008): 49–69.

Mühling, Jens. "The Permanent Exile of W. G. Sebald," *Pretext* 7 (2003): 15–26.

Niehaus, Michael. "W. G. Sebalds sentimentalische Dichtung," *W. G. Sebald. Politische Archäologie und melancholische Bastelei*. Eds. Michael Niehaus and Claudia Öhlschläger. [*Philologische Studien und Quellen* 196] Berlin: Schmidt, 2006. 173–187.

Öhlschläger, Claudia. *Beschädigtes Leben. Erzählte Risse: W. G. Sebalds Poetische Ordnung des Unglücks*. Freiburg i.Br.; Berlin; Vienna: Rombach, 2006.

——. "'Die Bahn des korsischen Kometen:' Zur Dimension 'Napoleon' in W. G. Sebalds literarischem Netzwerk." *Topographien der Literatur. Deutsche Literatur im transnationalen Kontext*. DFG-Symposium 2004. Eds. Hartmut Böhme, Inka Mülder-Bach, Bernhard Siegert, and Horst Wenzel. Stuttgart: Metzler, 2005. 536–558.

——. "Der Saturnring oder Etwas vom Eisenbau: W. G. Sebalds poetische Zivilisationskritik." *W. G. Sebald. Politische Archäologie und melancholische Bastelei*. Eds. Michael Niehaus and Claudia Öhlschläger. [*Philologische Studien und Quellen* 196] Berlin: Schmidt, 2006. 189–204.

——. "Unschärfe: Schwindel. Gefühle.: W. G. Sebalds intermediale und intertextuelle Gedächtniskunst." *Mémoire. Transferts. Images. / Erinnerung. Übertragungen. Bilder*. Ed. Ruth Vogel-Klein. *Recherches germaniques* Hors Série 2 (2005): 11–23.

Osborne, Dora. *Traces of Trauma in W. G. Sebald and Christoph Ransmayr*. Oxford: Legenda, 2013.

Pane, Samuel. "Trauma Obscura: Photographic Media in W. G. Sebald's *Austerlitz*." *Mosaic: A Journal for the Interdisciplinary Study of Literature* 38.1 (2005): 37–54.

Parry, Ann. "Idioms for the Unrepresentable: Postwar Fiction and the Shoah." *The Holocaust and the Text: Speaking the Unspeakable*. Eds. Andrew Leak and George Paizis. Basingstoke, England; New York, NY: Macmillan, 2000. 109–124.

Pearson, Ann. "'Remembrance … Is Nothing Other Than a Quotation:' The Intertextual Fictions of W. G. Sebald." *Comparative Literature* 60.3 (2008): 261–278.

Pic, Muriel. *W. G. Sebald – L'image papillon – suivi de W. G. Sebald: L'art de voler*. Paris: Les Presses du Réel, 2009.

Poljudow, Valerij. "Eins mit seinen Gegnern? Sebalds Sternheim-Polemik (1970)." *Sebald. Lektüren*. Eds. Marcel Atze and Franz Loquai. Eggingen: Ed. Isele, 2005. 56–58. [*Die Zeit* (August 14, 1970): 15]

Pralle, Uwe. "W. G. Sebald: Mit einem kleinen Sandspaten Abschied von Deutschland nehmen." *Süddeutsche Zeitung* Nr. 295 (December 22/23, 2001): 16.

Presner, Todd Samuel. "'What a Synoptic and Artificial View Reveals': Extreme History and the Modernism of W. G. Sebald's Realism." *Criticism* 46.3 (2004): 341–360.

Radvan, Florian. "W. G. Sebald – Schriftsteller und Scholar. Erinnerungen an einen Grenzgänger zwischen Literatur und Wissenschaft." *Kritische Ausgabe* Nr. 18 "Familie" (2010): 56–59. http://www.kritische-ausgabe.de/index.php/archiv/2661/ [Last accessed: March 16, 2010]

Remmler, Karen. "'On the Natural History of Destruction' and Cultural Memory: W. G. Sebald." *German Politics and Society* 23.3 (2005): 42–64.

Ribó, Ignasi. "The One-Winged Angel. History and Memory in the Literary Discourse of W. G. Sebald." *Orbis Litterarum* 64.3 (2009): 222–262.

Römhild, Juliane. "'Back in Sebaldland:' Zur Rezeption von W. G. Sebald in der britischen Tagespresse." *Zeitschrift für Germanistik* 15.2 (2005): 393–399.

Rosenfeld, Natania. "Enthrallments." *Hotel Amerika* 3.1 (2004): 19–23.

Santner, Eric L. *On Creaturely Life. Rilke, Benjamin, Sebald*. Chicago and London: The University of Chicago Press, 2006.

Sareika, Rüdiger, ed. *"Im Krebsgang": Strategien des Erinnerns in den Werken von Günter Grass und W. G. Sebald*. Iserlohn: Institut für Kirche und Gesellschaft, 2006.

Saturn's Moons: A W. G. Sebald Handbook. Eds. Jo Catling and Richard Hibbitt. Oxford: Legenda, 2011.

Schedel, Susanne. *'Wer weiss, wie es vor Zeiten wirklich gewesen ist?' Textbeziehungen als Mittel der Geschichtsdarstellung bei W. G. Sebald*. Würzburg: Königshausen & Neumann, 2004.

Schlant, Ernestine. "Post-Unification: Bernhard Schlink, Peter Schneider, W. G. Sebald." *The Language of Silence*. New York; London: Routledge, 1999. 209–234.

Schley, Fridolin *Kataloge der Wahrheit. Zur Inszenierung von Autorschaft bei W. G. Sebald*. Göttingen: Wallstein, 2012.

Schmidt-Hannisa, Hans-Walter. "Abberation of a Species: On the Relationship between Man and Beast in W. G. Sebald's Work." *W. G. Sebald and the Writing of History*, eds. Anne Fuchs and J. J. Long. Würzburg: Königshausen & Neumann, 2007. 31–44.

Schmitz, Helmut. "'...only signs everywhere of the annihilation.' W. G. Sebald's *Austerlitz*." *On Their Own Terms. The Legacy of National Socialism in Post-1990 German Fiction*. Birmingham, U. K.: University of Birmingham, University Press, 2004. 291–321.

——., ed. *A Nation of Victims? Representations of German Wartime Suffering from 1945 to the Present*. Ed. Helmut Schmitz. Amsterdam: Rodopi, 2007. 1–30.

Schmucker, Peter. *Grenzübertretungen: Intertextualität im Werk von W. G. Sebald*. Berlin [u.a.]: de Gruyter, 2012. (Spectrum Literaturwissenschaft 28)

Schönthaler, Philipp. *Negative Poetik. Die Figur des Erzählers bei Thomas Bernhard, W. G. Sebald und Imre Kertész*. Berlin: transcript, 2011.

Scholz, Christian. "'Aber das Geschriebene ist ja kein wahres Dokument.'" *Neue Zürcher Zeitung* 48 (2000): 51–52.

Schütte, Uwe. "Against *Germanistik*: W. G. Sebald's Critical Essays." *Saturn's Moons: A W. G. Sebald Handbook*. Eds. Jo Catling and Richard Hibbitt. Oxford: Legenda, 2011. 161–194.

——. *W. G. Sebald. Einführung in Leben und Werk*. Göttingen: Vandenhoeck & Ruprecht, 2011.

Searching for Sebald. Photography After W. G. Sebald. Ed. Lise Patt. Los Angeles: Institute for Cultural Inquiry and ICI Press, 2007.

Sebald. Lektüren. Eds. Marcel Atze and Franz Loquai. Eggingen: Ed. Isele, 2005.

Sebald, W. G. and Gordon Turner (Interviewer: Michaël Zeeman). "Introduction and Transcript of an Interview Given by Max Sebald." *W. G. Sebald. History – Memory – Trauma*. Eds. Scott Denham and Mark McCulloh. Berlin: de Gruyter, 2006. 21–29.

Seidel-Arpaci, Annette. "Lost in Translations? The Discourse of 'German Suffering' and W. G. Sebald's *Luftkrieg und Literatur*." *A Nation of Victims? Representations of German Wartime Suffering from 1945 to the Present*. Ed. Helmut Schmitz. Amsterdam: Rodopi, 2007. 161–179.

Seitz, Stephan. *Geschichte als bricolage. W. G. Sebald und die Poetik des Bastelns*. Göttingen: V & R Unipress, 2011.

Shaffer, Elinor. "W. G. Sebald's Photographic Narrative." *The Anatomist of Melancholy. Essays in Memory of W. G. Sebald*. Ed. Rüdiger Görner. Munich: iudicium, 2003. 51–62.

Sheppard, Richard. "Dexter – sinister: Some observations on decrypting the Mors code in the work of W. G. Sebald." *Journal of European Studies* 35 (2005): 419–463.

——. "The Sternheim Years: W. G. Sebald's *Lehrjahre* and *Theatralische Sendung* 1963–75." *Saturn's Moons: A W. G. Sebald Handbook*. Eds. Jo Catling and Richard Hibbitt. Oxford: Legenda, 2011. 42–107.

——. "'Woods, trees, and the spaces in between.' A report on work published on W. G. Sebald 2005–2008." *Journal of European Studies* 39.1 (2009): 79–128.

Shields, Andrew Jonathan. "Neun Sätze aus *Austerlitz*." *Akzente* 50.1 (2003): 63–72.

Sill, Oliver. "'Aus dem Jäger ist ein Schmetterling geworden.' Textbeziehungen zwischen Werken von W. G. Sebald und Vladimir Nabokov." *Poetica* 29 (1997): 596–623.

Silverblatt, Michael. "A Poem of an Invisible Subject." *The Emergence of Memory: Conversations with W. G. Sebald*. Ed. Lynne Sharon Schwartz. New York; London; Melbourne; Toronto: Seven Stories Press, 2007. 77–86.

Simic, Charles. "Conspiracy of Silence." *New York Review of Books*. 50.3 (February 27, 2003): 86–96.

Simon, Ulrich. "Der Provokateur als Literaturhistoriker. Anmerkungen zu Literaturbegriff und Argumentationsverfahren in W. G. Sebalds essayistischen Schriften." *Sebald. Lektüren*. Eds. Marcel Atze and Franz Loquai. Eggingen: Ed. Isele, 2005. 78–104.

Sontag, Susan. "A Mind in Mourning." *Times Literary Supplement* (February 25, 2000): 3–4.

Stahl, K. H. "W. G. Sebald: 'Carl Sternheim.'" *Wissenschaftler Literaturanzeiger* Heft 2 (1970): 41.

Steinaecker, Thomas von. *Literarische Foto-Texte. Zur Funktion der Fotografien in den Texten Rolf Dieter Brinkmanns, Alexander Kluges und W. G. Sebalds*. Bielefeld: transcript, 2007.

Streim, Gregor. "Der Bombenkrieg als Sensation und als Dokumentation. Gert Ledigs Roman *Vergeltung* und die Debatte um W. G. Sebalds *Luftkrieg und Literatur*." *Amsterdamer Beiträge zur neueren Germanistik* 57.1 (2005): 293–312.

Summers-Bremner, Eluned. "Reading, Walking, Mourning: W. G. Sebald's Peripatetic Fictions." *JNT: Journal of Narrative Theory* 34.3 (2004): 304–334.

Swales, Martin. "Intertextuality, Authenticity, Metonomy? On Reading W. G. Sebald." *The Anatomist of Melancholy. Essays in Memory of W. G. Sebald*. Ed. Rüdiger Görner. Munich: iudicium, 2003. 81–87.

——. Review of *W. G. Sebald. History – Memory – Trauma*, eds. Scott Denham and Mark McCulloh (Berlin: de Gruyter, 2006) in *Arbitrium* 26.1 (2008): 128–130.

Szentivanyi, Christina M. E. "W. G. Sebald and Structures of Testimony and Trauma: There are Spots of Mist that No Eye can Dispel." *W. G. Sebald. History – Memory – Trauma*. Eds. Scott Denham and Mark McCulloh. Berlin: de Gruyter, 2006. 351–363.

Tabbert, Reinbert. "Max in Manchester: Außen- und Innenansicht eines jungen Autors." *Akzente* 50.1 (2003): 21–30.

——. "Tanti saluti cordiali. Max: W. G. Sebald ... drei bislang unveröffentlichte Briefe an einen Studienfreund." *Literaturen* 5 (2004): 46–49.

Taberner, Stuart. "German Nostalgia? Remembering German-Jewish Life in W. G. Sebald's *Die Ausgewanderten* and *Austerlitz*." *Germanic Review* 79.3 (2004): 181–202.

Tennstedt, Antje. *Annäherungen an die Vergangenheit bei Claude Simon und W. G. Sebald* (Am Beispiel von *Le Jardin des plantes, Die Ausgewanderten* und *Austerlitz*). Freiburg im Breisgau: Rombach, 2007.

Tischel, Alexandra. "Aus der Dunkelkammer der Geschichte. Zum Zusammenhang von Photographie und Erinnerung in W. G. Sebalds *Austerlitz*." *W. G. Sebald. Politische Archäologie und melancholische Bastelei*. Eds. Michael Niehaus and Claudia Öhlschläger. [*Philologische Studien und Quellen* 196] Berlin: Schmidt, 2006. 31–45.

The Undiscover'd Country. W. G. Sebald and the Poetics of Travel. Ed. Markus Zisselsberger, Rochester, NY: Camden House, 2010.

Vees-Gulani, Susanne. "The Experience of Destruction: W. G. Sebald, the Airwar, and Literature." *W. G. Sebald. History – Memory – Trauma*. Eds. Scott Denham and Mark McCulloh. Berlin: de Gruyter, 2006. 335–349.

——. *Trauma and Guilt: Literature of Wartime Bombing in Germany*. Berlin and New York: de Gruyter, 2003.

Verschiebebahnhöfe der Erinnerung: Zum Werk W. G. Sebalds. Eds. Sigurd Martin and Ingo Wintermeyer. Würzburg: Königshausen & Neumann, 2007.

Vogel-Klein, Ruth. "Détours de la mémoire: La représentation de la Shoah dans la nouvelle 'Max Aurach' de W. G. Sebald." *L'indicible dans l'espace franco-germanique au XXe siècle*. Ed. Françoise Rétif. Paris: Harmattan, 2004. 153–173.

——. "Französische Intertexte in W. G. Sebalds *Austerlitz*." *W. G. Sebald. Intertextualität und Topographie*. Eds. Irene Heidelberger-Leonard and Mireille Tabah. Berlin: LIT Verlag, 2008. 73–92.

——. "Rückkehr und Gegen-Zeitigkeit. Totengedenken bei W. G. Sebald." *Mémoire. Transferts. Images. / Erinnerung. Übertragungen. Bilder*. Ed. Ruth Vogel-Klein. *Recherches germaniques* Hors Série 2 (2005): 99–115.

W. G. Sebald. Ed. Franz Loquai. Eggingen: Ed. Isele, 1997.

W. G. Sebald. Ed. Heinz Ludwig Arnold. *Text + Kritik* 158 (2003).

W. G. Sebald. Eds. Paul Michael Lützeler and Stephan K. Schindler. *Gegenwartsliteratur* 6 (2007).

W. G. Sebald. A Critical Companion. Eds. J.J. Long and Anne Whitehead. Seattle, WA: University of Washington Press, 2004.

W. G. Sebald. History – Memory – Trauma. Eds. Scott Denham and Mark McCulloh. Berlin: de Gruyter, 2006.

W. G. Sebald. Intertextualität und Topographie. Eds. Irene Heidelberger-Leonard and Mireille Tabah. Berlin: LIT Verlag, 2008.

W. G. Sebald. Politische Archäologie und melancholische Bastelei. Eds. Michael Niehaus and Claudia Öhlschläger. [*Philologische Studien und Quellen* 196] Berlin: Schmidt, 2006.

W. G. Sebald and the Writing of History. Eds. Anne Fuchs and J.J. Long. Würzburg: Königshausen & Neumann, 2007.

W. G. Sebald. Zerstreute Reminiszenzen. Gedanken zur Eröffnung eines Stuttgarter Hauses. Ed. Florian Höllerer. Warmbronn: Verlag Ulrich Keicher, 2008.

Wachtel, Eleanor. "Ghost Hunter." *The Emergence of Memory. Conversations with W. G. Sebald*. Ed. Lynne Sharon Schwartz. New York: Seven Stories Press, 2007.

Walkowitz, Rebecca. "Sebald's Vertigo." *Cosmopolitan Style. Modernism Beyond the Nation*. New York: Columbia University Press, 2006. 153–170.

Wandernde Schatten. W. G. Sebalds Unterwelt. Eds. Ulrich von Bülow, Heike Gfrereis, and Ellen Strittmatter. Marbach am Neckar: Deutsche Schillergesellschaft, 2008.

Ward, Simon. "Responsible Ruins? W. G. Sebald and the Responsibility of the German Writer." *Forum for Modern Language Studies* 42.2 (2006): 183–199.

Weber, Markus R. "Bilder erzählen den Erzähler: Zur Bedeutung der Abbildungen für die Herausbildung von Erzählerrollen in den Werken W. G. Sebalds." *Mémoire. Transferts. Images.* / *Erinnerung. Übertragungen. Bilder.* Ed. Ruth Vogel-Klein. *Recherches germaniques* Hors Série 2 (2005): 25–45.

——. "Die fantastische befragt die pedantische Genauigkeit: Zu den Abbildungen in W. G. Sebalds Werken." *W. G. Sebald. Text + Kritik* (2003): 63–74.

Weihe, Richard. "Wittgensteins Augen: W. G. Sebalds Film-Szenario *Leben Ws.*" *fair. Zeitung für Kunst und Ästhetik* 7.4 (2009): 11–12.

Williams, Arthur. "'Das Korsakowsche Syndrom:' Remembrance and Responsibility in W. G. Sebald." *German Culture and the Uncomfortable Past: Representations of National Socialism in Contemporary Germanic Literature. Warwick Studies in the Humanities.* Ed. Helmut Schmitz. Aldershot, [U.K.]: Ashgate, 2001. 65–86.

——. "W. G. Sebald: A Holistic Approach to Borders, Texts and Perspectives." *German-Language Literature Today: International and Popular?* Eds. Arthur Williams, Stuart Parkes, and Julian Preece. Oxford; New York: Lang, 2000. 99–118.

Wilms, Wilfried. "Speak no Evil, Write no Evil: In Search of a Usable Language of Destruction." *W. G. Sebald. History – Memory – Trauma.* Eds. Scott Denham and Mark McCulloh. Berlin: de Gruyter, 2006. 183–204.

——. "Taboo and Repression in W. G. Sebald's *On the Natural History of Destruction.*" *W. G. Sebald: A Critical Companion.* Eds. J. J. Long and Anne Whitehead. Seattle, WA: University of Washington Press, 2004. 175–189.

Wohlfarth, Irving. "Anachronie. Interferenzen zwischen Walter Benjamin und W. G. Sebald." *IASL. Internationales Archiv für Sozialgeschichte der Deutschen Literatur* 33.2 (2008): 184–242.

Wolff, Lynn L. "'Das metaphysische Unterfutter der Realität:' Recent Publications and Trends in W. G. Sebald Research." *Monatshefte* 99.1 (2007): 78–101.

——. "H. G. Adler and W. G. Sebald: From History and Literature to Literary Historiography." Special Issue: H. G. Adler. Eds. Rüdiger Görner and Klaus L. Berghahn. *Monatshefte* 103.2 (2011) 257–275.

——. "Literary Historiography: W. G. Sebald's Fiction." *W. G. Sebald: Schreiben ex patria* / *Expatriate Writing.* Ed. Gerhard Fischer. Amsterdam; New York: Rodopi, 2009. 317–332.

——. "'The Solitary Mallard': W. G. Sebald and Translation." *Journal of European Studies,* Special Issue: W. G. Sebald, ed. Richard Sheppard 41.3–4 (2011): 323–340.

——. "W. G. Sebald: A 'Grenzgänger' of the 20th/21st Century." *Eurostudia – Revue Transatlantique de Recherche sur l'Europe,* Special Issue 7.1–2 (2011): 191–198.

——., Jo Catling, and Richard Hibbitt. "W. G. Sebald: Secondary Bibliography." *Saturn's Moons: A W. G. Sebald Handbook.* Eds. Jo Catling and Richard Hibbitt. Oxford: Legenda, 2011. 495–543.

Zeugen der Zerstörung. Die Literaten und der Luftkrieg. Essays und Gespräche. Ed. Volker Hage. Frankfurt: S. Fischer, 2003.

Zilcosky, John. "Sebald's Uncanny Travels: The Impossibility of Getting Lost." *W. G. Sebald: A Critical Companion.* Eds. J. J. Long and Anne Whitehead. Seattle, WA: University of Washington Press, 2004. 102–120.

Zimmermann, Ben. *Narrative Rhythmen der Erzählstimme. Poetologische Modulierungen bei W. G. Sebald.* Würzburg: Königshausen & Neumann, 2012.

Zisselsberger, Markus. "A Persistent Fascination: Recent Publications on the Work of W. G. Sebald." *Monatshefte* 101.1 (2009): 88–105.
Zucchi, Matthias. "Zur Kunstsprache W. G. Sebalds." *Verschiebebahnhöfe der Erinnerung: Zum Werk W. G. Sebalds*. Eds. Sigurd Martin and Ingo Wintermeyer. Würzburg: Königshausen & Neumann, 2007. 163–181.

IV. W. G. Sebald-Related/-Inspired Films and Websites

Anon. "Stalking Sebald." http://stalkingsebald.blogspot.com/
"Chevalier, Sébastien." "Norwich. Du temps et des lieux, chez W. G. Sebald et quelques autres" http://norwitch.wordpress.com/
Gee, Grant. *Patience (After Sebald)*. 2011.
Honickel, Thomas. *W. G. Sebald. Der Ausgewanderte*. Munich: Bayerischer Rundfunk, 2007.
——. *Sebald: Orte*. 2007.
Hui, Barbara. http://barbarahui.net/litmap/#
Hui, Barbara and Jonathan Jones. "Mediated and Remediated Memories of Catastrophe: A Hypermedia Site Devoted to W. G. Sebald" http://dev.cdh.ucla.edu/~newmedia/barbara/ UCLA Project, May 2006.
Oberschelp, Peter. "Selysses. Kleine Sebaldstücke." http://peteroberschelp.blogspot.com/
Pitts, Terry. "Vertigo: Collecting & Reading W. G. Sebald. On Literature and Book Collecting, With an Emphasis on W. G. Sebald and the Novels with Embedded Photographs." http://sebald. wordpress.com/
Wirth, Christian. "W. G. Sebald. Ein Forum für den ausgewanderten Schriftsteller, Wanderer, Germanisten, Autor des Elementargedichts 'Nach der Natur' und weitere Werke." http:// www.wgsebald.de/

V. Related Primary and Secondary Literature

Addison, Joseph. *Spectator* No. 420 (Wednesday, July 2, 1712). *The Papers of Joseph Addison, Esq. in the Tatler, Spectator, Guardian, and Freeholder*. Together with his *Treatise on the Christian Religion*. To which are prefixed *Tickell's Life of the Author*, and extracts from *Dr. Johnson's Remarks on his Prose Writings*. With original notes never before published. Vol. III of IV. Edinburgh: William Creech, 1790.
Adler, Hans. "Günter Grass, *Novemberland*." *Günter Grass: Ästhetik des Engagements*. Eds. Hans Adler and Jost Hermand. New York: Lang, 1996. 93–109.
——. "Herder's Concept of *Humanität*." *A Companion to the Works of Johann Gottfried Herder*. Eds. Hans Adler and Wulf Koepke. Rochester, NY: Camden House, 2009. 93–116.
Adler, H. G. *Eine Reise*. Vienna: Zsolnay, 1999.
——. *Theresienstadt 1941–1945. Das Antlitz einer Zwangsgemeinschaft. Geschichte, Soziologie, Psychologie*. Tübingen: Mohr, 1955.

Adorno, Theodor W. "Jene zwanziger Jahre." *Kulturkritik und Gesellschaft II. Gesammelte Schriften*, vol. 10.2. Ed. Rolf Tiedemann. Frankfurt am Main: Suhrkamp, 1977. 503–506.

Albrecht, Andrea. "Thick descriptions. Zur literarischen Reflexion historiographischen Erinnerns 'am Beispiel Uwe Timms.'" *Erinnern, Vergessen, Erzählen. Beiträge zum Werk Uwe Timms*. Ed. Friedhelm Marx unter Mitarbeit von Stephanie Catani und Julia Schöll. Göttingen: Wallstein Verlag, 2007. 69–89.

Amann, Jürg. *Robert Walser. Eine literarische Biographie in Texten und Bildern*. Zurich; Hamburg: Arche, 1995.

Ankersmit, Frank R. *Historical Representation*. Stanford: Stanford University Press, 2001.

——. "Truth in History and Literature." *Narrative* 18.1 (2010): 29–50.

Aristotle. *Poetics. Aristotle's Theory of Poetry and Fine Art*. Ed. S. H. Butcher. New York: Dover Publications Inc., 1951.

——. *Poetik*. Übersetzt und erläutert von Arbogast Schmitt (Aristoteles, *Werke*, in deutscher Übersetzung. Band 5) Berlin: Akademie Verlag, 2008.

——. *Poetik*. Griechisch/Deutsch, Übersetzt und herausgegeben von Manfred Fuhrmann. Stuttgart: Reclam, 1994.

——. *Poetik*. Übersetzung, Einleitung und Anmerkungen von Olof Gigon. Stuttgart: Reclam, 1967.

Assmann, Aleida. *Der lange Schatten der Vergangenheit. Erinnerungskultur und Geschichtspolitik*. Munich: C. H. Beck, 2006.

——. "Speichern oder Erinnern? Das kulturelle Gedächtnis zwischen Archiv und Kanon." *Kakanien Revisted* (January 31, 2006): 1–8. http://www.kakanien.ac.at/beitr/theorie/AAssmann1.pdf [accessed: June 22, 2013]

Auerbach, Erich. "Philologie der Weltliteratur." *Philologie der Weltliteratur. Sechs Versuche über Stil und Wirklichkeitswahrnehmung*. Frankfurt am Main: Fischer Taschenbuch Verlag, 1992. 83–96.

——. "Philology and *Weltliteratur*." Trans. Maire and Edward Said. *The Centennial Review* 13.1 (1969): 1–17.

Baechtold, Jakob. *Gottfried Kellers Leben. Seine Briefe und Tagebücher*. Berlin: W. Hertz, 1894–1897.

Bal, Mieke. *Quoting Caravaggio. Contemporary Art, Preposterous History*. Chicago; London: University of Chicago Press, 1999.

Baqué, Dominique. *La photographie plasticienne. Un art paradoxal*. Paris: Éditions du Regard, 1998.

Barbetta, Maria Cecilia. *Änderungsschneiderei Los Milagros*. Frankfurt am Main: Fischer, 2008.

Barnstone, Willis. *The Poetics of Translation. History, Theory, Practice*. New Haven and London: Yale University Press, 1993.

Barthes, Roland. *Camera lucida. Reflections on Photography*. Trans. Richard Howard. New York: Hill and Wang, 1981.

——. "L'effet de réel." *Communications* 11 (1968): 84–89.

——. "Introduction to the Structural Analysis of Narratives." *Image, Music, Text*. Ed. and trans. Stephen Heath. New York: Hill & Wang, 1977. ["Introduction à l'analyse structural des récits." *Communications* 8 (1966): 1–27.]

Baudelaire, Charles. "The Salon of 1859." *The Mirror of Art. Critical Studies by Charles Baudelaire*. London: Phaidon Press, 1965. 144–216.

Benjamin, Walter. "Kleine Geschichte der Photographie." *Walter Benjamin. Gesammelte Schriften* 2.1. Eds. Rolf Tiedemann and Hermann Schweppenhäuser. Frankfurt: Suhrkamp, 1977 [1931]. 368–385.

——. "Das Kunstwerk im Zeitalter seiner technischen Reproduzierbarkeit." *Walter Benjamin. Gesammelte Schriften* 1.2. Eds. Rolf Tiedemann and Hermann Schweppenhäuser. Frankfurt: Suhrkamp, 1974 [1936] 431–469 [Erste Fassung]; 471–508 [Dritte Fassung].

——. "Lehre vom Ähnlichen." *Walter Benjamin. Gesammelte Schriften* 2.1. Eds. Rolf Tiedemann and Hermann Schweppenhäuser. Frankfurt: Suhrkamp, 1977 [1933]. 204–210.

——., trans. Phil Patton. "A Short History of Photography." *Artforum* 15.6 (1977): 46–61.

——. "Über das mimetische Vermögen." *Walter Benjamin. Gesammelte Schriften* 2.1. Eds. Rolf Tiedemann and Hermann Schweppenhäuser. Frankfurt: Suhrkamp, 1977 [1933]. 210–213.

Bergen, Ordnen, Restaurieren. Der Wiederaufbau des Historischen Archivs der Stadt Köln. Publication of the Historisches Archiv Amt für Presse- und Öffentlichkeitsarbeit. Cologne: Barz & Beienburg, 2012.

Berger, John. *Another Way of Telling.* New York: Vintage, 1995.

Berghahn, Klaus. "Ringelblums Milchkanne. Über Möglichkeiten und Grenzen der dokumentarischen Repräsentation des Holocaust." *Kulturelle Repräsentationen des Holocaust in Deutschland und den Vereinigten Staaten.* Eds. Klaus L. Berghahn, Jürgen Fohrmann, and Helmut J. Schneider. New York: Lang, 2002. 147–166.

Berman, Carolyn Vellenga. "The Known World in World Literature: Bakhtin, Glissant, and Edward P. Jones." *Novel* 42.2 (2009): 231–238.

Bernard-Donals, Michael F. and Richard Glejzer. *Between Witness and Testimony: The Holocaust and the Limits of Representation.* Albany: State University of New York Press, 2001.

Bertens, Hans. *The Idea of the Postmodern. A History.* London & New York: Routledge, 1995.

Beyer, Marcel. *Flughunde.* Frankfurt am Main: Suhrkamp, 1995.

——. *Spione.* Cologne: DuMont, 2000.

Blumenberg, Hans. "'Nachahmung der Natur.' Zur Vorgeschichte der Idee des schöpferischen Menschen." *Wirklichkeiten in denen wir leben. Aufsätze und eine Rede.* Stuttgart: Reclam, 1993. 55–103.

Böll, Heinrich. *Frankfurter Vorlesungen.* Cologne: Kiepenheuer & Witsch, 1966.

Brecht, Bertolt. "Die Dreigroschenprozeß. Ein soziologisches Experiment." *Werke, Große kommentierte Berliner und Frankfurter Ausgabe.* Vol. 21, *Schriften 1.* Eds. Werner Hecht, Jan Knopf, Werner Mittenzwei, and Klaus-Detlef Müller. Berlin; Weimar; Frankfurt am Main: Suhrkamp, 1992. 448–514.

——. "The Three Penny Trial: A Sociological Experiment." Trans. Lance W. Garmer. *German Essays on Film.* Eds. Richard McCormick and Alison Guenther-Pal. New York: Continuum, 2004. 111–132.

Bredow, Rafaela von. "Bilder machen Geschichte." *Der Spiegel* Heft 38 (September 18, 2006): 164.

Breisach, Ernst. *Historiography. Ancient, Medieval, & Modern.* Chicago and London: The University of Chicago Press, 1994[2].

Browning, Christopher R. *Ordinary Men. Reserve Police Battalion 101 and the Final Solution in Poland.* New York: Harper Collins, 1992.

Bürger, Peter. "Die Echtheit der alten Steine. Deutschland streitet über den Wiederaufbau historischer Gebäude." *Neue Zürcher Zeitung* (January 7, 2009): 25.

Burke, Peter, ed. *New Perspectives on Historical Writing.* University Park, PA: Pennsylvania State University Press, 2001[2].

Canetti, Elias. *Alle vergeudete Verehrung. Aufzeichnungen 1949–1960.* Reihe Hanser 50. Munich: Hanser, 1970.

——. *Die Stimmen von Marrakesch. Aufzeichnungen nach einer Reise.* Munich: Hanser, 1967.

——. *The Voices of Marrakesch. A Record of a Visit*. Trans. J.A. Underwood. New York: Seabury Press, 1978.

Cassin, Barbara, general ed. *Vocabulaire européen des philosophies: Dictionnaire des Intraduisibles*. Paris: Éditions du Seuil/ Le Robert, 2004.

Coetzee, J.M. "The Genius of Robert Walser." *The New York Review of Books* 47.1 (November 2, 2000).

Cunningham, Michael. "Found in Translation." *The New York Times* (October 3, 2010): WK10.

Damrosch, David. "Introduction. Goethe Coins a Phrase." *What is World Literature?* Princeton: Princeton University Press, 2003.

Dant, Tim and Graeme Gilloch. "Pictures of the Past. Benjamin and Barthes on Photography and History." *European Journal of Cultural Studies* 5.1 (2002): 5–23.

Didi-Huberman, Georges. *Images in Spite of All. Four Photographs from Auschwitz*. Trans. Shane B. Lillis. Chicago & London: University of Chicago Press, 2008.

Durrell, Martin. "Idris Parry: Scholar of German Literature." *The Independent (Obituaries)* (Wednesday, March 26, 2008).

Eigler, Friederike. *Gedächtnis und Geschichte in Generationenromanen seit der Wende*. Berlin: Schmidt, 2005.

Eliot, T.S. "Tradition and the Individual Talent." *The Sacred Wood. Essays on Poetry and Criticism*. New York: Barnes & Noble, 1960. 47–59.

Enzensberger, Hans Magnus, Jan Peter Tripp, and Justine Landat. *Blauwärts. Ein Ausflug zu dritt*. Frankfurt am Main: Suhrkamp, 2013.

Ermarth, Elizabeth Deeds. "The Trouble with History." *Historisierte Subjekte – Subjektivierte Historie. Zur Verfügbarkeit und Unverfügbarkeit von Geschichte*, eds. Stefan Deines, Stephan Jaeger, Ansgar Nünning. Berlin; New York: de Gruyter, 2003. 105–120.

Felman, Shoshana and Dori Laub. *Testimony. Crises of Witnessing in Literature, Psychoanalysis, and History*. New York and London: Routledge, 1992.

Foucault, Michel. "Of Other Spaces." Trans. Jay Miskowiec. *Diacritics* 16.1 (1986): 22–27.

Franke, Dörte, director. "Stolperstein." Germany, 2008, 76 minutes.

Franklin, Ruth. *A Thousand Darknesses. Lies and Truth in Holocaust Fiction*. Oxford: Oxford University Press, 2010.

——. "Identity Theft: True Memory, False Memory, and the Holocaust." *The New Republic* (May 31, 2004): 31–37.

Friedländer, Saul. *Wenn die Erinnerung kommt*. Munich: C.H. Beck'sche Verlagsbuchhandlung, 1998.

——. *When Memory Comes*. Trans. Helen R. Lane. New York: Farrar, Straus, and Giroux, 1979.

Genette, Gérard. *Figures III*. Paris: Éditions du Seuil, 1972.

Gerstner, Jan. "Nach der Erinnerung. Silke Horstkotte erschließt in 'Nachbilder' den Komplex von 'Fotografie und Gedächtnis in der deutschen Gegenwartsliteratur.'" *literaturkritik.de* http://www.literaturkritik.de/public/rezension.php?rez_id=13333 [accessed: August 20, 2009]

Glaser, Hermann. *1945. Ein Lesebuch*. Frankfurt am Main: Fischer, 1995.

Göpfert, Rebekka. "Susi Bechhöfer fragt zurück. W.G. Sebald lieh sich für *Austerlitz* ihre Biographie." *Frankfurter Rundschau* Nr. 63 (Saturday, March 15, 2003): 10.

Gossman, Lionel. *Between History and Literature*. Cambridge, MA and London: Harvard University Press, 1990.

Gourevitch, Philip and Errol Morris. "Annals of War. Exposure. The Woman Behind the Camera at Abu Ghraib." *The New Yorker* (March 24, 2008): 44–57.

——. *Standard Operating Procedure*. New York: Penguin, 2008.

Grass, Günter. *Die Blechtrommel*. Darmstadt: Luchterhand, 1959.

Grescoe, Taras. "Skeleton in the cupboard." *Independent on Sunday* (August 25, 1996): 46, 48.

Gross, Sabine. *Lese-Zeichen. Kognition, Medium und Materialität im Leseprozeß*. Darmstadt: Wissenschaftliche Buchgesellschaft, 1994.

Grossman, Edith. "Translating Cervantes: Lecture by Edith Grossman." *Encuentros* 52 (2005): 1–11.

Gubar, Susan. "The Long and Short of Holocaust Verse." *New Literary History* 35.3 (2004): 443–468.

Halliwell, Stephen. *The Aesthetics of Mimesis. Ancient Texts and Modern Problems*. Princeton, N. J.: Princeton University Press, 2002.

Hansom, Paul, ed. *Literary Modernism and Photography*. Westport, CT; London: Praeger, 2002.

Harvey, Robert. *Witnessness: Beckett, Dante, Levi and the Foundations of Responsibility*. London; New York: Continuum, 2010.

Hilsenrath, Edgar. *Jossel Wassermanns Heimkehr*. Munich: Piper, 1993.

──. *Der Nazi und der Friseur*. Cologne: Literarischer Verlag Helmut Braun KG, 1977.

Hirsch, Marianne. *Family Frames. Photography, Narrative, and Postmemory*. Cambridge, MA and London, England: Harvard University Press, 1997.

──. "The Generation of Postmemory." *Photography in Fiction*. Eds. Silke Horstkotte and Nancy Pedri. Special issue of *Poetics Today* 29.1 (2008): 103–128.

──. *The Generation of Postmemory. Writing and Visual Culture After the Holocaust*. New York: Columbia University Press, 2012.

Hoffman, Eva. *After Such Knowledge. Memory, History, and the Legacy of the Holocaust*. New York: Public Affairs, 2004.

Hutcheon, Linda. "Literature Meets History: Counter-Discursive 'Comix.'" *Literatur und Geschichte in der Postmoderne*. Eds. Stephan Kohl, Karl Reichl, Hans Sauer, Hans Ulrich Seeber and Hubert Zapf. *Anglia. Zeitschrift für Englische Philologie* 117.1 (Special Issue) (1999): 4–14.

──. "The Pastime of Past Time: Fiction, History, Historiographic Metafiction." *Genre*, Special Topics 12: *Postmodern Genres*. Ed. Marjorie Perloff. XX.3–4 (1987): 285–305.

Jacobson, Dan. *Heshel's Kingdom*. London; New York: Penguin, 1999.

Josephs, Jeremy, with Susi Bechhöfer. *Rosa's Child. The True Story of One Woman's Quest for a Lost Mother and a Vanished Past*. London; New York: I. B. Tauris Publishers, 1996.

Jürgensen, Chistoph. *"Der Rahmen arbeitet." Paratextuelle Strategien der Lektürelenkung im Werk Arno Schmidts*. Göttingen: Vandenhoeck & Ruprecht, 2007.

Kacandes, Irene. "Testimony: Talk as Witnessing." *Talk Fiction. Literature and the Talk Explosion*. Lincoln and London: University of Nebraska Press, 2001. 89–140.

──. "'When facts are scarce': Authenticating Strategies in Writing by Children of Survivors." *After Testimony. The Ethics and Aesthetics of Holocaust Narrative for the Future*. Eds. Jakob Lothe, Susan Rubin Suleiman, and James Phelan. Columbus: The Ohio State University Press, 2012. 179–197.

Kafka, Franz. "'Oktavheft B' (Januar/Februar 1917)." *Nachgelassene Schriften und Fragmente I*. Ed. Malcolm Pasley. *Schriften und Tagebücher. Kritische Ausgabe*. Eds. Jürgen Born, Gerhard Neumann, Malcolm Pasley, and Jost Schillemeit. Darmstadt: Wissenschaftliche Buchgesellschaft, 1993.

──. *Der Proceß*. Ed. Malcolm Pasley. *Schriften und Tagebücher. Kritische Ausgabe*. Ed. Jürgen Born, Gerhard Neumann, Malcolm Pasley, and Jost Schillemeit. Darmstadt: Wissenschaftliche Buchgesellschaft, 1990.

———. "Die Sorge des Hausvaters." *Drucke zu Lebzeiten*. Eds. Wolf Kittler, Hans-Gerd Koch, and Gerhard Neumann. *Schriften und Tagebücher. Kritische Ausgabe*. Eds. Jürgen Born, Gerhard Neumann, Malcolm Pasley, and Jost Schillemeit. Darmstadt: Wissenschaftliche Buchgesellschaft, 1994.

———. "The Worries of a Head of Household." Trans. Michael Hofmann. *Metamorphosis and Other Stories*. London: Penguin, 2007.

Kant, Immanuel. *Anthropology. From a Pragmatic Point of View*. Trans. Victor Lyle Dowdell. Ed. Hans H. Rudnick. Carbondale and Edwardsville: Southern Illinois University Press; London and Amsterdam: Feffer & Simons, Inc., 1978.

———. *Critique of Pure Reason*. Trans. and ed. Paul Guyer and Allen W. Wood. Cambridge: Cambridge University Press, 2000.

Kempowski, Walter. *Culpa. Notizen zum 'Echolot'*. Mit Seitenhieben von Simone Neteler und einem Nachwort von Karl Heinz Bittel. Munich: btb, 2007.

———. *Deutsche Chronik I–IX*. Munich: Knaus, 1971–1975, 1978–1979, 1981, 1984.

———. *Echolot. Ein kollektives Tagebuch*. Munich: Knaus, 1993, 1999, 2002, 2005.

———. *Haben Sie Hitler gesehen? Deutsche Antworten*. Nachwort von Sebastian Haffner. Munich: Hanser, 1973.

———. *Haben Sie davon gewusst? Deutsche Antworten*. Nachwort von Eugen Kogon. Munich: Knaus, 1979.

Kimmelman, Michael. "Art Survivors of Hitler's War." *The New York Times* (December 1, 2010): A1.

———. "Ghosts in the Lens, Tricks in the Darkroom." *The New York Times* (September 30, 2005).

Kluge, Alexander. "Der Luftangriff auf Halberstadt am 8. April 1945." *Neue Geschichten. Hefte 1– 18 'Unheimlichkeit der Zeit'*. Frankfurt am Main: Suhrkamp, 1977. 33–107.

Klüger, Ruth. *Dichter und Historiker: Fakten und Fiktionen*. Mit einem Vorwort von Hubert Christian Ehalt. Vienna: Picus Verlag, 2000.

Koselleck, Reinhart. "Einleitung."; "Die Herausbildung des modernen Geschichtsbegriffs." "Geschichte, Historie." *Geschichtliche Grundbegriffe. Historisches Lexikon zur politisch-sozialen Sprache in Deutschland*. Vol. 2. Eds. Otto Brunner, Werner Conze, and Reinhart Koselleck. Stuttgart: Ernst Klett Verlag, 1975. 593–595; 647–717.

———. "Historia Magistra Vitae. Über die Auflösung des Topos im Horizont neuzeitlich bewegter Geschichte." *Natur und Geschichte. Karl Löwith zum 70. Geburtstag*. Eds. Hermann Braun and Manfred Riedel. Stuttgart: Kohlhammer, 1967. 196–219.

Kracauer, Siegfried. "Die Photographie [1931]." *Aufsätze 1927–1931*. Vol. 5.2. *Schriften*. Ed. Inka Mülder-Bach. Frankfurt am Main: Suhrkamp, 1990. 83–98.

Kundera, Milan. *L'art du roman*. Paris: Gallimard, 1986.

———., trans. Linda Asher. *The Art of the Novel*. London; Boston: Faber and Faber, 1988.

Kunkel, Benjamin. "Still Small Voice. The Fiction of Robert Walser." *The New Yorker* (August 6, 2007): 68–71.

Lang, Berel. "The Post-Holocaust vs. the Postmodern. Evil Inside and Outside History." *Holocaust Representation. Art within the Limits of History and Ethics*. Baltimore: Johns Hopkins University Press, 2000. 140–157.

Langer, Lawrence L. "Fictional Facts and Factual Fictions." *Reflections of the Holocaust in Art and Literature*. Ed. Randolph L. Braham. New York: Institute for Holocaust Studies, 1990. 117–130.

Lehmbäcker, Heinz and Uwe Johnson. *Mecklenburg. Zwei Ansichten*. Mit Fotografien von Heinz Lehmbäcker und Texten von Uwe Johnson. Frankfurt am Main and Leipzig: Insel Verlag, 2004.

Lethem, Jonathan. "The Ecstasy of Influence. A Plagiarism." *Harper's Magazine* (2007): 59–71.

Linenthal, Edward. *Preserving memory. The Struggle to Create America's Holocaust Museum*. New York: Penguin Books, 1997.

Literatur und Geschichte. Ein Kompendium zu ihrem Verhältnis von der Aufklärung bis zur Gegenwart. Eds. Daniel Fulda and Silvia Serena Tschopp. Berlin; New York: de Gruyter, 2002.

The Literature of Fact. Ed. Angus Fletcher. Selected Papers from the English Institute. New York: Columbia University Press, 1976.

Lothe, Jakob. "Narrative, Memory, and Visual Image: W. G. Sebald's *Luftkrieg und Literatur* and *Austerlitz*." *After Testimony. The Ethics and Aesthetics of Holocaust Narrative for the Future*, eds. Jakob Lothe, Susan Rubin Suleiman, and James Phelan. Columbus: The Ohio State University Press, 2012. 221–246.

——. Susan Rubin Suleiman, and James Phelan. "Introduction: 'After' Testimony: Holocaust Representation and Narrative Theory." *After Testimony. The Ethics and Aesthetics of Holocaust Narrative for the Future*, eds. Jakob Lothe, Susan Rubin Suleiman, and James Phelan. Columbus: The Ohio State University Press, 2012. 1–19.

Lützeler, Paul Michael. "Fiktion in der Geschichte – Geschichte in der Fiktion." *Klio oder Kalliope? Literatur und Geschichte: Sondierung, Analyse, Interpretation*. [Philologische Studien und Quellen 145] Berlin: Erich Schmidt Verlag, 1997. 11–20.

——. *Poetik der Autoren. Beiträge zur deutschsprachigen Gegenwartsliteratur*. Frankfurt am Main: Fischer Taschenbuch Verlag, 1994.

Lyotard, Jean-Fraçois. *Le différend*. Paris: Minuit, 1983.

Madsen, Peter. "World Literature and World Thoughts: Brandes/Auerbach." *Debating World Literature*. Ed. Christopher Prendergast. London; New York: Verso, 2004. 54–75.

Mailer, Norman. *The Armies of Night. History as a Novel, the Novel as History*. New York: Signet, 1968.

Mann, Golo. "Geschichtsschreibung als Literatur." [Vortrag, gehalten im Rahmen der "Geistigen Begegnungen in der Böttcherstraße" in Bremen am 19. Oktober 1964] Angelsachsen: Verlag Bremen, 1964.

Marker, Chris. *Sans soleil*. France, 1982; 16 mm, 100 min. Text of the film: http://www.marker text.com/sans_soleil.htm [Last accessed: October 1, 2010]

Martinez, Matias and Michael Scheffel. *Einführung in die Erzähltheorie*. Munich: Verlag C.H. Beck, 2000.

McGlothlin, Erin. *Second-Generation Holocaust Literature: Legacies of Survival and Perpetration*. Rochester, NY: Camden House, 2006.

Mepham, John. "Narratives of Postmodernism." *Postmodernism and Contemporary Fiction*. Ed. E. J. Smyth. London: Batsford, 1991. 138–155.

Mitscherlich, Alexander and Margarethe. *Die Unfähigkeit zu trauern. Grundlagen kollektiven Verhaltens*. Munich: Piper, 1977.

Moretti, Franco. "Conjectures on World Literature." *New Left Review* 1 (2000): 54–68.

Mülder-Bach, Inka. "Einleitung [Section III. Literarische Räume]." *Topographien der Literatur. Deutsche Literatur im transnationalen Kontext*. DFG-Symposium 2004. Eds. Hartmut Böhme, Inka Mülder-Bach, Bernhard Siegert, and Horst Wenzel. Stuttgart: Metzler, 2005. 403–407.

Müller, Filip. *Eyewitness Auschwitz. Three Years in the Gas Chambers*. Trans. Susanne Flatauer. New York: Stein and Day, 1979.

Mulisch, Harry. *The Discovery of Heaven*. Trans. Paul Vincent. New York: Penguin, 1997.

Nabokov, Vladimir. *Speak, Memory. An Autobiography Revisited*. New York: Vintage International, 1989.

——. "The Paris Review (1967)." *Deutliche Worte. Interviews – Leserbriefe – Aufsätze*, vol. 20. *Gesammelte Werke*. Ed. Dieter E. Zimmer. Reinbek bei Hamburg: Rowohlt, 1993.

Nitschmann, Johannes. "Eine Stadt verliert ihr Gedächtnis." *Berliner Zeitung* (March 5, 2009): 2.

Nünning, Ansgar. "'Beyond the Great Story': Der postmoderne historische Roman als Medium revisionistischer Geschichtsdarstellung, kultureller Erinnerung und metahistoriographischer Reflexion." *Literatur und Geschichte in der Postmoderne*. Eds. Stephan Kohl, Karl Reichl, Hans Sauer, Hans Ulrich Seeber and Hubert Zapf. *Anglia. Zeitschrift für Englische Philologie* 117.1 (Special Issue) (1999): 15–48.

——. "Crossing Borders and Blurring Genres: Towards a Typology and Poetics of Postmodernist Historical Fiction in England since the 1960s." *European Journal of English Studies* 1.2 (1997): 217–238.

——. *Von historischer Fiktion zu historiographischer Metafiktion. Band I Theorie, Typologie und Poetik des historischen Romans*. Trier: Wissenschaftlicher Verlag Trier, 1995.

——. "'Verbal Fictions?' Kritische Überlegungen und narratologische Alternativen zu Hayden Whites Einebnung des Gegensatzes zwischen Historiographie und Literatur." *Literaturwissenschaftliches Jahrbuch* 40 (1999): 351–380.

Onega, Susana. *Telling Histories. Narrativizing History, Historicizing Literature*. Amsterdam; Atlanta, GA: Rodopi, 1995.

Paul, Gerhard. "Von der historischen Bildkunde zur Visual History. Eine Einführung." *Visual History. Ein Studienbuch*. Ed. Gerhard Paul. Göttingen: Vandenhoeck & Ruprecht, 2006. 7–36.

Photography. Essays & Images. Illustrated Readings in the History of Photography. Ed. Beaumont Newhall. New York: The Museum of Modern Art, 1980.

Plato. *The Republic*. London and New York: Penguin, 2003.

Prütting, Lenz. "Arno Schmidt." *Kritisches Lexikon der Gegenwartsliteratur*. 35. Nlg. (Stand 1.4.1990) 1–22.

Rauschenbach, Bernd. "Was 'Worte' sind, wißt Ihr –?" *"Arno Schmidt? – Allerdings!" Eine Ausstellung der Arno Schmidt Stiftung Bargfeld. Im Schiller-Nationalmuseum, Marbach am Neckar. 30. März–27. August 2006*. Ed. Deutsches Literaturarchiv Marbach. Deutsche Schillergesellschaft, 2006. 33–50.

Sartre, Jean-Paul. *L'imagination*. Paris: PUF, 1981.

Schäfer, Hans-Dieter. *Mein Roman über Berlin*. Passau: refugium, 1990.

Schwarz, Daniel. *Imagining the Holocaust*. New York: St. Martin's Press, 1999.

Schlegel, Friedrich. "Brief über den Roman." *Kritische und theoretische Schriften*. Stuttgart: Reclam, 1997. 202–213.

Schlink, Bernhard. *Der Vorleser*. Zurich: Diogenes, 1995.

Schmidt, Arno. *Julia, oder die Gemälde. Scenen aus dem Novecento, Bargfelder Ausgabe IV, 4*. Zurich: Haffmans, 1992.

——. *Die Schule der Atheisten. Bargfelder Ausgabe IV, 2*. Zurich: Haffmans, 1994.

Scott, A. O. "Never Forget. You're Reminded." *The New York Times* (November 23, 2008): AR1.

Shields, David. *Reality Hunger*. New York: Knopf, 2010.

Simon, Claude. *Le jardin des plantes*. Paris: Les Éditions de Minuit, 1997.

Simon, Ulrich E. *A Theology of Auschwitz*. London: Victor Gollancz Ltd., 1967.

Sontag, Susan. *On Photography*. New York: Farrar, Straus and Giroux, 1973, 1974, 1977.

——. *Under the Sign of Saturn*. New York: Farrar, Straus and Giroux, 1980.

Steinaecker, Thomas von. "'Im Grunde bin ich Ikonoklast.' Ein Gespräch mit Alexander Kluge über die Abbildungen in seinen Texten." *Kultur & Gespenster* 1 (2006): 28–34.

Steiner, George. *After Babel: Aspects of Language and Translation*. Oxford: Oxford University Press, 1992.

——. *Language and Silence. Essays on Language, Literature, and the Inhuman*. New York: Atheneum, 1967.

——. "The Writer as Remembrancer: A Note on *Poetics, 9.*" *Yearbook of Comparative and General Literature* 22 (1973): 51–57.

Stierle, Karlheinz. "Geschehen, Geschichte, Text der Geschichte." *Geschichte: Ereignis und Erzählung*. Eds. Reinhart Koselleck and Wolf-Dieter Stempel. (*Poetik und Hermeneutik* 5) Munich: Fink, 1973. 530–534.

Tawada, Yoko. "Das Tor des Übersetzers oder Celan liest Japanisch." *Ansichten und Auskünfte zur deutschen Literatur nach 1945*. Ed. Heinz Ludwig Arnold. *Sonderband Text + Kritik* 9 (1995): 179–186.

Timm, Uwe. *Am Beispiel meines Bruders*. Cologne: Kiepenheuer & Witsch, 2004.

——. *Der Freund und der Fremde*.Cologne: Kiepenheuer & Witsch, 2005.

——. *Halbschatten*. Cologne: Kiepenheuer & Witsch, 2008.

Turner, Joseph W. "The Kinds of Historical Fiction: An Essay in Definition and Methodology." *Genre* 12 (1979): 333–355.

Vico, Giambattista. *New Science. Principles of the New Science Concerning the Common Nature of Nations*. Trans. David Marsh. New York: Penguin, 1999.

Wackwitz, Stephan. *Ein unsichtbares Land*. Frankfurt am Main: Fischer, 2003.

Walser, Robert. *Aufsätze von Robert Walser*. Leipzig: Kurt Wolff Verlag, 1913.

——. *Aus dem Bleistiftgebiet. Mikrogramme 1924–1933*. Im Auftrag des Robert Walser-Archivs der Carl Seelig-Stiftung/Zürich entziffert und herausgegeben von Bernhard Echte und Werner Morlang. 6 Volumes. Frankfurt am Main: Suhrkamp, 1985–2000.

——. "Kleist in Thun." *Geschichten von Robert Walser. Mit Zeichnungen von Karl Walser*. Leipzig: Kurt Wolff Verlag, 1914.

——. *Microscripts*. Trans. and with an introduction by Susan Bernofsky. Afterword by Walter Benjamin. New York: New Directions/Christine Burgin, 2010.

——. *Selected Stories*, with a Foreword by Susan Sontag, trans. Christopher Middleton and others. New York: Farrar, Straus, Giroux, 1982.

Welzer, Harald, Sabine Moller, and Karoline Tschuggnall, eds., '*Opa war kein Nazi.*' *Nationalsozialismus und Holocaust im Familiengedächtnis*. Frankfurt: Fischer, 2002.

Wieviorka, Annette. *Déportation et genocide. Entre la mémoire et l'oubli*. Paris: Plon, 1995.

White, Hayden. "Commentary: 'With no particular place to go:' Literary History in the Age of the Global Picture." *New Literary History* 39.3 (2008): 727–745.

——. *The Content of Form. Narrative Discourse and Historical Representation*. Baltimore; London: Johns Hopkins University Press, 1987.

——. *Metahistory. The Historical Imagination in Nineteenth Century Europe*. Baltimore: Johns Hopkins University Press, 1973.

Wittgenstein, Ludwig. *Logisch-philosophische Abhandlung. Tractatus logico-philosophicus*. Eds. Brian McGuinness and Joachim Schulte. Frankfurt am Main: Suhrkamp, 1989.

——. *Philosophische Untersuchungen*. Kritisch-genetische Edition. Ed. Joachim Schulte. In Zusammenarbeit mit Heikki Nyman, Eike von Savigny und Georg Henrik von Wright. Frankfurt am Main: Suhrkamp, 2001.

——. Trans. G. E.M. Anscombe. *Philosophical Investigations*. Oxford: Basil Blackwell, 1968.

Wolin, Jeffrey A. *Written in Memory. Portraits of the Holocaust. Photographs by Jeffrey A. Wolin*. San Francisco: Chronicle Books, 1997.

Young, James E. *Writing and Rewriting the Holocaust. Narrative and the Consequences of Interpretation*. Bloomington and Indianapolis: Indiana University Press, 1988.

Zuckerman, Lord Solly. *From Apes to Warlords*. London: Hamish Hamilton, 1978.

Name Index

Subject Index

rhetoric 28, 38, 57, 84, 91, 137, 183, 228
rhythm 219
ruins 55, 89, 104, 158, 245

S
St. Gallen 8
Schelde River 160
schema 78, 122, 156, 164, 188
scholar, see academia
"Schreibkrise", see crisis
science 37–38, 49, 239
screen 143, 190
second generation 113–114, 186
Second World War, see World War II
section break 64, 166
self-referentiality 51, 130, 232, 240
semantics 40, 92, 130, 140, 218, 228
semiotics 20, 61, 66, 93–94, 115, 128, 214,
    216, 236, 238
semioticization 66, 84, 89, 94, 142, 230, 237
sense, see also meaning 74, 112–113, 137,
    154–158, 160–161, 163–165, 167, 176,
    178, 181, 189, 193–196, 199–201, 204,
    207–208, 219, 226–227, 234, 236, 239,
    248
senses 1, 12, 18, 46, 56, 78, 89, 93, 105, 160,
    172, 184, 192, 194, 196, 198, 205, 208,
    210–211, 216, 237
shadow 75, 80, 163, 170, 203
sign 35, 48, 66–67, 84, 94, 116, 128, 131,
    134, 144, 170, 174, 192, 205, 212–213,
    217, 226, 234
silence 7, 46, 83–84, 147
simulacrum 118
simultaneity viii, 18, 20, 30, 33, 42, 50, 61,
    64, 71, 80, 97, 120, 122, 124, 130,
    150–151, 155–156, 158, 160, 164, 169,
    174, 178–180, 194, 198, 230, 234, 236,
    238–239, 247, 249
skepticism 3–4, 11, 38, 51–52, 57, 65, 67, 71,
    87, 96
snow 76, 159, 196, 234
solitude 189–190, 223–224
"Sonderkommando" 116–118
Sonthofen 141
sound 46, 173, 203, 207, 212, 216–218, 222,
    225, 230, 232

source 23, 29, 35, 47, 49, 52, 66–68, 87–88,
    90–91, 93–94, 108, 110–111, 120, 122,
    129, 131, 133–136, 138–139, 152–154,
    172, 186, 213, 220, 226–227, 236, 247
South Africa 174
space 17–18, 30, 50, 62, 64, 67, 73–74, 80,
    90, 94–95, 107, 118, 122, 150–151, 153,
    156–160, 162–163, 168, 175, 178–179,
    185, 196–197, 207, 244, 248
species 1, 50, 179
spectator 38–39
spirit 5, 14
"Sprachkrise", see crisis
State Archive, Prague 164, 171, 191–192,
    230
"Stolperstein" 132, 174
story 3, 8, 24, 36–39, 42, 45–47, 49–51, 53,
    62–68, 75, 87–89, 94, 97, 110, 116,
    119–120, 124–125, 131–134, 151–152,
    163–164, 171, 173, 175, 188–190, 194,
    198, 204, 206, 208, 229–230, 246
Stower Grange 158, 167
structure vii–viii, 18–19, 28, 30–31, 37, 41,
    49–50, 52, 60–61, 63–64, 66, 75, 88,
    92, 115, 131, 136, 152, 170, 176, 182, 185,
    187–191, 212, 215, 220–221, 225, 233,
    238, 240
style 15, 28, 31, 64, 76, 88, 92, 98, 108, 150,
    152–153, 155, 220–222, 224, 238, 241,
    244
subjectivity 25, 56, 71, 106, 173
subjunctive mood 219
substance 118, 216
substratum 238
survivor 44, 57, 89, 93, 112–114, 146, 167,
    182, 186, 211, 238
suspense 39, 157, 221
synonymy 218
synoptic 82, 87, 90, 92–93
syntax 31, 64, 88, 115–116, 192, 219,
    221–222, 224, 234
synthesis 53, 87, 137

T
tableau vii, 30, 150, 161
taboo 82–83
technology 17–18, 62, 104–107, 144, 248

CPSIA information can be obtained
at www.ICGtesting.com
Printed in the USA
BVHW091254260421
605879BV00009B/233